D1196358

C. P. E. BACH

C. P. E. BACH

════

Hans-Günter Ottenberg

TRANSLATED BY
PHILIP J. WHITMORE

Oxford   New York
OXFORD UNIVERSITY PRESS
1987

Oxford University Press, Walton Street, Oxford OX2 6DP
Oxford New York Toronto
Delhi Bombay Calcutta Madras Karachi
Petaling Jaya Singapore Hong Kong Tokyo
Nairobi Dar es Salaam Cape Town
Melbourne Auckland
and associated companies in
Beirut Berlin Ibadan Nicosia

Oxford is a trade mark of Oxford University Press

Published in the United States
by Oxford University Press, New York

First published in 1982 by Verlag Philipp Reclam jun. Leipzig
First published in English in 1987 by Oxford University Press

British Library Cataloguing in Publication Data
Ottenberg, Hans-Günter.
C. P. E. Bach.
1. Bach. Carl Philipp Emanuel
I. Title   II. Carl Philipp Emanuel Bach.
English
780'.92'4   ML410.B16
ISBN 0-19-315246-0

Library of Congress Cataloging in Publication Data
Ottenberg, Hans-Günter.
C. P. E. Bach
Translation of: Carl Philipp Emanuel Bach. 1982.
Bibliography: p.
Includes indexes.
1. Bach, Carl Philipp Emanuel, 1714–1788.
2. Composers—Germany—Biography. I. Title.
ML410.B160873   1987   780'.92'4 [B]   86-23904
ISBN 0-19-315246-0

Set from captured data by H Charlesworth & Co Ltd, Huddersfield
Printed in Great Britain
at the University Printing House, Oxford
by David Stanford
Printer to the University

CONTENTS

LIST OF ILLUSTRATIONS

(between pp. 148 and 149)

TRANSLATOR'S PREFACE

In preparing an English translation of Hans-Günter Ottenberg's fine biography of Carl Philipp Emanuel Bach, I hope to have helped to fill a conspicuous gap in the literature that is available in English on eighteenth-century German music. While there are several books and articles which deal with particular areas of Bach's work, and while more general histories of the music of the period do not neglect him, this is the first complete biographical study to have appeared in English in book form. There are signs that scholarly interest in C. P. E. Bach is on the increase: a complete edition of his works is in preparation, and the thematic catalogue produced by Alfred Wotquenne at the beginning of the present century is about to be superseded by Eugene Helm's new catalogue (see p. 215). Thus the time appears ripe for a life-and-works study of this kind to be made more widely available.

The present work was written and originally published in the German Democratic Republic. In one or two details, consequently, it reflects a local point of view, as for example in the remarks on pp. 215ff. about research projects, concert series, compositional developments, and so on taking place in the German Democratic Republic. These have been retained, together with a number of comments reflecting a Marxist outlook, because it is felt that the particular perspective from which Ottenberg discusses this music, emphasizing the cultural and intellectual environment in which it arose, and the *Sitz im Leben* which it has occupied ever since, especially in Bach's native Germany, constitutes one of the principal merits of the book.

Bearing in mind the needs of an English readership I have endeavoured to replace many of the source references used by Ottenberg with references to English translations of the texts in question. Although many of the translations of quotations which appear in the present text are my own, I have still supplied references in the footnotes to other existing translations, so that the interested reader may more easily investigate the context of the passages quoted. References to the original German texts are frequently retained, either in the footnotes or in the Bibliography. Paragraph references have been given for quotations from the first volume of Bach's *Versuch über die wahre Art das Clavier zu spielen*, and also for quotations from Quantz's *Versuch einer Anweisung die Flöte traversiere zu spielen* and Mattheson's *Der vollkommene Capellmeister*, so that it should be possible to locate the passage quoted in either the English or the German version of the text. Page references, not paragraph references, are given for quotations from the second volume of Bach's *Versuch*, however, since the numbering of chapters adopted by W. J. Mitchell in his English translation is so markedly different from Bach's own.

The Bibliography has been reserved for books, articles etc. that deal specifically with an aspect of the work of C. P. E. Bach, or that are otherwise of direct significance to the student of his music. Many other texts are mentioned in the footnotes, some of them frequently. For ease of reference, and in order to avoid unnecessary duplication of material, I have indicated in square brackets at each subsequent reference the place where the original (full) reference to such texts may be found. Where cross-references are lacking, full details of the text quoted may be found either in a recent footnote or in the Bibliography. I have amplified the Glossary and the Bibliography to some extent; with the exceptions of minor amendments and corrections, however, the text has remained unaltered. Where it appeared necessary to add a translator's note, I have done so in the footnotes, indicating by the use of square brackets that the comment was my own.

Given that the new thematic catalogue by Eugene Helm had not appeared at the time of going to press, it was thought advisable to retain the more familiar Wotquenne catalogue numbers in the text, although a table of concordances between the different numberings has been appended to facilitate comparison (Appendix IV, pp. 245ff.).

In some instances where it has seemed impossible to capture in translation the full flavour of certain frequently-used expressions, the original German form has been retained. Such words as *Originalgenie*, *Empfindsamkeit*, and *Akademie* are in this category.

Where it has been necessary to specify the register in which certain pitches occur, the American Standard names have been used. Thus Middle C is called C_4, the note below it is B_3, and the C below is C_3 etc.

The following abbreviations are used in source references:

AMZ	= *Allgemeine musikalische Zeitung*
B-Jb	= *Bach-Jahrbuch*
HUC	= *Hamburgischer unpartheyischer Correspondent*
JAMS	= Journal of the American Musicological Society
MQ	= The Musical Quarterly
MGG	= *Die Musik in Geschichte und Gegenwart*, ed. F. Blume, 14 vols. (Kassel and Basel, 1949–68); suppl. 2 vols. (1973–9)
New Grove	= The New Grove Dictionary of Music and Musicians, ed. S. Sadie, 20 vols. (London 1980).
RISM	= *Répertoire internationale des sources musicales*
SIMG	= *Sammelbände der internationalen Musikgesellschaft*

It remains only for me to record my thanks to those who have assisted me in the preparation of this translation, and especially to Dr S. L. F. Wollenberg, whose encouragement, advice, and innumerable detailed suggestions for improvements to the translation have been a source of support at every stage. Needless to say, any imperfections that remain are my own responsibility. The author, Dr H.-G. Ottenberg, has rendered my task much easier by kindly suggesting additional items for the Bibliography and numerous minor amendments which have served to bring the book up to date. I am grateful to Professor Eugene Helm for giving permission to publish the work-list (Appendix III), an abbreviated version of the work-list originally published in *New Grove* in his article 'Bach, III (9) Carl Philipp Emanuel', and also for kindly supplying a list of corrections incorporating the results of recent research. Finally I should like to record my gratitude to the publishing and production staff of Oxford University Press, with whom it has been a pleasure to work.

P. J. W.

INTRODUCTION

Carl Philipp Emanuel Bach—An Original Genius?

As we study his portrait [Plate I] we see a face no less formidable than his musical personality. It is of a kind which will always make an impression in the world. Between the eyebrows, in the expression of the eyes, one can detect a hint of his creative energy. With such an appearance, he can, he will, he must surely make his mark in many places with grace and advantage. And it is at once apparent that he is not a man to compromise. It is always so where true genius is found. Accepted or rejected; valued or ignored—the organizing genius transforms everything in unity, wholeness, and sufficiency . . .[1]

Yet the painter has politely disguised the defect of the left eye . . . thereby inevitably losing some of the unique forcefulness of Bach's expression. None the less, spirit enough remains in the eyes and the eyebrows. The nose, rather too rounded, still manages to convey an impression of refinement and creative power. The mouth, for all its simplicity, such a fine expression of delicacy, richness, dryness, assurance, and security; the lower lip somewhat artful and weak—with only a faint hint of awkwardness! The slight dip in the lower jaw more than compensates.

Firmness, cheerfulness, courage, and conviction can be seen on the forehead. I do not know whether it is simply an illusion, but it seems to me at least that in most portraits of virtuosi the lower part of the face is not entirely successful; here, though, the outline of the chin is masterly.[2]

This description of Carl Philipp Emanuel Bach's features—based on an engraving by Johann Heinrich Lips—is taken from the third volume of Lavater's *Physiognomische Fragmente zur Beförderung der Menschenkenntnis und Menschenliebe* [Fragments of physiognomy for the promotion of knowledge and goodwill among men] (1777). It was no coincidence that the second son of Johann Sebastian Bach, together with Jean-

---

[1] Up to this point, according to Lavater, the description is supplied by a 'musician and physiognomist', who may have been P. C. Kayser or C. F. D. Schubart. See G. Busch, *C. Ph. E. Bach und seine Lieder* (Regensburg, 1957), p. 129n. The text given in paragraphs 2 and 3 was written by Lavater himself. (See n. 2.)

[2] J. C. Lavater, *Physiognomische Fragmente zur Beförderung der Menschenkenntnis und Menschenliebe*, iii (Leipzig and Winterthur, 1777), pp. 200f. Lavater had written to Bach on 13 May 1775 to ask for a portrait for the *Fragmente*; Bach sent one in August of the same year. See Busch, op. cit., p. 129.

Philippe Rameau and Niccolò Jommelli, should have been one of the few musicians among a vast array of politicians, philosophers, poets, painters, and scientists to have attracted the attention of Johann Caspar Lavater.

A Swiss theologian, poet, and friend of Goethe, Lavater was at the time one of the most influential writers of the *Sturm und Drang* generation. For his *Fragmente* he was looking for a musician who was both popular and at the same time committed to the intellectual outlook of the *Sturm und Drang* movement. He found what he was looking for in Carl Philipp Emanuel Bach. Even if Goethe was right to criticize the excessive rationalism of Lavater's approach,[3] according to which the inner, personal disposition of a subject could be accurately deduced from his appearance, the characterization he offers of Bach contains much that is correct. His description corresponds remarkably well with the picture that contemporaries of C. P. E. Bach have left—that of an *Originalgenie* [original creative genius]. In both composition and keyboard performance, his genius is amply attested. Christian Friedrich Daniel Schubart, a prominent critic, editor of the *Deutsche Chronik* (1774–6), and a distinguished authority on the musical life of Germany, writes in his *Ideen zu einer Ästhetik der Tonkunst* [Ideas towards a musical aesthetic] (1784–5):

The innumerable keyboard compositions by this master all bear the imprint of his extraordinary genius. There is no other so rich in invention, so inexhaustible in new turns of phrase, so perfect in harmony.[4]

'Had you but heard', wrote Johann Friedrich Reichardt enthusiastically, having met the already famous Bach in Hamburg in 1772, 'how Bach brings his clavichord to life—an instrument which many people, perhaps with some justification, have long held to be dead and inexpressive, and how he manages to convey every nuance of emotion and passion—in a word, how he puts his entire soul into the music!'[5] And the English music historian Charles Burney confirms:

However, each candid observer and hearer, must discover, in the slightest and most trivial productions, of every kind, some mark of originality in the

---

[3] See *Goethe: Berliner Ausgabe*, xiii, 'Aus meinem Leben. Dichtung und Wahrheit' (Berlin, 1960), pp. 651ff., 804ff.

[4] C. F. D. Schubart, *Ideen zu einer Ästhetik der Tonkunst*, written c.1784–5, published by L. Schubart (Vienna, 1806), p. 178. (R/Hildesheim, 1969).

[5] J. F. Reichardt, *Schreiben über die Berlinische Musik* (Hamburg, 1775), p. 8. [According to a note included in the original edition of this work, it was intended as a supplement to the first part of Reichardt's *Briefe eines aufmerksamen Reisenden*, first published the previous year [Chapter 3, n. 68 below]. The facsimile reprint of the latter work issued by the Da Capo Press (Hildesheim etc., 1977) does not in fact include the supplement, although, according to Ottenberg, the reprint issued in Leipzig in 1976 does include it.]

modulation, accompaniment, or melody, which bespeak a great and exalted genius.[6]

The list of such tributes could be extended much further.

Any reference to the 'great Bach' in the second half of the eighteenth century almost always meant C. P. E. Bach. No wonder that he was immediately hailed as the foremost musical exponent of the *Sturm und Drang* movement: of a musical language based on individual self-expression, which set out to 'touch the heart' and 'awaken the passions',[7] which was able to convey a wide variety of mood-changes, from exuberance to tranquillity, from unbridled excitement to a delicate inner sensibility, and in which close attention to compositional detail was achieved within an improvisatory overall framework. In Bach's music there are extraordinarily daring harmonic progressions; articulation and dynamics are worked out in minute detail; the strongly characterized theme carries with it a high potential for developmental treatment. It is pioneering music, marking the beginning of a new phase in musical history with all the merits and demerits that this involves, reaching out after new modes of expression with a zest for the unconventional, but sometimes marred by traces of immaturity and underdevelopment.

None the less, in view of the intrinsic quality of this music it would be unjust to dismiss the composer as a mere 'forerunner' or 'precursor'. C. P. E. Bach's work did in fact influence that of his immediate successors considerably, but it was then quickly forgotten. Beethoven's remark in a letter to the Leipzig publishing house of Breitkopf & Härtel in 1809 is well known:

I have only one or two of Emanuel Bach's keyboard compositions, and yet there are some which every true artist should know, not only for the great enjoyment to be derived from them, but also for the purpose of study; and my greatest pleasure is to play at the homes of true music-lovers works [of Bach's] which I have never or only seldom seen.[8]

By this time, however, C. P. E. Bach's symphonic compositions and larger vocal works had long since passed out of the concert repertoire, while his keyboard music—the core of his output—and the songs were

---

[6] C. Burney, *The Present State of Music in Germany* (London, 1773), quoted from *Dr. Burney's Musical Tours in Europe*, ed. Percy A. Scholes, 2 vols. (London etc., 1959), ii, p. 214.

[7] These are central aesthetic formulations, influenced by contemporary musical thought and frequently employed by Bach.

[8] L. van Beethoven, letter of 26 July 1809 to Breitkopf & Härtel. German text in *Beethovens Sämtliche Briefe*, ed. A. C. Kalischer, 2nd edn. (incomplete), 3 vols. (Berlin and Leipzig, 1909–11), i, p. 284. For an English version see *The Letters of Beethoven*, trans. and ed. Emily Anderson, 3 vols. (London, 1961), i, p. 235.

at best relegated to the intimacy of domestic musical gatherings. The tenth issue of the *Allgemeine musikalische Zeitung* (1807–8) contains reviews of works for the pianoforte by the following composers: Beethoven, Caudella, Danzi, Dotzauer, Dussek, Goldmann, C. G. Hering, Jadin, Kozeluch, Meinecke, Nägeli, Reicha, Riotte, Starke, Steibelt, F. Stein, Steinacker, Wilms, and Wölfl.[9] Neither in this nor in subsequent issues of the journal is there any detailed discussion of works by C. P. E. Bach; much the same picture emerges from a comparison with other musical periodicals of the time.[10]

Ever since 1829, the year of the famous revival of the St Matthew Passion conducted by Felix Mendelssohn Bartholdy, the 'great Bach' has been unambiguously identified in the minds of the wider public with Johann Sebastian Bach, which clearly makes sense in view of the elder Bach's monumental achievement. Yet direct comparisons between the music of father and son were unfair to the latter. Robert Schumann's comment of 1833, that Philipp Emanuel remained very far behind his father as a creative musician,[11] hardly does him justice. The differences between father and son, both in their artistic aims and in the social environments in which they grew up, make it impossible to measure them against each other. Even today such fruitless viewpoints persist as that C. P. E. Bach's music is technically too straightforward and unconvincing (as if a 'learned' style were the sole guarantee of quality), and that his works were merely the more distinguished products of a 'fallow period' in musical history, generally dismissed as 'pre-Classical'.

For a number of years now, C. P. E. Bach's music has received increasing attention. Both instrumental and vocal works—though still relatively few—are being rediscovered for the repertoire. Musicologists have made studies of several areas of his output, and a number of extended monographs has appeared. Musical historiography, if it is to be taken seriously, will not concern itself exclusively with the highlights of musical history, but will broaden its outlook and cover a wider field, including, for example, investigation of the transition period between the works of J. S. Bach, Handel, and Telemann, and those of the Viennese Classical composers, during which C. P. E. Bach produced an outstanding life's work.

His work contains elements which might well strike a chord with

[9] *AMZ*, x (1807–8), cols. v f. (R/Amsterdam and Hilversum, 1964).

[10] See the discussion in the final chapter of this book.

[11] R. Schumann, *Gesammelte Schriften über Musik und Musiker*, 5th edn., 2 vols. (Leipzig, 1914), i, p. 11, also found in R. Schumann, *On Music and Musicians*, ed. K. Wolff, trans. P. Rosenfeld (London, 1947), p. 67.

modern listeners. Bach's advocacy of an unlimited though not un-disciplined subjectivity in art is reflected in his expressive style. An improvisatory habit of thought led him to a freer handling of inherited forms, for which his music was repeatedly dubbed 'bizarre' in his lifetime. Even for the present-day listener this music still opens up new and little-explored avenues. That C. P. E. Bach's music manages to have an immediate impact on the listener is a consequence of Bach's insistence that a composer must himself be gripped by the *Affekt* he sets out to convey. The abrupt changes of mood and the fluid dynamics which so often stand side by side in Bach's music, reflect the state of mind of a remarkably unstable, intense, highly excitable artistic personality; these tensions are not left unresolved, however. To take an example, in the A major Fantasia from the fourth collection 'für Kenner und Liebhaber' (1783) there is a great deal of virtuoso display. Hemi-demisemiquaver passage-work, wild arpeggios, and triplet runs of uncertain direction gradually achieve an intensification of the *Affekt*, a process which is reinforced by the appearance of a brief Adagio that slows down the rhythmic impetus. After a period of harmonic and metrical instability there follows an Andante in regular metre, in which a clear tonality is established and the melody assumes a cantabile character: in other words a more peaceful *Affekt* is estab-lished. There is no Classical equilibrium here; instead, the composer darts from one mood to another at a moment's notice. Written in a highly refined idiom, if relatively conventional by twentieth-century standards, Bach's music remains fundamentally expressive, impas-sioned, and not without a flavour of Romanticism. His compositional style with all its personal traits impresses both 'Kenner' and 'Lieb-haber'—to borrow two eighteenth-century concepts—as fascinating and aesthetically stimulating.

It is hoped that the present study will contribute towards making C. P. E. Bach better known, both as a man and as a musician.

Weimar—Cöthen—Leipzig—Frankfurt an der Oder (1714–1738)

The Years in Weimar and Cöthen

On 2 March 1714 Johann Sebastian Bach, who had been court organist and chamber musician (*Cammer-Musicus*) to Duke Wilhelm Ernst of Weimar since 1708, was promoted to the rank of Konzertmeister, an important event in his career. One week later—on 8 March—his second son, Carl Philipp Emanuel, was born. Baptismal records reveal one of the godparents to have been none other than the 'Kapellmeister to the Imperial Free City of Frankfurt on the Main', Georg Philipp Telemann.[1]

At the end of 1716 a further important appointment loomed in which Johann Sebastian Bach had an interest. The post of Kapellmeister fell vacant on the death in December 1716 of Johann Samuel Drese, and Bach, well aware of his ability, hoped to be appointed himself. The Duke, however, chose Drese's son, Johann Wilhelm, who had studied in Italy many years previously. The breach that was already developing between J. S. Bach and his patron could no longer be avoided. The following year Bach accepted an offer to become Court Kapellmeister to Prince Leopold of Anhalt-Cöthen.[2] Only then did he ask to be relieved of his duties in Weimar, rather too emphatically, for the Duke had him arrested forthwith 'for too stubbornly forcing the issue of his dismissal'.[3]

In the Weimar years Bach composed organ music of various kinds, including most of the *Orgelbüchlein*, a masterpiece of musical word-painting, a number of organ transcriptions of Vivaldi's concertos, as well as preludes, fugues, and church cantatas, in which the beginnings of Bach's characteristic 'expressive melody' (Besseler's term[4]) can already be observed.

---

[1] See *The Bach Reader. A Life of Johann Sebastian Bach in Letters and Documents*, ed. H. T. David and A. Mendel, 2nd edn. (London, 1966), p. 429. See also *Bach-Dokumente*, ii: 'Fremdschriftliche und gedruckte Dokumente zur Lebensgeschichte Johann Sebastian Bachs 1685–1750' (Kassel etc., 1969), p. 54.

[2] J. S. Bach signed the contract on 5 Aug. 1717.

[3] See *Bach Reader*, p. 75, and *Bach-Dokumente*, ii, p. 65.

[4] H. Besseler, 'Bach als Wegbereiter', *Archiv für Musikwissenschaft*, xii (1955), p. 3. See also H. Besseler, *Aufsätze zur Musikaesthetik und Musikgeschichte* (Leipzig, 1978), p. 368.

When J. S. Bach arrived in Cöthen in December 1717 with his wife Maria Barbara and their four children, Catharina Dorothea, Wilhelm Friedemann, Carl Philipp Emanuel, and Johann Gottfried Bernhard, he found a lucrative job awaiting him. He was now paid almost twice his former salary. The music-loving prince kept a small orchestra, and Bach soon came to value its considerable proficiency. The Kapellmeister's task was to write and perform *Gebrauchsmusik* in the broadest sense of the term: music for mealtimes, for evening chamber concerts, for feast-days and holy days. The freedom to make use of every form and genre of the latest French and Italian music was for Bach a piece of great good fortune.

Among the many instrumental works written in Cöthen, the Inventions and Sinfonias, the first part of the *Well-tempered Clavier* and the 'Brandenburg Concertos' are outstanding. In these works, marked thematic invention and development of material is combined with a rich harmonic vocabulary, showing a masterly command of inherited forms and styles without concealing Bach's unmistakable personal idiom; such music could scarcely fail to make an impression on amateurs and experts alike. At the same time Bach was an organ virtuoso of the first rank. Consequently his reputation spread. The famous meeting in Dresden with the French organist and harpsichordist Marchand, mentioned in almost every Bach biography, was to have taken place as early as 1717.[5] The well-known Hamburg composer and theorist Johann Mattheson took note, and asked Bach to supply biographical details for inclusion in his *Neu zu errichtende Musicalische Ehren-pforte*[6] [New Musical Gate of Honour].

Early Musical Education

Carl Philipp Emanuel Bach thus grew up in a well-to-do middle-class family. He may have been a high-spirited child, much given to playful pranks, for, as Rochlitz later records,[7] he possessed 'great liveliness'. His parents were greatly concerned to provide their children with a

---

[5] As is well known, the competition on the organ did not take place because Marchand retreated at the last moment. Soon after Bach's death, various accounts of this incident appeared in a number of different versions. See *Bach Reader*, pp. 218f., 287, 303f., 444f., and 452f., and *Bach-Dokumente*, iii: 'Dokumente zum Nachwirken Johann Sebastian Bachs 1750–1800' (Kassel etc., 1972), p. 296 *et passim*.

[6] See *Bach Reader*, pp. 228f., and *Bach-Dokumente*, ii, p. 65.

[7] F. Rochlitz, *Für Freunde der Tonkunst*, 4 vols. (Leipzig, 1824–32), iv, pp. 277f. [Translator's note. See also C. P. E. Bach, *Essay on the True Art of Playing Keyboard Instruments*, trans. and ed. W. J. Mitchell (New York and London, 1949), Translator's Introduction, p. 12, where a remark made by J. F. Doles about C. P. E. Bach is quoted as follows: 'Like many boys of active mind and body, he was afflicted from childhood on with the malady of the roguish tease.']

thorough, all-round education; like his brother Wilhelm Friedemann, four years his senior, Philipp Emanuel attended the Lutheran Latin school in Cöthen. In July 1720 his mother died; J. S. Bach now had to look after the four children alone, which he did with great devotion, making sure that his sons' musical education was not neglected. In his autobiography C. P. E. Bach says, 'In composition and keyboard playing I never had any other teacher than my father.'[8] J. S. Bach began to teach his children to play on keyboard instruments quite early; the *Clavierbüchlein für Wilhelm Friedemann Bach*, written in 1720 for the then ten-year-old boy primarily as a collection of various models in composition, already assumes a fair degree of keyboard proficiency.[9] It seems likely that Carl Philipp Emanuel was also taught from this *Clavierbüchlein*, in other words, that he probably received his earliest keyboard instruction around 1720–1.

Presumably J. S. Bach was already thinking of seeking alternative employment at this stage. Although he had good opportunities to develop as a composer in Cöthen and even hoped at first 'to spend the rest of [his] life' there,[10] his name appears in a memorandum dated 21 December 1722 as one of the applicants for the post of Cantor at the Thomaskirche in Leipzig.[11] After Telemann and Graupner had declined the post, the way was clear for Bach. Equipped with good references from his employer in Cöthen he moved to Leipzig with his new wife, Anna Magdalena Wilcke, whom he had married on 3 December 1721, in order to take up his new appointment. The local newspaper reported as follows:

Last Sunday at midday four carriages laden with household effects arrived here from Cöthen, belonging to the former princely Kapellmeister of that place, who has been summoned to Leipzig as Cantor Figuralis; at 2 o'clock he arrived himself with his family in two coaches, and moved into the newly restored residence in the Thomasschule.[12]

[8] C. P. E. Bach, 'Autobiography', contained in C. Burney, *Tagebuch einer musikalischen Reise*, trans. C. D. Ebeling and J. J. C. Bode, 3 vols. (Hamburg, 1772–3; R/Kassel etc., 1959), iii, p. 199. English translation by W. S. Newman, 'Emanuel Bach's Autobiography', *MQ*, li (1965), p. 366. [Translator's note—the 'Autobiography' is not contained in Burney's original text, *The Present State of Music in Germany* (London, 1773), but was included in the German translation published soon afterwards in Hamburg. See W. S. Newman, loc. cit., pp. 363ff. Throughout the present book page-references will be made both to the German original and to Newman's translation.]

[9] See W. Plath, *Kritischer Bericht zur Neuen Bach-Ausgabe*, v.5, 'Klavierbüchlein für Wilhelm Friedemann Bach' (Kassel etc., 1963), p. 70.

[10] J. S. Bach, letter of 28 Oct. 1730 to Georg Erdmann, quoted from *Bach Reader*, p. 125. See also *Bach-Dokumente*, i: 'Schriftstücke von der Hand Johann Sebastian Bachs' (Kassel etc., 1963), p. 67.

[11] See *Bach Reader*, pp. 87f., and *Bach-Dokumente*, ii, p. 88.

[12] See *Bach-Dokumente*, ii, p. 104.

J. S. Bach in Leipzig

Bach's reasons for moving to Leipzig are explained in a letter written some years later, on 28 October 1730, to his childhood friend Georg Erdmann:

Though, at first, indeed, it did not seem at all proper to me to change my position of Kapellmeister for that of Cantor. Wherefore then, I postponed my decision for quarter of a year; but this post was described to me in such favourable terms that finally (particularly since my sons seemed inclined towards [university] studies) I cast my lot, in the name of the Lord, and made the journey to Leipzig, took my examination, and then made the change of position.[13]

What might have been the Bach family's first impressions of the great trading city, which even at that time numbered well over 30,000 inhabitants? Business and commercial enterprise were the dominant themes of city life. Leipzig was surrounded by attractive countryside, and by extensive pleasure gardens designed on the French model. The three annual fairs drew people from far and wide: 'Leipzig has now achieved such prestige as a commercial centre, that in the whole empire, only Hamburg . . . can compare with it.'[14] The intellectual outlook of the university was somewhat disparate. On the theological side, orthodox Lutheran, almost scholastic positions were rigidly maintained; on the other hand Johann Christoph Gottsched, attached to the University since 1724, was an enthusiastic advocate of the Enlightenment, while the renowned historian Johann Burkhard Mencke, founder of the *Deutschübende poetische Gesellschaft* (1722) and himself well known as a poet under the pseudonym Philander von der Linde, was formulating his advanced theory of history. Leipzig was also a leading city in another respect: as a centre of the book and sheet music trade. These favourable circumstances were later to prove advantageous to C. P. E. Bach in many ways.

If these and other matters made Leipzig seem an ideal environment for the growth of bourgeois art and culture, it must also be said that it was not free from bureaucracy or provincialism. J. S. Bach was to encounter precisely this over and over again in the course of more than twenty-five years spent working in Leipzig. On the one hand it was certainly true that after recovering from the ravages of the Thirty Years War the city enjoyed 'a remarkable upsurge in musical activity in which Church, town, and gown all played a part'.[15] Two *Collegia*

---

[13] J. S. Bach, letter to Georg Erdmann. See n. 10 above.

[14] Quoted in *Erläuterungen zur deutschen Literatur: Aufklärung* (Berlin, 1971), p. 45.

[15] R. Eller, Section 'Vom Westfälischen Frieden bis zum Ausgang des 18. Jahrhunderts' in the article 'Leipzig', *MGG*, viii, col. 546.

musica had existed since the turn of the century, the origins of which went right back to the first decades of the seventeenth century. Yet even St Thomas's Choir was in a fairly poor state when Bach took it over, and his repeated attempts to achieve a 'well-regulated church music to the glory of God'[16] were largely unsuccessful. Bach's 'Short, but most necessary draft for a well-appointed church music with certain modest reflections on the decline of the same',[17] which he sent to the city council on 23 August 1730, remained unanswered. Disputes over the directorship of music in the University Church constituted a further source of irritation to Bach during his years in Leipzig. His work with the 'Scottish' *Collegium musicum*[18] he found much more rewarding; technically it was certainly more proficient.

J. S. Bach was burdened with an immense quantity of work. As 'Director musices', a title which he preferred to 'Cantor', he was responsible for the music in church services and—an important addition—for composing and performing the music for funerals, weddings, and various ecclesiastical or civic festivities. He took these duties very seriously, and never descended to carelessness in spite of unfavourable conditions, poor singers and instrumentalists, and frequent clashes with the authorities. The first few years in Leipzig alone saw the composition of five annual cycles of cantatas, the Magnificat (1723), the St John Passion (1724), and the St Matthew Passion (*c.*1729).

School and University in Leipzig

In Leipzig C. P. E. Bach attended the Thomasschule. An act of 14 June 1723 declares him to be in his first year [*Sexta*] there.[19] His name appears in a later catalogue as an 'externus' (day-boy) numbered twenty-fifth out of thirty-six students in the uppermost class [*Prima*].[20] As a result of the special musical responsibilities of the Thomasschule, which had to provide 'music for the city churches as well as for weddings and funerals',[21] there were often unfortunate disagreements between the teaching staff. The Rector had to ensure that the weekly allocation of twenty-one hours to academic instruction, rather less than that of the Nikolaischule, should be exploited to the

---

[16] See *Bach Reader*, p. 60, and *Bach-Dokumente*, i, p. 19.
[17] See *Bach Reader*, pp. 120ff., and *Bach-Dokumente*, i, pp. 60ff.
[18] This had developed from the *Collegium musicum* founded in 1702 by G. P. Telemann.
[19] See *Bach-Dokumente*, ii, p. 112.
[20] See H. Miesner, *Philipp Emanuel Bach in Hamburg* (Leipzig, 1929), p. 115. (R/Wiesbaden, 1969).
[21] See B. Knick, ed., *St Thomas zu Leipzig* (Wiesbaden, 1963), p. 141.

greatest advantage. The Cantor was allowed seven hours of musical instruction per week, very little time in which to train and maintain a choir at a reasonable level of competence. Under Johann Heinrich Ernesti, Rector of the Thomasschule from 1684 to 1729, neither Kuhnau nor his successor J. S. Bach could hope for any sympathy for their problems. The aged Ernesti was much too unyielding to offer any real support to the Cantors in their reasonable demands for the improvement of working conditions in the music department.

While Carl Philipp Emanuel was registered as a pupil of the Thomasschule, the educational reforms already started under Jakob Thomasius began to bear fruit.[22] Latin was replaced by the vernacular both in the classroom and in the textbooks. But it was only through Johann Matthias Gesner, whom the young Bach came to know as Rector and perhaps as teacher, that an enlightened, broadly neo-humanistic educational approach was adopted. In teaching Greek and Latin, Gesner placed emphasis on reading Classical literature. Not only did this serve as a model for the development of good taste, but it also enshrined the basic principles of Gesner's philanthropy. His pupils learned rhetoric and grammar from the writings of Herodotus, Plutarch, and Euripides. Importance was also attached to the study of history, geography, and mathematics.

Thus Carl Philipp Emanuel received a good schooling which prepared him well for University. On 1 October 1731 he matriculated at the Faculty of Law where from 1726 to 1734 Michael Heinrich Gribner was Ordinarius. Those who opted to study law had to sit examinations in a variety of disciplines.[23] Roman law was one—here the works of Heineccius, Böhmer, and Hellfeld served as a basis. 'Collegia' in natural and civil law were open to the public, and this served to strengthen the good reputation of the Law Faculty at Leipzig. The young Bach would have devoted his time to the study of these subjects, but also to German private law, Saxon particular law, and other branches of jurisprudence. He may possibly have attended lectures by Gottsched, who held a chair in poetry at the Faculty of Philosophy.

Further Musical Studies

Naturally the artistic development of the young Carl Philipp Emanuel was greatly assisted by the varied musical environment of Leipzig,

---

[22] Jakob Thomasius, father of the Enlightenment jurist Christian Thomasius, was Rector from 1675 to 1684.
[23] See C. C. Carus, *Die Universität Leipzig* (Leipzig, 1830).

despite its limitations. For some time the German musical world had been showing increasing interest in the 'great composer and organist' Johann Sebastian Bach;[24] thus his son was able to write in his autobiography:

I had from an early age the special good fortune of hearing the most excellent music of all kinds all around me, and of making the acquaintance of many first-rate masters, some of whom became my friends. In my youth I had this advantage in Leipzig, for there was hardly a distinguished musician who passed through that place without making the acquaintance of my father and playing for him. My father's particular greatness in composition and in organ and harpsichord playing was far too renowned for any respected musician to miss the opportunity, if it arose, of getting to know the great man better.[25]

J. S. Bach was a strict teacher: 'His pupils had to begin straight away with works of his own that were by no means easy.'[26] Thanks to numerous surviving accounts and references by his sons and other pupils Bach's teaching methods can be more or less reconstructed. Carl Philipp Emanuel's training as a keyboard performer was most probably based on the *Clavierbüchlein* mentioned above, a collection composed chiefly of works by Bach with a few by Telemann, G. H. Stölzel, and J. C. Richter. Unconvinced by the earlier view that the *Clavierbüchlein* was intended as a keyboard tutor, Wolfgang Plath has suggested that Bach's contributions were 'primarily models in composition, even if they may also have served as performing pieces'.[27] And he deduces from the layout of the *Clavierbüchlein* that 'the composition manual proceeds gradually from the simple to the complicated, persists in difficulty through the three-part fantasias, and concludes at the point where the noble art of fugue comes within the student's grasp'.[28]

Keyboard instruction and familiarization with the basic principles and techniques of composition thus went hand in hand. Bach's method of working out keyboard pieces with a view to their usefulness as models in composition proved to be extraordinarily beneficial, and what is more, it stimulated both horizontal and vertical thinking as well as expressive playing. C. P. E. Bach had this early, solidly-based education to thank especially for his later successes as a composer and keyboard performer. Whether he also used the *Clavierbüchlein für Anna*

---

[24] See the references quoted in O. E. Deutsch, *Handel. A Documentary Biography* (London, 1955), p. 232, *Bach Reader*, pp. 81f., 151, 441 etc., *Bach-Dokumente*, ii, pp. 185ff., 197, 279 etc.

[25] See C. P. E. Bach, 'Autobiography', p. 201. Newman, p. 367.

[26] C. P. E. Bach, *Versuch über die wahre Art das Clavier zu spielen*, 2 vols. (Berlin, 1753–1762; R/Leipzig, 1957), i, Introduction, par. 24. For details of W. J. Mitchell's English translation, see n. 7 above.

[27] Plath, op. cit., p. 70 [n. 9 above].

[28] Ibid., p. 71.

Magdalena Bach in the course of his studies is uncertain. In any event he composed five short pieces for this collection, written no earlier than 1730–1.[29]

It is clear that this thorough training with his father enabled the young Bach to develop his musical talents continuously. After the *Clavierbüchlein* he would have worked on the Inventions and the Sinfonias, and eventually on the *Well-tempered Clavier*. This compendium of keyboard music had been written and compiled 'for the use and profit of the musical youth desirous of learning as well as for the pastime of those already skilled in this study' by J. S. Bach himself.[30] Naturally Carl Philipp Emanuel also took part as a chorister in various performances of church music.

Although Carl Philipp Emanuel's participation in his father's *Collegium musicum* is not documented, it is none the less probable that the young Bach appeared in public from time to time as continuo harpsichordist, a task well within his technical powers. A later source from the second half of the eighteenth century suggests this indirectly: 'Almost every day during his long stay in Leipzig...Jacob von Stählin enjoyed the company of the famous Carl Philipp Emanuel Bach and from time to time played a solo or a concerto in his father's *Collegium musicum*.'[31] The fact that there are one or two surviving manuscript copies in the hand of the young Carl Philipp Emanuel of works by the elder Bach, including the simpler version of the D minor Harpsichord Concerto, BWV 1052a,[32] adds further weight to the suggestion. Similarly it is easy to imagine the sons as soloists in the concertos for two harpsichords. In the letter to Erdmann mentioned earlier, J. S. Bach reports proudly, 'But they [Bach's children] are all born musicians, and I assure you that I can already form an ensemble both *vocaliter* and *instrumentaliter* within my family, particularly since my present wife sings a good, clear soprano, and my eldest daughter, too, joins in not at all badly.'[33]

It appears from the autobiography that Carl Philipp Emanuel was familiar with the musical life of Dresden. Like Wilhelm Friedemann he probably accompanied his father from time to time on journeys to the

---

[29] The pieces in question are two marches in D and in G, BWV Anh. 122 and 124, two polonaises in G minor, BWV Anh. 123 and 125, and the *Solo per il Cembalo* in E flat major, BWV Anh. 129.

[30] Title-page of the first book of the *Well-tempered Clavier* (1722), quoted from *Bach Reader*, p. 85. Original in *Bach-Dokumente*, i, p. 219.

[31] From a letter by Jacob von Stählin to his son Peter; for original text see *Bach-Dokumente*, iii, p. 408.

[32] See in this connection U. Siegele, *Kompositionsweise und Bearbeitungstechnik in der Instrumentalmusik Johann Sebastian Bachs* (Neuhausen-Stuttgart, 1975), pp. 101ff.

[33] J. S. Bach, letter to G. Erdmann; see n. 10 above.

Saxon capital.[34] J. S. Bach's organ improvisations acted like a magnet—he was personally acquainted with Hasse, Quantz, Pisendel, and Zelenka.[35] These men were both performers and composers, and since they were in part responsible for new stylistic trends it is reasonable to assume an influence on the compositional development of Bach's second son as well.

So Carl Philipp Emanuel's formative years were filled with musical stimuli of many different kinds. We know, moreover, that C. P. E. Bach along with other members of the family helped his father with the preparation of performing material. In addition to the copy of a harpsichord concerto mentioned above, some of the parts for the Kyrie and Gloria of the B minor Mass exist in his handwriting, together with parts for the cantatas *Herr Gott, dich loben wir*, BWV 16, *Ich liebe den Höchsten von ganzem Gemüte*, BWV 174, and the motet *Der Geist hilft unsrer Schwachheit auf*, to name but a few examples.[36] Given his father's interest in the development of instrument manufacture and his reputation as an outstanding authority on the organ, the young Bach's familiarity with the mechanics of the harpsichord is hardly surprising. He tuned harpsichords himself[37] and would also have quilled the jacks. Although still a law student at Leipzig University, C. P. E. Bach made his first attempt to start a musical career in August 1733: he applied for the post of organist at St Wenceslas' Church in Naumburg—albeit without success.[38] Consequently the young Bach remained at university.

Earliest Compositions

It has already been mentioned that in addition to keyboard tuition the young Bach received instruction in the basics of composition from his father. These included figured bass and its realization, the stylistic characteristics of various dance-movements like the Allemande, the Sarabande, the Courante, and the minuet, and mastery of polyphonic techniques. C. P. E. Bach himself wrote a revealing account of his father's teaching methods:

He started his pupils in composition with practical exercises straight away, and omitted all the *dry species* of counterpoint that are given in Fux and others. His pupils had to begin their studies by learning pure four-part figured bass.

[34] During C. P. E. Bach's time in Leipzig his father is known to have visited Dresden three times—19–20 December 1725 (when he gave concerts on the Silbermann organ in the Sophien-kirche in Dresden), in September 1731, and finally in July 1733.

[35] See also *Bach Reader*, p. 279, *Bach-Dokumente*, iii, p. 289.

[36] In this connection see G. von Dadelsen, *Bemerkungen zur Handschrift Johann Sebastian Bachs, seiner Familie und seines Kreises* (Trossingen, 1957), pp. 39f.

[37] This is evident from certain extant account books. See *Bach-Dokumente*, ii, p. 122.

[38] See *Bach-Dokumente*, i, p. 271.

From this he moved on to chorales; first he added the basses himself, leaving the pupils to invent the alto and tenor. Then he taught them to devise the basses themselves. He particularly insisted on good part-writing. In teaching fugues, he began with two-part ones, and so on. The realization of a figured bass and the introduction to chorales are without doubt the best ways of studying composition, as far as harmony is concerned. As for the invention of ideas, he required this from the very beginning, and anyone who had none he advised to stay away from composition altogether. Neither with his children nor with other pupils would he begin the study of composition until he had seen work of theirs in which he detected talent.[39]

C. P. E. Bach was seventeen years old when he wrote his first surviving works. No doubt earlier attempts were also made. (The dating of Bach's extant works, especially of the autograph material, poses few problems, since the *Verzeichnis des musikalischen Nachlasses des verstorbenen Capellmeisters Carl Philipp Emanuel Bach* [Catalogue of the musical estate of the late Kapellmeister Carl Philipp Emanuel Bach, see Bibliography], which in all probability derives from a thematic catalogue prepared by Bach himself, gives precise information as to dates and places of composition.) Naturally enough, small-scale works such as marches, minuets, and polonaises predominate at first. And yet Bach soon turns his attention to sonatinas, sonatas, trios, and keyboard concertos.[40] The young composer's first published work, a 'Menuet pour le clavessin', Wq. 111,[41] appeared in 1731. From an analytical point of view these pieces are startling: from the very beginning Bach's desire to be different and to break away from established patterns can be observed. This is not to suggest, of course, that his style represented a deliberate rejection of his father's musical language—the music of J. S. Bach had too strong an influence on his son to be thrown off so lightly. It was actually through the younger composer's struggle to master the various forms of 'learned' music and through his upbringing as a Bach pupil that he was prevented from yielding to the easy option of a simplified style. Personal, original traits are felt even in the earliest works of the young Bach. That they are thoroughly convincing, while highly unconventional, is just one result of the rapid development of an extraordinarily gifted composer. From a stylistic point of view, the early works present a somewhat kaleidoscopic picture. Within a rich

---

[39] From a letter by C. P. E. Bach to J. N. Forkel dated 13 Jan. 1775, quoted from *Bach Reader*, p. 279. For original see *Bach-Dokumente*, iii, p. 289.

[40] In many instances autographs, performing parts etc. have been lost, so that the number of works written in Leipzig must be assumed to be considerably greater.

[41] 'Wq.' is the standard abbreviation for A. Wotquenne, *Thematisches Verzeichnis der Werke von Carl Philipp Emanuel Bach* (Leipzig, 1905). [See Concordance, pp. 245ff., for the corresponding catalogue numbers used in E. E. Helm's thematic catalogue.]

yield of musical genres is found a remarkable self-assertiveness and an exploration of all manner of technical possibilities.

The Sonata in B flat, Wq. 62 no. 1 (1731), seems to be a direct product of his father's teaching. As in the Inventions of J. S. Bach, the thematic idea is treated in contrapuntal style, that is to say observing strict part-writing. Among the pieces which C. P. E. Bach contributed to the *Clavierbüchlein für Anna Magdalena Bach* (1725), the March in D major is the most original. The composer sets to work confidently. The theme is both simple and concise (Ex. 1).

Ex. 1. March, BWV Anh. 122

In his elaboration of the theme, Bach uses the mandatory sequences and some conventional repetitions in the bass, but the given framework is filled with lively invention. Where technical problems arise, let it be said in passing, Bach knows how to deal with them. After the initial eight-bar phrase, the dominant key is reached, as expected, with A_4 in the uppermost part. In case the change in register arising from the entry of the theme in the second section should appear too abrupt, Bach adds a fanfare figure rising to A_5 which gives added emphasis to the cadence and introduces a pleasing asymmetry into the first section.

More interesting from the point of view of Bach's stylistic development are one or two sonatas and sonatinas from the Leipzig period and the *Solo per il Cembalo* in E flat major, BWV Anh. 129. Sonata form is the prevailing structural model used by the young Bach and it remains so, along with the free fantasia, in the Berlin and Hamburg periods. There have been several studies of Bach's contribution to the emergence of Classical sonata form.[42] Erich Beurmann sees the essential features of this form in the F major Sonata, Wq. 65 no. 1, written in Leipzig as early as 1731: contrasting material in a secondary key and a development section which is no mere transposed repeat of the exposition, but involves much more advanced treatment of the thematic material.[43] According to Beurmann, this makes Bach one of the

---

[42] See the writings of P. Barford, E. Beurmann, W. Müller, E. Randebrock, R. Wyler. (For details see Bibliography, pp. 249ff.)

[43] See E. Beurmann, *Die Klaviersonaten Carl Philipp Emanuel Bachs*, Diss., Göttingen, 1953, pp. 36ff.

principal pioneers of this new form.[44] The listener, of course, is more likely to be struck by the novel detail of these works. The music sounds playful, unconcerned, and in the slow movements there are occasional traces of impassioned *Empfindsamkeit*. The unbridled passion of later works, the preference for unusual harmonic turns of phrase, the musical depiction of strong contrasts in mood—all these traits are present in embryo even in the light *galant* works of the sixteen- and seventeen-year-old composer.

To give three examples: in the *Solo per il Cembalo* in E flat major, C. P. E. Bach presents a lively theme which is subjected to *Fortspinnung*—a technique for which the young composer could not possibly have had a better teacher than his father—thereby sustaining motivic interest and achieving rhythmic variety. As the closing group is approached, in place of the expected completion of the cadence, a diminished seventh chord appears, which Bach prolongs for a further two bars before allowing it to resolve (Ex. 2).

Ex. 2

A harmonic joke, one might think; certainly, but at the same time it is also a manifestation of a highly individual creative imagination. Or consider the dramatic intensification of expression towards the end of the C minor Andante from the Sonatina Wq. 64 no. 1 (Ex. 3).

Ex. 3

Such a turn of phrase would be unthinkable in J. S. Bach's music. It is a sign of a completely different kind of artistic personality. The younger Bach follows the feeling of the moment unhesitatingly. Hence the frequently unexplained changes in mood. In slow movements such as the Largo from the Sonatina Wq. 64 no. 2 there are already signs of the powerful emotional world of the later works (Ex. 4).

Ex. 4

Let there be no misunderstanding: this is not a matter of mere waywardness, a succession of new and original ideas simply for the sake of novelty. C. P. E. Bach is adept at handling the techniques learned from his father: the invention of original and pliable themes, combined with at times astonishing powers of motivic development. Naturally enough there are also mechanical and disconnected passages, where chains of triplets are spun out over long stretches, frequently interrupted by caesuras. Short phrases are highly characteristic of this music. Ornaments are still used sparingly. As C. P. E. Bach developed as a composer his handling of detail grew increasingly refined.

The Leipzig works reveal one further stylistic feature: the prominence of melody, bringing with it a shift of emphasis on to the upper part. The idea of the 'vocally inspired' composer ['*singend denkender*' *Komponist*][45]—an essential element of C. P. E. Bach's musical philosophy—is expressed in cantabile melodies and free declamation. Melodic configurations such as Ex. 5 from the Adagio non molto of the E minor Sonatina, Wq. 64 no. 4, offer good examples of *empfindsam* expressiveness.

Ex. 5

Through the nature of the genre, the five so-called 'Leipzig Trios' (Wotquenne's label), Wq. 143–7, come closer to J. S. Bach's musical

---

[45] Bach, *Versuch*, i, Ch. III, par. 12. [Mitchell's translation of '*singend denken*' is 'think in terms of song'.]

idiom than do the solo sonatas and sonatinas; so close in fact that some of the chamber works hitherto attributed to J. S. Bach may well prove to be by his second son, or at least to be student compositions written under the elder Bach's guidance and assistance.[46] The Sonata in G for two flutes and continuo, BWV 1039, is one of a number of the Leipzig Cantor's instrumental works which illustrate what Siegele describes as the 'union of pure polyphony and perfect harmony in a fixed number of voices'.[47] C. P. E. Bach needed to tackle this style of composition, and he did so in his first chamber works. At the same time he knew that his father's achievement was unrepeatable. Both Carl Philipp Emanuel and Wilhelm Friedemann admitted to Forkel that they were 'driven to adopt a style of their own by the wish to avoid comparison with their incomparable father'.[48]

The path which led C. P. E. Bach to a homophonic style within the relatively short space of four years can be traced quite clearly. A comparison between the D minor Trio, Wq. 145[49] and the A minor Trio, Wq. 148[50] (see p. 27f. below) illustrates how one technique was replaced by the other.

What is remarkable is the way in which Bach builds the theme of the first movement of Wq. 145 so as to define the tonal space gradually (Ex. 6).

Ex. 6

[46] See K. and I. Geiringer, *Johann Sebastian Bach. The Culmination of an Era* (New York, 1966), pp. 302f. n., and Siegele, op. cit., pp. 23ff. [n. 32 above].

[47] Siegele, op. cit., p. 68.

[48] J. N. Forkel, *Johann Sebastian Bach. His Life, Art, and Work*, trans. and ed. C. S. Terry (London, 1920), p. 105.

[49] In the *Verzeichnis des musikalischen Nachlasses des verstorbenen Capellmeisters Carl Philipp Emanuel Bach* (Hamburg, 1790), [see Bibliography] it is indicated that this trio was revised by Bach in 1747 in Berlin. Further details are not known. There are unlikely to have been any major alterations. Bach may simply have polished the upper parts to make them more fluent. For a contrary view, see U. Siegele, op. cit., p. 44 [n. 32 above], where attention is drawn to the close resemblances between two pairs of corresponding movements in Wq. 145 and BWV 1036. Siegele suggests that Wq. 145 may represent the revised version, made *c.*1747, and that BWV 1036 may be the original version of this work, composed by C. P. E. Bach in Leipzig.

[50] This trio was also revised by Bach in 1747.

This method of shaping the theme can be explained first and foremost by practical considerations. In Leipzig the trios were performed by a flautist who was evidently very capable.[51] Whether he contributed at all to the shaping of this or that run or figure, we will never know, but in any case the young composer knew well how to exploit the tone qualities of the instruments for which he was writing. By using different registers he also achieved greater melodic variety.[52] The main theme is left open, that is to say it demands immediate continuation, and indeed its principal motives are treated polyphonically immediately afterwards in the *Fortspinnung* section: the second melody instrument enters as expected at the interval of a fifth. The other two movements of the trio are also characterized by an imitative style.

To clarify: it is melodic *Fortspinnung* that is involved here rather than thematic development. Even though the opening fragment of the theme is from time to time quoted out of context in order to allow greater variety in harmonic treatment, even though close imitations bring about a thickening of texture, and even though the two upper parts intertwine in learned fashion (see Ex. 7), the theme remains a constant, both in shape and in expression: unity of *Affekt* is maintained throughout the movement.

Ex. 7

This is the compositional framework which Bach acquired from his father. Yet the manner of elaboration and the shaping of detail do not conceal the distance which the young Bach has already begun to travel from his model. Everything is simplified. Alfred Dürr speaks of a style in which Bach's 'à la mode *galanterie* and expressiveness must have formed a singular contrast to the "carefully worked" and broad-outlined compositions of his father'.[53]

The expressive aims of the younger Bach's music were quite different

---

[51] A. Dürr expresses this view in the preface to his performing edition of the D minor Trio (Edition Moeck, Nr. 1074, Celle, 1963).

[52] The range of the violin part in the first movement is from A_3 to E_6 flat, that of the flute part from D_4 to E_6.

[53] Dürr, loc. cit.

and led to different stylistic features. In the D minor Trio, C. P. E. Bach reveals his mastery of the art of shaping a movement by means of imitative counterpoint. Yet in so doing he imposes certain restrictions on himself, for example the 'laws' of part-writing. The constant flow of even semiquavers in this work is just one consequence of this convention. Sharp contrasts in mood are excluded, as is the strongly individual shaping of the melodic line later so typical of C. P. E. Bach. The subsequent development of his artistic personality was to lead him away from the 'learned style' although he would never abandon it entirely. While they have much to do with the composer's artistic temperament, these trends are not entirely unrelated to the prevailing *Zeitgeist*.

The Enlightenment, the predominant intellectual movement of the eighteenth century, had a decisive impact on musical developments in the period. A new ideal in music was championed and actually realized by the young generation of composers born around 1710, of whom C. P. E. Bach was one. It took account in a broad sense of the musical demands of both 'Kenner' and 'Liebhaber'. *Galanterie* and *Empfindsamkeit*, simplicity and accessibility are its outstanding attributes. It was given polemical expression in Johann Adolph Scheibe's attack on J. S. Bach:

This great man would be the admiration of whole nations if he had more grace [*Annehmlichkeit*], if he did not render his music unnatural by adopting a turgid [*schwülstig*] and confused style, and if he did not obscure its beauty by an excess of art.[54]

The historical distance of more than two centuries allows us to perceive the matter rather more clearly. Certainly the contrast between Bach's work and that of the younger generation—besides Scheibe, mention might be made of Georg Anton Benda, C. P. E. Bach, and Georg Christoph Wagenseil—was correctly noted by contemporary critics. J. S. Bach was rightly seen as an exponent of a 'learned style'. And yet the approach used in earlier histories of music to explain the contrast by opposing the 'Baroque' and the 'pre-Classical', or similar concepts, is inadequate, because coloured by value judgements.[55] The concept of Enlightenment permits a more sophisticated view; when applied to music it cannot simply be reduced to the ideal of simplicity and naturalness embodied in Scheibe's

---

[54] *Bach Reader*, p. 238. For original text see J. A. Scheibe, *Critischer Musikus* (complete edn., Leipzig, 1745; originally pubd. 1737; R/Hildesheim etc., 1970), p. 62.

[55] In H. J. Moser, *Geschichte der deutschen Musik*, 2 vols. (Stuttgart and Berlin, 1920–4), ii.1, p. 309, the author writes in connection with the new compositional practices that were appearing around the middle of the century of 'a serious breakdown of technique'. Moser, in an unacceptable generalization, declared the Enlightenment to be essentially 'anti-Baroque' (op. cit., p. 312).

formulation, for it also covers many qualities of the music of J. S. Bach.[56] There are numerous points of contact between the two styles. It is in the music of C. P. E. Bach that the strong links between the old and the new styles can be observed most clearly—understandably more so in the Leipzig trios than in the later works.

In many of the works written in Leipzig, stereotyped figures such as stepwise moving bass-lines and conventional transitional flourishes appear again and again. Sequences occur at every corner, and the thematic material is not always adequate to sustain interest for a whole movement. Yet these faults can hardly be held against a young composer, just setting out on his musical career.

The Town of Frankfurt an der Oder in the Eighteenth Century and its Musical Life

In the late summer of 1734 C. P. E. Bach moved to Frankfurt in order to continue his studies at the Viadrina University. One can only guess at the reasons for the move. Was Bach looking for more self-sufficiency and greater independence from his parents? A significant question, certainly, is whether he really intended to obtain a professional qualification in law. After three years of academic training in Leipzig he could have taken the necessary examinations which would have entitled him to practise in the Saxon provinces.[57] Did he wish to avoid a decision of this kind by going to Frankfurt? It is likely, however, that he was merely using his legal studies—just as composers like Heinrich Schütz, Johann Mattheson, George Frideric Handel, and his own brother Wilhelm Friedemann had done—in order to obtain better opportunities to develop as a musician. Education was certainly an asset in this respect; the teaching post which Bach held at the Johanneum in Hamburg from 1768 until his death in 1788 was tenable only by those who had received an academic training.[58] Was Bach perhaps looking for an opening in the nearby Prussian capital? Undoubtedly the social situation there at the time was so bleak that it could not have seemed attractive either to a prospective lawyer or to a musician. These questions must remain unanswered for the present.

---

[56] Evidence of many features of the Enlightenment in the music of J. S. Bach was reported at the conference held in Leipzig in connection with the Third International Bach Festival of the German Democratic Republic in 1975. An interdisciplinary colloquium was held on the theme 'J. S. Bach and the Enlightenment'. See *Bericht über die Wissenschaftliche Konferenz zum III. Internationalen Bach-Fest der DDR* (Leipzig, 1977).

[57] See Carus, op. cit., p. 127 [n. 23 above].

[58] See C. H. Bitter, *Carl Philipp Emanuel und Wilhelm Friedemann Bach und deren Brüder*, 2 vols. (Berlin, 1868), i, p. 9. The various documents—letters, cantata texts, etc.—supplied in the appendices to Bitter's study are full of errors. The text also contains inaccurate quotations.

Just as in Leipzig, the trade fairs had been a part of the commercial life of Frankfurt for centuries. And yet in the first half of the eighteenth century distinct signs of decline could be observed. As Berlin grew in importance, being the capital of Prussia, so Frankfurt, formerly the most important trading centre for the East and strategically situated on the North–South route from Scandinavia down to Hungary, became less important. Frederick William I declared Frankfurt a garrison town. Even as late as 1713 the debts which Frankfurt had accumulated through the Thirty Years War were still running at over 60,000 Thalers. The history of the city's intellectual centre, the university founded in the sixteenth century, was played out against the background of a tension between feudalism and the desire of the middle classes for emancipation. The Prussian King despised scholarship and art, except in so far as they served to promote military aims. Nor was Frederick William I above inflicting personal humiliation; on 12 April 1737 a number of university professors were obliged by order of the King and in his presence to oppose the court jester Morgenstern in a public debate on the subject of his essay 'Sensible thoughts on fools and folly'.[59] Maybe C. P. E. Bach witnessed this disgraceful episode. None the less there were some scholars who tried to spread the ideas of the Enlightenment in their own faculties. Böhmer's reform of penal law was one of the pioneering achievements of Frankfurt University. Johann Jakob Moser, author of the fifty-volume *Teutsches Staatsrecht* [German civil law] (1737–54) had been struggling since 1736 to update the legal training offered there, admittedly without success. In 1739 Moser left the University. His account of his time in Frankfurt presents a fairly bleak picture.[60]

That C. P. E. Bach was one of his students may be safely assumed. Further details concerning Bach's legal studies cannot be established, however. Naturally he needed to consider his advancement as a

[59] Johann Jakob Moser describes this meeting. See J. J. Moser, *Lebensgeschichte . . . von ihm selbst beschrieben* (Frankfurt am Main and Leipzig, 1777), pp. 169ff. For an abbreviated but more readily accessible version, see *J. J. Moser. Ein schwäbischer Patriot*, ed. S. Röder (Heidenheim, 1971), pp. 59ff. See also G. Köster, *Frankfurt an der Oder. Natur und Geschichte* (Frankfurt an der Oder, 1928), pp. 88f.

[60] There follows a further extract from Moser's autobiography: 'The University is in any case rather remote, and, except at the Jubilee, was never well attended: after Halle was founded and grew to prominence, so that even the Elector's endowment was transferred there, most of the local people were more or less obliged to go there. And especially at the time when I was there it was not possible for the University to flourish, because: (1) Silesia was still in the hands of the Austrians and no Silesian would have dared to study there. (2) All sorts of peculiar things had happened about which respect requires me to be silent [Moser was referring primarily to the poor quality of the teaching staff] . . .(4) In particular the Law Faculty, on which everything there depended, appeared to be in a bad way . . . When I arrived there was not a single Collegium in Law to be heard.' See J. J. Moser, op. cit., pp. 157ff. Abbreviated in *Schwäbischer Patriot*, p. 58.

musician. Frankfurt could not begin to compare with Leipzig as a musical centre, and yet Friedrich Rochlitz's remark that 'In Frankfurt there was practically no music at all'[61] is quite misleading.

Rooted as it was in the city's social institutions, the musical life of Frankfurt was hardly different in kind from that of other German cities. Church, City, and University required music for all kinds of occasions and were all subject to similar conflicting developments. The guild of town pipers was superseded or perhaps absorbed by the emerging middle-class musical societies.

At the same time Frankfurt could claim a number of distinguished musical achievements.[62] Jodocus Willich, humanist and versatile Renaissance scholar, established a *Collegium musicum* there around 1530, one of the earliest in Europe. The Frankfurt lutenists, among them Benedict de Drusina, Matthäus Waissel and Gregor Krengel were known far beyond the city boundaries. Among the most influential Cantors were Gregor Lange (in Frankfurt 1574–9), Friedrich Pittanus (1591–3), and above all Bartholomäus Gesius (Cantor 1593–1613). Michael Praetorius, author of the famous *Syntagma musicum*, studied there from 1585 and held the post of organist at the Marienkirche from 1586 to 1589. The Thirty Years War destroyed the city's musical life, which subsequently re-emerged only in fits and starts. A little information is available about various musical occasions in the eighteenth century, mostly in the context of University ceremonies. In most cases the performing material has been lost. For an academic jubilee in 1706—to name but one example—R. L. Mensching, a student from Hanover, composed a serenade.[63] This work was performed under his direction and consisted of an Overture, a Gigue, an *Air chanté alternativement avec les instruments*, a Sarabande, an Entrée, an *Air de Flûtes accompagné des Violons*, and a Menuet. There was music during the solemn procession as well. The students 'alternated with one another in such a way that the trumpets would sometimes stop, echoed gently by the violins or very softly by the *flûtes douces*, and finally all three groups would come together in chorus'.[64] In the same way other academic festivities, such as the birthdays of professors or pageants celebrating the election of a rector, were also supplied with music.

---

[61] Rochlitz, op. cit., iv, p. 282.

[62] General studies of Frankfurt's musical history include: C. Sachs, *Musik und Oper am kurbrandenburgischen Hof* (Berlin, 1910; R/Hildesheim, 1977), C. Sachs, 'Abriss einer brandenburgischen Musikgeschichte', *Landeskunde der Provinz Brandenburg*, ed. E. Friedel and R. Mielke, iv: 'Die Kultur' (Berlin, 1916), E. Kirsch, 'Zur Musikpflege an der Universität Frankfurt an der Oder', (sixteenth to eighteenth centuries), *Volk und Heimat* (Breslau, 1924), and H. Grimm, *Meister der Renaissancemusik an der Viadrina* (Frankfurt an der Oder and Berlin, 1942).

[63] See Kirsch, op. cit.   [64] Ibid.

A few years before Bach's move to Frankfurt, Johann Gottlieb Janitsch, later to enter the service of Frederick II, had studied in the Law Faculty at the Viadrina and was at the same time active in musical circles. On 14 November 1729 he performed a serenade of his own with the University *Collegium musicum* to mark the occasion of a visit from Frederick William I. Two further serenades by Janitsch were played on similar occasions in subsequent years.

Even after Bach had left Frankfurt there were still plenty of music-loving students there who were to influence the development of the city's musical life in all sorts of ways. Among them was Christian Gottfried Krause, student of law from February 1741. In Johann Adam Hiller's 1766 Leipzig publication *Wöchentliche Nachrichten die Musik betreffend*, the following observation appeared: 'Both at school in Breslau and later for the *Akademie* in Frankfurt an der Oder, he [Krause] wrote a great deal of church music.'[65] Krause, although he practised as a lawyer from 1753 onwards, was one of the leading music theorists in Berlin.

C. P. E. Bach's Musical Activity in Frankfurt

Information about C. P. E. Bach's Frankfurt years is given in three documents. University matriculation records confirm that 'Carolus Philippus Emanuel Bach Vinariensis Thuringus' became a student in the Law Faculty on 9 September 1734.[66] In the genealogy of the Bach family the following entry is found against the name Philipp Emanuel: 'at present a student at Frankfurt an der Oder; is also giving lessons in keyboard playing'.[67] Thus we learn that Bach also gave keyboard tuition, in order to earn a little extra money. Finally we read the following in the autobiography written in 1773:

After completing my studies at the Thomasschule in Leipzig I studied Law both in Leipzig and later in Frankfurt an der Oder, and while I was in the latter place, I directed and composed not only for a musical *Akademie* but also for all the public concerts on ceremonial occasions at that time.[68]

So Bach led some sort of musical ensemble in Frankfurt as well as writing occasional music of all kinds. We know of five cantatas which

[65] J. A. Hiller, ed., *Wöchentliche Nachrichten und Anmerkungen die Musik betreffend*, i (Leipzig 1766–7), p. 84 (R/Hildesheim, 1970).

[66] Staatsarchiv Potsdam, Pr. Br. Rep. 86 Universität Frankfurt an der Oder, Nr. 59, fo. 238. (Also printed in *Ältere Universitäts Matrikeln*, I: 'Universität Frankfurt an der Oder', ed. E. Friedlaender, ii [1649–1811] (Leipzig, 1888), p. 339.)

[67] See *The Origin of the Family of Bach Musicians*, [*Ursprung der musicalisch-Bachischen Familie*], ed. with a facsimile C. S. Terry (London, 1929); Facs., entry no. 46, Trans., p. 16.

[68] C. P. E. Bach, 'Autobiography', p. 199. Newman, loc. cit., p. 366.

were written between January 1736 and March 1737. The texts of three have been preserved, but without mention of the composer's name;[69] only the titles of the other two are extant.[70] If we are to believe Bach's statement that he composed 'for all the public concerts on ceremonial occasions', then we must regard him as the composer of these cantatas. The matter might, of course, be confirmed by a stylistic analysis, but for the fact that the music has not survived. The artistic merit of these works was probably not very great, for Bach normally took care to preserve good compositions. This was simply *Gebrauchsmusik* that was hardly likely to outlive the occasion of its composition. The surviving manuscripts of keyboard and chamber music from the Frankfurt period, however, tell a different story. These works too had a specific purpose to fulfil. The six surviving keyboard sonatas[71] Bach undoubtedly used for teaching purposes. The chamber music[72] as well as a concerto for harpsichord and strings[73] and the cantatas may have been written for the *Akademie* to which he refers in the autobiography.

One work from the Frankfurt period illustrates how far the individualization of C. P. E. Bach's style has progressed already: the Trio in A minor for flute, violin, and continuo, Wq. 148. Unlike the Leipzig trios, this work, dating from 1737, is strongly characterized by homophonic writing.

The first movement contains such typical stylistic traits as appoggiaturas and runs of parallel thirds. These features are present from the very beginning of the Allegretto (Ex. 8).

[69] Reference is made to the following works: 'Oratorio performed on the First Sunday of Advent 1736 at the solemn Consecration of the Frankfurt Unterkirche. Printed by Sigismund Gabriel Alex at Frankfurt an der Oder' (see Bitter, op. cit., i, pp. 325ff.). 'When His Royal Highness the Most Illustrious Prince and Lord Frederick William, Prince of Prussia and Margrave of Brandenburg and His lady wife ... honoured the town of Frankfurt with Their Highness's presence, the students of the University expressed their most humble joy at the occasion in the following Cantata. 18 March 1737. Printed by Philipp Schwarz, Royal Prussian University Press' (see Bitter, op. cit., i, pp. 328ff.). 'When the Most Illustrious and Powerful Prince and Lord Frederick William, King of Prussia and Margrave of Brandenburg ... honoured the town of Frankfurt an der Oder with His Highness's presence at St Martin's fair in 1737, the students of the University wanted to demonstrate their most humble respect and joy. Printed by Sigismund Gabriel Alex at Frankfurt an der Oder' (see Bitter, op. cit., i, pp. 331ff.).

[70] 'Cantata by C. P. E. Bach which was performed at the Ungnad-Thiel wedding feast.' (Wedding cantata of 18 Jan. 1736.) 'Cantata by C. P. E. Bach ... which was performed at the royal birthday celebrations ... of the Crown Prince of Prussia ... 24 January 1737.' These titles are given in the alphabetical catalogue of the Stadtarchiv Frankfurt an der Oder. The manuscript was lost during the Second World War.

[71] The sonatas referred to are those in E minor, Wq. 65 no. 5 (1735), G major, Wq. 65 no. 6 (1736), E flat major, Wq. 65 no. 7 (1736), C major, Wq. 65 no. 8 (1737), B flat major, Wq. 65 no. 9 (1737), and A major, Wq. 65 no. 10 (1738).

[72] In Frankfurt an der Oder in 1735 Bach wrote a trio in A minor for flute, violin, and continuo, Wq. 148, followed in 1735 and 1737 by two solos for flute, in G major and E minor respectively, Wq. 123 and 124.

[73] The concerto in question is Wq. 3 in G major (1737).

Ex. 8

They bring the work close to the *empfindsamer Stil*. In his treatment of thematic material Bach follows not so much the principle of motivic *Fortspinnung* as that of the juxtaposition of blocks of heterogeneous material. These are frequently marked off from one another by abrupt changes of key, for example from C major to D major (bars 18–19) or from F major to G major (bar 35). Such an emphasis on contrast goes against the demand for unity of *Affekt* which appears again and again in writings on musical aesthetics in this period. Here we observe rather the first indications of that improvisatory style of thought later to become characteristic of C. P. E. Bach. There is little in this trio to call to mind the long-breathed melodic style of his father.

Short phrases are also typical of the other movements. Yet superimposed on this relatively informal style were many different contrapuntal effects and variation techniques. During the first movement there are a number of *piano* episodes followed by abrupt changes of mood (Ex. 9).

Ex. 9

The whole is a masterpiece of chamber style, improvisatory in its detail, lively in its musical expression, pleasing, entertaining, and spirited.

If Bach's preference for unusual compositional procedures can be observed in embryo in this trio, it becomes fully evident in the G major Harpsichord Concerto, Wq. 3. In the first movement Bach presents a bold main theme, unstable in its direction, caught in continual upward and downward movement. It is an early example of the 'characteristic theme',[74] and manifests the unbridled, passionate artistic temperament of the composer (Ex. 10).

Ex. 10

To see these fast runs merely as a mechanical play with scales would be a great misunderstanding. In fact they possess unique expressive force. They are energetic melodic lines, treated at first very freely by Bach, resulting in an impression of aimlessness. After a few bars of such diffuse writing comes the first point of repose: movement is halted on the note D_4, accented by a trill and a pause sign. This is another instance of Bach's individuality: the focus of attention on to single notes. At once the musical scenery changes. First *piano*, then *pianissimo*, Bach introduces a subsidiary idea, which provides as it were a counterweight to the main theme (Ex. 11).

Ex. 11

Here a more restful cantabile element comes into play, followed immediately by an energetic motive which recalls the mood of the opening (Ex. 12).

Ex. 12

As far as the formal design of the movement is concerned, Bach proceeds very deliberately. Each of the three solo sections is longer

[74] This term [*Individualthema*] was used extensively by Heinrich Besseler. See Besseler, 'Bach als Wegbereiter' [n. 4 above]. *Individualthemen* are much more clearly evident in C. P. E. Bach's Berlin and Hamburg works.

than the previous one. In the same way increasing technical demands are made on the performer. While still making cautious use of runs and passage-work at the beginning, the composer gives the final episode an unmistakably virtuoso character; the scene is set by pounding semiquavers (Ex. 13).

Ex. 13

It was natural to assign considerable prominence to technical display in a harpsichord concerto. Bach, himself an outstanding harpsichordist, weaves in plenty of effective keyboard figurations, which can hardly have failed to impress the listener. As far as the overall structure of the movement is concerned, some passages in the concerto are quite ingenious. In the opening bars of the first solo episode, running scales (the main theme), pass through the entire orchestra, cementing the ensemble, starting with the first violins and moving down into the bass instruments, against rising syncopated arpeggio figures. In passing it may be mentioned that Bach avoids literal repetition during the corresponding passage at the beginning of the second solo section by using a different succession of instruments.[75]

In other works from the Frankfurt period Bach does not achieve such a high degree of artistic individuality. The keyboard sonatas, for example, with the exception of the second movement of the Sonata in E minor, Wq. 65 no. 5, a highly expressive Siciliano, or the opening movement of the Sonata in G, Wq. 65 no. 6, with its rather subtle structure, are mostly *galant* pieces. They have little originality in structure or keyboard style. The thematic ideas are often very short and their elaboration consists of conventional chains of triplets and semiquavers. And yet the best of the youthful works show clearly that Bach had already discovered a new and individual musical language, which he was to refine further in the years to come.

Seen in this light, the Frankfurt episode was important in two ways. It was a period of creative productivity and stylistic growth. It was also, however, an important period in Bach's personal development. As

---

[75] The scales begin in the violas, continue in the second violins and finally pass into the first violins.

we have seen, there are no documents to give more detailed information about this process, no comments by contemporaries, no remarks made in letters, no references in the press. But there is the music itself, and this testifies strongly to Bach's personal growth. Such works as the G major Harpsichord Concerto or the A minor Trio are to be understood as the expression of a richly developed personality.

If we consider the conclusions drawn from our analysis of these two early works in this light, then C. P. E. Bach will appear to us as a lively, intellectually highly adaptable individual with an undeniable tendency towards eccentricity. And yet his psyche is also stamped with emotion, sensitivity, strong inwardness, and humour. His works, especially his slow movements, frequently give the impression of an artist turning more and more in on himself, one for whom music means communication, self-expression of the most intimate kind. Thus did Bach mature both as man and musician. Here are the beginnings of a new view of humanity—appropriate to the new era—which was to be fully established in the next phase of Bach's creative life, his Berlin period. The gradual disappearance of the 'learned style', to be replaced first by the *galant* and finally by the *empfindsam* style is merely a symptom of this process.

2

Berlin (1738–1768)

Harpsichordist at the Prussian Court

> In 1738, when I had completed my studies and travelled to
> Berlin, I received a most propitious invitation to escort a young
> gentleman on his travels abroad; an unexpected gracious sum-
> mons to Ruppin [fifty miles north-west of Berlin] from the then
> Crown Prince in Prussia, now King, caused me to abandon this
> plan. Conditions were such that I did not formally enter the
> service of His Majesty until His accession to the throne in 1740,
> when I had the honour of accompanying on the harpsichord in
> Charlottenburg the first flute solo which His Majesty performed
> as King. From this time onwards until November 1767 I was
> continuously in the service of the King of Prussia, even though I
> received one or two lucrative offers from elsewhere. His Majesty
> was gracious enough to increase my salary substantially each
> time this happened.[1]

With these few words from the autobiography, C. P. E. Bach
describes his Berlin years, not omitting the mandatory tribute to his
former patron. Bach, then, was active in Berlin for almost thirty years,
closely involved in the musical life of the city. His contact with the
leading representatives of the bourgeois Enlightenment was highly
stimulating. Bach composed more than 300 works during these years,
consisting mainly of keyboard and chamber music, but also including
at least nine symphonies, thirty-eight keyboard concertos, a Magnificat, an Easter Cantata and numerous songs. His keyboard works
exerted a lasting influence on the evolution of a new keyboard style. In
spite of the somewhat doctrinaire rationalism which was coming to
dominate music theory, and the rigid adherence to old-fashioned ideas
prevailing in Berlin court music, which must have had an inhibiting
effect on a composer trying to forge a personal musical style, Bach
managed to achieve a high degree of artistry. His music soon became
widely known and was regarded highly throughout Germany and even
abroad.

The biographical sources are once again little help in illuminating
the period immediately after Bach's student years in Frankfurt. He had

[1] C. P. E. Bach, 'Autobiography', pp. 199f. Newman, loc. cit., p. 366.

turned down an opportunity to accompany the son of Graf von Keyserlingk as Master of the Household on a journey to France, Italy, and England,[2] which might have led to a great many useful contacts; apparently the invitation from the Crown Prince seemed more attractive. And indeed Bach could certainly hope for excellent professional opportunities in the musical establishment of the music-loving Prince of Prussia, which already included an impressive number of leading musicians.

The link with Frederick came about through the two sons of the Prussian minister von Happe, who were also studying at the University of Frankfurt an der Oder.[3] At first Bach divided his time between Ruppin and Rheinsberg, not at this stage officially in permanent employment. Here he made the acquaintance of Johann Gottlieb Graun, who had been leader of the small orchestra since 1732. He also became a friend of the Benda family from Bohemia. Franz Benda, according to Johann Joachim Quantz, was called to Ruppin as a violinist in 1733, to be followed one year later by his brother Johann Georg, also a violinist (Georg Anton Benda did not become a court musician in Berlin until 1742). In 1735 Frederick appointed Carl Heinrich Graun [Plate 7] Kapellmeister. When Frederick moved to Rheinsberg the following year in order to take up residence at Wasserburg, the old castle newly enlarged by Georg Wenzeslaus von Knobelsdorff, he took with him a total of seventeen musicians: a Kapellmeister, a harpsichordist, seven violinists, a violist, a cellist, a bass-player, a flautist, two horn-players, a harpist, and a theorbo player.[4]

Even at that date the band was of a fairly high standard, according to at least one contemporary report. Knobelsdorff wrote from Rome: 'The instrumental music here has not impressed me at all, and I should very much like to let these Romans hear one of our concerts at Ruppin.'[5] Quantz, too, expressed words of praise: 'Even between 1731 and 1740 in Ruppin and Rheinsberg the orchestra was so constituted as to attract every composer and soloist and to satisfy them fully.'[6] The court musicians had to wear full livery during their daily performances. In outward appearance nothing was to change in the

[2] See P. Spitta, *Johann Sebastian Bach*, 3 vols., trans. C. Bell and J. A. Fuller-Maitland (London, 1884–5), iii, p. 236. See also H. Miesner, 'Graf von Keyserlingk und Minister von Happe, zwei Gönner der Familie Bach', *B-Jb*, xxxi (1934), pp. 108f.

[3] Miesner, 'Graf von Keyserlingk . . .', p. 115.

[4] See C. Mennicke, *Hasse und die Brüder Graun als Symphoniker* (Leipzig, 1906), pp. 468f.

[5] See T. Fontane, 'Die Grafschaft Ruppin', *Wanderungen durch die Mark Brandenburg*, i, 2nd edn. (Munich, 1977), p. 88n.

[6] See F. W. Marpurg, *Historisch-Kritische Beyträge zur Aufnahme der Musik*, 5 vols. (Berlin, 1754–78; R/Hildesheim, 1970), i, p. 249.

following decades. (The well-known oil-painting by Adolph Menzel can at least claim authenticity on this point [Plate 3].) The repertoire consisted mostly of instrumental music, chiefly the symphonies and chamber music of Hasse and Johann Gottlieb Graun. Chamber cantatas were also heard, however, the vocal parts frequently being taken by Carl Heinrich Graun and Franz Benda. In addition, Quantz's flute compositions appeared more and more as time went by. The Crown Prince also composed music himself.[7]

After Frederick's accession to the throne in 1740 the orchestra was enlarged to include thirty-nine musicians. An annual salary of 300 Thalers was allocated to Bach,[8] one of the 'court musicians engaged in 1741'. For the first harpsichordist this was remarkably little. Quantz, who was flautist and musical adviser to the King, was paid considerably more. In addition to an annual salary of 2,000 Thalers, Frederick II paid him extra for each new composition and each new flute that he built. In the musical life of the Court noticeable changes were taking place. The King commissioned Knobelsdorff to build an opera-house and Carl Heinrich Graun travelled to Italy in order to engage singers. On 7 December 1742 the Royal Opera House [Plate 4] was opened ceremonially with a performance of Graun's *Cesare e Cleopatra*. The duties of the orchestra were thereby considerably increased. According to Marpurg, operas—exclusively those of Graun and Hasse—were performed every Monday and Friday in December and January, while 'on the other days of the week, during the Carnival season, balls, concerts, plays, and other entertainments took place at the Court. At other times, concerts were held every evening from seven until nine in the King's chamber [mostly in Sanssouci and Charlottenburg], during which His Majesty would usually demonstrate his fine discriminating taste and his exceptional dexterity on the flute.'[9]

C. P. E. Bach's duties as harpsichordist required a high degree of skill in various forms of practical musicianship. It goes without saying that he had to be an accomplished keyboard player. He also had to be able to improvise a satisfactory polyphonic continuo part over a figured bass, and to be skilled in various styles of accompaniment. According to the character of each work, the keyboard player had to choose either a single-voiced or a polyphonic accompaniment. The latter style, using maybe four or five parts, was needed, in Bach's own words, 'for heavily-scored music, for learned pieces, contrapuntal

[7] See Mennicke, op. cit., pp. 456f.
[8] See E. E. Helm, 'Bach', section III (9), 'Carl Philipp Emanuel', *New Grove*, i, p. 845; *The New Grove Bach Family* (London, 1983), p. 257.
[9] See Marpurg, op. cit., i, pp. 75f.

movements, fugues etc., and particularly for works consisting of music alone, in which taste plays a relatively small part'.[10] At the same time the harpsichordist had to be familiar with the lighter *galant* style, in which the accompanist had to allow the soloist to be heard clearly during instrumental solos or arias, only to assert himself again in the appropriate places with all manner of passage-work, such as leaps, runs, and chains of trills. In addition, experience of directing and of work with both singers and instrumentalists was required. Bach carried out all these tasks with great skill and sensitivity. The experience he gained during his first years in Berlin was later to be written down in his *Versuch über die wahre Art das Clavier zu spielen* [Essay on the true art of playing keyboard instruments].

The Prussian Capital around 1740

Frederick William I, King of Prussia from 1713 until 1740, was chiefly interested in building up his army; trade and industry had to meet the enormous demand for military equipment thus produced. Almost 80 per cent of the state's annual budget was directed towards military purposes (this was to remain so during the reign of Frederick II!). Out of almost 75,000 inhabitants in Berlin in 1730 (by 1750 there were already more than 100,000), as many as a fifth belonged to the army. Intellectual and cultural life stagnated, as can be clearly seen, for example, from the fact that the Royal Academy visibly declined, and that the philosopher Christian Wolff, persecuted as a 'free-thinker', was forced out of Prussia by the threat of execution. The court musical establishment was soon dissolved, for the 'Soldier' King's interest in music seemed to extend only to one or two regimental trumpeters.

When Frederick II became King in 1740, there were some significant changes in society. Economic policy, while admittedly still based on old commercial principles, was now directed towards independence from foreign markets. Wool became the most important commodity, and textiles the most important industry. In the legal system one or two reforms, such as the abolition of torture, were put into effect. Four years after Frederick's accession came the solemn reopening of the Royal Academy. Over the next few years leading scholars such as the mathematicians Maupertuis and Euler, the philosophers d'Alembert, Voltaire, and Lamettrie, and the botanist Linnaeus, became members of this distinguished learned society. The King corresponded with leading representatives of the French Enlightenment. He indulged his musical interests both at opera performances and as a flautist during

---

[10] Bach, *Versuch*, ii, p. 5 (Mitchell, p. 175).

the evening chamber concerts. Many new buildings (the Opera, Sanssouci, the Potsdamer Stadtschloss and others) offer convincing evidence of a new cultural splendour in the Prussian capital, 'where one saw or wanted to see Versailles in Germany' [Plate 5].[11]

And yet the Enlightened ideas of the flute-playing Frederick II were in every case subordinated to military interests, which were aimed at making Prussia into the foremost European power; this could only be achieved by military means. None other than Voltaire exposed Frederick's real ambitions in the aphorism: 'The Prince throws off his philosopher's cloak and reaches for his sword as soon as he catches sight of a province which he fancies.'[12] Only a few months after ascending the throne Frederick II began the first Silesian War and thereby sparked off the great Austro-Prussian rivalry which was to last for some decades. In subsequent years military exploits brought untold suffering and great material losses to the people. In the light of such aggressive expansionism, the view of Frederick as an 'Enlightened monarch', presented in bourgeois histories, needs some qualification. The Marxist historian Ingrid Mittenzwei has described Frederick II as a 'nobleman who died shortly before that great turning point in human affairs, the French Revolution; he undoubtedly responded to some impulses of the newly-dawning era, and tried to bring his somewhat backward country into line with new ideas, but at the same time—true to the outlook of his class and of his country—he erected barriers against the new society'.[13]

Because of the largely post-feudal economic and social conditions in Prussia, the middle classes were still denied the exercise of political power in the 1740s. The lack of a class in 'civil law' at the Academy[14] shows how concerned the feudal absolutist state was to limit the social influence of the middle class. In these conditions bourgeois art and culture could develop only hesitatingly. Since French was spoken at the Court, the Academy had no option but to publish its Enlightened writings in that language. Soon, however, such figures as Lessing, Nicolai, and Moses Mendelssohn emerged, who promoted the German language, literature, and philosophy with great vigour.

[11] J. K. F. Triest, 'Bemerkungen über die Ausbildung der Tonkunst in Deutschland im achtzehnten Jahrhundert', *AMZ*, iii, (1800–1), col. 279.

[12] Quoted from G. Vogler and K. Vetter, *Preussen. Von den Anfängen bis zur Reichsgründung* (Berlin, 1970), p. 121.

[13] I. Mittenzwei, *Friedrich II von Preussen. Eine Biographie* (Berlin, 1979), p. 206. In connection with the history of eighteenth-century Prussia, see this work, also G. Schilfert, *Deutschland von 1648 bis 1789* (Berlin, 1962), Vogler and Vetter, op. cit., and W. Hubatsch, *Frederick the Great of Prussia. Absolutism and Administration*, trans. P. Doran (London, 1975).

[14] F. Nicolai, *Beschreibung der Königlichen Residenzstädte Berlin und Potsdam und aller daselbst befindlicher Merkwürdigkeiten* (Berlin, 1769), p. 235.

The middle class began to develop its own forms of music-making. Johann Gottlieb Janitsch, bass viol player in the court orchestra, had founded an amateur concert series in Rheinsberg as early as 1738, which was continued in Berlin as an *Akademie*. A few years later additional concert enterprises were started. As yet there was no permanent middle-class musical theatre. *Singspiele* were performed now and then by travelling groups of players. Song-writing became noticeably more popular.[15] By 1750 middle-class musical life in Berlin already presented an imposing picture.[16]

The Prussian and Württemberg Sonatas

In addition to his regular duties at the Court, which must in time have become monotonous, C. P. E. Bach sought further musical opportunities. He gave keyboard tuition as he had done in Frankfurt. Bach's reputation as a teacher was excellent, and many a famous composer passed through his hands, including his youngest brother Johann Christian, and Friedrich Wilhelm Rust, who was later to become musical director at Dessau. The young duke Carl Eugen of Württemberg also received keyboard lessons—the same man who was later to achieve notoriety through disgraceful political activity, in particular through trading soldiers with America.

Bach, however, was more strongly inclined towards composition than teaching. In his first few years in Berlin he wrote prolifically, producing over twenty keyboard sonatas and ten keyboard concertos by 1744. He was not only hard-working but also extremely shrewd in business matters: he was to remain so throughout his life. Two collections of sonatas appeared in rapid succession from the Nuremberg publishing houses of Balthasar Schmid and Johann Ulrich Haffner: in 1742 the *Sei Sonate per Cembalo*, Wq. 48, known as the Prussian Sonatas, and in 1744 the *Sei Sonate per Cembalo*, Wq. 49, known as the Württemberg Sonatas [Plate 6]. It may have been through the influence of his father that he acquired this contact with the Nuremberg publishers.[17]

These two collections, apart from one or two less mature individual movements, are perhaps the most significant examples in the sonata literature for solo keyboard instruments of the stylistic changes that were in the air. Some individual movements remain firmly within the

---

[15] See 'Berlin', *New Grove*, ii, p. 567. See also 'Berlin', *MGG*, i, cols. 1712f.

[16] See below (pp. 62ff.).

[17] See L. Hoffmann-Erbrecht, 'Johann Sebastian und Carl Philipp Emanuel Bachs Nürnberger Verleger', *Die Nürnberger Musikverleger und die Familie Bach, Materialien zu einer Ausstellung des 48. Bach-Fests der Neuen Bach-Gesellschaft* (Nuremberg, 1973), pp. 5ff.

musical language of J. S. Bach, and are clearly influenced by the form of the trio sonata,[18] the gigue,[19] and the invention,[20] yet it would be wrong to dismiss them as merely derivative. On the contrary, they offer a further illustration of the way in which the growth of Bach's creative personality necessarily involved coming to terms with the inherited repertoire of polyphonic techniques and its structural principles, which he then adapted to suit new expressive aims.

The confidence with which C. P. E. Bach was able to handle contrapuntal techniques may be seen in Ex. 14 from the slow movement of the Sonata in E, Wq. 48 no. 3.

Ex. 14

This movement is written in three-part texture throughout. Its even rhythmic flow produces unity of *Affekt*, giving rise to unity of expression. The linear part-writing suggests a contrapuntal exercise (a trio sonata), but the appearance is deceptive: in bars 7 and 8 come typically Bachian turns of phrase (Ex. 15).

Ex. 15

The composer presents a dynamic contrast here, reinforced by harmonic effects (a falling diminished seventh) and the wide spacing of the hands. The result is not simply a loosening of the texture—the long

---

[18] Examples of this are to be found in the slow movements of Sonatas Wq. 48 no. 3, Wq. 49 no. 4, and Wq. 49 no. 5. See E. Randebrock, *Studien zur Klaviersonate Carl Philipp Emanuel Bachs*, Diss. Münster 1953, pp. 35ff.

[19] See the Finale of Wq. 48 no. 4.

[20] See the Finale of Wq. 49 no. 6.

lines of J. S. Bach's polyphony are generally absent—but rather a hint
of a new keyboard style, of new possibilities of motivic treatment.

The sonata as it evolved in Berlin normally contained three
movements. The minuet, an integral part of the South German sonatas
of Wagenseil, Monn, Steffan, and others, expressing a lighter, more
relaxed mood, is rejected, together with the rondo, on aesthetic
grounds.[21] Still, the first two movements in Bach's keyboard sonatas
are unquestionably weightier than the Finales.

It is the themes themselves, full of original and memorable details,
that are immediately striking. They belong to the category of the
'characteristic theme', a phenomenon which Besseler has traced
throughout much of the harpsichord and organ music of J. S. Bach,
not omitting a brief discussion of its further development at the hands
of C. P. E. Bach.[22] The 'characteristic' quality is revealed in the subtle
refinements of the individual musical elements. Let us consider
Ex. 16—the Vivace from the B flat major Sonata, Wq. 48 no. 2.

Ex. 16

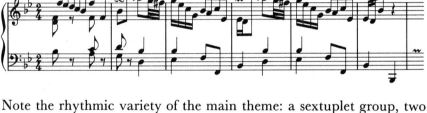

Note the rhythmic variety of the main theme: a sextuplet group, two
quaver leaps, a dotted quaver, two demisemiquavers, and several
semiquavers are juxtaposed in an apparently arbitrary succession. The
melody line changes direction restlessly. The harmonic scheme is also
unconventional, for as early as the second bar the tonic is treated as a
secondary dominant. In adding a trill over the seventh, and on a weak
beat, Bach achieves a definite impression of musical irregularity. In
other words every detail in this brief passage works against the
listener's logical expectations. And yet it is in this very discontinuity
that his individuality is manifested: at the heart of it lies the artistic
personality of Carl Philipp Emanuel Bach.

The surprise effect on the listener is carefully calculated. Here we are
dealing with a composer who takes it upon himself 'to stir the heart of the

---

[21] Hiller takes the view that minuets give the symphony 'an effeminate appearance'. See
Hiller, op. cit., i, p. 243 [Chapter 1, n. 65].

[22] See Besseler, 'Bach als Wegbereiter', pp. 1ff. [Chapter 1, n. 4].

listener into a gentle emotion and thence to lead him wherever he wishes'.[23] The close links with the idea of fantasia and of improvisation are striking and will be considered in more detail later. This does not mean, of course, that such thematic formulations as that in Ex. 16 are met throughout Bach's music. Other themes may be much more evenly structured when the underlying artistic purpose so requires. Bach is perfectly capable of working out the basic formal plan, that of sonata form, in many different ways. Again and again he looks for new solutions, and presents the motivic material in constantly new guises. This must have made quite an impression on contemporary audiences; 'Some time ago, our Herr Bach', wrote Marpurg in his *Der critischer Musicus an der Spree*, 'played the sixth sonata from his second published set for a good friend of mine.[24] This friend confessed to me that he normally suffered the misfortune of losing concentration before a piece of music was over; in this piece, however, he was able to perceive the formal design, and the performance was such as to retain his ardent and unshakeable attention throughout. This good friend is not a trained musician, and yet he understood the language of the music without the assistance of a text.'[25]

As a further illustration of the novelty of these works, let us consider the exposition of the first movement of the A minor Sonata, Wq. 49 no. 1 [Plate 6]. Once again Bach presents a main theme with an irregular rhythmic-melodic profile (Ex. 17).

Ex. 17

---

[23] Bach, *Versuch*, i, Ch. III, par. 1.
[24] Reference is made to the Sonata in B minor, Wq. 49 no. 6.
[25] F. W. Marpurg, *Der critische Musicus an der Spree* (pubd. collectively as *Des critischen Musicus an der Spree erster Band*, Berlin, 1750; R/Hildesheim, 1970), p. 217.

As such it has plenty of potential for developmental treatment, and Bach takes full advantage of this. Even in these three bars a number of rhythmically differentiated motivic patterns can be seen, which give an urgent impetus to the music. Out of a powerful 'tutti' idea, the central motivic element, emerges a demisemiquaver figure which is followed each time by a characteristic Bachian long appoggiatura. The melodic direction is strongly upward. The highest note of the theme is reached at the A_5 in bar 2, and is then followed by a cadence in the tonic. Here, as in the following extracts, Bach shows his mastery of a new method of shaping material, 'the thematic treatment of pliable motives'.[26] The range of thematic-motivic developmental possibilities thus produced seems almost inexhaustible.

Bach isolates and prolongs the long appoggiatura so as to produce a contrasting *piano* secondary idea which both softens the impassioned rhetoric of the opening and gives the music an expression of pleading. After this the two hands enter into a lively dialogue, at the same time reverting to the varied rhythms of the main theme (Ex. 18).

Ex. 18

In bars 8 and 9 the 'tutti' idea is transformed into passage-work (demisemiquaver runs in parallel sixths) (Ex. 19).

Bach tries out a further possibility of motivic treatment by restating the opening idea as if in its original form, but then placing the continuation in the left hand while the right hand takes up the secondary idea (Ex. 20).

[26] R. Steglich, 'Karl Philipp Emanuel Bach und der Dresdner Kreuzkantor Gottfried August Homilius im Musikleben ihrer Zeit', *B-Jb*, xii (1915), p. 112.

Ex. 19

Ex. 20

In this way the composer constantly creates new and unexpected motivic patterns. The sensitive articulation and ornamentation of the melodic line, the dynamic contrasts (such as echo effects) and original harmonic combinations (the diminished seventh is a favourite expressive device) in this sonata movement offer yet one more proof of Bach's sovereign mastery of a great variety of compositional procedures.

Such stylistic details, however, are invariably a means to an end. C. P. E. Bach is principally concerned with the representation of *Affekt*. According to an inherited aesthetic principle, unity of *Affekt* must always be preserved throughout a piece or movement.[27] This is achieved by unity of thematic material. For Bach, however, the *Affekt* is far from being a rigid abstraction, but is rather a reflection of changing human emotions, the finest gradations of which—he speaks of 'light and shade'—it is the composer's task to depict.[28] It is precisely this variety of expression, manifesting itself in personal stylistic details of thematic invention and treatment, which gave rise to Bach's later reputation as an *Originalgenie*.

The Mozart biographer Hermann Abert has written an accurate characterization of C. P. E. Bach the keyboard composer:

The popular slogan '*galant* style' does not remotely do justice to the art of this remarkable man, in whom features of the old-style Enlightenment are

---

[27] Quantz speaks of the prevailing *Affekt* as the bearer of the expression in a piece of music. See J. J. Quantz, *Versuch einer Anweisung die Flöte traversiere zu spielen* (Berlin, 1752), trans. and ed. E. R. Reilly as *On Playing the Flute*, 2nd edn. (London, 1985), Ch. XI, par. 15.

[28] Bach, *Versuch*, i, Ch. III, par. 7.

constantly crossing paths with the spirit of *Sturm und Drang*, and even of the later Romantic movement. He is in many respects the very antithesis of the *galant* spirit, if that is understood to mean the preference for a partly graceful, partly *empfindsam* interplay of thoughts and feelings. In spite of his fashionable exterior and in spite of the occasional over-exuberance characteristic of such innovators, Bach demands much more from the listener in these sonatas, he frequently wrenches him away through strange heights and depths, and forces him, like a true son of J. S. Bach, by means of a harmonic vocabulary which is often almost wildly daring, into areas of the soul which were quite unknown to the *galant* composers, even to his brother Johann Christian.[29]

It is above all in the slow movements of Bach's keyboard sonatas that the subjective, emotional *Empfindsamkeit* predominates, about which his contemporaries had so much to say. Even in the first set of sonatas Bach was aiming at the ideal of an expressive 'musical speech' (Mattheson), thereby placing himself firmly within the prevailing musical aesthetic of the middle of the century. The resemblance of music to rhetoric was taken for granted by the theorists. Attempts were made in a great many treatises to apply linguistic phenomena and modes of expression to the realm of music and to deduce analogous musical structures. 'The object is to imitate a form of speech observing the rules of grammar and syntax, suggesting concrete concepts and connecting them. Music must speak.'[30] Hence the large number of figures of speech discussed in a musical context, for example *Abruptio*,[31] *Ellipsis*,[32] *Multiplicatio*,[33] *Extensio*,[34] but also the 'redendes Prinzip' (rhetorical principle)[35] and the dialogue. Bach frequently employs these devices; he refers in his *Versuch* to the 'speaking' passages in his music.[36] The question of the character of Bach's keyboard style is also important. Geiringer speaks of a 'technique of transferring elements of the dramatic vocal style into keyboard music'.[37]

The F minor slow movement of the first Prussian Sonata serves as a

---

[29] H. Abert, *Wolfgang Amadeus Mozart*, 2 vols., 3rd edn. (Leipzig, 1955–6), i, pp. 65ff.

[30] See A. Schering, 'Carl Philipp Emanuel Bach und das "redende Prinzip" in der Musik', *Jahrbuch der Musikbibliothek Peters für 1938*, xlv (1939), p. 15.

[31] See 'Rhetoric and music', *New Grove*, xv, pp. 793ff. Here *Abruptio* is described as 'a general pause or silence within a musical texture where silence is not expected' (p. 800).

[32] Ellipsis. 'The omission of an otherwise essential consonance which alters the normal formation of a suspension or passing-note passage . . . More generally (according to Scheibe), an unexpected new direction taken by a passage that has led up to an expected conclusion.' ('Rhetoric and music', *New Grove*, xv, p. 797.)

[33] Diminution or *Multiplicatio* refers to the division of a note into several smaller note-values.

[34] *Extensio* or *Prolongatio*. 'The extension of the normal value of a dissonance, whether a suspension or a passing-note.' ('Rhetoric and music', *New Grove*, xv, p. 797.)

[35] Schering's term. See Schering, op. cit.

[36] Bach, *Versuch*, i, Ch. III, par. 15.

[37] See K. and I. Geiringer, *The Bach Family. Seven Generations of Creative Genius* (London, 1954), p. 353.

good illustration of this. In this movement, probably for the first time in his career, C. P. E. Bach makes use of an instrumental recitative. J. S. Bach's Chromatic Fantasia and Fugue, BWV 903, also contains a passage of recitative in the middle section of the fantasia, but in this case, one that is called forth by the nature of the genre as a necessary counterweight to the strict polyphony of the fugue. His son uses the recitative formally and expressively as 'musical speech' in the literal sense. By contrasting two different types of sonority he attempts to create the impression of a dialogue in this movement. The Andante begins with a cantilena, flowing in declamatory style into a broad melodic line. At the same time the melody, already rich in appoggiaturas, acquires sharper dissonances—in bar 2 the immediate juxtaposition of G and G flat creates tension—and these are undoubtedly intended to effect an increase in intensity (Ex. 21).

Ex. 21. Sonata in F major, Wq. 48 no. 1

The ensuing recitative not only creates a contrast in mood with what has gone before, but also gives a rhetorical meaning to the arioso passage which follows (Ex. 22).

Ex. 22

The alternation of recitative and arioso remains central to the subsequent progress of the movement. Bach discovers some surprising harmonic solutions: for example, he modulates in just a few bars from G major to E flat major.

It may have been a movement like this, surely one of Bach's most expressive musical creations, which Johann Friedrich Reichardt had in mind many years later when he wrote in the *Musikalischer Almanach* (1796):

... but there had never before then appeared any instrumental music in which such a rich, yet well-ordered harmony was combined with such noble lyricism, nor so much beauty, order, and originality achieved, as in the first two sets of sonatas printed in Nuremberg and the first concertos of this master.[38]

Keyboard Concertos

Reichardt's reference to some 'concertos' by Bach in which a high degree of artistic originality may be seen applies particularly to the first movement of the Harpsichord Concerto in E major, Wq. 14. This work was composed in 1744, just around the time of the first two collections of keyboard sonatas. The fact that it was printed in Berlin one and a half decades later shows that C. P. E. Bach valued it highly enough to want to offer it to a wider public.

What is the formal scheme that Bach uses for his concertos? To what tradition do they belong? How is the concept of 'concerto', the element of 'competition' between orchestra and soloist, realized? The key position occupied by this genre in Bach's total output is amply attested by the fact that he composed thirty-eight keyboard concertos in Berlin alone.[39] There are several reasons for this. As a harpsichordist-composer, active not only in the court orchestra, where his concertos were certainly performed from time to time,[40] but also in a variety of amateur musical gatherings, he must have needed to supply works of his own in order to help provide suitable repertoire. The great demand for solo concertos, especially marked at a time when middle-class concert life was establishing itself increasingly, can be explained by the desire of both 'Kenner' and 'Liebhaber' to be entertained by virtuoso solo playing, but at the same time to be moved by a heartfelt, emotional style of performance. Among the keyboard concertos there are a few works of which Bach could say that he had composed them in 'complete freedom'.[41] Certain formal and textural innovations in these works gain for them an important place in the history of the keyboard concerto. It is in these concertos that the link with the tradition of Vivaldi and J. S. Bach is most clearly evident.

[38] *Musikalischer Almanach*, ed. J. F. Reichardt (Berlin, 1796), Part IV, section 'C. P. E. Bach'.

[39] Fuller details concerning date of composition, scoring etc. are to be found in R. W. Wade, *The Keyboard Concertos of Carl Philipp Emanuel Bach. Sources and Style* (Ann Arbor, 1981). See also Pippa Drummond, *The German Concerto. Five Eighteenth-Century Studies* (Oxford, 1980) and Wotquenne, op. cit.

[40] See H. Miesner, 'Porträts aus dem Kreise Philipp Emanuel und Wilhelm Friedemann Bachs', *Musik und Bild. Festschrift Max Seiffert* (Kassel, 1938), p. 102.

[41] C. P. E. Bach, 'Autobiography', p. 209. Newman, loc. cit., p. 372.

The composite opening ritornello with its sequence of ideas allowed for a process of selection and permutation which could give rise to a different version of the ritornello at each statement; the relationship of the solo sections to the ritornellos could range from complete contrast to thematic identity.[42]

This formal principle, practised by Vivaldi, had a far-reaching influence on the development of the German concerto. J. S. Bach's preoccupation with Vivaldi began no later than 1713–14 in Weimar. To these years belong the harpsichord and organ transcriptions, and there is evidence to suggest that a few of Bach's original concertos also belong to the Weimar period; the majority of Bach's concertos, however, probably date from the years spent at Cöthen.[43] In Leipzig Bach revised the three extant violin concertos, BWV 1041–3, as well as several lost concertos for one or more solo instruments, by substituting a harpsichord as the solo instrument, apparently in order to provide new repertoire for the city's *Collegium musicum*. By this time, if not before, C. P. E. Bach must himself have had some early experience of the keyboard concerto. This provided him with a starting-point for his own work in Berlin. Most of all it was J. S. Bach's technique of linking the ritornellos with the solo episodes motivically that was adopted by his son, and then further enriched through his newly-gained experience in the field of the keyboard sonata, which had taught him to handle the structural outline of sonata form, to write individually characterized themes, and to combine different motivic groups.

A fairly advanced stage in the gradual transition from Baroque ritornello movement to Classical concerto-allegro movement can already be observed in the E major Concerto, Wq. 14. As in most of C. P. E. Bach's concertos, four ritornellos alternate with three solo episodes. Thematic differentiation is not the aim here, but rather unification by the use of similar thematic material in solo and tutti, a principle which suits the general requirement of unity of *Affekt*. The main theme of the E major Concerto with its wide intervals and triadic

Ex. 23

---

[42] R. Eller, 'Antonio Lucio Vivaldi', *MGG*, xiii, col. 1861.
[43] The author is indebted to Dr K. Heller, Rostock, for kindly providing this information.

melody in the upper part over a stepwise descending bass—a relic of the old style—is present in all the tutti sections (Ex. 23).

The solo thematic material in turn consists of a considerably embellished version of the tutti theme. It is written in a more characteristic keyboard idiom. Bach ornaments the melody discreetly with appoggiatura figures and animates it with smaller note-values (Ex. 24).

Ex. 24

Regarding the proportional lengths of tutti and solo sections, an interesting pattern emerges. In the course of the movement the solo sections become noticeably longer, so that the third solo is actually twice as long as the first tutti section, as the table below illustrates.

Tutti (= T)	T1		T2		T3		T4
Solo (= S)		S1		S2		S3	
No. of bars	50	45	40	55	20	100	40
Length expressed as a proportion of that of the first tutti.	1.0	0.9	0.8	1.1	0.4	2.0	0.8

Translator's Note: lengths of sections as listed above are not exact, but are rounded off to facilitate comparison.

It is in keeping with the very nature of the concerto to place the emphasis on solo concertante writing, as Bach does here. In the solo sections with their short tutti interruptions he unfolds a richly motivic tapestry. The statement of the thematic material in the first solo is followed by passages with marked developmental character: Bach uses many sequences, sets up an interesting exchange between the hands and then leads from motivic material into figurative passage-work. In the second and third solos the display element is increased. For long stretches full of harmonic movement, runs and arpeggios predominate: the rippling semiquavers in the second and third octave above middle C—played on the upper manual—bring out effectively the bright silvery tone of the harpsichord. Yet here too the theme is ever-present in the shape of the *Kopfmotiv* in the bass. The whole movement is pervaded by a sense of urgency which fully reflects Bach's impassioned inspiration.

This impassioned style is even more evident in later works. The first movement of the Harpsichord Concerto in D minor, Wq. 23, written in 1748, with its jagged themes and its boldly expressive character, actually anticipates Beethoven (Ex. 25).

Ex. 25

The slow movements are of particular interest in the light of the contemporary remark: 'The stronger and more moving . . . the slow movement of a concerto is, the greater the effect it will have, and the more successfully an accomplished performer will be able to project his personality when playing it.'[44] In one or two slow movements, such as that of the C minor Concerto, Wq. 31, written in 1753, Bach returns to the instrumental recitative and the 'rhetorical' style of the keyboard sonatas in order to intensify the dialogue between soloist and orchestra (see pp. 196f. below). The finales, while similar in construction to the first movements, are more relaxed in mood. A few concertos were arranged by the composer as concertos for flute, oboe, or violoncello.

J. S. Bach's Visits to Berlin

'In the year 1744 in Berlin I married Johanna Maria Dannemann, youngest daughter of a local wine-merchant.'[45] Bach's wife, who was ten years his junior, bore him three children. The first, Johann August

[44] Scheibe, op. cit., p. 633 [Chapter 1, n. 54].
[45] C. P. E. Bach, 'Autobiography', pp. 202f. Newman, loc. cit., p. 368.

(? Adam), was born on 30 November 1745; Bach's only daughter, Anna Carolina Philippina, followed on 4 September 1747, and finally one year later in September 1748 came Johann Sebastian. According to Rochlitz, C. P. E. Bach was anxious that his children should continue the family musical tradition:

Bach had a son and a daughter. Neither child appeared to be especially talented musically: the former eventually became a lawyer and the latter occupied herself with domestic duties all her life. When he was already fairly advanced in years [!] to his great joy a further son was unexpectedly born to him. 'This child', he exclaimed, 'will be the one to continue the family tradition!' And in this consoling hope he christened the child Sebastian, explaining to his friends on numerous occasions: 'Through this child I shall bequeath to the world all that I have learnt from my great father and all that I have discovered for myself.'[46]

Although this tale has a strongly anecdotal flavour, and is somewhat hyperbolic, it is nevertheless true that Bach's youngest son was artistically talented: he was to become a painter.

It was early in C. P. E. Bach's Berlin period that the two visits from his father occurred. The first visit took place in August 1741, soon after Emanuel had been officially appointed chamber harpsichordist to the King, and on this occasion the elder Bach enjoyed the hospitality of the King's personal physician, Dr Georg Ernst Stahl, a friend of Emanuel. J. S. Bach's journey to Berlin may have been planned as a family visit, although the cultural atmosphere of the city would itself have provided sufficient attraction; we read in a letter from Johann Elias Bach, since 1737 a member of the Leipzig Cantor's most intimate family circle, that 'in Berlin the golden age of music seems to have dawned'.[47]

A second visit followed in 1747, this time at the invitation of Frederick II, who received J. S. Bach in audience on 7 and 8 May. In the obituary of J. S. Bach written by C. P. E. Bach and Johann Friedrich Agricola the meeting is described as follows:

In the year 1747 he [J. S. Bach] made a journey to Berlin and was graciously allowed on this occasion to perform in the presence of His Majesty the King of Prussia at Potsdam. His Majesty himself played a fugue subject for him,[48] on which Bach improvised a fugue at once on the piano, to the especial pleasure of His Majesty. Hereupon His Majesty demanded to hear a six-part fugue, which command was also fulfilled at once, on a theme selected by Bach, to the astonishment of the King and the assembled musicians. After his return to

---

[46] See Rochlitz, op. cit., iv, pp. 290f.

[47] See Geiringer, *The Bach Family*, p. 187.

[48] Arnold Schoenberg's hypothesis that C. P. E. Bach may have written this theme himself is one of several suggestions. See A. Schoenberg, 'Bach' (10 Mar. 1950), quoted in *Style and Idea. Selected writings of Arnold Schoenberg*, ed. L. Stein (London, 1975), pp. 393ff.

Leipzig, he wrote a three-part and a six-part *Ricercar* besides various other smaller pieces based on the same theme presented to him by His Majesty, and dedicated the copper engraving of the work to the King.[49]

Thus did J. S. Bach's Musical Offering come to be written.

There can be no doubt that father and son would have exchanged ideas on compositional matters during these two visits. Given their widely differing approaches, this might have led to heated debate. And yet it would be a mistake to view the father–son relationship solely in terms of Bach's aphoristic (and unsubstantiated) comment regarding the music written by his second son: 'It's Prussian blue; it fades!',[50] or to attribute too much weight to the quip about the 'old wig', as the sons allegedly referred to their father. It is well known that throughout his life the Berlin Bach expressed appreciation of his father's genius in letters, theoretical writings, and recorded conversations, and he frequently quoted him in support of his own views.[51]

Still stronger testimony to the extraordinarily fertile influence of his father's music is offered by C. P. E. Bach's actual compositions. Even in connection with the two sonata collections, Wq. 48 and Wq. 49, and earlier works, it has been argued above that the new 'taste' did not consist of a radical break with tradition, but was essentially built on to the elder Bach's musical language, while admittedly distinguished from an early stage by many idiosyncratic, pioneering stylistic innovations. And in order to appreciate just how gifted a composer his son was, J. S. Bach need only have compared his music with that of other contemporary musicians like Schaffrath, Agricola, even Quantz and J. G. Graun. Several of C. P. E. Bach's Berlin works, which must have been known to his father through manuscript copies and printed editions, possessed a far higher degree of originality than the music of these others, a fact which can hardly have escaped his father's notice. This originality, with which Burney was later to credit only Bach and Franz Benda among all the Berlin composers,[52] was achieved in part through the integration of stylistic features from J. S. Bach's music. There are numerous instances of this, in pungent harmonies, for example, in polyphonic effects, or in the *Fortspinnung* applied in many sonatas.

W. F. Bach, his father's favourite son, stood even closer to the elder

---

[49] C. P. E. Bach and J. F. Agricola, *Obituary of J. S. Bach*, quoted in *Bach Reader*, pp. 215ff. (this particular passage p. 220). Originally published in L. Mizler, *Musikalische Bibliothek*, iv (Leipzig, 1754; R/Hilversum, 1966), pp. 166f.

[50] *Bach Reader*, p. 447; *Bach-Dokumente*, iii, p. 519.

[51] See, for example, Bach, *Versuch*, i, Introduction, par. 24, and Ch. I, par. 7; ii, pp. 12 (Mitchell, p. 181) and 322 (Mitchell, pp. 426f.).

[52] Burney, *Musical Tours*, ii, p. 206.

Bach's music. C. P. E. Bach said of his brother: 'He could provide a better substitute for our father than the rest of us put together.'[53] Features of the *empfindsamer Stil*, sighing appoggiaturas, and deeply-felt melancholy are combined in his music, which is full of strokes of genius, passionate and exalted, directed entirely at the connoisseur.[54]

The Magnificat

In 1749 C. P. E. Bach wrote his Magnificat in D for solo quartet, choir, and orchestra, Wq. 215. The occasion of its composition is something of a mystery. Perhaps Bach wrote it in the hope of securing the title of Court Kapellmeister to Princess Anna Amalia of Prussia. Herself a composer, the princess possessed an extensive music library.[55] As an eager champion of the 'learned style' she greatly esteemed the music of J. S. Bach, but also valued Handel, Hasse, C. H. and J. G. Graun, and C. P. E. Bach. Another possibility is that Bach may have written the Magnificat as a test-piece with a view to applying for the post of Cantor at the Thomasschule in Leipzig at some later date. There seems to have been a performance of this work in Leipzig quite early on. Johann Friedrich Wilhelm Sonnenkalb, pupil of the Thomasschule from 1746 to 1754, and later Organist and Cantor, has this to say: 'I can still recall with pleasure the splendid Magnificat which Herr Bach of Berlin performed during my time in the Thomaskirche on a feast-day of Our Lady shortly before his father died—quite some time ago now.'[56] This would suggest 2 February, 25 March, or 2 July 1750 as possible dates for the performance.[57]

Carl von Winterfeld describes the Magnificat as a 'collection of model examples of many different movement types',[58] and indeed this large-scale choral work presents an amalgam of inherited forms with new features that point towards the Viennese Classical style.

In any musical setting of the liturgical Magnificat in this period, a strong element of tradition comes into play. Not only will the

---

[53] See *Bach-Dokumente*, iii, p. 613.

[54] For a thematic catalogue of W. F. Bach's music see M. Falck, *Wilhelm Friedemann Bach* (Leipzig, 1913). See also the work-list supplied in *New Grove*, i, pp. 843f., and in *The New Grove Bach Family*, pp. 247ff.

[55] See E. R. Blechschmidt, *Die Amalien-Bibliothek. Musikbibliothek der Prinzessin Anna Amalia von Preussen (1723–1787). Historische Einordnung und Katalog mit Hinweisen auf die Schreiber der Handschriften* (Berlin, 1965).

[56] 'Herrn Sonnenkalbs Fortsetzung der unpartheyischen Gedanken über den Tractat des Herrn Daube selbst', F. W. Marpurg, *Historisch-Kritische Beyträge*, iv, pp. 236f. [n. 6 above]. See also *Bach-Dokumente*, iii, p. 148.

[57] See *Bach-Dokumente*, iii, p. 148.

[58] C. von Winterfeld, *Der evangelische Kirchengesang und sein Verhältnis zur Kunst des Tonsatzes*, 3 vols. (Leipzig, 1843–7), iii, p. 431.

particular *Affekt* of each individual movement be common to all
settings, but to some extent common techniques will be used to achieve
it. The 'Sicut locutus est' is treated as a fugue by J. S. Bach in his
Magnificat in D, BWV 243, as is the 'Sicut erat in principio' in the
present work. Both works are written in the key of D major, a
customary practice, intended to make possible the use of natural
D trumpets in the outer movements and one or two of the inner
movements, but also a deliberate means of achieving the *Affekt* of joy
and glory, the 'triumphal mood'.[59] The resemblance of the orchestral
introductions in the two settings extends as far as compositional detail:
running semiquavers in the strings and woodwind, accents and triadic
figures in trumpets and drums. Yet as soon as the chorus enters the
picture changes noticeably: J. S. Bach constructs a skilful polyphonic
vocal texture (Ex. 26), whereas his son prefers more homophonic
effects and a much simpler texture (Ex. 27). The vocal part-writing is
also less 'instrumental' in C. P. E. Bach's setting.

Ex. 26. J. S. Bach, Magnificat, BWV 243, Opening Chorus

The historical outlooks and ideals manifested here differ markedly.
Whereas J. S. Bach attaches prominence to polyphony and includes a
greater number of choruses, thus achieving a more dramatic mood,
C. P. E. Bach by contrast stresses the uppermost voice and writes in a
predominantly lyrical style.

[59] See Schubart, *Ideen*, p. 379 [Introduction, n. 4].

Ex. 27. C. P. E. Bach, Magnificat, Wq. 215, Opening Chorus

The solo numbers, in which imitative counterpoint is less prominent, become the focus of attention. None the less much of the choral writing is unmistakably indebted to J. S. Bach. The opening motives of 'Fecit potentiam' and 'Deposuit potentes' are borrowed almost literally from the elder Bach's Magnificat. The resemblance to Italian opera is made clear in more than one instance by the use of certain aria-types. According to the character of the text before him, C. P. E. Bach will select either an *empfindsam*, a lyrical, or a triumphant mode of expression. Thus the 'Quia respexit' makes ample use of appoggiaturas, small intervals with a preference for motives moving by step, and finely graded dynamics. By means of skilful melodic exchanges between soprano and violins Bach achieves a deeply-felt 'scena' reflecting the smallest nuances of meaning in the text. The antithesis of this is found in the subsequent tenor aria 'Quia fecit' which opens with a rising triadic figure, a concise, energetic scale climbing to D_6 and an outline of the tonic chord leading strongly to the first cadence (Ex. 28).

Ex. 28

The powerful impetus of this thematic idea is intrinsic to the entire piece, and places it in the category of the 'victory aria'. There are numerous anticipations of the later vocal works of Mozart, and not only in those instances where a similar melodic formula appears (Exx. 29 and 30).

Ex. 29. C. P. E. Bach, Magnificat, Wq. 215, 'Sicut erat'

Si - cut   e - rat   in   prin - ci - pi - o

Ex. 30. W. A. Mozart, Requiem, K. 626, 'Kyrie eleison'

Ky - ri - e   e - le - i - son

J. S. Bach's Estate

J. S. Bach died on 28 July 1750. The obituary for Lorenz Mizler's *Societät der Musicalischen Wissenschaften*, to which Bach had belonged since June 1747, was written jointly by C. P. E. Bach and Johann Friedrich Agricola. It appeared in 1754 in the fourth volume of Mizler's *Musikalische Bibliothek*.

This document has become significant for the history of the reception of Bach's music. Notwithstanding some anecdotal insertions it contains important details about J. S. Bach's life from a reliable source. In the first place it includes an outline—albeit not a very detailed one—of his total *œuvre*. The authors of the obituary also try to mention the place of composition for each work, and in this they were to influence Bach scholarship considerably in the following decades, in fact right up to the present day. Two central ideas are of particular interest: firstly Bach's mastery of the most 'esoteric secrets of harmony', which is viewed as a symptom of 'serious, elaborate, and profound music'[60]—contemporaries saw him as the 'great master of fugues'[61] and 'author of profound music'[62]—and secondly his reputation as the greatest 'organist and harpsichord virtuoso',[63] and as a master of the art of improvisation. From the subjective vantage point of the *empfindsamer Stil* C. P. E. Bach and Johann Friedrich Agricola identify certain 'special', 'strange' features in Bach's music,[64] but they underline its distinctive and stylistically influential character with such labels as 'novel', 'expressive', and 'beautiful'.

[60] Bach and Agricola, *Obituary*, loc. cit., p. 222.

[61] J. Mattheson, *Der vollkommene Capellmeister* (Hamburg, 1739; R/Kassel and Basel, 1954; trans. and ed. E. C. Harriss, Ann Arbor, 1981), Part III, Ch. XXIII, par. 66.

[62] *Bach Reader*, p. 236; *Bach-Dokumente*, ii, p. 410.

[63] Bach and Agricola, *Obituary*, loc. cit., p. 223.

[64] Ibid., p. 223.

C. P. E. Bach took the fifteen-year-old Johann Christian into his house and gave him instruction in keyboard playing. The younger brother left Berlin in 1754, or possibly 1755, and went to Italy in order to complete his musical studies with the famous Padre Martini. He became a Roman Catholic, a step which his elder brother took very much amiss, and on which he commented ironically, 'inter nos, he has behaved very differently from honest old Veit'.[65] In 1760 J. C. Bach became cathedral organist in Milan and composed his first operas. In 1762 he moved to England, to take up a lucrative post at the King's Theatre in London.

A large part of J. S. Bach's estate, including the autographs of the two surviving Passions, the Christmas Oratorio, and the B minor Mass, fell to Carl Philipp Emanuel, whose interests were represented by his brother Wilhelm Friedemann during the distribution of the estate. In addition to these and many other works by J. S. Bach, Carl Philipp Emanuel's own Nachlassverzeichnis (1790) names works by other composers from the Bach family. Emanuel took great care of the manuscripts he had inherited. It is true that in 1756 he offered for sale the original plates of the 'Art of Fugue', first published in late 1750 or early 1751,[66] but he did so in the hope that they would be acquired by a publisher who would make available this 'most complete and practical fugal work . . . for the benefit of the public'.[67] Bach's hopes were not fulfilled. Presumably the copper plates were sold for their metal value and then melted down.

The post of Cantor at the Thomasschule, left vacant upon J. S. Bach's death, attracted applications from Carl Philipp Emanuel Bach himself as well as from Johann Gottlieb Görner, Johann Ludwig Krebs, and August Friedrich Graun; the successful candidate, however, was Gottlob Harrer, thanks to the support of Count Heinrich von Brühl. At this time the various tensions arising out of Bach's court service in Berlin had grown particularly acute, not least as a result of his meagre salary. He was still receiving his initial salary of 300 Thalers, which was bound to cause resentment, given that Nichelmann, the second harpsichordist, was paid 500 Thalers, while Quantz and the Graun brothers were still receiving 2,000 and 1,200 Thalers respectively. The King took no steps to improve his chief harpsichord-

---

[65] *The Origin of the Family of Bach Musicians.* Veit Bach (died before 1577), the first to appear in this genealogy, probably fled from Hungary to Germany in order to escape the Counter-Reformation. For a discussion of the date of J. C. Bach's journey to Italy, see H.-J. Schulze, 'Wann begann die "italienische Reise" des jüngsten Bach-Sohnes?', *B-Jb*, lxix (1983), pp. 119ff.

[66] The 'Art of Fugue' appeared in 1752 in a second edition with a detailed introduction by F. W. Marpurg.

[67] *Bach Reader*, p. 269.

ist's wages, which must surely have been among the reasons for Bach's renewed efforts in 1753 to find alternative employment. He applied for the post of organist at Zittau, as did his brother Wilhelm Friedemann, organist and Director of Music at the Marktkirche in Halle since 1746, and also Gottfried August Homilius, Johann Christoph Altnickol, and Johann Trier. The last-named, a student at Leipzig University and director of the students' *Collegium musicum*, was appointed to the post.

The matter of Bach's salary had still not been resolved by the middle of 1755. Frederick's private chamberlain, Michael Gabriel Fredershoff, reported to the King as follows:

Lautensack [privy councillor and adviser to the King on military and financial affairs] has forwarded to me Bach's letter in obedience to Your Most Gracious Majesty's command. His other complaints are 'too numerous [to list], but his principal grievance is that he can no longer survive on 300 Thalers. In every year of service he has needed to spend a further 600 Thalers—Nichelmann and Agricola were his pupils, and they get 600 Thalers, he humbly requests Your Majesty to increase his salary, or else to release him from his duties. He has been driven by necessity to make this request, for he would serve Your Majesty with the greatest pleasure, were it not that he is unable to support his family.[68]

The King's comment in the margin reads as follows:

Bach is lying; Agricola gets only 500 Thalers. He once played in a concert here, and now he's getting cocky. His pay will be increased, but he must wait for the next round of financial measures.[69]

So Bach had to fight hard for a secure social position (which, it should be said, was never seriously endangered either in Berlin or later in Hamburg). When Harrer died on 9 July 1755, Bach applied once again for the post of Cantor at the Thomasschule. The then mayor of Leipzig took this view: 'I have received a recommendation for Bach from Telemann in Hamburg, but he would not be able to undertake any teaching duties in the school, and this is an essential requirement.'[70] Johann Friedrich Doles was appointed. Once again Bach's attempt to find alternative employment was unsuccessful. In any case the King now granted him a pay rise of 200 Thalers, bringing his total stipend to 500.[71]

[68] See H. Miesner, 'Aus der Umwelt Philipp Emanuel Bachs', *B-Jb*, xxxiv (1937), p. 139.
[69] Ibid.
[70] Stadtarchiv Leipzig, Tit. VIII 66, fo. 98; see H.-J. Schulze, '. . . da man nun die besten nicht bekommen könne . . .', *Bericht über die Wissenschaftliche Konferenz zum III. Internationalen Bach-Fest der DDR 1975* (Leipzig, 1977), p. 76.
[71] See Miesner, 'Umwelt Bachs', loc. cit., p. 139.

Chamber Music

In spite of these unfortunate set-backs, Bach's composing flourished. In 1751 Balthasar Schmid's Nuremberg publishing business, by then in the hands of his widow, issued some chamber music by Bach with the following title: 'Two trios, the first for two violins and bass, the second for flute, violin, and bass; in both works, however, one of the upper parts can also be performed at the keyboard.' The first is the Trio in C minor, Wq. 161 no. 1,[72] which bears the programmatic title 'Conversation between a Sanguineus and a Melancholicus'. Hardly any other work by Bach has generated so much discussion. According to the printed preface,

An attempt has been made in the first trio to express as far as is possible by means of instruments alone something for which the resources of voices and a text are perhaps more suitable. It is meant to portray a conversation between a Sanguineus and a Melancholicus, who are in disagreement throughout the first and most of the second movement; each tries to draw the other over to his own side, until they settle their differences at the end of the second movement, at which point the Melancholicus gives up the battle and assumes the manner of the other.[73]

There then follows a detailed explanation of 'all the main events' in the work, so that each individual mood, each element of the situation portrayed can be grasped and followed by the listener. The range of characteristics depicted is considerable: complaining, playfulness, pleading, questioning, melancholy, high spirits, bitterness, sadness, and so on. A pictorial, associative musical language is attempted here.

In this chamber work C. P. E. Bach confronts one of the most controversial aesthetic questions of his day: what is the essence of instrumental music, and how can it be defined? Writers such as Christian Gottfried Krause, Quantz, Nichelmann, and Marpurg, arguing from a rationalist standpoint, had given pride of place to vocal music over instrumental forms, since the presence of words supplies a clear notional content to the former.[74] This attitude carried implicitly a fundamental misjudgement of instrumental music. 'Sonate, que me veux-tu?' asked Bernard le Bovier Fontenelle.[75] Sonata, chamber music, and symphony were all more or less relegated to the category of

---

[72] This trio was written in 1746.

[73] See H. Mersmann, 'Ein Programmtrio Karl Philipp Emanuel Bachs', *B-Jb*, xiv (1917), p. 139, for complete preface. See also C. P. E. Bach, *Sonata c-moll 'Sanguineus und Melancholicus'*, ed. K. Hofmann (Neuhausen-Stuttgart, 1980), Preface, p. 4.

[74] See for example C. G. Krause, *Von der musikalischen Poesie* (Berlin, 1752), p. 41.

[75] Quoted in Peter le Huray and James Day, *Music and Aesthetics in the Eighteenth and Early-Nineteenth Centuries* (Cambridge, 1981), pp. 4, 195.

meaningless entertainment, and attempts were made to define the content of such music in terms of a variety of affections. If one remembers that some writers classified over thirty emotional states together with their corresponding musical idioms, it is easy to see how difficult it must have been in practice to apply this 'dictionary aesthetic'[76] to instrumental music. Ideas of this kind could only be formulated with any certainty in connection with vocal music, where the text could be drawn upon to elucidate the 'content'. In this connection Quantz writes, 'Vocal music has some advantages that instrumental music must forgo. In the former the words and the human voice are a great advantage to the composer, both with regard to invention and effect.'[77]

While this problem may fairly tax the minds of theorists and aestheticians it scarcely troubled composers themselves, least of all C. P. E. Bach, who entertained no doubts as to the expressivity and the profundity that could be achieved in instrumental music. Bach did not require a vocal medium in order to express his ideas fully: he actually discovered a number of advantages in the instrumental genres, among which were the effects of 'surprise and passion, which instruments can achieve better than voices'.[78] A link with language and with vocal music is present none the less in his instrumental works, through the 'rhetorical principle' (Schering's phrase)—and the idea of a 'vocally inspired' composer.[79]

In the C minor Trio, Bach demonstrates that definite musical meaning can exist even in the absence of a text; and yet he appears to call this whole thesis into question once again, for he has found it necessary to give the listener a programme explaining the 'Conversation between a Sanguineus and a Melancholicus'. The communication of meaning in this particular case also involves recourse to long-established and widely familiar expressive pictorial devices. Bach saw clearly the difficulties to which this gave rise and the constraints placed upon the invention, and for this reason he later avoided such experiments. When Gerstenberg asked him to write programme music, believing that it must be possible to express 'the marked emotions contained in a text with equal force in instrumental music',[80]

---

[76] This term [*Wörterbuchästhetik*] is used by a number of writers including D. Zoltai in *Ethos und Affekt. Geschichte der philosophischen Musikästhetik von den Anfängen bis zu Hegel* (Budapest and Berlin, 1970), p. 181.

[77] Quantz, op. cit., Ch. XVIII, par. 28 [n. 27 above].

[78] Bach, *Versuch*, i, Ch. II, 1st section, 'General', par. 8.

[79] Ibid., i, Ch. III, par. 12.

[80] H. W. von Gerstenberg, letter of summer 1773 to C. P. E. Bach (survives only as a draft); see E. F. Schmid, *Carl Philipp Emanuel Bach und seine Kammermusik* (Kassel, 1931), p. 56.

Bach evasively replied that the presence of words made the task easier.[81]

In spite of some occasionally rather obvious pictorial details, best seen as a concession to the fashionable taste for programmatic music deriving particularly from the influence of the French *clavecinistes*, the experiment attempted in this trio may be considered a success. Out of two contrasted expressive types, described in the programme, and achieved by means of thematic differentiation and constant changes of tempo, metre, and mode (Ex. 31)

Ex. 31. Trio in C minor, Wq. 161 no. 1

a most interesting piece of music is developed. Here, as in other works, Bach's ability to manipulate motivic material with great variety is clearly illustrated. Whether it is achieved through imitative counterpoint or through novel harmonic treatment, the effect of each movement is startlingly original (Ex. 32).

Ex. 32

Some of the chamber music written in Berlin was intended for performance at the Court. Much of it would have been written in

---

[81] See Bach's reply to Gerstenberg, quoted in E. E. Helm, 'The "Hamlet" Fantasy and the Literary Element in C. P. E. Bach's Music', *MQ*, lviii (1972), p. 291, and Helm's discussion of it on pp. 293f.

haste, especially since the King disliked unusual, experimental music. Bach now draws on a wider range of solo instruments than he had done in his Frankfurt chamber works. In Berlin he composed for obbligato cembalo, violin, flute, oboe, viola da gamba, cello, and harp. As a result of daily contact with his colleagues at the Court, Bach was able to study in detail all the instruments in general usage. He came to know the character of each instrument and its technical possibilities astonishingly well. After the harpsichord, the flute was his favourite instrument.

The solo part in the opening Andante of the Sonata in A minor for flute and continuo, Wq. 128, written in 1740, is shaped with remark- able freedom (Ex. 33). The melody is wide-ranging and colourful, enlivened by carefully placed peaks and troughs.

Ex. 33

Here, as in so many of his slow movements, Bach is obviously influenced by the ideal of the 'vocally inspired' composer.

In the faster and more brilliant outer movements of the solos, duets, and trios for flute or violin, arpeggio figures, scales, and chains of triplets constantly reappear in new variants and combinations.

From a stylistic point of view there are two technical procedures used in the trio sonatas. On the one hand there is the 'Baroque conception',[82] in which the two melody instruments are treated on an equal footing; but there are also works where one or other of the two is given priority. In the D minor Sonata for two violins and continuo, Wq. 160, a work from the mid-Berlin period, the first violin is unmistakably the principal part. This already represents a first step towards the Classical ideal of chamber music. Haydn's early string quartets illustrate this same emphasis on the upper part, in which the musical expression is concentrated into a single melody. Only later was equilibrium restored by the equalization and individualization of all four parts, in Haydn's case with the 'Russian Quartets', op. 33, written

---

[82] Geiringer, *Bach Family*, p. 362.

in a 'completely new and special way',[83] and in Bach's case at least in part with the 'Quartets for Keyboard, Flute, Viola, and Bass', Wq. 93–5.[84] The texture of these works is no longer governed by older polyphonic concepts, but rather by the more recent techniques of thematic development and fragmentation.

Musical Life in Berlin

C. P. E. Bach's distinction as a composer had long since won him wide acclaim, as his colleagues must certainly have recognized. Frederick, however, preferred the music of Hasse, Quantz, and the Graun brothers. His harpsichordist and resident composer wrote in a style which pleased him less. As Burney later remarked, the King was not particularly 'partial' to it.[85] Bach for his part had much to criticize in the King's flute-playing, and did so quite openly. 'When a guest once gushingly remarked to the august player: "What rhythm", Bach murmured audibly, "What rhythms!"'[86]

Official court culture with its exclusive orientation towards French literature and Italian opera may have offered Bach some stimulation, but intellectually he was more at home with the bourgeois Enlightenment, which was ideologically in direct opposition to feudal absolutism; Bach was the movement's chief musical representative. The upper bourgeoisie in the Prussian capital had access to a wide range of educational opportunities, and Bach took full advantage of them. Music-lovers could attend the performances of various amateur musical societies—initially private affairs, but soon developing into public concerts— and they could even take part themselves, if they played an instrument and were prepared to abide by the regulations. The earliest such venture was the *Akademie* founded by Johann Gottlieb Janitsch. From 1749 onwards the *Musikübende Gesellschaft* assembled weekly at the home of Johann Philipp Sack. Also popular were the *Musikalische Assemblées* run by Christian Friedrich Schale, and the concerts which took place at the home of Johann Friedrich Agricola.[87] As is well known, Bach was greatly involved in the activities of these groups. On

[83] Haydn used this phrase to describe the op. 33 quartets in seve al letters written towards the end of 1781. See H. C. Robbins Landon, *Haydn: Chronicle and Works*, ii, 'Haydn at Esterháza 1766–1790' (London, 1978), pp. 454f.

[84] See especially the Finale of the D major Quartet, Wq. 94.

[85] See C. Burney, *A General History of Music*, 4 vols. (London, 1776–89), iv, p. 604 (also ed. F. Mercer, 2 vols. (London, 1935, R/1957), ii, p. 961).

[86] Quoted from Geiringer, *The Bach Family*, p. 339.

[87] [Translator's note. At this point Ottenberg adds the following sentence: 'Geiringer believes that there may also have been concerts in Bach's house.' The German translation of Geiringer, *The Bach Family*, as *Die Musikerfamilie Bach* (Munich, 1958), in the passage on p. 375 to which

22 March 1755 he played continuo in the first performance of Carl Heinrich Graun's Passion oratorio *Der Tod Jesu.*[88]

In his *Beschreibung der Königlichen Residenzstädte Berlin und Potsdam und aller daselbst befindlicher Merkwürdigkeiten* [Description of the Royal Residences of Berlin and Potsdam and all matters of interest to be found there] (1769) Friedrich Nicolai says of Berlin's concert life:

Public concerts generally take place throughout the winter, supported by the subscriptions of a few music-lovers, and in addition to this concerts have recently begun to be held once a week in the auditorium of the Opera. There are numerous concerts and for the most part there is no shortage of performers, for besides the court orchestra and the various establishments maintained by other members of the Royal Family, Berlin can boast a great many private musicians and connoisseurs of music.[89]

Among the leading musicians were the Graun brothers, the Benda brothers, Johann Joachim Quantz, Johann Gottlieb Janitsch, Christoph Schaffrath, Christian Friedrich Schale, Johann Philipp Sack, Friedrich Wilhelm Marpurg, Christoph Nichelmann, Johann Friedrich Agricola, and Johann Philipp Kirnberger. Bach established close contacts with many of these composers and performers since, like himself, the majority were employed in the service of the King. To the same circles belonged Berlin's principal music theorists and critics. Their discussions touched both on instrumental matters and a wide range of aesthetic issues.

Looking back over this period, Bach wrote in his autobiography:

Of all the music that one heard in those days, particularly in Berlin . . . I need say but little; who does not know that this was a time when music in general, but especially the standard of performance, reached a peak, from which I fear that it has since fallen.[90]

However stimulating Bach's musical environment in Berlin may have been initially, the years ahead were to see an increasing rigidity in musical philosophy and theory, which restricted creativity and gave the so-called Berlin school a reputation in South Germany and elsewhere for pedantry.[91]

Ottenberg refers in a note, does indeed suggest this. A glance at the punctuation of the English original, however (pp. 341f.), reveals that this was not Geiringer's meaning. The passage in the English original is as follows: '. . . were among the friends he met at the Berlin Monday Club, at the Saturday concerts taking place at Agricola's house, and in his own hospitable home'.]

[88] See Miesner, *Bach in Hamburg*, p. 69.

[89] Nicolai, op. cit., p. 404 [n. 14 above].

[90] C. P. E. Bach, 'Autobiography', p. 201. Newman, loc. cit., p. 367.

[91] Schubart writes in his *Ideen zu einer Ästhetik der Tonkunst* of the 'pedantic stiffness' of the music of the Berlin school; see Schubart, op. cit., p. 83 [Introduction, n. 4]. In Burney's *The Present State of Music in Germany* we find the following remark: '. . . and Graun's compositions of thirty years

Of particular importance for Bach's creative development was the exchange of ideas with leading Berlin poets promoted in the first instance by a few joint publications of songs. Not only is Bach's handling of the poetry in his odes and songs remarkably sensitive, following 'every strand of the poet's thought',[92] but the 'rhetorical principle' is itself central to his work in all genres. Some of the instrumental music was actually supplied with words during the 1770s precisely because of this 'speaking' style. (The extent to which the structures and forms of poetry, and even poetic imagery, may have influenced Bach's instrumental music, remains a matter for further research.) Bach was a friend of the poet Johann Wilhelm Ludwig Gleim, a leading figure in the German Anacreontic tradition. They remained in touch after Gleim moved away to Halberstadt in 1747. Ten years later the poet wrote this description of the circles in which he and Bach had moved.

Ramler, Lessing, Sulzer, Agricola, Krause (the musician, not the stupid journalist, Heaven help him!), Bach, Graun, in short all those belonging to the Muses and liberal arts, daily got together, either on land or on water. What a pleasure to glide in such company on the Spree [the name of the river on which Berlin is built] competing with the swans! What a joy to lose one's way with this group in the Thiergarten among a thousand girls.[93]

Lessing became acquainted with Bach in 1748. If Bach profited as a song-composer through this opportunity to widen his knowledge of language and literature, we may also assume that Lessing's occasional reflections on music, contained in his *Kollektaneen* and in the *Hamburg-ische Dramaturgie* (sections 26 and 27) were influenced by Bach. Nevertheless they differed on some important questions, such as the relationship between vocal and instrumental music, or the problem of unity of *Affekt*. Karl Wilhelm Ramler, who became a teacher at a cadet school in 1748, also belonged to the same circle of Berlin writers. Bach contributed five settings to his publications of *Oden mit Melodien* (1753 and 1755). The joint editor of this collection, Christian Gottfried Krause,[94] was a lawyer to the municipal council and French court in

ago, were elegant and simple, as he was among the first Germans to quit fugue and laboured contrivances, and to allow, that such a thing as melody existed, which, harmony should support, not suffocate; but though the world is ever rolling on, most of the Berlin musicians, defeating its motion, have long contrived to stand still'. See Burney, *Musical Tours*, ii, p. 207.

[92] F. W. Marpurg, *Kritische Briefe über die Tonkunst, mit kleinen Clavierstücken und Singoden*, 3 vols. (Berlin, 1760–4; vols. i-ii R/Hildesheim, 1974), i, p. 169.

[93] J. V. L. Gleim, letter of 16 Aug. 1758 to J. P. Uz—quoted in Busch, op. cit., p. 56. A translation of this extract appears in Geiringer, *The Bach Family*, p. 342.

[94] Krause's authorship, while not indicated on the title-page, is nevertheless assumed by M. Friedlaender in *Das deutsche Lied im 18. Jahrhundert*, 2 vols. (Stuttgart and Berlin, 1902; R/Hildesheim, 1962), i.1, p. 115.

Berlin, who in addition to his professional activity had established a good reputation as a composer and music theorist. His treatise *Von der musikalischen Poesie* [On musical poetry] (published in 1752), was widely circulated in Germany at the time.

Meetings would take place in literary clubs, based on the English model, including the Monday Club (from 1746) and the Thursday Club (from 1749). Bach was a welcome guest in affluent upper-middle-class circles. It was probably through the Jewish banking family Itzig that he made the acquaintance of the philosopher Moses Mendelssohn, who in turn knew Friedrich Nicolai, the editor of the *Allgemeine Deutsche Bibliothek*, a journal in which many of Bach's works were reviewed. Sara Levy, great-aunt of Felix Mendelssohn-Bartholdy, acquired a large collection of the music of W. F. and C. P. E. Bach. The latter had his own way of repaying kindnesses received; he was admired as an improviser and was thus frequently in demand as a performer on the clavichord or the harpsichord at social gatherings, and he would often play musical portraits of ladies from among his circle of acquaintances. Bach's own home also served as a venue for such gatherings: he was reputed to be one of the leading living composers and was moreover the famous son of the great J. S. Bach. In conversation he was a spirited and accomplished participant.

To present a picture of Bach's personality and to describe his manner, life-style, and habits, is by no means easy. The relevant sources which might yield further information on the Berlin years are largely unavailable. This need come as no surprise. It was not until the era of *Sturm und Drang* that interest in the artist's personality, in the creative ego, developed to any great extent, an interest which was to find expression in many personal diaries, autobiographies, and physiognomical studies. Material of this kind relating to Bach's Hamburg period, however, is available in considerable quantity. The musicologist and Bach scholar Rudolf Steglich has drawn a sketch of C. P. E. Bach's character which is probably reasonably accurate[95]—here it is amplified in one or two respects. He describes him as a man of great sensitivity, self-aware, full of healthy ambition, and, not least, shrewd enough in financial matters to make a successful career as a composer. His volatile temperament had something of the Latin about it, an impression reinforced by his outward appearance: he was dark-skinned, dark-eyed, had black hair, and was fairly short in stature. With a keen sense of humour and plenty of good spirits, he knew how to enjoy life. All in all he seems to have had an honest, worldly-wise, and many-sided personality.

---

[95] Steglich, op. cit., pp. 41f.

C. P. E. Bach's achievement in the fields of composition, music theory, interpretation, and concert organization must be seen first and foremost in relation to the Enlightenment. The resemblance between Bach's avowed aims and intentions and those of the leading representative of the literary Enlightenment, Gotthold Ephraim Lessing, is unmistakable. Lessing's opposition to the view of man put across by French Classical tragedy as an effeminate creature, moralizing in the abstract, together with his admiration for Shakespeare's work with its dramatic characterization and strong passions, his concept of the function of tragedy as the awakening of 'fear and sympathy', his search for originality and personal creative expression—all these things correspond closely to the aesthetic precepts represented by C. P. E. Bach: passion and sensitivity in expression, subjective involvement of the listener, and a high degree of craftsmanship.

The ideas of the Enlightenment influenced a wide range of scholarly and artistic activity. Prominent thinkers, writers, and artists set out to bring universal knowledge and freedom of thought into the public domain, filled as they were with optimism and a sense of progress, and drawing inspiration from their own powers of reasoning. The development of a bourgeois German culture became their first priority. Lessing launched an attack on the belief that tragedy should concern itself only with characters drawn from the nobility. The protagonists of his own tragedy *Miss Sara Sampson* (1753) are simple folk, hitherto assigned by Gottsched exclusively to the realm of comedy. Lessing wrote critical reviews for the *Berlinische privilegierte Zeitung* of new literary works, including some by Gottsched and Georg Friedrich Meier.[96] At around the same time Winckelmann published his *Gedanken über die Nachahmung griechischer Werke in der Malerei und Bildhauerkunst* [Thoughts on the imitation of Greek works in painting and sculpture] (1755), a work which was to have a lasting influence on German interest in antiquity.

Baumgarten's *Aesthetica* (1750) was another pioneering work, even though it was written in Latin, the traditional language of scholarship. Subsequent editions of this work appeared in German, however, entitled *Anfangsgründe aller schönen Künste und Wissenschaften* [Rudiments of all the fine arts and sciences] (1754–9),[97] and it thus became accessible to a wider public. Baumgarten, who became Professor of Philosophy and Theology at the University of Frankfurt an der Oder in 1737, is to be credited with introducing aesthetics into the curriculum of philosophical disciplines; he understood it to be an essential

---

[96] See *Lessings Werke*, ed. J. Petersen and W. von Olshausen, ix: 'Zeitungsartikel und Rezensionen' (Berlin etc., n.d.), pp. 40ff.

[97] This three-volume work was dictated to G. F. Meier by Baumgarten.

component of 'worldly wisdom',[98] and saw as one of its most urgent tasks the improvement of taste and the promotion of virtue.[99] This view was shared by the musical theorists in Berlin.

The ideas of the Enlightenment also affected discussions about the nature, styles, and genres of music, discussions which were conducted with extraordinary intensity and passion. The rationalist ideas which Christian Wolff was largely responsible for introducing into the teaching of the Berlin Academy remained the predominant philosophical trend in music theory until well into the second half of the eighteenth century. Musical criticism developed greatly in Berlin in the 1750s. Didactic treatises appeared covering a wide range of subject-matter. The standard works of those years include Quantz's *Versuch einer Anweisung, die Flöte traversiere zu spielen* (1752), Krause's *Von der musikalischen Poesie* (1752), Bach's *Versuch über die wahre Art das Clavier zu spielen* (1753–1762), Marpurg's *Handbuch bei dem Generalbasse und der Composition* (1755–8), and Agricola's *Anleitung zur Singekunst* (1757).[100] Musical periodicals and the so-called 'Schreiben an . . . ' [Letters to . . .] could be almost as sharply polemical as the pamphlets written in France or Italy. The great debate on the relative merits of French and Italian music, recently rekindled by Rousseau's strongly-worded attack on the music of his country, was brought to the attention of German readers by Marpurg's *Historisch-Kritische Beyträge zur Aufnahme der Musik* [Critical-Historical Contributions to the Reception of Music]. Feelings ran equally high in Germany; Marpurg published the titles of nine anti-Rousseau pamphlets in the second and fifth issues of this Berlin musical journal, having prepared the ground for such a discussion by publishing the essay, 'A letter to the Marquis of B. on the difference between French and Italian music'[101] as well as a long review of 'Lettre sur la musique française'.[102]

In combative spirit and fully aware that eighteenth-century music had reached a new, higher level of development, the theorists began to tackle some fundamental aesthetic questions. At the same time they turned their attention from abstract speculation towards the actual performance of music. A genuine 'Enlightenment' in all musical matters became the avowed object of theoretical endeavour.

---

[98] See G. F. Meier, *Auszug aus den Anfangsgründen aller schönen Künste und Wissenschaften* (Halle, 1758), par. 4.

[99] Ibid., par. 6.

[100] Titles in translation: Quantz, *On playing the flute*, Krause, *On musical poetry*, Bach, *Essay on the true art of playing keyboard instruments*, Marpurg, *Handbook on composition and figured bass*, Agricola, *Introduction to the art of singing*.

[101] See Marpurg, *Historisch-Kritische Beyträge*, i, pp. 1ff. [n. 6 above].

[102] Ibid., pp. 57ff.

According to C. P. E. Bach and his contemporaries, music had to reflect human nature; it was a language of the affections, a mirror of the emotional world of man. Its task consisted in 'stirring the heart to a gentle emotion'.[103] Christoph Nichelmann, another harpsichordist employed at the Berlin Court and a pupil of J. S. Bach, formulated an idea that was central to the musical outlook of the time:

The ultimate objective of all artistic mixtures and combinations of sounds is to engage the feelings of the listener through the emotional appeal of those same sounds, to hold his attention completely, and by cleansing his passions and emotions, to bring about a greater state of inner contentment.[104]

Two essential qualities of music are described here: its affective nature and its cathartic function, with the aid of which the great ethical objective—the virtuous man—was to be realized. As Mattheson asserted, 'Where there is no passion, no emotion, there is no virtue either.'[105]

A large stock of conventional affective models stood at the composer's disposal. Human emotions had been systematically classified and each could be musically represented. Krause's description of thirty-three different affections includes the following remarks about regret: 'Regret is portrayed by a sad, sighing, and occasionally self-accusing tone, which at the same time betokens unrest.'[106] In C. P. E. Bach's view the *Affekt* should reflect the soul, the spiritual disposition of the composer, which is communicated to the listener through the equally subjective participation of the performer:

Since there is no other way in which a performer can move the hearts of his audience, he must himself be moved; so it is essential that he should be able to immerse himself in whichever emotion he wishes to arouse in his audience; he communicates his own emotions to them, and thus he is most likely to succeed in stimulating a response. In subdued and sad passages he must himself be subdued and sad . . .[107]

Here, then, is a musical philosophy which lays particular stress on music's function of releasing and of stirring the emotions.

[103] Bach, *Versuch*, i, Ch. III, par. 1.
[104] C. Nichelmann, *Die Melodie nach ihrem Wesen sowohl, als nach ihren Eigenschaften* (Danzig, 1755), p. 11.
[105] J. Mattheson, *Capellmeister*, Part I, Ch. III, par. 53 [n. 61 above].
[106] Krause, op. cit., p. 95 [n. 74 above].
[107] Bach, *Versuch*, i, Ch. III, par. 13. C. Dahlhaus points out in a short report 'Si vis me flere . . .', *Die Musikforschung*, xxv (1972), pp. 51f., that the passage 'Since there is no other way in which a performer can move the hearts of his audience . . .' in C. P. E. Bach's *Versuch* 'is nothing other than a scarcely concealed quotation from one of the canonical texts of Classical civilization, Horace's *Ars poetica*'. In the original the passage reads: 'Si vis me flere, dolendum est primum ipsi tibi: tum tua me infortunia laedent, Telephe vel Peleu.' Quintus Horatius Flaccus, *De arte poetica liber*, vv. 102–4.

Versuch über die wahre Art das Clavier zu spielen

In his capacity as a theorist, C. P. E. Bach exerted a considerable influence on the discussion of aesthetic and technical issues and of questions specifically related to musical instruments. His *Versuch über die wahre Art das Clavier zu spielen* [Essay on the true art of playing keyboard instruments] should be regarded together with Quantz's treatise on playing the flute and Leopold Mozart's *Gründliche Violinschule* as one of the most important didactic works of the century. In the introduction to his English translation of the *Versuch*, William J. Mitchell estimates that each of the two parts of the *Versuch* sold altogether between 1,000 and 1,500 copies before they appeared in revised editions in 1787 and 1797 respectively.[108] In order to demonstrate how extraordinary this figure is, Mitchell makes a comparison with Georg Joachim Göschen's edition of the works of Goethe (1787–90); of the 2,000 copies that were printed only 602 were sold by subscription, and the sales of individual volumes were even smaller.

Bach's *Versuch* provides the foundation of modern keyboard technique.[109] Haydn, Mozart, and Beethoven all studied this work attentively, and Carl Maria von Weber was also to derive much inspiration from it. To music-lovers, performers, and scholars of today the *Versuch* still conveys a great many important insights into keyboard playing as well as continuo playing and other aspects of contemporary performing practice. It also contributes towards a better understanding of stylistic and technical aspects of Bach's own music and of the problems of interpretation that are involved. C. P. E. Bach had set himself a difficult task in writing the *Versuch*. In discussing keyboard performance he wanted to evaluate critically the great heritage built up over many years, but also to take account of new musical ideals at the level of technical detail. Bach relied heavily on 'French keyboard pieces', which he describes as 'a good training for keyboard players',[110] especially in the form in which they had developed under the influence of François Couperin's *L'art de toucher le clavecin*. Still more important was the example of his father's teaching:

It is harmful to hold pupils back with too much easy music—in this way they remain at the same stage; just a few elementary pieces should be enough at the beginning. A wise teacher gradually accustoms his pupils to more difficult pieces. Everything depends upon the method of instruction and upon a good early foundation; in this way the pupil will not even notice that he is being led

---

[108] See Bach, *Essay*, Translator's Introduction, p. 3 [Chapter 1, n. 7].
[109] Ibid., p. 13.
[110] Bach, *Versuch*, i, Introduction, par. 4.

towards more difficult pieces. My late father achieved good results by this approach.[111]

The wide circulation which this work achieved at the time can be explained by its practical orientation; it steers clear of speculative theory and concerns itself entirely with specific problems of performance, aiming in the broadest sense to contribute to the education of musical taste. The many reissues of the *Versuch* make clear how real the demand was for such a work. After the favourable reception of the first part (1753) from both connoisseurs and amateurs, Bach decided in 1759 to reissue it.[112] Encouraged by its success, he followed it in 1762 with an even more comprehensive second part, of which 'the principal concern is the art of accompaniment'.[113] The strength of this treatise derives from almost twenty active years both as harpsichordist and teacher on which Bach could look back and so draw on an immense fund of experience. At this time many questions concerning technique and the nature of musical meaning were in the air. The *Versuch* concerns itself not only with practical details, but also with significant ideas in the fields of musical expression and taste. The pupil must become familiar with different styles, techniques, genres, and a wide selection of 'good music'.[114] Bach intends as the primary aim of his treatise 'to explain how to play simple pieces [*Handsachen*] with the approval of competent judges'.[115] After an Introduction in which individual keyboard instruments are described, their strengths and weaknesses listed, their temperament, their acoustic and mechanical properties explained, and more besides, Bach addresses himself in three main chapters to the problems of fingering, ornaments, and finally execution, this last chapter including detailed treatment of the free fantasia.

Bach's knowledge of the individual qualities of each keyboard instrument is extensive. His favourite is the clavichord, the flexible and tender sound-quality of which is especially well suited to reproducing the finest nuances of expression. Moreover by using *Bebung*, an effect achieved when the performer sets the key into a vibrato-like motion, the music can be considerably enlivened. This is why Bach recommends the use of the clavichord as a means of learning a good style of performance, applicable to keyboard playing in general. 'A good clavichordist will also be a good harpsichordist, but not vice versa.'[116]

The harpsichord is used first and foremost in orchestral music; it is

---

[111] Ibid., par. 24.

[112] Further reissues of Bach's *Versuch* in the eighteenth century appeared as follows: Part I—1780 and 1787, Part II—1780 and 1797.

[113] Bach, *Versuch*, ii, Foreword.   [114] Ibid., i, Introduction, par. 6.

[115] Ibid., i, Foreword.   [116] Ibid., i, Introduction, par. 15.

indispensable as a continuo instrument in ensembles, and it can also serve as the solo instrument in concertos. Concerning the piano, which was just beginning to establish itself, Bach was somewhat sceptical. Initially it suffered from too many technical deficiencies and the tone quality lacked the sensitivity which Bach required. In the *Versuch* he affirms:

> The new fortepianos, if they are built to last, have many fine qualities, although special and painstaking study is required to master the touch. They are effective as solo instruments and in chamber music, but I still consider a good clavichord, apart from its weaker tone, to possess all the advantages of the former, with the added assets of *Bebung* [vibrato] and *Tragen* [portato],[117] which can be produced by renewing the pressure after striking the key. Hence the clavichord is the instrument on which one may judge the ability of a keyboard player most accurately.[118]

In the first chapter, 'On Fingering', Bach advocates equal use of all five fingers. In this he differs from earlier writers who did not make use of the thumb. Bach attributes this to the more chordal style of earlier keyboard writing.[119] More recent music on the other hand made use of a 'variety of passage-work',[120] in which the right-hand fingers particularly were exercised more than previously. In this, no doubt, C. P. E. Bach was applying certain of his father's teachings, for it is well known that J. S. Bach was skilled in the use of the thumbs.[121] Here, then, Bach recommends 'equal use of all the fingers', which is 'particularly necessary in order to preserve the line when inner parts are passed from one hand to another, as in Example 65b pertaining to par. 94 of the first chapter [see Ex. 34], the fingering of which may also be regarded as typical for genuine polyphony'.[122]

Ex. 34

---

[117] Mitchell's translation. *Tragen* describes a means of sustaining the notes by renewed pressure, indicated by a slur with dots. See Mitchell's note in Bach's *Essay*, p. 156 [Chapter 1, n. 7].

[118] Bach, *Versuch*, Introduction, par. 11.

[119] Ibid., i, Ch. 1, par. 6.

[120] Ibid., i, Ch. 1, par. 6.

[121] See Bach and Agricola, *Obituary*, p. 223 [n. 49 above].

[122] H. Hering, 'Klavierspiel', *MGG*, vii, col. 1177.

On the other hand, Bach recommends that one should 'avoid as far as possible placing accompanying parts . . . in whichever hand is playing the most important line, so as to leave it completely free to project the melody skilfully and without hindrance'.[123]

The first chapter also contains detailed instructions about various techniques of 'crossing-over' fingering in the performance of scales, arpeggios, and other '*Passagien*' as well as the technique of finger substitution, so that all in all Bach's *Versuch* offers a systematic and forward-looking account of fingering technique.

In the second chapter, the longest in the *Versuch*, Bach deals with ornamentation. Here too, new ground is broken. He influenced contemporary performing practice by helping 'to bring about uniformity of interpretation of certain types of ornament, thereby enlarging the range of ornaments available'.[124] Some older scholars, such as Riemann,[125] Baumgart,[126] and Mennicke[127] have reproached Bach for overloading his music with ornaments. The reason for their use, it was alleged, was simply to compensate for the lack of sustaining power in eighteenth-century keyboard instruments. Such views, which led to the publication of inaccurate performing editions,[128] do not stand up to examination. Bach regarded ornaments not as mere decoration or embellishment, but as essential elements of musical expression, which served to differentiate and refine the top line in a melodic texture. The ornamented notes were highlighted because they were the weighty and significant ones.

[Ornaments] bind the notes together, give them life; when needed they add a special emphasis and weight; they are pleasing and awaken attention; they help to express the meaning of the music; whether it is happy or sad or whatever else, the ornaments always contribute to the correct expression; a good style of execution depends to a considerable extent on a mastery of the art of ornamentation; a mediocre composition can be improved by ornaments, while on the other hand the finest melody could only appear empty and monotonous without them, and the clearest expression would inevitably be obscured.[129]

[123] Bach, *Versuch*, i, Ch. III, par. 11.
[124] A. E. Cherbuliez, *Carl Philipp Emanuel Bach. 1714–1788* (Zurich and Leipzig, 1940), p. 41.
[125] See H. Riemann, 'Die Söhne Bachs', *Präludien und Studien*, 3 vols. (Leipzig, 1895–1901, R/Hildesheim, 1967), iii, pp. 173ff.
[126] See E. F. Baumgart, 'Ueber harmonische Ausfüllung älterer Claviermusik, hauptsächlich bei Ph. Em. Bach', [*Leipziger*] *Allgemeine musikalische Zeitung*, v (1870), pp. 185ff.
[127] See Mennicke, op. cit., pp. 86f. [n. 4 above].
[128] In this connection see H. Schenker, 'A Contribution to the Study of Ornamentation', trans. Hedi Siegel, *The Music Forum*, iv (1976), p. 17. Blatant misrepresentations of Bach's original text are found in H. von Bülow's edition of six keyboard sonatas, published by Peters in Leipzig in 1862.
[129] Bach, *Versuch*, i, Ch. II, 1st section, 'General', par. 1.

In every case the composer must take into account the chief purpose, the correct representation of *Affekt*, in his choice of ornaments. They must be applied 'without doing violence to the *Affekt* of the piece'.[130] At the same time Bach warns against excessive ornamentation, for the 'necessary clarity and noble simplicity of line' can thereby be lost.[131] After some general reflections of this kind he discusses individual ornaments and their stylistic, technical, and expressive features. He distinguishes eight types of ornament: appoggiaturas, trills, turns, mordents, double appoggiaturas, slides, snaps, and embellished pauses. The effects of each ornament are discussed at length. Appoggiaturas were to be used 'to enhance both melody and harmony' and thereby to achieve a 'particularly pleasing effect'.[132] 'Trills enliven the melody and are thus indispensable.'[133] 'The turn is a simple ornament which renders the melody both attractive and brilliant.'[134]

Ex. 35. Summary of the most important ornaments

(*a*) Appoggiaturas

Long appoggiaturas

Short appoggiaturas

... The 'invariable short appoggiaturas ... are written with single, double, triple, or even more tails, and are to be played so quickly that it is scarcely apparent that the following note loses any of its duration.' (*Versuch*, i, Ch. II, 2nd section, 'Appoggiaturas', par. 13.)

[130] Ibid., i, Ch. II, 1st section, 'General', par. 8.
[131] Ibid., i, Ch. II, 1st section, 'General', par. 4.
[132] Ibid., i, Ch. II, 2nd section, 'The Appoggiatura', par. 1.
[133] Ibid., i, Ch. II, 3rd section, 'The Trill', par. 1.
[134] Ibid., i, Ch. II, 4th section, 'The Turn', par. 1.

(*b*) Trills

Ascending trill

Descending trill

Half or short trill [*Pralltriller*]

(*c*) Turns

Trilled turn

Snapped turn

Ascending turn

(*d*) Mordent

long

short

(*e*) Double appoggiatura

(*f*) The Slide

with two notes

with three notes

or

or

or

(*g*) The Snap

[The realizations given here of the long appoggiaturas and of the snap do not in fact occur in Bach's *Versuch*; all the other examples are quoted from Bach.]

Two examples will serve to illustrate the extent to which ornaments were integrated into the fabric of the music. In the Finale of the third

Sonata from the *18 Probestücke* the upper part reaches a peak on B_5 in
bar 4 (Ex. 36).

Ex. 36

This ascent is preceded by a trilled turn on the note A_4. Setting aside
for the moment its resemblance to the previous motivic segment, the
function of the turn seems to be to propel the melody line forward
through that rising arpeggio. The ascent derives its inner dynamic
from the energy released by the decoration of the A_4.

There are several reasons for the abundance of ornaments in slow
movements. In his desire to refine the melodic line, Bach often uses
very small note-values as units of rhythmic animation— hemi-demi-
semiquavers are not uncommon. Embellishments such as trills, mordents, and turns are closely integrated into the line and give it colour
and variety. Bars 13 and 14 from the middle movement of the fifth
sonata of the *18 Probestücke* take the form of a masterly sequence. The
ornaments here are an indispensable part of the variation procedure
(Ex. 37).

Ex. 37

This art of diminution is fascinating both to listeners and performers
largely because of Bach's mastery of ornamentation in an improvisatory style.

In the third chapter of the *Versuch* the problems of execution are
considered. Avoiding brilliant virtuosity of the kind which astonishes
the listener but fails to 'stir the heart to a gentle emotion',[135] Bach seeks
to move his listeners, without thereby indulging in sentimentality.
After allowing himself to be filled with the particular *Affekt* of the piece
he was about to play, the musician had to assume control over the

---

[135] Ibid., i, Ch. III, par. 1.

feelings of his audience, he had to render them sad and pensive, greatly agitated, or jubilant: in short he had to stir them. Bach requires that degree of immediacy of expression which a 'vocally inspired' composer[136] can achieve through imitation of the human voice. This means more than mere lyricism, however. 'Vocal inspiration' also involves impassioned declamation, exclamation, lament, meditation. A phrase such as that quoted in Ex. 37, if it were to be sung, would suggest a gradual increase in volume towards the highest note, then a sudden diminuendo and finally a clear accent on the A_5 flat followed by a softer G_5 flat. Such detailed and unwritten dynamic gradations had also to be achieved by an instrumentalist. Hence Bach's preference for the clavichord. 'Vocal inspiration', however, has implications for harpsichord performance as well. Bach's works for double-manual harpsichord offer innumerable examples of a finely-nuanced expression modelled on the human voice. The interpretation of these passages requires 'a freedom and a skill in handling the musical text . . . which harpsichordists have only recently rediscovered'.[137]

'Vocal inspiration' therefore refers in general terms to an animated, emotionally charged style of performance. 'Play from the soul'[138] is one of Bach's constant demands on the keyboard player. And he regards the essence of good performance to be 'nothing other than the facility of rendering audible the true content and *Affekt* of musical ideas. The same idea can be interpreted in so many different ways that one scarcely perceives that it is always the same idea.'[139] One of the great strengths of the *Versuch*, frequently mentioned above, is that every aesthetic judgement is tested in practice; in other words, Bach's musical outlook as described in this chapter is well grounded in his performing experience:

The variables in performance are the strength and weakness of the notes, their emphasis, use of the snap, legato and staccato, vibrato, arpeggiation, sustaining, and rubato. Anyone who either omits to use these refinements, or uses them wrongly, is a poor performer.[140]

An immediate practical illustration of Bach's theoretical approach is

[136] 'In par. 8 above the practice of listening to accomplished musicians was recommended as a means of acquiring a good style of performance. Here it is more particularly advised that no opportunity should be missed of hearing good singers; in this way one learns to *think vocally* [author's italics]. Indeed it is a good idea to sing a melody to oneself in order to perceive how it should be performed correctly.' Ibid., i, Ch. III, par. 7. [Translator's note. Ottenberg's frequent references to what is here translated as 'thinking vocally' or 'vocal inspiration' (*singend denken*) are in fact references to this passage; see n. 79 above and Chapter 1, n. 45.]

[137] J. H. van der Meer, *Die klangfarbliche Identität der Klavierwerke Carl Philipp Emanuel Bachs* (Amsterdam, 1978), p. 12.

[138] Bach, *Versuch*, i, Ch. III, par. 7.

[139] Ibid., i, Ch. III, par. 2.

[140] Ibid., i, Ch. III, par. 3.

found in the *18 Probestücke in 6 Sonaten* [18 test-pieces in the form of 6 sonatas] which were published together with the *Versuch*.[141] Here more than anywhere else in his keyboard music, Bach has notated in great detail his exact requirements. Expression and content are specified by tempo indications such as *allegretto tranquillamente, andante ma innocentemente, andante lusingando, allegretto arioso ed amoroso*. Tempo, phrasing, and articulation are clearly marked. Dynamics range from *ppp* through all intermediate stages to *ff*. Bach leaves behind the old terraced dynamics and adopts the newer art of dynamic transition.

The Fantasia Principle

Bach underlines again and again the importance of expression. He even goes so far as to sanction departure from strict metre if the expression should require it and 'if one is playing alone or with a small circle of connoisseurs'.[142] Such ideas were novel in the middle of the eighteenth century; they suggest a preoccupation with a genre which held a key position for C. P. E. Bach more than for any other contemporary composer: the 'free fantasia'. An inclination towards the improvisatory is characteristic of Bach's artistic personality. His skill in improvisation on the clavichord must be regarded as part of his inheritance from his father; it matured during Bach's many years of service as court harpsichordist to Frederick the Great, and was widely admired.

This improvisatory quality permeates all Bach's music, not only the fantasias. The characteristic features of improvisation—extended rhapsodic passages, instrumental recitatives, an imaginative arrangement of surprise effects, *adagio* insertions—are found equally in sonata and concerto movements. Thematic ideas which avoid all rhythmic and metrical regularity also indicate a close relation to the fantasia. While on the one hand Bach's actual improvisations, often lasting for hours and conveying great emotional excitement, were such as to defy transcription, on the other hand Bach particularly insisted on an accurate interpretation of any given text in accordance with the composer's intentions. The careful differentiation of dynamics, articulation, and ornaments in his scores suggests that Bach wished to leave a faithful record of his personal idiom. This does not mean that he had abandoned all specific forms of improvisation in his written compositions: they are still found where the genre and the conventions of style require them, as, for example, in the realization of figured bass or the instrumental cadenza.

---

[141] These six sonatas have been published by B. Schott (Mainz, 1935) in an edition by E. Doflein. Permission from Schott & Co. Ltd. to reproduce the C minor fantasia (Ex. 38 below) from this edition is gratefully acknowledged.
[142] Bach, *Versuch*, i, Ch. III, par. 8.

Bach's preference for the 'free fantasia' and its improvisatory qualities can be explained by his intention to achieve 'beauty in diversity'.[143] He was of the opinion that:

It is primarily by means of fantasias, consisting not of previously memorized passages or borrowed ideas, but arising spontaneously from a good and musical soul, that the keyboard player more than any other musician, can achieve the effect of speech, the abrupt surprise of changes in mood; I have sketched a brief illustration of this genre in the last of the *Probestücke*. Common time is indicated, although not observed throughout—as is customary in this genre; for this reason bar-lines are always omitted in the fantasia. The duration of the notes is determined partly by the 'moderato' indication, but mainly by the relative values of the notes themselves. Triplets can be identified wherever the notes are grouped in threes. Rhapsodic improvisation[144] seems particularly appropriate for the expression of emotions, because every type of regular metre carries with it a certain constraint. Accompanied recitatives are a good illustration of the way in which tempo and metre need to be changed frequently in order to arouse and to quieten many different emotions in rapid succession.[145]

Here a significant dramatic principle of Bach's music is mentioned: the way in which emotions are aroused and then quieted. This can be observed in Bach's C minor Fantasia, Wq. 63 no. 6 (Ex. 38), to which Bach was specifically referring in the passage quoted above.

Ex. 38

---

[143] Bach, *Versuch*, ii, p. 336 (Mitchell, p. 438).

[144] In omitting bar-lines Bach may possibly be referring to the tradition of the French *clavecinistes*, that is, to the *préludes* of Louis Couperin and Jean Henri d'Anglebert. See P. Schleuning, *Die Freie Fantasie*, Diss., Freiburg (Göppingen, 1973), pp. 64f., 154.

[145] Bach, *Versuch*, i, Ch. III, par. 15.

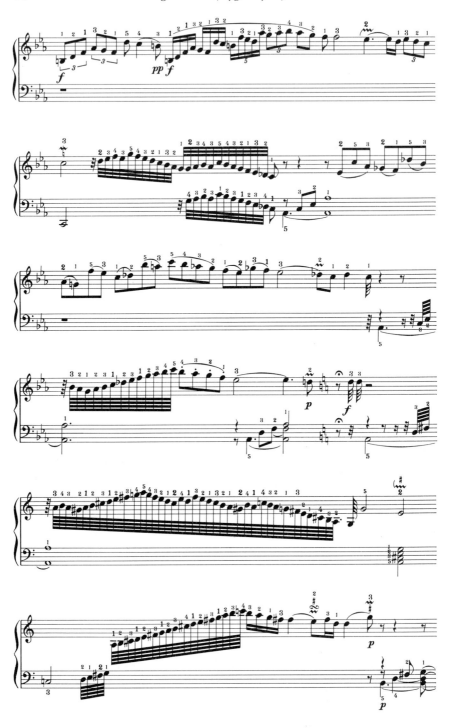

Note: the fingering in the above example is by C. P. E. Bach, with changes of
hand position indicated by the numerals in the larger size.

The work is divided into three main sections, each defined by a
different tempo indication: *allegro moderato—largo—allegro moderato*,
and it follows a wide-ranging tonal scheme: C minor—A flat
major—D⁷—G major—G minor—E flat major, etc. Both outer sections are articulated by the juxtaposition of rising arpeggios culminating
in virtuoso rhapsodic figures, and free instrumental recitative. The
whole of the first section is constructed out of an alternation of these two
contrasting elements. Recitative, being a form of musical declamation,
is able to portray 'many different emotions in rapid succession'. It was
surely the composer's intention that the recitative passages should
suggest a question-and-answer dialogue. It is noticeable that Bach
consistently observes the pattern of build-up and release. In a passage of
growing intensity, arpeggios and recitative elements alternate rapidly.
Short-phrased melody, bold chromatic and enharmonic modulations,
as well as dynamic contrasts help to increase the emotional intensity,
and an initial climax is reached with a quasi-rhetorical figure which
cadences on to a *pp* G minor chord (p. 81 line 3). This has the effect of a
question; the 'answer' corresponds to the 'quieting' of the emotion just
aroused, and it follows in a short passage of lyrical character, coming to a
close on a fermata. Then the figurative motive returns, but this time it is
dramatically accented. Once again a more restful passage is required for
contrast, and Bach supplies this in the second main section of the piece,
an extended Largo of predominantly lyrical expression. Again the
intensity increases. Bach achieves a build-up through *fortissimo-piano*
effects combined with a diatonically rising top line and a chromatically
rising bass-line. The climax occurs on a dominant seventh chord (p. 82
line 3). The release of emotional energy is achieved provisionally
through resolution of the harmonic tension of the dominant seventh
chord, but fully only in the course of a long-drawn-out decrescendo. An

instrumental recitative leads into the final main section, which functions as a recapitulation, matching the opening Allegro Moderato in content. Immediately before the end a few reminiscences of the Largo are heard, more particularly of the lively middle section with its impassioned and emotional expression.

The range of expression within a Bach fantasia is extraordinarily large; it can extend from pure lyricism to 'fury, rage . . . or other violent emotions'.[146] It is possible to decode the emotional content of the music fairly accurately. Bach referred to the C minor Fantasia in a letter to Forkel dated 10 February 1775 as a 'dark fantasia'.[147] If this darkness is taken to represent one end of the spectrum of moods, at the opposite end from 'lightness' or 'brightness', then it is possible to classify various expressive types in between the two extremes. With reference to the beginning of the Largo: E flat major, a slow beat, consonant, cantabile upper-voice-centred texture, *Empfindsamkeit*, and a sense of 'consoling meditation'[148] all contribute to the *Affekt*. A clear articulation of this definition of content is supplied by the text (paraphrased from Hamlet's soliloquy) which Bach's friend Gerstenberg subsequently added to this part of the fantasia. According to Gerstenberg, the Largo represents 'a kind of middle state of Hamlet's shattered soul';[149] the text at this point begins: 'ins Licht zum Seyn erwachen! . . .' [To awaken in the light of being! . . .][150]

This procedure for rousing and quieting emotions and the resultant swing between dramatic and lyrical modes of expression is far removed from a narrowly *galant* style. It was Schubart who was later to draw attention to the pioneering quality of much of C. P. E. Bach's music: 'All the trifles of today's clavichord music, all that pretty light-hearted stuff, all the tinkle of modern composers is an outrage to a giant like him. In spite of all fashions he remains what he is—Bach!'[151]

Day-to-day Professional Life and Travel

Bach's work with Frederick the Great's orchestra brought little variety. His constant duties as accompanist were soon made lighter by the

---

[146] Ibid., i, Ch. III, par. 4.

[147] The letter is quoted in Bitter, op. cit., i, pp. 340ff. The relevant phrase occurs on p. 341.

[148] Schleuning, op. cit., p. 221.

[149] From a letter to Nicolai dated 5 Dec. 1767; see E. E. Helm, 'The "Hamlet" Fantasy', loc. cit., p. 279.

[150] The full text is quoted both in F. Chrysander, 'Eine Klavier-Phantasie von Karl Philipp Emanuel Bach mit nachträglich von Gerstenberg eingefügten Gesangsmelodien zu zwei verschiedenen Texten', *Vierteljahrsschrift für Musikwissenschaft*, vii (1891), pp. 5–14, and in E. E. Helm, 'The "Hamlet" Fantasy', loc. cit., pp. 281–2. [Translator's note. The text in question is a free paraphrase of the famous soliloquy in *Hamlet*, III. i. 56ff.]

[151] Schubart, op. cit., p. 179 [Introduction, n. 4].

appointment of a second harpsichordist—from 1742 to 1745 Christian Friedrich Schale, from 1745 to 1756 Christoph Nichelmann, and from 1756 onwards Karl Friedrich Fasch. The two harpsichordists would take it in turns to spend four weeks at a time on duty, mainly in Potsdam. Even after more than fifteen years had elapsed since Bach's appointment, the King still persisted in his strong likes and dislikes. In the opera-house he would only tolerate works by Graun, Hasse, and occasionally some by Vinci and Agricola, while in the concerts the repertoire was drawn from Quantz, the Benda brothers, and the King himself.[152] Only on rare occasions were works by Bach performed in the King's presence. The picture, then, had hardly changed since Frederick's accession to the throne in 1740. Burney, who spent a few days in Berlin during his European travels of 1772, described the musical establishment there not without a light touch of irony: '. . . but with respect to the *general* and *national* styles of composition and performance, it seems at present, to be formed so much upon *one model*, that it precludes all invention and genius'.[153] There were at least two composers to whom he did not apply this judgement: C. P. E. Bach and Franz Benda. Bach's creative thought was original and individual enough to resist the influence of the prevailing Italianate taste.

Much to his regret the constant and time-consuming duties at Court did not leave Bach time for extensive foreign travel of the kind that so many artists of his day undertook for study purposes. None the less many eminent musicians took the trouble to visit the famous Bach in Berlin. He was later to write:

If I wished to be verbose and to tax my memory, I should not find it difficult to write out a long list of names of composers, singers, and instrumentalists of all kinds with whom I am acquainted. This much I know for certain—that among their number there were geniuses of a stature and quality such as have yet to reappear. This being said, I do not deny that the opportunity to visit foreign lands would have been a source of great pleasure and advantage to me.[154]

Among the few journeys Bach is known to have made was a visit to Bad Teplitz in Bohemia as early as 1743 because of his gout. In 1751 Bach stayed with Gleim in Halberstadt; from there he journeyed via Brunswick to Hamburg where he met Johann Mattheson. A hand-written note added to the *Grundlage einer Ehren-Pforte* describes the

---

[152] See Mennicke, op. cit., p. 489 [n. 4 above]; for a more general discussion of musical life at Frederick's court see E. E. Helm, *Music at the Court of Frederick the Great* (Norman, Okla., 1960), pp. 81ff.

[153] See Burney, *Musical Tours*, ii, p. 206.

[154] C. P. E. Bach, 'Autobiography', p. 202. Newman, loc. cit., pp. 367f.

meeting as follows: 'On 15 June Mattheson received three unexpected visitors, whose conversation on musical matters was most entertaining—namely the famous harpsichordist, C. P. E. Bach, the great Italian violinist, [Philippo Maria] Pio, and Seliger, the gifted Swedish campanologist from Stockholm.'[155]

In the person of Mattheson, Bach made the acquaintance of a leading representative of the musical Enlightenment, whose ideas also met with a broad resonance in Berlin.[156] A statement such as this—everything in music which 'occurs without commendable emotion means nothing, does nothing and is worth nothing'[157]—is in perfect accord with the views expressed in the *Versuch*. Bach may also have met his godfather Georg Philipp Telemann in Hamburg.

Bach made a further journey in 1754, this time to Gotha, where Georg Benda had been Kapellmeister since 1750. Bach had already made the acquaintance of this Bohemian composer and performer in the early 1740s, when both were employed at the Berlin Court. Bach gave two concerts in the Thuringian town.[158] In the same year he went to Kassel, which was probably where Johann Friedrich Reifenstein painted his portrait of Bach aged forty [Plate 2].[159] Finally we know of a visit to Strelitz[160] and of a period of several months in 1758 which the Bach family spent at the home of Johann Friedrich Fasch,[161] Court Kapellmeister in Zerbst, on account of the wars.

Among the innumerable visitors that Bach received in Berlin was Baldassare Galuppi, the well-known Italian *opera buffa* composer and principal *maestro di cappella* at St Mark's Venice, who stayed in Berlin in 1765 on his way to St Petersburg. When in the autobiography Bach mentions a certain decline in some of the music written in the second half of the eighteenth century, and expresses agreement with 'many men of insight that the comic style, so popular today, is the chief offender',[162] he is referring to remarks made by Galuppi during his visit to Berlin. When Hasse visited the Prussian capital in March 1753, he had occasion to hear Bach perform on the harpsichord. The great

---

[155] J. Mattheson, *Grundlage einer Ehren-Pforte* (Hamburg, 1740), ed. M. Schneider (Berlin, 1910; R/Kassel etc., 1969), Anhang, p. 28.

[156] J. F. Agricola quotes extensively from Mattheson, *Das neu-eröffnete Orchestre* (1713) in his *Schreiben an Herrn . . .* (1749). Reviews of the writings of this Hamburg Enlightenment figure are to be found in F. W. Marpurg, *Historisch-Kritische Beyträge*, i, pp. 142ff., 477f. [n. 6 above]. See also one or two remarks in Quantz, op. cit., Ch. XVIII, par. 84 [n. 27 above].

[157] Mattheson, *Capellmeister*, Part II, Ch. V, par. 82 [n. 61 above].

[158] See F. Lorenz, *Die Musikerfamilie Benda. Georg Anton Benda* (Berlin and New York, 1971), p. 38.

[159] See P. M. Young, *The Bachs* (London, 1970), p. 173.

[160] See Miesner, 'Bachs Umwelt', p. 141.

[161] See Busch, op. cit., p. 57.

[162] C. P. E. Bach, 'Autobiography', p. 201. Newman, loc. cit., p. 367.

master of *opera seria* was full of praise for his performance.[163] Johann
Gottfried Müthel, one of the leading innovators in keyboard music
after 1750, visited Bach in Potsdam.[164]

In spite of all the restrictions, Bach's years in Berlin afforded him a
great many opportunities for learning about the musical life of the
period, thanks in part to his many business contacts; as he wrote in his
autobiography, 'I was able to hear not only the greatest masters of
Germany, but all that was best in what came from abroad; and I do
not believe that there is any form of music left of which I have not
heard some of the greatest exponents.'[165]

Organ Music and Symphonies

Bach turned in the 1750s to a medium which occupies a relatively
small position in his output, namely the organ. If it was above all the
great organist-composer and master of improvisation that the musical
world had admired in J. S. Bach, his second son moved further away
from his father in this field than in any other. Even in 1773 in
Hamburg, where his duties as director of the town's main churches
frequently brought him into contact with matters concerning organ
playing and organ composition, Bach expressed to Burney his regret
that he had 'lost the use of the pedals'.[166] The reasons for his neglect of
the organ are obvious. Whereas for centuries and still as late as
J. S. Bach's lifetime the Church had been a leading patron of music,
now the music-making of the middle classes took on greater importance. The emergence of public concerts, musical salons and other
middle-class domestic musical gatherings gave rise to a huge demand
for music which was met by a complex network of music publishers,
music shops, and various forms of publication by subscription. The
centre of gravity in the social setting of music-making had shifted to
meet the demand of the middle classes for their own kind of music. The
harpsichord, the clavichord, and increasingly the pianoforte too were
now the most popular keyboard instruments, against which the organ
as an instrument of worship could assert itself only with difficulty.

C. P. E. Bach's few organ works—one or two sonatas and fugues, and
two concertos, all written between 1754 and 1762—sound like transcriptions of music originally conceived for other keyboard instruments. With
only one exception Bach writes *senza pedale*. A greater contrast to the
masterly use of pedal technique in the toccatas, preludes, and fugues of

---

[163] See Mennicke, op. cit., p. 392 [n. 4 above].
[164] See Lothar Hoffmann-Erbrecht, 'Müthel, Johann Gottfried', *New Grove*, xii, p. 877.
[165] C. P. E. Bach, 'Autobiography', p. 202. Newman, loc. cit., p. 367.
[166] See Burney, *Musical Tours*, ii, p. 221.

J. S. Bach could scarcely be imagined, yet it was Carl Philipp Emanuel who boasted that his father could 'play things on the pedals which many not unskilful harpsichord players would find it hard enough to have to play with five fingers'.[167] Melodic style, thematic treatment, the whole idiom and technique are conceived in terms of other keyboard instruments. In the two organ concertos, which significantly carry the title 'Concerto per l'organo overo il Cembalo', Bach aspires towards the transparent sound of the harpsichord. Where polyphony is employed, it is of a fairly straightforward kind.

Some of the Berlin Bach's fugues were quoted by his friend Marpurg, the theorist, in order to illustrate the principle of the 'learned style'.[168] In two instances it is known that Bach sat on a committee to assess the ability of organists applying for vacant posts.[169]

Whereas organ music is not an area of Bach's output in which a continuous development can be traced, the symphony is: Bach concerned himself more and more with the genre after 1755. An isolated early example dates from 1741, and there are a further eight symphonies from the Berlin period, written in 1755, 1756, 1758, and 1762; the high point of the series, however, was reached only after the move to Hamburg, with the four 'Orchestral symphonies with twelve obbligato parts', Wq. 183.

The symphony was subject to many different influences—from the suite, the Neapolitan opera overture, and the concerto, especially the ripieno concerto. It developed in the course of the eighteenth century into a principal genre offering unrivalled opportunities to explore new artistic aims and objectives. In the various musical centres throughout Germany and Austria it appeared in many different forms. The Berlin composers adhered principally to the three-movement scheme fast–slow–fast. The minuet was excluded, as it had been from the keyboard sonata, and for similar reasons. Hiller was surely expressing a widely-held view when he wrote:

Minuets in symphonies always seem to us like beauty-patches on the face of a man; they give to the music an effeminate appearance, and weaken the virile impression made by the uninterrupted sequence of three well-matched serious movements, wherein lies one of the greatest beauties of execution.[170]

Of decisive significance for the future development of the Classical

[167] Bach and Agricola, *Obituary*, loc. cit., p. 223.

[168] For example the fugue Wq. 119 no. 4 is included in F. W. Marpurg, *Raccolta delle più nuove Composizioni di Clavicembalo di differenti Maestri ed Autori per l'anno 1757* (Leipzig, 1757), pp. 42ff. It is also to be found with a commentary by Marpurg in his *Clavierstücke mit einem practischen Unterricht für Anfänger und Geübtere*, 1. Sammlung (Berlin, 1762), commentary pp. 8ff., music Tab. IIff.

[169] See C. Sachs, *Musikgeschichte der Stadt Berlin bis zum Jahre 1800* (Berlin, 1908), pp. 164, 181.

[170] Hiller, op. cit., i, p. 243 [Chapter 1, n. 65].

symphony at the hands of Haydn, Mozart, and Beethoven were not
only the Italian and the Viennese models, but also those of the
Mannheim composers such as Johann Wenzel Anton Stamitz, Franz
Xaver Richter, and Carlo Giuseppe Toeschi. Characteristic stylistic
features included melodic gestures such as the 'orchestral tremolo', the
'Mannheim sigh', and the use of contrasting secondary themes; the
excellence of the orchestra led by Stamitz at the Court of the Elector
Palatine in Mannheim[171] was widely acknowledged. Bach's symphonies also had a lasting influence on the Viennese Classical style.

   C. P. E. Bach observed developments in contemporary musical life
attentively and was thoroughly well placed to reproduce compositional
innovations and the new *gusto* of the younger generation; in the
symphony he recognized not only the important experiments taking
place and the new stylistic issues raised, but also its inherent potential
for powerful public effects. His symphonies were performed by amateur musical societies. Although the circle of listeners was still relatively
small, it grew substantially as the symphony established itself more and
more in the concert-hall. Of the Berlin works admittedly only one
appeared in print, the Symphony in E minor, Wq. 177. Yet a great
many manuscript copies of the other works exist which spread all over
Europe in the course of the century. They reached England, France,
Holland, Denmark, Latvia, Estonia, Russia, Austria, and Switzer-
land.[172] Moreover, Bach made keyboard arrangements of some symphonies and published them in miscellaneous collections. Hiller's
Raccolta delle megliore Sinfonie (1761–2) contains works by C. P. E. Bach,
Kirnberger, Rolle, Hasse, Hiller, Leopold Mozart, Wagenseil, Abel,
and Georg Benda.

   The range of styles covered in the symphonies from the early work of
1741 to the Hamburg symphonies is considerable. Relics of the old
style—fugal passages, *Fortspinnung*, and features of the concerto grosso
with its prominent ripieno-concertino contrast—are combined with
more modern principles of construction. Sonata form, hitherto developed mainly in keyboard music, is used here in symphonic works,
especially in the outer movements. The layout and character of the
middle movements is similar to that found in the keyboard sonatas. As
was seen to be the case with the keyboard music, Bach develops his

---

[171] 'It was here [Mannheim] that the *Crescendo* and *Diminuendo* had birth; and the *Piano*, which
was before chiefly used as an echo, with which it was generally synonymous, as well as the *Forte*,
were found to be musical *colours* which had their *shades*, as much as red or blue in painting.'
Burney, *Musical Tours*, ii, p. 35.

[172] Concerning the dissemination of Bach's symphonies as well as their style, see the thorough
study by E. Suchalla, *Die Orchestersinfonien Carl Philipp Emanuel Bachs nebst einem thematischen
Verzeichnis seiner Orchesterwerke* (Augsburg, 1968), to which the author is indebted on many accounts.

melodic ideas from a thematic base. His skill at handling tiny motives and groups of motives in constantly new guises, new juxtapositions and combinations, his bold treatment of dissonance and modulation (seventh-chords and ninth-chords occur frequently), his rhythmic and dynamic nuances, all these things help to achieve the surprise effects so typical of Bach and to give marked individuality to some of the Berlin symphonies. With regard to instrumentation, Bach does not yet achieve the degree of tonal differentiation found in the later Hamburg works. To the usual body of strings are added normally two each of flutes, oboes, and horns, whose function is simply to fill out and strengthen the texture. In all the symphonies, the harpsichord is used as a continuo instrument.

The E minor Symphony mentioned above was very popular in its day.[173] Hasse told Burney that it was the best symphony he had ever heard.[174] The powerful, energetic main theme of the first movement contains an abundance of motives which serve as a rich source of material for a colourful and varied movement (Ex. 39).

Ex. 39. E minor Symphony, Wq. 177

A secondary idea is clearly contrasted with this opening (Ex. 40): it consists of a few lyrical bars, containing suspensions and syncopations at a *piano* dynamic with light scoring.

Ex. 40

It would be wrong to speak of a 'second subject' in the Classical sense, because the function of the theme is simply to provide a contrast in

---

[173] The same symphony exists in a version with woodwind as Wq. 178.
[174] Burney, *Musical Tours*, ii, p. 118.

colour, or rather in mood, with the main theme. It cannot be seen as a self-contained, structural contrast. It is the main theme which establishes the overall mood. This main theme is used as a means of articulation, being quoted in whole or in part at key points in the structure, such as the opening of the middle section and of the recapitulation. It also pervades the movement at the level of detail. In bar 22 the bass and oboe/flute begin an exchange which is both simple and attractive (Ex. 41, taken from the version with added wind parts, Wq. 178); the connection with bar 4 of the main theme is easy to see.

Ex. 41

In the *Fortspinnung* passages the motivic material is seized upon, dissected into tiny fragments and scales, and extended sequentially according to the modulatory scheme; here one finds many conventional patterns such as stepwise-moving bass-lines, tremolo figures, and cadential flourishes which offer a marked contrast to the otherwise richly individual traits of the E minor Symphony. Such patterns are frequently found even in the later Hamburg works.

Overall, however, the handling of individual instruments is more skilful in the Hamburg works. The title 'Orchestral symphonies with twelve obbligato parts' itself suggests this. By that time, though, Bach had learnt a number of stylistic devices from the Classical symphonies of Haydn, just as he had himself influenced the Classical style through his dense motivic treatment and his enlargement of the expressive range.

The Seven Years War

Between 1756 and 1763 Prussia and the neighbouring provinces of Silesia and Saxony formed the battleground for one of eighteenth-century Europe's most devastating wars, the Seven Years War. More than 180,000 soldiers died, to say nothing of all the deaths inflicted on the civilian population. This war was merely a violent expression of Prussia's already long-established militaristic aims: it sought to turn itself into the foremost European power. Within months of his accession to the throne Frederick's troops invaded the Austrian province of Silesia and annexed large areas. In the course of the second Silesian War (1744–5), and finally during the Seven Years War, Prussia secured Silesia once and for all. By this means it was able to enlarge its territory considerably and to gain control over new raw materials and industrial resources. The damaging economic side-effects and consequences of the war were felt not only by the inhabitants of the occupied territories in the form of heavy taxes, but also by the Prussian tax payer; means had to be found to pay off the enormous war debts which ran to a total of 139 million Thalers. Trade and industry were directed chiefly towards meeting the demand for weapons and armaments from the Prussian army. The serious economic crisis of 1763 placed further burdens on the population.

Many bourgeois artists, trapped in narrow political attitudes, praised Frederick's aggressive policies lavishly. Gleim's *Preussische Kriegslieder in den Feldzügen 1756 und 1757 von einem Grenadier* [Prussian War-songs of a Grenadier in the Campaigns of 1756 and 1757], published in 1758, are a typical instance of such triumphalist tendencies. Given that C. P. E. Bach set one of these poems to music, namely 'Herausforderungslied vor der Schlacht bei Rossbach' ['Song of Challenge before the Battle of Rossbach'], it may be concluded at least that his attitude towards such apologetic literature was unreflecting. As far as we know, it remained his only song on this theme. Lessing, too, was at first deceived by Frederick's victories in the Seven Years War, though he soon revised his opinion. Having often wished to settle in Berlin, he finally reacted against the restrictions that were placed on cultural life. Lessing left the Prussian capital at about the same time as C. P. E. Bach. He too went to Hamburg, though only for a short time. Later, in a letter to Nicolai dated August 1769, he attacked the Prussian establishment with his characteristic acerbity.

Just let anyone in Berlin try to write about other matters as freely as Sonnenfels did in Vienna; let them try to tell the truth to the aristocratic court rabble as he did, let them speak out for the rights of the people to be defended against exploitation and despotism, as happens now even in France and Denmark: they will soon discover which country remains even today the most servile in Europe.[175]

The long years of war had led to hardship and personal distress in Berlin's musical circles as much as elsewhere, and had brought much

---

[175] G. E. Lessing, letter of 25 Aug. 1769 to F. Nicolai, *Gesammelte Werke in zehn Bänden*, ed. P. Rilla, ix (Berlin, 1957), p. 327.

disorder into professional activity. The chamber concerts took place only sporadically, for the King was frequently away. At times Bach even served in the ranks of the Berlin home guard. Ramler reported to Gleim:

The rich nobility are fleeing, leaving the poor to gather their mites, and daring to abandon the town to fire and looting. Such is the talk here on our parade grounds where Sulzer, Baron Pöllnitz, Bach, the Commandant, Doctor Stahl, and Gröber the Chamberlain etc. etc. together with many other patriots are gathered together.[176]

During the war, when the Russian army advanced dangerously close to Berlin in August 1758, Bach fled to Zerbst with his family to Johann Friedrich Fasch, a friend of several years' standing.[177] Not until the beginning of December did the family return to Berlin.

The musicians expressed anger over their considerable financial losses. As court employees they were paid in paper money, which lost its value more and more as the war progressed. Bach, who received a steady income from his numerous private pupils, was not so badly affected as some of his colleagues. When Frederick II took no steps to reimburse his musicians after the peace treaty with Austria, his court harpsichordist, so Zelter informs us, 'made no attempt to conceal his fury'.[178]

Songs and Keyboard Works

Bach continued to compose during the Seven Years War. In 1757–8 he set a selection of no fewer than fifty-four poems, which appeared in print under the title *Herrn Professor Gellerts geistliche Oden und Lieder mit Melodien.* This first original collection of songs made Bach into one of the most highly-regarded song-composers in Germany overnight. The fact that five issues appeared in his lifetime (in 1758, 1759, 1764, 1771, and 1784) is enough to indicate the extraordinary popularity of the *Gellert-Lieder.*

Even before this publication Bach had written a few secular songs which had been included in various contemporary collections. The earliest known song, 'Eilt, ihr Schäfer' ['Make haste, ye shepherds'], dates from 1741. Bach published it in Johann Friedrich Gräfe's *Sammlung verschiedener und auserlesener Oden, zu welchen von den berühmtesten Meistern in der Music eigene Melodeyen verfertiget worden* [Collection of

---

[176] C. W. Ramler, letter of 28 July 1759 to J. W. L. Gleim, quoted in Busch, op. cit., p. 54n.

[177] Karl Friedrich Christian Fasch, son of Johann Friedrich Fasch, the Court Kapellmeister at Zerbst, had come to Berlin in 1756 as second harpsichordist, and had lived with Bach's family.

[178] See Karl F. Zelter, *Karl Friedrich Christian Fasch* (Berlin, 1801), p. 19.

various choice odes, to which original melodies have been added by the most famous masters in music]. After a silence of more than ten years he returned to this medium, no doubt inspired by the enormous vogue for song in Germany. Bach's song-settings were included in Ramler's and Krause's *Oden mit Melodien* (1753 and 1755), Marpurg's *Neue Lieder zum Singen beym Claviere* (1756), and in *Berlinische Oden und Lieder* (1756 and 1759). In the musical journal *Historisch-Kritische Beyträge zur Aufnahme der Music* appeared the 'Scherzlied vom Herrn Lessing', presumably intended to provide light relief from all the theoretical essays.

The song was a decidedly popular musical genre which stood outside the realm of courtly art. By around 1750 Berlin was by far the largest centre of song-writing in Germany. Gellert, Hagedorn, Gleim, Gräfe, Ramler, and Lessing were the most popular poets, while Agricola, Kirnberger, Marpurg, Quantz, Carl Heinrich Graun, and C. P. E. Bach were the most prolific composers. Not only were aesthetic and technical questions discussed in detail, but also the social function of the song. Krause speaks of the great prestige enjoyed by the French chanson, the model for the Berlin song, among all social classes:

It is such a happy sight for an impartial citizen and general philanthropist to see a peasant of that nation [i.e. the French] clutching a grape or an onion, singing merrily and joyfully ... If our composers would write their songs as naturally as possible, without using a keyboard instrument and without thinking that there should be a bass-line to go with the melody, then the taste for singing would rapidly spread among our people.[179]

The texts of the songs belonged for the most part to the Anacreontic tradition, a type of literature widely cultivated in middle-class circles in Germany since the 1740s, which depicted idyllic scenes from Classical mythology; typically there were numerous shepherds and shepherdesses with names like Damon, Doris, Phyllis, or Thyrsis, who would yield to entirely sensual pleasures.[180] Even though the subject-matter was drawn from antiquity, this poetry was rich in folk elements, and it gave a voice to the worldly aspirations of the lower classes. The social and political abuses of their generation were admittedly either ignored or trivialized by the Anacreontic poets, as can be seen, for example, in the following lines by Gleim.

[179] C. W. Ramler and C. G. Krause, *Oden mit Melodien*, 2 vols. (Berlin, 1753–5), i, Introduction. Quoted in Friedlaender, op. cit., i, p. 116 [n. 94 above].
[180] See *Geschichte der deutschen Literatur*, vi: 'Vom Ausgang des 17. Jahrhunderts bis 1789' (Berlin, 1979), pp. 214ff. See also J. M. Ritchie, 'The Anacreontic Poets: Gleim, Uz, and Götz', *German Men of Letters*, ed. A. Natan and B. Keith-Smith, vi (London, 1972), pp. 123ff.

Drum, O Deutschland
Willst du Frieden?
Wein und Liebe
Kann ihn stiften.[181]

(Now, my country,
Do you want peace?
Wine and women
Are what you need.)

Moralizing fables and playful love poems are found side by side in the
song collections. Most were set strophically, that is to say, in the
simplest musical form available. Tunefulness and accessibility were the

desired qualities; the melody had to be 'easy to understand ... and
easy for anyone to sing'.[182] Originality can only be achieved in this
medium if the composer rises above the conventional and commonplace and develops an unmistakably personal idiom.

  C. P. E. Bach's 'Eilt, ihr Schäfer' is a setting of a poem by Mariane
von Ziegler, who also supplied cantata texts for J. S. Bach. This small-
scale piece stands right at the beginning of the history of the German
Lied, and derives its subject matter from contemporary pastoral
poetry. In view of the then widespread use of contrafacta, it is
remarkable for the unity it achieves between text and music (Ex. 42).
The poem tells of a girl who asks some shepherds to deliver a message
of love to her sweetheart.

Ex. 42

---

[181] *Geschichte der deutschen Literatur*, vi, p. 221.
[182] Marpurg, *Kritische Briefe*, ii, p. 63.

Bach attempts here to render musically the pictorial and highly refined 'poetic devices'.[183] The vocal line rises to its first climax on G_5 at the words 'meinem Thyrsis', the most important part of the sentence, this being the name of the girl's sweetheart; the ascent is part of an inner crescendo, musically depicting both her unrest and her longing. The syncopations serve to intensify the build-up; none the less the stereotyped repeated bass-notes show that this verbal-musical unity does not permeate the entire texture.

Most of Bach's secular songs are technically fairly straightforward and would be well within the ability of amateur singers. The *Gellert-Lieder* on the other hand are more demanding, as a review in the *Allgemeine Deutsche Bibliothek* (1766) confirms.

These *Odenmelodien* also bear the unmistakable imprint of Bach's fiery and imaginative spirit. Indeed they seem to have been conceived more in terms of the keyboard than the voice. None the less a well-trained and technically accomplished singer will find ample scope to improve his execution of small ornaments, to practise the accurate rendering of certain difficult melodic configurations and to develop his powers of expression.[184]

Under the influence of Pietist thought Bach intended that these songs should serve as music for edification and instruction. The contemporary ideal of the virtuous man serves as a central theme. The song 'Wider den Übermuth' ['Against wantonness'], for example, contains the words: 'If perhaps I serve the world better than my neighbour does'[185]—a clear indication of a utilitarian ethic. On the whole the handling of melodic and harmonic resources in the *Gellert-Lieder* is more original than in the earlier songs. The keyboard writing has also become more refined.

Bach discusses his aesthetic principles as a song-composer in the preface to this collection:

In writing these melodies, I have considered the song in its entirety as far as possible. I say 'as far as possible', because, as every competent musician must know, one cannot demand too much of a melody to which more than one stanza is to be sung; the differences in punctuation, in distribution of monosyllabic and polysyllabic words and frequently in subject-matter etc. can seem to demand substantial differences in musical expression.[186]

The difficulty Bach describes here turned out in fact to be a problem of

---

[183] Ibid., i, p. 169.

[184] *Allgemeine deutsche Bibliothek*, ed. F. Nicolai, 118 vols. (Berlin and Stettin, Kiel, 1766–96), i.1 (Berlin and Stettin, 1766), p. 302.

[185] German original: 'Wenn ich vielleicht der Welt mehr, als mein Nächster nütze ...'

[186] C. P. E. Bach, *Herrn Professor Gellerts geistliche Oden und Lieder mit Melodien* (Berlin, 1758), Preface.

some significance for musical history: how could contrasting human emotions be expressed in the song? The through-composed Lied had not yet been 'discovered'. Bach found a partial solution to the growing problem of representing changes in mood:

In the *Gellert-Lieder* he uses a technique peculiarly his own, that is the addition of preludes, interludes, and postludes. The postludes in particular loosen the strict sequence of strophes, and serve not only to effect transitions, but also—especially after stanzas which end with a question mark—to express the different character of different stanzas.[187]

In the song 'Bitten' ['Pleading'] syllabic underlay predominates, with a few significant exceptions. The words 'so weit die Wolken gehen' ['as far as the clouds'] are set melismatically, no doubt to capture the picturesque quality of the image (Ex. 43).

Ex. 43

Bach chooses a simple homophonic accompaniment here, remaining largely within E minor and arousing gentle emotions. The expressive contrast contained within the strophe at the words 'Herr, meine Burg, mein Fels . . .' ['Lord, my rock, my stronghold'] is worked out in detail in Bach's music: emphatic note-repetitions interwoven with flowing accompaniment figures in a major key area are followed by an abrupt switch to the original key of E minor at the words 'Vernimm mein Fleh'n' ['Accept my pleading']; the strophe finally dwindles away into a *pianissimo* (Ex. 44).

187 Busch, op. cit., p. 356.

Ex. 44

Almost half a century later Beethoven adopted a very different solution in his setting of this poem.[188] It seems, though, that he must have known Bach's setting, for the resemblances between certain passages are quite striking (Ex. 45).

Ex. 45

If we compare Bach's songs with other contemporary Gellert settings,[189] it becomes clear that his are far more powerful emotionally. Gellert's own judgement is recorded in a letter to his sister: 'Bach, a court musician in Berlin, has composed settings of all my songs and has

---

[188] Reference is made to Beethoven's *Gellert-Lieder*, op. 48, written in 1803.
[189] Gellert's poems were also set by Johann Friedrich Doles and Friedrich Wilhelm Marpurg among others. See Busch, op. cit., p. 64, and H. G. Hoke, 'Marpurg, Friedrich Wilhelm', *MGG*, vii, col. 1670.

recently sent me a copy . . . They are good, but too good for a singer who is not musical.'[190]

Bach ventured into new territory with a further collection of keyboard works in the early 1760s. His Berlin publisher Winter published the *Sechs Sonaten fürs Clavier mit veränderten· Reprisen* [Six keyboard sonatas with varied (or 'altered') repeats] in 1760. What was Bach setting out to achieve with this collection? Performing practice in the eighteenth century involved many techniques of improvisation, including the universal practice of adding *ad libitum* variations and embellishments to repeats within movements, often, however, running counter to the composer's intentions.

Bach spoke out strongly against such practices in the introduction to these sonatas:

It is indispensable nowadays to alter repeats. One expects it of every performer. A friend of mine goes to endless trouble to play a piece as it is written, flawlessly, and in accordance with the rules of good performance; how can one not applaud him? Another, often pressed by necessity, makes up by his audacity in alteration for the lack of expression he shows in the written notes; the public nevertheless extols him above the former. Almost every thought is expected to be altered in the repeat, irrespective of whether the arrangement of the piece or the capacity of the performer permit it. But then it is just this alteration which makes most hearers cry Bravo, especially when it is accompanied by a long and at times exaggeratedly ornate cadenza. This leads to much abuse of those two true ornaments of performance! Such players have not even the patience to play the notes as written the first time; the overlong delay of Bravos is unendurable. These untimely alterations are often quite contrary to the style, contrary to the spirit, and contrary to the relation of one thought to another, an annoyance to most composers.[191]

The wider significance of these statements is obvious. They indicate a new concept of the nature and purpose of a musical work. For Bach, music is a uniquely personal expression of the composer's creativity, which, if it is to be accurately rendered in performance, needs to be written out in full detail. For this reason Bach gave precise instructions concerning the various musical elements in many of his sonatas, trios, concertos, and symphonies. These instructions were not restricted to exact tempo and mood indications, pointing to a definite *Affekt*, but applied also to the detail of a composition, which now appears much more finely wrought and polished. Subtle use of dynamics in itself gives

---

[190] C. F. Gellert, letter of 25 Mar. 1758 to his sister, *Gellert's sämmtliche Schriften*, 6 vols. (Leipzig, 1853–4), v, p. 267.

[191] C. P. E. Bach, *Sechs Sonaten fürs Clavier mit veränderten Reprisen* (Berlin, 1760), ed. E. Darbellay (Winterthur, 1976), Preface (p. xiii in Darbellay edition).

added colour to the inner life of a piece. If Bach writes out the repeats in full in these six sonatas, and thereby determines the variations to be played, he does not do so at the expense of expression. The unity of thought and the correct relationship of ideas is maintained throughout.

Bach sees the text of a musical work as the final stage in a creative process determined throughout by the composer. The 'thus-and-not-otherwise' quality of a musical score requires the performer to give a rendering in complete fidelity to his instructions. Schubart noted that while performing Bach's keyboard sonatas he had the experience of 'losing his personal identity and expressing instead a Bachian idiom'.[192] In view of his great concern to protect the authentic text, Bach took pains to ensure that his works were accurately printed, and he reacted strongly against printing errors or pirated editions.[193] The *Sonaten mit veränderten Reprisen*, aimed principally at beginners and amateurs, are rich in thematic invention and development; the phrasing is well balanced, the two- or three-part keyboard texture is transparent and carefully written. The varied repeats, as can be seen in Ex. 46 from the F major Allegretto, Wq. 50 no. 1, achieve unexpected refinements of expression.

Ex. 46

On account of the great demand for this collection Bach issued two supplements, each containing six sonatas, in 1761 and 1763. The principle of written-out repeats is not applied in these two publica-

[192] Schubart, op. cit., p. 295 [Introduction, n. 4].

[193] See H. von Hase, 'Carl Philipp Emanuel Bach und Joh. Gottl. Im. Breitkopf', *B-Jb*, viii (1911), pp. 86ff.

tions,[194] but it returns a few years later in *Kurze und leichte Clavierstücke mit veränderten Reprisen* [Short and simple keyboard pieces with varied repeats] (1766–8).

At the end of 1760 the Berlin firm of Birnstiel began to issue *Musikalisches Allerley von verschiedenen Tonkünstlern*, a periodical publication including many works by Bach. The editors have this to say about the purpose of the collection:

These pages will be continued every Saturday, and are intended to offer a collection of the most recent musical essays by good composers of vocal and instrumental music, keyboard, violin, and flute solos, smaller and larger pieces, odes, arias, polonaises, minuets, marches, duets, trios, fugues, symphonies, character pieces, and sonatas in the German, French, and Italian styles, and to bring them more and more to the attention of the public.[195]

The contributors included Kirnberger, Marpurg, Carl Heinrich Graun, Quantz, Agricola, Johann Friedrich Fasch, Rameau, Rolle, and Franz Benda. C. P. E. Bach was represented by keyboard miniatures—'La Xénophon-La Sybille', and others—as well as variations and songs.

About a year later there followed a similar publication, the *Musikalisches Mancherley*. The circle of contributors had narrowed to Kirnberger, Johann Friedrich Fasch, Agricola, and Bach. The latter contributed four sonatas written in 1749, 1754, and 1757, a minuet for three trumpets, drums, two violins, and bass as well as smaller character pieces—'L'Herrmann', 'La Buchholz', 'La Boehmer', 'La Stahl', and 'La Gleim'. These miniatures did not fail to create a stir among the public. The following extract is taken from *Ephemeriden der Menschheit*:

C. P. E. Bach, while still in Berlin, made musical portraits of several young ladies known to him in the form of short keyboard pieces; and several people who knew the ladies concerned have assured me that their temperament and general conduct has been happily expressed in the same; admittedly they must have heard the pieces played by Bach himself.[196]

'La Gleim', for example, an Allegro in 6/8, is a gracious and pleasant musical portrait (Ex. 47).

The pieces contained in these collections are simple, full of charming ideas, accessible, and easy to play, thus ideally suited to meet the demand of a middle-class public for light, entertaining music.

---

[194] Some of these sonatas were written before 1750.
[195] *Musikalisches Allerley*, 9 vols. (Berlin, 1761–3), i, Introduction to the first issue, dated 22 Nov. 1760.
[196] *Ephemeriden der Menschheit*, n.d.; quoted in Bitter, op. cit., i, p. 86n.

Ex. 47

Berlin—The Final Years

Bach's last few years in Berlin were occupied with work on many different forms of music. In 1765 he wrote the delightful chamber cantata 'Phillis und Thirsis', Wq. 232, for two sopranos, two flutes, and continuo. Declamation, word-painting, and instrumental accompaniment are superbly handled. The vocal line follows closely the expression of the text, at times sorrowful, at times joyful, to an attractive accompaniment in the flute parts, frequently moving in parallel thirds and sixths, and endowing this miniature work of art with intimacy and grace (Ex. 48).

Ex. 48

More keyboard pieces by Bach appeared in print during the 1760s including *Clavierstücke verschiedener Art* (1765) and *Sechs leichte Clavier-*

Sonaten (1766). Numerous individual songs were collected together and published as *Oden mit Melodien* (1762). C. P. E. Bach rescued a part of his father's *œuvre* from oblivion by publishing a collection of four-part chorales which he had extracted from individual Passions, cantatas, and other vocal works by J. S. Bach. The first hundred chorales appeared in 1765 in Berlin and Leipzig with a highly illuminating introduction:

> I hope to bring great pleasure and to achieve much of value through this collection. I need hardly offer any words in praise of the harmony of these songs; the late author of them needs no recommendation from me. The public is accustomed to seeing only masterpieces from him. Experts of music will not wish to make an exception of the present collection, if they pay due attention to the entirely special harmony and the natural flow of the inner parts and the bass, the distinguishing excellences of these harmonizations. How valuable such a collection can be for the student of composition, and who indeed would now deny the advantage of beginning such a study with chorales instead of dry, pedantic contrapuntal exercises?[197]

The publication of the remaining chorales was delayed through disagreements with the publishers, who had other priorities, until well into the 1780s.[198]

For many years C. P. E. Bach had been in contact with Georg Philipp Telemann, musical director of the five principal churches in Hamburg since 1721. Perhaps Telemann had his godson in mind as a possible successor from quite early on, and had helped him to secure useful contacts among influential circles in Hamburg.[199] In any event, when the opportunity arose, Bach was no doubt strengthened in his resolve to leave the Prussian Court by the stifling conditions of musical life in Berlin, especially in the aftermath of the Seven Years War. His social position as a court employee and his resulting lack of independence was bound to prove intolerable in the long term. Bach's decision to leave Berlin was an assertion of the independent status of the free artist. The lives of Haydn, Mozart, and Beethoven also offer instances of this desire to escape the restrictions of court service.

When Telemann died on 25 June 1767, his grandson Georg Michael Telemann temporarily took over his job. The post was soon advertised and C. P. E. Bach was appointed, his chief rivals being his brother Johann Christoph Friedrich, the so-called Bückeburg Bach, Hermann Friedrich Raupach, and Johann Heinrich Rolle. Frederick released his

---

[197] *Bach Reader*, p. 271. See also *Bach-Dokumente*, iii, p. 180.

[198] See F. Smend, 'Zu den ältesten Sammlungen der vierstimmigen Choräle J. S. Bachs', *B-Jb*, lii (1966), pp. 5ff.

[199] Bach already knew the Hamburg town official Jacob Schuback, for example. See his letter to Telemann of 29 Dec. 1756, quoted in Geiringer, *The Bach Family*, pp. 343–4.

harpsichordist most reluctantly, and only 'after repeated, most respectful requests'.[200]

Bach had been active in the Prussian capital for nearly thirty years.
During this time he had composed assiduously, and, always receptive
to new influences, had forged a highly individual style, which made
him one of the most respected composers in the German-speaking
world. In Bach, artists and music-lovers recognized the most important
representative of modern trends in composition. Bach, however, was
aware of a conflict between the potential freedom of the composer as a
result of his newly-found social independence on the one hand, and the
less discriminating requirements of the musical amateur, who nevertheless determined the commercial value of music on the other
hand.[201] 'In my whole output, especially of keyboard music, there are
just a few trios, solos, and concertos which I wrote in complete freedom
and for my own use.'[202]

For publishers in Berlin, Leipzig, and Nuremberg, most of Bach's
works were a safe investment. They ensured that the music was
widely disseminated at home and abroad. Bach tackled most of the
major genres during his Berlin period—chamber music, concertos,
symphonies, and songs—and in each he discovered much new
territory.

His principal area of activity, however, remained keyboard music.
From the first published collections, the Prussian and Württemberg
Sonatas, Bach worked out a new style and achieved a high degree of
originality and expressive power. The source and origin of musical
development was for him the 'characteristic theme'. In his best
keyboard music Bach shows himself to be a 'master of richly varied and
imaginative interweaving and transformation of themes and motives,
and able at the same time to preserve thematic unity within diversity.
His thematic treatment no longer takes the form of a succession of
contrapuntal variations, nor is it yet true thematic-motivic development, but instead a progressive unfolding of a creative idea in varied
forms enlivened by unexpected contrasts in texture, rhythm, harmony,
and dynamics as well as changes in metre, tempo, and register.'[203]
Modernity and originality went hand in hand with the Enlightened
musical outlook which found its theoretical expression first and
foremost in the *Versuch über die wahre Art das Clavier zu spielen*. As

---

[200] C. P. E. Bach, 'Autobiography', p. 200. Newman, loc. cit., pp. 366f.

[201] These problems are considered in detail by Schleuning, op. cit., pp. 146ff. [n. 144 above].

[202] C. P. E. Bach, 'Autobiography', p. 209. Newman, loc. cit., p. 372.

[203] 'Carl Philipp Emanuel Bach', *Riemann-Musiklexikon*, 12th edn., 3 vols. (Mainz, 1959–67),
Personenteil, i, p. 71.

harpsichordist in the court orchestra and as a harpsichord teacher he had built up an excellent reputation.

As Charles Burney declared: 'Of all the musicians which have been in the service of Prussia, for more than thirty years, Carl P. E. Bach, and Francis Benda, have, perhaps, been the only two, who dared to have a style of their own; the rest are imitators.'[204] Equipped with such ability and such a reputation, at the peak of his creative powers, and with unique imagination and energy, C. P. E. Bach set about his new tasks in Hamburg.

[204] Burney, *Musical Tours*, ii, p. 206.

3
Hamburg (1768–1788)

Bach's Tasks and Duties

> After the numberless questions and vexatious taxes to which
> myself and baggage had been subjected in passing through the
> despotic states of Germany, it was a very agreeable and
> unexpected circumstance to me to find the entrance into this
> city free from examination, or custom-house embarassments, the
> name only of a traveller being demanded at the gates. The
> streets are ill built, ill paved and narrow, but crowded with
> people who seem occupied with their own concerns; and there is
> an air of chearfulness, industry, plenty, and liberty, in the
> inhabitants of this place, seldom to be seen in other parts of
> Germany.[1]

Thus begins the account written by the English music historian
Charles Burney of his stay in Hamburg. About ten days earlier during
his visit to Berlin Burney had had to wait for three quarters of an hour
in front of the toll-pike and had been subjected to a distressingly
detailed customs examination, before being allowed to enter the city
accompanied by a soldier 'with his musket on his shoulder, and
bayonet fixed'.[2] We know that Burney was disappointed by Berlin's
musical life. Hamburg was different: here he recorded healthier
musical conditions. He praised the town's key musical figures—Handel, Telemann, and Mattheson—was surprised by the openness of the
intellectual climate he encountered in middle-class circles, and he
made the personal acquaintance of 'one of the greatest composers that
ever existed, for keyed instruments'[3]—C. P. E. Bach.

Bach too, after leaving Berlin in March 1768, not least because of the
restrictions of court service disrupted by the war and its aftermath,
found the more open atmosphere of Hamburg refreshing and stimulating. His social and economic position was much more secure here; in
this city, where the middle class exercised a decisive influence on
musical life, he found the ideal conditions for his development as a
composer. His keyboard sonatas and symphonies, songs and oratorios
were heard in public concerts. Many middle-class families in Hamburg
diligently studied the music of the 'great Bach' in order to perform it

---

[1] Burney, *Musical Tours*, ii, p. 208.   [2] Ibid., p. 159.   [3] Ibid., p. 219.

domestically—more than once they came to grief. They could hardly have been expected to cope with the technical and musical requirements of those often extremely complicated works which repeatedly brought on Bach the charge of *Bizarrerie*[4] and which belonged to the category of music written by Bach 'in complete freedom' and for his 'own use'. Yet on the other hand Bach followed in his own music the advice he gave to a young composer: 'In works that are to be printed, in other words, intended for general consumption, be less abstruse and put in more sugar.'[5] This distinction between 'public' and 'private' styles can be recognized in all Bach's Hamburg works.

The Senate, not the Church, was Bach's official employer, and it was to the Senate too that he had to turn in legal questions. His salary was paid to him by the City Treasury. In November 1767, while still in Berlin, Bach received his letter of appointment from the Hamburg Senate, which read: 'We are pleased to confirm your appointment, the more so as we place our full confidence in your excellent reputation and celebrated skills.'[6] Bach's candidacy was strongly supported by Senator, later Mayor, Anton Wagener.[7] Although there were several months of delay before Bach was able to leave Berlin, he was able to prepare himself during this period for his new responsibilities. In letters to Georg Michael Telemann, Bach asked for information about the state of church music in Hamburg, about texts, censorship, musicians, copyists, and so on.[8]

Not until the end of March 1768 did Bach enter his new employment as musical director of the five principal churches in Hamburg and Cantor of the Johanneum. In his autobiography he states:

In 1767 I was summoned to Hamburg as musical director replacing the late Kapellmeister Telemann. After repeated and most respectful requests I was granted leave by the King; and His sister, Her Royal Highness Princess Amalia, did me the honour of appointing me as Her personal Kapellmeister on my departure. Since coming here I have received a few more most tempting invitations elsewhere, but have always declined them.[9]

[4] Schubart (*Ideen*, p. 179—see Introduction, n. 4) expresses a widely held view when he says, 'The complaints one hears about his music are made against its singular taste, verging on the bizarre, its studied difficulty, individualistic style . . . and unyielding resistance to fashionable tastes.'

[5] C. P. E. Bach, letter of 31 Aug. 1784 to J. C. Kuhnau. Quoted in Schmid, *Kammermusik*, p. 81 and in Schleuning, op. cit., p. 236 [Chapter 2, n. 144].

[6] Letter of appointment from the Hamburg Senate, quoted in H. Miesner, *Philipp Emanuel Bach in Hamburg* (Berlin, 1929, R/Wiesbaden, 1969), p. 8.

[7] Ibid., p. 7.

[8] See S. L. Clark, 'The Letters from Carl Philipp Emanuel Bach to Georg Michael Telemann', *The Journal of Musicology*, iii (1984), pp. 177ff.

[9] C. P. E. Bach, 'Autobiography', p. 200. Newman, loc. cit., pp. 366f.

Bach's solemn installation took place on 19 April 1768. Telemann's grandson composed two cantatas for the occasion, and Bach made an inaugural speech in Latin 'De nobilissimo fine artis musicae'.[10]

The Hamburg post brought with it an entirely different field of activity from that which Bach had known in Berlin, resembling to some extent his father's duties in Leipzig. The school timetable at the Johanneum, a city Gymnasium, required Bach to give a singing lesson every day to the upper forms and at the same time to give instruction in the 'theory and history of music'.[11] In practice, however, these duties were mainly carried out by a suitably qualified singer, a custom which went back at least to Telemann's time. Bach, soon in any case to be overwhelmed with public responsibilities, saw no reason to alter this arrangement, especially since there were discipline problems in the school.

Owing to the nature of Bach's new tasks, he now turned his attention to genres which he had previously neglected, with the sole exception of the Magnificat, namely the great vocal forms: Passions, oratorios, and cantatas. The church year alone contained more than sixty feast-days for which Bach had to compose music. Although he made use of cantata cycles and other works by his predecessor Telemann as well as some by his father, and frequently borrowed whole pieces unaltered, this still involved a great deal of work. The large number of extant manuscripts of Passion settings, Easter pieces, Christmas pieces, numerous wedding cantatas, funeral music, and ceremonial music intended for liturgical use, testify to this.[12]

For civic celebrations Bach wrote a few secular cantatas and *Bürgerkapitänsmusiken*. Evidence that he was not spared unexpected demands is provided by a note on the score of the chorus 'Spiega Ammonia fortunata':

With this chorus, Hamburg expressed its joy and respect on the occasion of the visit of His Highness the Swedish Crown Prince with His youngest brother in 1770. C. P. E. Bach had to write it in twelve hours. It was performed twice, heavily scored, copied, and sent to the King in Stockholm. No one has ever done this before.[13]

Much of the 'vocal music for liturgical and other festivities'[14] was quickly forgotten, but a great deal has found its place in musical

---

[10] See Miesner, *Bach in Hamburg*, p. 10.   [11] Quoted in Bitter, op. cit., i, p. 186.
[12] In reality the total number of occasional works may have been much greater—there have been substantial losses of performing material. See Miesner's indications as to extant sources: Miesner, *Bach in Hamburg*, pp. 51ff.
[13] See Miesner, *Bach in Hamburg*, p. 22.
[14] C. P. E. Bach, 'Autobiography', p. 207. Newman, loc. cit., p. 371.

history, including the Passion Cantata (1770), the oratorios *Die Israeliten in der Wüste* [The Israelites in the Desert] (composed in 1769, published in 1775), and *Carl Wilhelm Rammlers Auferstehung und Himmelfahrt Jesu* [C. W. Rammler's Resurrection and Ascension of Jesus] (composed in 1777, published in 1787). Contemporary audiences valued these works very highly indeed, critics reviewed them enthusiastically,[15] and rightly so. The *empfindsam* expression, coupled with a profound affective content, perfectly matched the expectations of the new middle class, and it fascinated Reichardt, Voss, Claudius, and Gerstenberg. Yet these works are not entirely free from traces of sentimentality, a concession to an audience which delighted in stirring, lyrical utterances.

For the performance of his vocal works, Bach had at his disposal numerous singers, regular town players, extra players, and church choirs. To all appearances he got on well with them. The extant account books, which Bach kept with his usual meticulousness, offer evidence relating to matters of scoring, repertoire, fees, and other matters.[16] Trumpeters and timpanists, for example, were regularly brought in to accompany the *Te Deum laudamus*. From time to time rehearsals took place in Bach's home, which gave the composer occasion to regale his musicians with 'sandwiches, wine, and cakes'.[17]

Bach was in charge of church music in St Nicholas's, St Catherine's, St James's, St Peter's, and St Michael's. The artistic standard was for the most part low. Owing to insufficient rehearsals, too many performances—sometimes as many as ten Passions in thirteen days—and an inadequately trained body of singers, the music (usually hastily compiled in any case) aroused little interest. Moreover Bach frequently used pre-existent cantata texts, which were no longer to the taste of the Hamburg public. These deficiencies were by no means isolated instances, but were part of a widespread decline in German church music, lamented by Hiller, for example.[18] Reichardt too was later to express similar dissatisfaction:

Unpardonable and godless is the desecration of church music, and its degradation from the noble propriety after which it has striven for centuries,

---

[15] Reviews and critical accounts are found among other places in various issues of the *Staats- und Gelehrte Zeitung des Hamburgischen unpartheyischen Correspondenten* (henceforth abbreviated as *HUC*), in both parts of Reichardt's *Briefe eines aufmerksamen Reisenden die Musik betreffend* [n. 68 below], and in *Magazin der Musik*, ed. C. F. Cramer [n. 45 below]. See also Miesner, *Bach in Hamburg*, pp. 68ff. and Bitter, op. cit., ii, pp. 1ff. Two of the named vocal works have been published in modern editions by Editio Musica Budapest.

[16] See Miesner, *Bach in Hamburg*, pp. 15ff.   [17] Ibid., p. 19.

[18] See J. A. Hiller, 'Von der Kirchenmusik', *Wöchentliche Nachrichten*, i, pp. 395ff. [Chapter 1, n. 65].

to a miserable state of silly trifling and cheap sentimentality. That art so noble, so sublime, so divine, which surely has the power to improve and ennoble mankind, is now reduced to sensational frivolity![19]

Although it is not explicitly stated, Reichardt is obviously referring here to the adoption of elements derived from Italian *opera buffa* in church music.[20]

The congregation wanted edification, but at the same time entertainment. Even the sermons would sometimes contain ideas bordering almost on free-thinking. Hamburg, the city of trade and shipping, was in this respect unlike other German cities. Heinrich Miesner mentions a sermon preached in 1773: 'How much the arts and the sciences are indebted to commerce.'[21] That even the lottery and the value of money were discussed from the pulpit, shows the extent to which mercantilist thinking was ingrained in Hamburg.[22] Bach himself made no efforts to improve the state of church music. With regret he remarked to Burney: ' . . . I meet with men of taste and discernment, who deserve better music than we can give them here.'[23] Let there be no misunderstanding: such declining standards apply mainly to the music heard during church services, but not to public concerts and oratorio performances. Bach was particularly devoted to the latter; his liturgical music he regarded more as a means of earning his daily bread.

Bach's income was substantial. His basic annual salary came to 1,200 Thalers, and if one also takes into account his housing allowances and the fees for additional sacred and secular performances, his regular income came close to 2,000 Thalers. Further earnings from his concerts, his keyboard lessons, and his numerous publications enabled him to live in some luxury. No doubt he was thinking of this financial security when he said to Burney, 'I am now reconciled to my situation.'[24] Certainly the cost of living in Hamburg was high.

[19] J. F. Reichardt, *Musikalisches Kunstmagazin*, 2 vols. (Berlin, 1782–91), i, p. 179.

[20] Bach wrote in his autobiography: 'I believe, together with many men of insight, that the comic style, so popular today, is the chief offender. Without appealing to the authority of those who have written little or no comedy, I can quote one of the greatest masters of the genre now living, Signor Galuppi, who fully agreed with me when staying in my house in Berlin, and related some very amusing incidents which he had witnessed, even in some Italian churches.' C. P. E. Bach, 'Autobiography', pp. 201f. Newman, loc. cit., p. 367.

[21] See Miesner, *Bach in Hamburg*, p. 25.   [22] Ibid.   [23] Burney, *Musical Tours*, ii, p. 213.

[24] Ibid. [Translator's note. It is amusing here to compare Burney's original text with the translation into German of 1773 as *Tagebuch einer musikalischen Reise*, iii, p. 191. In the original version, Burney quotes C. P. E. Bach as having said: 'I am now reconciled to my situation, except indeed, when I meet with men of taste and discernment, who deserve better music than we can give them here.' In place of the word 'reconciled', the German version gives 'sehr zufrieden', that is 'very contented'. So it is hard to be sure whether the remark did in fact refer to Bach's satisfaction with his material comforts, or whether it meant instead that he had simply resigned himself to the uninspiring task of providing church music that would be badly performed.]

Our desperately heavy currency renders our transaction more difficult, because we cannot get nearly as much for it here as we do in Berlin, Leipzig, etc. for your currency; hence it is that if you have a louis d'or in your pocket, or a well-filled purse, in the foreign fashion, you get rid of its contents in a moment, scarcely knowing why or wherefore![25]

Bach's activities in Hamburg ranged far beyond the composition and performance of church music. With great enthusiasm he initiated his own series of public concerts from April 1768 onwards. His improvisations on the clavichord and harpsichord thrilled music-lovers from far and near. As ever he was in great demand as a keyboard teacher.[26] He was also called in as an expert to help with the appointment of organists.[27] His contacts with leading German publishing firms were further expanded and many of his works appeared in his own editions. Where sales threatened to drop, he knew how to spur them on. In various parts of Germany, musicians, music-sellers, and other tradesmen had taken advantage of Bach's subscription schemes, that is, they would distribute and sell works offered to them at a bargain rate. When one of his middlemen no longer wished to work for him, Bach without hesitation put an announcement in the *Berlinische Nachrichten von Staats- und Gelehrten Sachen* on 17 December 1774: 'Since Herr Cantor Pochhammer in Berlin is not subscribing to my oratorio [*Die Israeliten in der Wüste*], music-lovers should apply to Herr Hering for it.'[28] This was virtually to compromise Pochhammer publicly. A few days later, on 29 December, Pochhammer published the following explanation: 'I wish to inform the distinguished public herewith that the allegation that I did not wish to subscribe to Herr Kapellmeister Bach's oratorio is unfounded and untrue, because I had not received any instructions concerning it.'[29]

During the Hamburg years Bach was extraordinarily prolific. Sonatas, trios, quartets, fantasias, concertos, symphonies, songs, and the large choral works mentioned earlier were all produced, but his greatest skill was once again manifested in keyboard works:

Every element of Emanuel's style in the Berlin period reappears in maturer and more concentrated form in the composer's masterwork, the six collections

---

[25] C. P. E. Bach, letter of 10 Apr. 1780 to the Leipzig publisher Schwickert. Quoted from *Letters of Distinguished Musicians*, collected L. Nohl, trans. Lady Wallace (London, 1867), p. 64.

[26] Bach's Hamburg pupils included Jan Ladislav Dussek, Nicolas-Joseph Hüllmandel, Dietrich Ewald von Grotthuss, Christian Friedrich Gottlieb Schwenke, Niels Schiørring, Carl August Friedrich Westenholz, and Zierlein.

[27] See Miesner, *Bach in Hamburg*, p. 21.

[28] See K. Hortschansky, 'The Musician as Music Dealer in the Second Half of the 18th Century', *The Social Status of the Professional Musician from the Middle Ages to the 19th Century*, ed. W. Salmen, trans. H. Kaufman and B. Reisner (New York, 1983), p. 198.

[29] Ibid., pp. 198f.

'für Kenner und Liebhaber' ['for connoisseurs and amateurs'—Wq. 55–9 and 61], published between 1779 and 1787.[30]

In Hamburg Bach was able to assume the social position which had been denied him in Berlin on account of the court structures prevailing there: that of a free, creative, economically more or less independent, emancipated artist. This status, which was admittedly called into question once again by new social currents to be discussed later, was made possible by the advanced state of bourgeois art and culture in Hamburg.

Musical Life in Hamburg

During the first decades of the eighteenth century Hamburg, which had been Germany's chief port and centre of overseas trade since the seventeenth century, experienced a marked economic upsurge. Thanks to its political neutrality, the Hanseatic city was largely spared the damaging consequences of the warring disputes of the period, particularly the War of the Spanish Succession; what is more, it was able to negotiate profitable trading agreements not only within Germany but also with the Netherlands, France, and England. Linen from Silesia and Westphalia was a profitable export commodity, while preference was given to imports from the German colonies, especially of sugar and coffee. In 1712 the political structures of the city-state were revised. The need for this had arisen during the open conflicts that broke out around the turn of the century between groups of small merchants and workers on the one hand and aristocratic councillors and their commercial allies on the other. None the less such administrative reforms achieved only a partial solution of social conflicts. It was only those who possessed at least 1,000 Thalers and were free of debt who were eligible to vote,[31] with the result that both the small merchants and the working class were excluded from political life.

Economic prosperity derived from trade and shipping created favourable conditions for the cultivation of music. The wealthy Hamburg bourgeoisie sponsored numerous cultural activities. The opera-house 'am Gänsemarkt' was built in 1678, and the establishment there of popular opera was to set an example to the rest of Germany for decades. The people of Hamburg 'showed unswerving devotion to the theatre and helped to produce a shift of emphasis towards popular opera on the musical stage'.[32] Kusser, Keiser, Handel, Mattheson, and

---

[30] Geiringer, *The Bach Family*, p. 358.

[31] See *Heimatchronik der Freien und Hansestadt Hamburg*, ed. E. von Lehe *et al.* (Cologne, 1960), p. 116.

[32] K. Stephenson, article 'Hamburg', *MGG*, v, col. 1393.

Telemann all wrote effectively for the stage. As many as 116 works were written by Keiser alone. Plots drawn from the ancient world of gods and heroes were just as popular as everyday scenes from Hamburg, like those portrayed in the operas *Der Hamburger Jahr-Marckt* and *Die Hamburger Schlacht-Zeit* (both 1725), or incidents from student life, as in *Le bon vivant oder die Leipziger Messe*. These works were permeated by a robust realism and their often sharply satirical tone did not spare the upper classes. As burlesques and platitudes penetrated the opera more and more, however, its aesthetic quality declined correspondingly. During the 1720s and 30s rumours multiplied among the affluent middle classes that the opera was damaging trade. According to one contemporary account, the citizens of Hamburg had become too preoccupied with business concerns, and had no desire to sit on one spot for three or four hours.[33] Financial support for what were usually extremely costly productions was withheld by these very circles. Hellmuth Christian Wolff sees the principal cause of the decline of the opera after about 1725 in the emergence of a new rationalistic outlook, especially under the influence of Gottsched, which entailed the 'rejection of everything "unnatural", and this included all forms of opera . . . Gottsched's criticisms were directed not solely against the apparitions of gods and spirits or against the surprising and often implausible plots, but also against the dominating, autonomous role of music. He rejected all purely musical devices in opera, coloratura as well as text-repetition etc.'[34] In this way the life-blood of the Hamburg opera, which had maintained a continuous existence for over half a century, was cut off. In 1738 the opera-house 'am Gänsemarkt' closed its doors.

Concert life in Hamburg achieved a more lasting success. Under Telemann's direction regular public concerts had taken place in the hall of the Drillhaus since 1722, to which the townspeople were admitted for a small fee. During more than forty years in office, Telemann had performed a large number of his own works and those of contemporaries such as Handel, Graun, and Hasse. In another area too Hamburg was a leading centre in German musical life at the beginning of the century: musical journalism. On the model of the English weekly periodicals Johann Mattheson had issued first the *Vernünfftler* (1713–14) and then a number of musical journals: *Critica Musica* (1722–5) and *Der musicalische Patriot* (1728). At a time when in

---

[33] See H. C. Wolff, *Die Barockoper in Hamburg (1678–1738)*, 2 vols. (Wolfenbüttel, 1957), i, p. 342. The source quoted is C. L. von Griesheim, *Die Stadt Hamburg nach ihrem politischen, oeconomischen und sittlichen Zustande* (Schleswig, 1759), p. 195.

[34] Wolff, *Barockoper*, pp. 341f.

Prussia Frederick William I had abolished municipal self-government and was recklessly repressing the middle class, Mattheson, addressing himself to the bourgeoisie, was advocating 'the improvement of the human intellect and will'.[35]

When Carl Philipp Emanuel Bach took up his duties in Hamburg, one of his first tasks was to revive the concert-life of the city, which had suffered a decline since the death of Telemann. On 16 April 1768 an announcement appeared in the *HUC* that a concert would take place on 28 April under Bach's direction and with his participation as harpsichordist.[36] Only a few days later this was followed by another such occasion:

It is hereby announced that permission from the authorities has been given to Kapellmeister and Musikdirector Bach to hold his second and final grand concert of the season on 5 May in the newly-built *Konzertsaal auf dem Kamp*, for the greater comfort of the audience, during which, among a wide variety of musical entertainments, he will himself perform on the harpsichord. On this occasion the highly popular cantata on the poem Ino[37] by the famous Herr Professor Ramler will be performed.[38]

This was to be the start of an active concert life for Bach stretching over many years. Most of the concerts were held on Mondays between 5 p.m. and 8 p.m., which placed considerable demands on the stamina of performers and audience alike; venues included the rooms in the Drillhaus, the *Konzertsaal auf dem Kamp* (*Valentinskamp*), and the hall in the *Handelsakademie*, an educational establishment. For the sake of financial security, Bach went over to organizing subscription concerts. Twenty such concerts were planned for the autumn and winter season 1768–9. Doubts have been expressed as to whether these actually took place.[39]

As far as the repertoire was concerned, Bach exercised great care and discernment over the choice of music possessing both popular appeal and artistic merit. Emphasis was placed mainly on first performances and revivals of works by German composers.[40] Besides his own works he performed oratorios, operatic excerpts, secular

[35] J. Mattheson, *Der Musicalische Patriot* (Hamburg, 1728), p. 6. [On Mattheson's journalism generally, see *New Mattheson Studies*, ed. G. J. Buelow and H. J. Marx (Cambridge etc., 1983).]

[36] *HUC*, no. 62, 16 Apr. 1768; see also J. Sittard, *Geschichte des Musik- und Concertwesens in Hamburg* (Altona and Leipzig, 1890), p. 102.

[37] Reference is made to G. P. Telemann's cantata, *Ino*.

[38] *HUC*, no. 70, 30 Apr. 1768; extracts quoted in Sittard [n. 36 above] p. 102.

[39] See Sittard [n. 36 above] p. 105. Sittard suggests that these concerts probably did not happen on the grounds that Hamburg daily newspapers at the time contain no references to their having taken place. Yet it must be borne in mind that during Bach's lifetime there was still no such thing as regular concert criticism.

[40] See Sittard [n. 36 above] pp. 102ff., and Miesner, *Bach in Hamburg*, pp. 19ff.

cantatas, symphonies, and instrumental concertos by Johann Sebastian Bach, Handel, Telemann, Graun, Hasse, and Haydn. Even works far removed from Carl Philipp Emanuel Bach's own aesthetic aims and musical style, such as Gluck's *Alceste* and *Orfeo ed Euridice*, were included in the programmes. Thanks to a surviving letter from Matthias Claudius to Heinrich Wilhelm von Gerstenberg we have the names of a few of the works which were performed. Claudius mentions among other works Handel's *Messiah*, Hasse's *Romolo ed Ersilia*, Jommelli's *Requiem*, Salieri's *Armidia*, and Carl Philipp Emanuel Bach's *Die Israeliten in der Wüste*.[41]

Rehearsals took place in conditions much more favourable than those prevailing in church music. Bach had at his disposal a large number of orchestral players and soloists of no mean ability. On 19 August 1776 the *HUC* reported on an orchestral rehearsal as follows:

The day before yesterday ... Herr Kapellmeister Bach rehearsed his four recently completed great symphonies in the *Konzertsaal auf dem Kamp*.[42] The orchestra was probably larger than any seen in Hamburg for many years. It was composed of some forty professionals from Hamburg and a few amateurs who rendered these incomparable and unique symphonies with great vigour and precision; Herr Bach did complete justice to their skill, and those present made a lively show of approval.[43]

The performances were for the most part of high quality[44] and were evidently well received by Hamburg audiences; many years later a reference was made to this period in Cramer's *Magazin der Musik*: 'The best and most frequented concerts at that time were those of the great Bach.'[45]

During almost fifteen years of concert activity Bach saw some memorable performances. In 1772 Michael Arne conducted the first German performance of Handel's *Messiah* in Hamburg. Its success must have been considerable, for at the end of 1775 and early in 1777—this time under Bach's direction—the work was heard again. The poet Johann Heinrich Voss, after hearing a performance, wrote enthusiastically to his fiancée, 'Oh Handel, Handel! who is there among the singers of this world who can produce such magical sounds

---

[41] The relevant passage from Claudius's correspondence is quoted in Sittard [n. 36 above] p. 108.

[42] Reference is made to the four 'Orchestral symphonies with twelve obbligato parts', Wq. 183.

[43] *HUC*, no. 133, 19 Aug. 1776; quoted in Sittard [n. 36 above] p. 107.

[44] See Sittard [n. 36 above] pp. 102ff.

[45] *Magazin der Musik*, ed. C. F. Cramer, 2 vols. (Hamburg, 1783–6, R/Hildesheim and New York, 1971), ii.1, p. 3.

in bold flight as you?'[46] This enthusiasm, not unlike the reception given to Goethe's *Werther* in certain respects, was a consequence of the Handel revival of the 1770s. Reichardt devoted lengthy sections of his *Musikalisches Kunstmagazin* to this great composer.[47] Schubart called Handel 'one of the most perfect geniuses that has ever lived'.[48] It is to Carl Philipp Emanuel Bach's credit that he played a practical part in this Handel Renaissance.

Equally, Bach's inclusion in concert programmes of works which the audience found difficult to understand testifies to his high artistic standards. In performing extracts from his father's B minor Mass he was taking a risk in this respect. The fact that these were extremely well received redounds to the credit of the Hamburg audience and testifies to the high quality of the performance. In the *HUC* on 11 April 1786 one reads the following:

An opportunity arose . . . of admiring especially the five-part Credo by the immortal Sebastian Bach, one of the most magnificent works ever written, but one in which a good number of voices is needed on each part if it is to achieve its full effect. Once again, above all in the Credo, our worthy singers demonstrated their justly famed skill in a correct and sensitive rendering of the most difficult passages.[49]

All in all Bach's concerts became a focus of attention for musical circles in Hamburg, not least because he knew how to captivate the audience repeatedly with his harpsichord playing. Naturally concert-goers were drawn mainly from the ranks of the wealthy middle classes. Richard Petzoldt makes an interesting comparison in his essay 'On the social position of the musician in the eighteenth century':

At the end of G. P. Telemann's life a North German day-labourer working a twelve-hour day would earn six shillings in winter and eight shillings in summer, while a haymaker would earn sixteen. With sixteen shillings he would be able to buy six pounds of pork. (1 Mark = 16 shillings.) The average admission charge at G. P. Telemann's Hamburg concerts, however, was twenty-four shillings, in other words three days' wages for that peasant labourer.[50]

In this respect the situation had hardly changed significantly by Carl Philipp Emanuel Bach's time. The price of a ticket to his concert on 28 April 1768, for example, was two Marks.[51]

---

[46] Quoted in Sittard [n. 36 above] p. 110.
[47] See Reichardt, *Kunstmagazin*, i, pp. 42ff., 92f., 191ff., 202 [n. 19 above].
[48] Schubart, op. cit., p. 104 [Introduction, n. 4].
[49] *HUC*, no. 57, 11 Apr. 1786; quoted in *Bach-Dokumente*, iii, p. 421.
[50] R. Petzoldt, 'The Economic Conditions of the 18th-century Musician', *Social Status*, ed. W. Salmen, p. 188 [n. 28 above].
[51] *HUC*, no. 70, 30 Apr. 1768; in this connection see also Sittard, p. 105 [n. 36 above].

Die Israeliten in der Wüste

Bach's extensive concert activity obliged him also to turn his attention more and more to composition in the larger forms: symphonies, concertos, and vocal works. At the very beginning of his Hamburg period, in the latter half of 1768 and early 1769, he composed the oratorio *Die Israeliten in der Wüste*. Bach's explicit remark that this work might be performed 'not only on a solemn occasion but at any time, inside or outside the Church',[52] as indeed it was, illustrates a tendency to transplant music formerly reserved mainly for the Church into the concert-hall. This is only partly explained by the fact that external circumstances in the concert-hall—the availability of better singers and orchestral performers, better rehearsal conditions, the possibility of organizing subscriptions, and so on—were so much better suited to the performance of such a technically difficult oratorio; the public concert had become one of the principal institutions of musical life in the period. This shift was not without its consequences for the aesthetic and social character of the oratorio in general, nor for the style of this particular work. The phenomenon of a 'public idiom', a 'popular style',[53] confronted Bach with new artistic problems: in choice of subject-matter no less than in questions of style.

According to Friedrich Blume, the *Israeliten* contains 'no oratorio-like contemplative elements and is rather more like a sacred drama in the style of Handel'.[54] Bach's normally unbridled, passionate idiom gives way in this oratorio to an *empfindsam* tone, no doubt in keeping with the contemporary demand that music should stir the emotions. All the same Bach does not omit dramatic contrasts and similar bold effects, particularly in the arias and choruses. Yet these are always used for the same purpose: to underline more clearly the dramatic situations and the stirring *Affekte*. The *Israeliten* is a work in the *empfindsamer Stil*. Even the choice of subject and the treatment of the text reflect this musical ideal. In place of literal quotation from Scripture, the Hamburg poet Daniel Schiebeler, author of other oratorio libretti and song texts, provides poetic reflections on extracts from the Old Testament describing the journey of the thirsty and dispirited Jews through the desert. Only when Moses indicates the life-giving spring does the community recover its faith and give praise to God.

---

[52] See Bach's announcement of the publication of the score in *HUC*, 14 Sept. 1774, quoted in Miesner, *Bach in Hamburg*, p. 74.

[53] This concept was used by Forkel among others. See Forkel, *Johann Sebastian Bach*, p. 104 [Chapter 1, n. 48].

[54] See F. Blume, *Protestant Church Music* (London, 1975), p. 300.

This narrative is extended in the second part of the oratorio by the introduction of the Messianic theme; while this is understandable in view of the popularity of Handel's masterpiece in Hamburg, it is dramatically inappropriate in this instance. Schiebeler sketches a series of poetic images and moods that are ideally suited to musical portrayal in an expressive, cantabile style. Thus the slow instrumental introduction to the oratorio is to be understood in the light of the imagery and expressive content of the text of the opening chorus, 'The tongue cleaves to the parched mouth';[55] hence the halting melodic flow, the muted strings and flutes (strings are marked *con sordino*), the minor key, and the *adagio* tempo.[56] This opening is highly suggestive. In a few bars, Bach constructs a crescendo laden with tension out of shifting harmonies and evocative chromatic progressions, producing constantly changing colours and awakening in the listener a sense of yearning, of aimlessness (Ex. 49).

This symbolic *Tonmalerei* is comparable with that of Haydn's *Creation*. The treatment of the chorus also follows the expression of the text. While the literary quality of the libretto should not be overestimated, in this setting it cannot have failed to make an impression on

Ex. 49

[55] 'Die Zunge klebt am dürren Gaum'.
[56] Slow tempos predominate in this work, matching the overall *empfindsam* character of the oratorio. The numbering used here for references to individual arias, choruses etc. is taken from the edition by Editio Musica Budapest, ed. Gábor Darvas (Budapest, 1971), as are also Exx. 49–51.

contemporary audiences. Specially significant words such as 'Gott',
'Klagen', or 'Grab' are sensitively depicted (Ex. 50).

Ex. 50

Individual choruses serve to portray a wide range of moods. Some are
reminiscent of the angry outbursts of the high priests in J. S. Bach's
passions, some convey a spirit of lamentation, and others are cast in a
mood of triumph and rejoicing. Bach's principal aim, however, is to
achieve a lyrical *empfindsam* tone. With one or two exceptions, the
choral items in the *Israeliten*, like those in the Magnificat, are homophonic in style. The orchestral writing is seldom independent; on the
whole it follows the chorus parts quite closely.

In his handling of recitatives, Bach shows remarkable assurance.
Accents, caesuras, and punctuation are accurately observed. Some of

the *recitativo secco* passages contain brief Adagio insertions, characteristically bearing some such label as 'traurig' [sadly] or 'aufgebracht' [angrily]. In particularly affective passages Bach provides string accompaniment,[57] a formula familiar to us from his father's St Matthew Passion. In places where the text contains especially expressive images, Emanuel Bach uses *recitativo accompagnato*, even where the chorus is involved.[58] This penchant for the extended 'scena', possibly influenced by Hasse's and Gluck's operas, is also demonstrated in the arias. The da capo structure is modified in such a way that it reproduces the sequence of human emotions experienced by the protagonists. Two outer sections enclose a contrasting middle section in a different key and tempo. In some cases Bach introduces as many as four tempo changes within a single duet.[59]

Perhaps the most beautiful aria in the oratorio is Moses' 'Lord, see your people lying in the dust'.[60] In a peaceful, flowing cantilena, the solo bassoon and the singer enter into an expressive dialogue. Nowhere are there any traces of ostentatious virtuosity. Coloratura is entirely avoided. The thematic material of this aria is all designed to assist the expression of the lament: the skilful declamation of the voice part, its striking melodic descent, and the ubiquitous appoggiatura motive in the strings—a survival from the doctrine of musical figures (Ex. 51).

This is the *empfindsamer Stil par excellence*, and could be compared with many passages in Bach's instrumental slow movements.

Ex. 51

---

[57] See nos. 4 and 14.   [58] See no. 14.
[59] See no. 13: Largo—Vivace—Poco adagio—Vivace—Largo.
[60] 'Gott, sieh dein Volk im Staube liegen'. No. 15.

lie - gen,   sieh dein Volk   im Stau-be   lie - gen!   O Va - ter   der Er - bar -

The *Israeliten* occupies an important position in the history of the oratorio as a genre. Together with other contemporary works it forms the 'basis of a repertoire of oratorios less exclusively associated with performance in church buildings than hitherto'.[61] The attention which this work received at the time was phenomenal,[62] so much so that the composer found it worth his while to have it published. A copy of the first edition of 1775 was acquired by Johanna Elisabeth von Winthem, Klopstock's future wife. She was herself an accomplished soprano, and she probably sang the part of the second Israelite woman a few times, to judge from the evidence of some handwritten additions made by Bach in the copy of the score mentioned above.[63]

There is no doubt that Klopstock, resident in Hamburg from 1770 onwards and a close friend of Bach, had encouraged and supported both the composition and the publication of the *Israeliten*.[64] Bach addressed the musical public as follows:

[61] See G. Feder, section 'Das Oratorium in Deutschland bis J. Haydn', article 'Oratorium', *MGG*, x, col. 148.

[62] For references to various Hamburg performances see Sittard [n. 36 above] pp. 108, 114, 125. A performance in Berlin under Rellstab is mentioned in O. Guttmann, *Johann Karl Friedrich Rellstab: ein Beitrag zur Musikgeschichte Berlins* (Berlin, 1910), p. 33. The *Israeliten* was also heard in Leipzig during the Gewandhaus concerts in 1784 and 1798. See A. Dörffel, *Festschrift zur hundertjährigen Jubelfeier der Einweihung des Concertsaales im Gewandhause zu Leipzig*, i: 'Statistik . . .' (Leipzig, 1881), p. 2.

[63] According to Bitter, Bach made some additions in the vocal part on pages 21 and 94 of this score, 'which point to no small degree of coloratura technique'. See Bitter, op. cit., ii, p. 5. See also Miesner, *Bach in Hamburg*, p. 36.

[64] See Bach's letter to Forkel of 15 Sept. 1774: 'Now I am completely absorbed by my oratorio . . . Herr Klopstock and some other friends have been the cause of my taking up a dramatic form once again.' Quoted in Bitter, op. cit., i, p. 339.

I wish to make available to my friends a printed full score of *Die Israeliten in der Wüste*, an oratorio which I have composed . . . On account of the great expense involved, I have chosen on this occasion the safe method of publication by subscription. All the gentlemen correspondents who belong to Herr Klopstock's *Deutsche Gelehrten-Republik*, from whom I beg and promise myself this same favour for love of music, will take out a subscription forthwith until 10 January 1775, according to Herr Klopstock's plan and recommendation. I undertake to provide all those services rendered by Herr Klopstock to these gentlemen, and hope that they will return the compliment. I shall do my best to ensure good quality paper and a clean, clear style of print . . . The gentlemen correspondents are asked to be so good as to send their subscriptions directly to me at the appropriate time.[65]

Another important stimulus to Bach's involvement with the genre of the oratorio came undoubtedly from the works of George Frideric Handel. The preference for Old Testament subject matter, the Messianic theme, the stirring choral effects, the 'Enlightened' approach whereby the oratorio was intended to be 'equally suitable for performance by members of all Christian denominations'[66]—all this serves to indicate a close connection with Handel's art.[67]

What was it about the music of both men which so fascinated contemporary audiences? Johann Friedrich Reichardt praised Handel's *Judas Maccabaeus* and Bach's oratorio with equal exuberance and used the same language and the same turns of phrase to describe the individual arias and choruses of each work:

I reach for my pen in a burst of enthusiasm for the harmonies of Handel . . . My joy begins to border on pain. Never, never have I experienced the like. But nor have I ever heard the magical sounds of that conqueror of hearts before; nor the way in which his mighty harmonies fill the souls of his listeners with the fear of approaching thunder, how they cause their bones to tremble and their blood to freeze in terror; how pure celestial harmonies return to soothe their souls, and sweet, melodious song pours peace and rapture into their hearts and fills their eyes with tears of the sweetest and noblest joy. When they are thoroughly saturated with such exalted feelings, the desperate cry of a

---

[65] See *HUC*, no. 174, 14 Sept. 1774. Quoted in Miesner, *Bach in Hamburg*, p. 36.

[66] See Bach's announcement of the publication of the score in *HUC*, 14 Sept. 1774, quoted in Miesner, *Bach in Hamburg*, p. 74.

[67] Sittard provides evidence that there was a performance of the *Messiah* under Bach's direction in one of Hamburg's Masonic lodges on 23 Feb. 1777. 'Last Sunday the concert series organized for charity by the city's four united Masonic lodges came to an end. Non-Freemasons were also admitted to these concerts, in which Herr Kapellmeister Bach directed some excellent vocal works, chief among them his own *Die Israeliten in der Wüste*, *St Elena* by Hasse, Klopstock's *Erscheinung* in settings by Gluck, Pergolesi, and Zoppis, and the *Messiah* by Handel. The company was always large and dazzling, for many members of the nobility in this region, from the Council, and from the Church, honoured the occasion with their presence. The final concert ended with Handel's *Messiah* . . .' *HUC*, 26 Feb. 1777. Quoted in Sittard [n. 36 above] p. 112.

people in agony digs even more deeply into their souls and fills them with turmoil, leaving behind a sting which not even the subsequent triumphant hymn of joy sung by a liberated people can quite dispel. Thus does the mighty master take possession of the hearts of his audience and thus is he able to arouse in them any emotion he chooses.[68]

And concerning the *Israeliten*, after getting to know the work at Bach's house—admittedly only in a keyboard reduction—Reichardt has this to say:

This is one such masterpiece by Herr Kapellmeister Bach . . . for here is found such flowing, pleasing, and natural lyricism as only Kayser and Graun have ever been able to achieve.

It astonished me to see how far this great man was able to descend from those Olympian heights, which are as natural to him as flying close to the sun is to an eagle, in order to put simple song within the reach of us poor mortals.

And how fittingly, how perfectly each expression is conveyed; how strong, how overpowering the cry of the despairing people, how original the expression of their mockery and contempt of God and of their leader, how majestic the voice of Moses addressing the people, and how imploring, how deeply humble his prayer to God as he bows into the dust, how overwhelming the joy of the liberated people, how utterly delightful the whole of the final scene, in contrast to the horror of the earlier scenes of misery: none of this can I begin to convey to you, for there is no other language adequate to express it than that of Bach's music.[69]

In both works Reichardt finds an increased degree of artistic subjectivity. In this he represents the outlook of the *Sturm und Drang* movement, according to which works of art are the products of an unbounded artistic creativity. Strong emotions, genuine passions of shattering, almost painful intensity, these Reichardt expects to find expressed in music. Thus he is able to identify personally with the music he hears. Reichardt's experience of music, like that of countless other listeners, feeds entirely on the human feelings and emotions released by it.

It will not have escaped the attentive reader that Reichardt's enthusiastic appraisal of Bach's oratorio none the less contains a faint hint of criticism. The Berlin Kapellmeister and musical journalist mentions some concessions to public taste. It is true that Bach avoids the often rather sentimental tone of many contemporary oratorios,[70]

---

[68] See J. F. Reichardt, *Briefe eines aufmerksamen Reisenden die Musik betreffend*, 2 vols. (Frankfurt am Main and Leipzig, 1774, Frankfurt am Main and Breslau, 1776, R/Hildesheim etc., 1977), i, pp. 82f.

[69] Ibid., ii, pp. 14f.

[70] See A. Schering, *Geschichte des Oratoriums* (Leipzig, 1911, R/Hildesheim, 1966), pp. 343ff., 360ff.

but he does make use of a style of writing which, according to Rochlitz, was also used 'worthily and effectively by other composers'[71]—what might be termed a 'popular' style.

'. . . a style of performance and composition as close as possible to that of singing'

'Carl Philipp Emanuel Bach ... went out into the world sufficiently early to discover how to compose for a wide audience. Hence in the clarity and intelligibility of his melodies', continued Forkel in his book *Johann Sebastian Bach* (1802), 'he approaches the popular style, though he scrupulously avoids the commonplace.'[72] This judgement by Forkel is open to misinterpretation in so far as it suggests a tendency towards simplification throughout Bach's Hamburg works. The facts tell a different story. Many works contain an abundance of formal intricacies and complex meanings. All such phenomena can nevertheless—to pursue Forkel's line of argument—be linked to the common denominator of popular art.

An important element of Bach's musical philosophy is summed up in this concept of popular art. Throughout his life the Hamburg master displayed a certain scepticism towards theoretical-aesthetic speculation, and it would be mistaken to regard Bach's ideas about music as an attempt to set up a theoretical system. Even the *Versuch über die wahre Art das Clavier zu spielen* was intended primarily as a practical performance guide, and it is significant that only a few months before his death Bach was still occupied with a projected treatise on composition 'as practised today'.[73] Little of what Bach had to say in the 1770s and 80s about musical aesthetics advanced beyond the long-established doctrine of the affections. The inadequacy of this doctrine had to be demonstrated in practice before it could be superseded in theory. When Bach emphasizes the 'precise determination of musical expression',[74] a principle of classification is invoked which had lain at the basis of the old catalogues of affections. On the other hand, Bach's contemporaries valued those very passages in his fantasias 'which do not correspond precisely to particular emotions or ideas'.[75] The development of musical aesthetics here enters a transitional phase. The

---

[71] Rochlitz, op. cit., iv, pp. 313f. [Chapter 1, n. 7].

[72] Forkel, *Johann Sebastian Bach*, p. 104 [Chapter 1, n. 48].

[73] C. P. E. Bach, letter of 8 Mar. 1788 to a publisher (Musée de Mariemont, RISM B-MA), quoted in Schmid, *Kammermusik*, p. 72n.

[74] See Bach's review of the first volume of J. N. Forkel, *Allgemeine Geschichte der Musik* in *HUC*, 9 Jan. 1788, quoted in Bitter, op. cit., ii, p. 110.

[75] *Magazin der Musik*, i.2, p. 1250 [n. 45 above].

musical outlook of the Berlin circle—Marpurg, Krause, Quantz etc.—is supplanted by new aesthetic ideas, frequently derived from diametrically opposed philosophical positions (Herder, Kant, Wackenroder etc.).[76]

It is not to be held against Carl Philipp Emanuel Bach that he failed to pursue such aesthetic developments in detail and to adopt them in his own musical philosophy.[77] He was primarily a practical musician. And yet the aesthetic observations scattered throughout his letters, his reviews, and in the autobiography are undeniably progressive in tone:

My principal study, especially in recent years, has been directed towards achieving on keyboard instruments a style of performance and composition as close as possible to that of singing, in spite of the lack of sustaining power. This is no easy task, if the ear is neither to be left too empty, nor the noble simplicity of the melody ruined by too much noisy accompaniment.[78]

The affinity between the aesthetic formulation 'a style of performance and composition as close as possible to that of singing' and that of the 'vocally inspired' composer, which Bach had expressed years earlier in the *Versuch*, is clear. As before, the main objective is to stir the listener's heart, which means neither more nor less than rousing him emotionally. In this typically man-centred musical philosophy, Bach reveals himself to be a true son of the Enlightenment.

Bach's style did not remain unaffected by these ideas. During his first ten years in Hamburg there were a number of changes of emphasis in his compositional activity. The chief obligation placed on him by his job as the city's director of music was to compose church music of all kinds. In the instrumental field genres which had hitherto been used frequently receded into the background, while others assumed a new importance. To give just one example: from the Berlin period we have over a hundred keyboard sonatas, whereas in Hamburg between 1769 and 1775 Bach composed only seven. Even some of the sonatas published in the collections 'für Kenner und Liebhaber' from 1779 onwards had been written in the 1750s. Bach was to become more

---

[76] More detailed consideration of theoretical and aesthetic matters would be out of place here. See in this connection Zoltai, op. cit. [Chapter 2, n. 76], and the author's dissertation, *Die Entwicklung des theoretisch-ästhetischen Denkens innerhalb der Berliner Musikkultur von den Anfängen der Aufklärung bis Reichardt* (Leipzig, 1978).

[77] The following remark in Reichardt's autobiography is very revealing: 'At that time our young artist's first thought was that the true art of music lay in the conscious realization of the inner secret processes of the soul which continue uninterruptedly and unknown to any other. Bach did not share this idea; he seemed in fact not to grasp it, in spite of his first-rate mind.' J. F. Reichardt, 'Autobiography', *AMZ*, xvi (1814), col. 32. [The passage quoted occurs during the fourth and last instalment of Reichardt's autobiography, the first having appeared in *AMZ*, xv (1813), cols. 601ff.]

[78] C. P. E. Bach, 'Autobiography', p. 209. Newman, loc. cit., p. 372.

involved with the larger forms of keyboard music—sonata, fantasia, and rondo—during the later Hamburg period, that is to say after 1780. In the field of chamber music, the predominant items were solos, marches, and polonaises—genres calculated to meet the rapidly increasing demand among a wide circle of amateurs for music that was simple to play and easy to listen to. This same tendency towards simplification left its mark on the title-pages of many publications from around this time: in 1770 Bach issued the anthology *Musikalisches Vielerley* [Musical Miscellany], also in that year the *Six Sonates pour le Clavecin à l'usage des Dames*, and one year later the *Sechs leichte Flügel-Concerte mit Begleitung* [Six easy harpsichord concertos with accompaniment]. Bach also explored new possibilities of scoring by using unusual instrumental combinations; in addition to the more traditional chamber groupings, one finds the horn, the clarinet, and the bassoon treated as obbligato instruments.[79] Other works from the first ten years in Hamburg included: six 'string symphonies' (1773), *C. P. E. Bach's keyboard sonatas with an accompaniment for violin and violoncello* (1775),[80] four 'Orchestral symphonies with twelve obbligato parts' (1776),[81] and several sonatas from the collections 'für Kenner und Liebhaber'.

Short, simple keyboard pieces, then, are found alongside highly technical symphonies, and light-hearted dance-movements alongside complex keyboard sonatas. Even the most seemingly trivial work bears the imprint of Bach's originality.

The extent of his interest in miniature forms is illustrated in the *Twelve short two- and three-part pieces for flute (or violin) and harpsichord* (1770).[82] Printed in miniature format, so as to be suitable for music-making 'while on a journey or a planned visit to friends, or out on a stroll',[83] these small-scale pieces fulfilled an important function. They provided the amateur with music to play [*Spielmusik*] in the literal sense of the word—music that is simple and easy to understand without being plain, music that is sometimes attractive and dance-like in character—Tempo di Menuetto, Alla Polacca, Allegro scherzando—and sometimes *empfindsam*. The twelve pieces are grouped in pairs; after each even-numbered movement there is an instruction to repeat the preceding odd-numbered movement. Bach achieves a clear contrast in

---

[79] Examples from Bach's Hamburg period include: 'VI Piccole Sonate a due Corni, due Flauti, due Clarinetti e Fagotto', 1775, Wq. 184, and '6 Kleine Stücke oder Märsche für 2 Hörner, 2 Oboen, 2 Klarinetten und Fagott', Wq. 185.

[80] The first set of these sonatas was published in 1776, the second in 1777. Original title: *C. P. E. Bachs Clavier-Sonaten mit einer Violine und einem Violoncello zur Begleitung.*

[81] The 'Orchestral symphonies' were published in 1780 by Schwickert in Leipzig. Original title: *Orchestersinfonien mit zwölf obligaten Stimmen.*

[82] German title: *Zwölf zwei- und dreistimmige kleine Stücke für die Flöte (oder Violin) und das Clavier.*

[83] Quoted from the preface.

colour between the movements of each pair—with only one exception the even-numbered movements are labelled 'Cembalo tacet'.

The Andante pair, numbered 11 and 12 in the collection, offers a model example of Bach's imaginative handling of the miniature form. Nowhere does the music appear trite. Neither the gestures of pathos nor virtuoso exuberance are required in this music. Its means of expression consist in a tender sound quality, remaining at a *piano* dynamic over long stretches. Bach achieves a fine balance in the part-writing between motion and relative stability. He is not afraid to use surprising harmonic progressions: the diminished seventh chord in bar 3 of the first Andante greatly enlivens the predominantly tonic and dominant harmony. The shaping of the upper part in the second Andante is particularly sensitive; the melody begins rather dreamily, then ascends rapidly through one and a half octaves, immediately drops back again, then moves towards a second peak, finally rounding off the first eight-bar phrase with a cadence formula (Ex. 52).

Ex. 52. Andante, Wq. 82 no. 12

Suspensions and appoggiaturas serve here to refine the melodic outline, but also, more importantly, they colour the musical expression. In the *Versuch*, Bach extols the 'beauty and sweetness of appoggiaturas'.[84]

If this music is intended to communicate through its gestures and attitudes, then the impression conveyed is one of constant, gentle flattery. Whether such extra-musical connotations ever existed in the mind of the composer seems a matter of secondary importance; far

[84] Bach, *Versuch*, ii, p. 210 (Mitchell, p. 341).

more important is the fact that this Andante possesses an attractive and pleasing quality, *Empfindsamkeit*, and here and there a touch of passion. Inasmuch as Bach still managed to be original in this piece while writing specifically for the 'public as regards both taste and technical ability',[85] he satisfied the demand for popular art.

The Rondo

As mentioned earlier, musical theorists in North Germany banished the minuet from the symphony; at the beginning of the 1770s another fierce aesthetic debate took place concerning the rondo. No doubt owing in part to its frequent use by South German composers it was completely rejected by some theorists. The musical scholar and friend of Bach, Johann Nikolaus Forkel from Göttingen, commented 'how little genuine intrinsic merit most of the fashionable pieces in this form possess'.[86] This view, however, was sharply at odds with the musical tastes of many amateur musicians, who showed a marked preference for the rondo, and it would have been both arrogant and short-sighted for Bach to ignore this popular demand. To him as a musician the rondo cannot have seemed *a priori* good or bad. He judged each individual work on its own merits. To use the rondo as a means of musical expression, as a medium in which to experiment with all manner of compositional devices, especially variation technique, to entertain and stimulate the listener, this Bach felt to be a worthwhile artistic exercise. He composed a large number of rondos; it seems that they were still widely admired in later years, to judge from a letter Bach wrote to a business colleague:

The demand for rondos is as great here as in London, so I have included some in this collection in order to boost sales. I know from experience that many people buy these collections of my keyboard works purely on account of the rondos.[87]

Forkel wrote a detailed analysis of the G major rondo from the first volume of *C. P. E. Bach's keyboard sonatas with an accompaniment for violin and violoncello*. He began by discussing the aims of his analytical investigation, namely 'to give the musical amateur a few hints on how to enjoy [the sonatas] and admire them in an informed way'.[88] Forkel developed an approach to analysis which involved not only the

[85] Quoted from the preface.

[86] J. N. Forkel, *Musikalisch-kritische Bibliothek*, 3 vols. (Gotha, 1778–9, R/Hildesheim, 1964), ii, p. 281.

[87] Quoted in O. G. Sonneck, 'Zwei Briefe C. Ph. Em. Bach's an Alexander Reinagle', *SIMG*, viii (1906–7), p. 114.

[88] Forkel, *Bibliothek*, ii, p. 277.

discussion of formal and technical matters but also the evaluation of the 'character' and 'intrinsic value' of a musical work. Admittedly Forkel's musical ideals and his general artistic standards are by no means free from prejudice. His lack of sympathy for the works of the Classical masters, Haydn, Mozart, and Beethoven, and his strong attacks on Gluck have frequently led to accusations of conservatism.[89]

Forkel describes the rondo as a 'round . . . in which a beautiful, memorable, and significant idea recurs from time to time, mixing and alternating with other subsidiary ideas that issue from it'.[90] Of the characteristics of the main theme he has this to say:

Every musical phrase, like every idea in poetry or rhetoric, if it is to be delivered with its own particular sparkle or repeated several times, must possess an intrinsic merit, in order to justify that sparkle or repetition.[91]

This constant reference to the laws of verbal language is easily explained: Forkel had himself formulated a system of musical rhetoric in which he derived the various structural components of music—motive, theme, caesura, etc.—from analogous linguistic phenomena.[92]

The 'principal idea' of this Bach rondo, he tells us, is 'so beautiful, that one feels one could never tire of hearing it (Ex. 53). It is highly attractive, simple, clear and intelligible without being dull, and at each repetition one hears it with renewed pleasure.'[93]

Ex. 53. Rondo, Wq. 90 no. 2

Bach has in fact produced here a thematic idea with the potential for extensive variation, so constituted as 'not to weary the listener by excessive uniformity, but instead to satisfy the necessary condition of diversity common to all the arts'.[94]

[89] See F. Peters-Marquardt and A. Dürr, 'Johann Nikolaus Forkel', *MGG*, iv, cols. 518f. There are a number of essays on Gluck in Forkel, *Bibliothek*, i, pp. 53ff.

[90] Forkel, *Bibliothek*, ii, pp. 281f.   [91] Ibid., ii, pp. 282f.

[92] See J. N. Forkel, *Allgemeine Geschichte der Musik*, 2 vols. (Leipzig, 1788–1801), i, Introduction, pp. 1ff.

[93] Forkel, *Bibliothek*, ii, pp. 283f.

[94] Ibid., ii, p. 284.

With the help of one or two musical examples Forkel demonstrates different aspects of Bach's compositional procedures (Ex. 54). He is particularly interested in the tonal scheme, since Bach guides the listener through 'the entire harmonic labyrinth'.[95]

Ex. 54

At the start of bar 95 the key is E flat major, but Bach modulates in the space of a few bars back to G major, a progression on which Forkel comments as follows: since this modulation to E flat major is 'bolder and more remote' than earlier modulations, therefore 'the return from it is also correspondingly more daring, yet still so finely achieved that one very gradually loses the sense of a distinct tonality and is drawn gently back into the security of the tonic key'.[96]

Forkel's appreciative comments are thoroughly justified. In his variation of the rondo theme and in his handling of the interludes (*Couplets*) Bach displays an astonishingly fertile and varied imagination. On its initial restatement the theme is immediately ornamented by means of a figurative embellishment which serves as an element of contrast and appears in constantly new guises during later restatements: in this way many different nuances of expression are achieved in the course of the rondo. Structural notes are decorated from above and below (as in Ex. 55),

Ex. 55

[95] Ibid., ii, p. 289.
[96] Ibid., ii, p. 291.

and the texture is at some points reduced to a single line. By quoting
motivic material in extreme registers Bach achieves some fine effects of
timbre.

Forkel's analysis raises one of the problems which confronted Bach:
how to write music in such a way as both to appeal to the musical
amateur and to satisfy the desire of the professional for originality in a
work of art. Bach's G major rondo is a good example of 'popular'
music. The *Hamburgischer unpartheyischer Correspondent* on 22 February
1777 described it as a work that shone 'ut luna inter stellas minores'.[97]
For the complete set Bach attracted 390 subscribers who between them
bought 534 copies[98]—a very high sales figure indeed. This is a measure
of his success in balancing the evolution and constant refinement of his
personal style against the aesthetic requirements of a wider circle of
music-lovers. There is another genre, however, in which his creative
individuality was able to reach still higher levels than were possible in
this rondo: a genre in which from the outset technical limitations were
fewer and concessions to popular taste more clearly evident, namely
the symphony.

The Six 'String Symphonies'

One of the subscribers to *C. P. E. Bach's keyboard sonatas with an
accompaniment for violin and violoncello* was Baron Gottfried van Swieten,
who had established cordial relations with Bach after being appointed
Austrian Imperial ambassador in Berlin in 1770. Swieten, an enthusiastic music-lover, greatly admired the music of Haydn and Mozart,
and actively promoted it. He was to prove an extremely useful contact
for Bach, and became a keen supporter of his music. It is well known
that Mozart discovered C. P. E. Bach's works at the Baron's musical
gatherings,[99] and made 'a collection of the fugues of Bach—not only of
Sebastian, but also of Emanuel and Friedemann'.[100]

---

[97] *HUC*, no. 31, 22 Feb. 1777; quoted in Bitter, op. cit., i, p. 210n.

[98] These figures are supplied in Bitter, op. cit., i, pp. 208f. See also the lists of subscribers
published with the first editions of these works.

[99] See W. A. Mozart, letter of 10 Apr. 1782 to his father, *The Letters of Mozart and his Family*,
trans. and ed. Emily Anderson, 3rd edn. (London, 1985), p. 800.

[100] Ibid.

Swieten may be considered the key figure in the dissemination of Bach's music in Austria, especially in Vienna.[101] At the beginning of the 1770s Swieten commissioned the Hamburg Bach to compose some symphonies, in which, according to the express wish of the commissioner, he might 'give himself free rein, without regard to the difficulties of execution which were bound to arise'.[102] In the six symphonies for four-part string orchestra with continuo a landmark was achieved in the growth of Bach's style. Reichardt was fascinated by their 'original and bold flow of ideas' and he praised the 'great diversity and novelty in their forms and surprise effects'.[103] He concluded his appraisal thus: 'Hardly has ever a more noble, daring, or humorous musical work issued from the pen of a genius.'[104]

Reichardt used similar language to describe the instrumental works of Haydn. And indeed Haydn's symphonies of the 1770s resemble Bach's 'string symphonies' in several respects. In both cases an equally powerful musical personality sets out to give artistic expression to passionate feelings. The frequent use of surprise effects creates the impression of a symphonic fantasia. In Haydn's symphonies from this period 'rhythmic contrasts and the sophisticated development of rhythmic motives' are typical. 'The forceful individuality of these works also leaves its mark on the harmony, most strikingly perhaps in certain highly characteristic examples of long-range harmonic tensions.'[105] The image of the *Sturm und Drang* composer, therefore, seems quite appropriate.

From the opening bars of Bach's C major Symphony, Wq. 182 no. 3, there is no doubt that a new note is being sounded: a forceful, impulsive main theme (Ex. 56), its pent-up energy strengthened still further by the unison texture, establishes a powerful momentum.

Ex. 56

[101] See R. Bernhardt, 'Aus der Umwelt der Wiener Klassiker, Freiherr Gottfried van Swieten', *Der Bär. Jahrbuch von Breitkopf & Härtel* (1929–30), pp. 74ff.

[102] Reichardt, 'Autobiography', *AMZ*, xvi, col. 29 [n. 77 above].

[103] Ibid.

[104] Ibid.

[105] J. P. Larsen and H. C. Robbins Landon, 'Franz Joseph Haydn', *MGG*, v, col. 1902.

In this extract the listener's conventional expectations are thwarted in two ways. Firstly, the irregular structure of the theme is striking. Here Bach has deliberately avoided any hint of symmetry or regular periodicity, and with it an important means of orientation for the listener.[106] The eleven-bar (!) main theme falls into three unequal sections: the thematic 'antecedent' (bars 1–6), and a link (bar 7) to the thematic 'consequent' (bars 8–11). Secondly, the music comes to a halt on A flat in bar 6; after a rest there follows another chromatic note, F sharp, this time emphasized by a trill and lasting for a whole bar. By this point the tonic area is already left behind. The new key of G major is immediately used as a springboard into other keys: Bach was practised at negotiating 'harmonic labyrinths'. Within just a few bars Bach touches sequentially on the following tonalities: C, F, D, G, E, and A minor. After the first *Fortspinnung* section, the music loses its energetic drive completely. Everything seems to suggest that Bach is about to relieve the forcefulness of the opening section by introducing a *piano* cantabile secondary idea. Yet once again expectations are thwarted! After only four bars of G major comes an abrupt switch to a *forte* E major harmony (Ex. 57).

Ex. 57

One must try to imagine the effect of such harmonic and expressive daring on contemporary listeners, given that musical theorists in the 1770s were still teaching them to regard unity of *Affekt* as an immutable compositional norm. Lessing held on to this view:

[106] Irregularity is created in this example immediately after the repetition of the head-motive, which is then extended by one bar (bar 5).

A symphony which expresses different passions in different sections is a musical monster; in a symphony there must be only one dominant passion, and each individual phrase must allow this same passion to emerge clearly, simply modifying it in various ways, either in its degree of strength and vigour, or by mingling with it various other related passions; it must be the composer's aim to arouse this same passion within us.[107]

It goes without saying that such statements were not allowed to pass unchallenged. In essence the following remarks by Gerstenberg about one of Bach's keyboard fantasias[108] apply equally well to the third 'string symphony':

Besides, I cannot but add that this fantasia by Bach provides a fairly conclusive refutation of Herr Lessing's contention in the 27th section of his *Dramaturgie* that the musician cannot pass from one passion to its opposite within a single piece, from restfulness to rage, for example, or from tenderness to ferocity. Herr Lessing appears not to have considered the possibilities offered by the skilful use of transitions, of which there are such remarkable examples in this fantasia, and also, it seems to me, in many other sonatas by Bach.[109]

Faced with the undeniable originality of Bach's music, Reichardt found himself obliged to qualify in at least one respect his earlier highly conservative statements on instrumental music, in which he had adopted a position not far removed from Lessing's:

Were we to give to each of our instrumental compositions one single character, or, in the case of those made up of several movements, to seek to portray in them the true refinements of one single *Affekt*, or the nuanced transitions from one to another, and were we also to abandon those empty, constricting rules about how to handle nearly-related keys, and how to pass from major to minor and vice versa in supposedly well-written pieces, were we instead to give free rein to joyous élan and a more sedate, troubled pace to sorrowful music, much would be gained thereby.[110]

Such ideas, coming as late as 1784, find as little resonance in the Classical music of Haydn and Mozart as they do in that of C. P. E. Bach. Consequently Reichardt modified his position: 'It is only Bach and Haydn who need a wider range of expression in order to convey their highly original ideas.'[111]

The slow movement of the C major Symphony, which follows the

---

[107] G. E. Lessing, 'Hamburgische Dramaturgie', 27th section, *Gesammelte Werke in zehn Bänden*, ed. P. Rilla, vi (Berlin, 1954), p. 142.

[108] Reference is made to the C minor Fantasia from the *18 Probestücke in 6 Sonaten*, Wq. 63.

[109] H. W. von Gerstenberg, letter of 27 Apr. 1768 to F. Nicolai, quoted in Schmid, *Kammermusik*, p. 53.

[110] Reichardt, *Kunstmagazin*, i, p. 25 [n. 19 above].

[111] Ibid.

first movement without a break, is extraordinarily deeply felt. This is not the only instance of linked movements in Bach's music: the other 'string symphonies' contain further examples, an indication that Bach was aiming at a cyclical unity whereby the single movement was to become an organic part of the symphonic whole. It is only through such large-scale planning that an imbalance between tension and release can be avoided; thus the expressive weight of the first two movements of the C major Symphony requires, from the listener's point of view, to be offset by the lighter style of the Finale. In the Adagio, Bach strikes up an expressive duet for the violins (Ex. 58).

Ex. 58

Yet this lyricism is not unbroken. The movement had opened with

Ex. 59

weighty dissonant *fortissimo* strokes followed by a descending figure played *piano* and repeated *pianissimo* (Ex. 59), and this passage re-appears three times to interrupt the melodic flow.[112]

After the seriousness of the first two movements, the Finale seems positively lightweight. With its frequent sequential patterns and its alternation of tutti and solo passages, it resembles a concerto move-ment somewhat. There is much in this movement that fits the image of a humorous Bach, whether it is the carefree main theme, in the manner of a street song (Ex. 60),

Ex. 60

or the vigorous unison passage which marks the conclusion of both exposition and recapitulation (Ex. 61).

Ex. 61

Ernst Suchalla has an important observation to make about antici-pations of 'Classical techniques' in a passage from the first movement of the B flat major Symphony, Wq. 182 no. 2 (Ex. 62).

Ex. 62

[112] Bach builds the opening of this movement over a bass-line consisting of the notes B—A—C—H—E, a little bow to the commissioner, Baron van Swieten. [In German musical nomenclature, H = B natural, B = B flat.]

All four parts are motivically constructed. Three motives drawn from the main theme are developed simultaneously for the first time. Viola and cello take the bass of the *Kopfmotiv* and subject it to traditional ostinato treatment. Two other motives, standing in question-and-answer relation to each other, and likewise borrowed from the opening of the movement, are found in the two violin parts. These motives constitute the thematic content of the passage. Such dualism, based on thematic-motivic work ... lies at the heart of Classical developmental techniques ...[113]

Reichardt had said of these symphonies:

It would be a great loss for art if these masterpieces were to remain hidden away in private hands. Nowhere does there yet exist a complete collection of the works of this great composer and humorist, from whom even Haydn, as he frequently and willingly admitted, learned and profited more than from any other.[114]

Unfortunately even today the situation regarding the dissemination of Bach's works has not changed so significantly that Reichardt's remarks have lost their relevance; they can still be understood as an invitation to perform these symphonies and other works by Bach in our concert-halls, and to rediscover them for the recording and broadcasting industries. Bach's symphonies demand attentive listening. They reveal to the music-lover an imaginative musical language, impassioned and sensitive in its detail and ever full of surprises. These works testify eloquently to Bach's richly developed artistic personality in their

[113] Suchalla, op. cit., pp. 52f.
[114] Reichardt, 'Autobiography', *AMZ*, xvi, col. 29 [n. 77 above]. Bach's string symphonies were lost for several decades until Hugo Riemann discovered manuscript copies of them in the Library of the Thomasschule in Leipzig, mistook them for string quartets and published them as such. Not until Ernst Fritz Schmid's discovery of the autographs of four of the symphonies in the library of the Conservatoire Royal de Musique in Brussels was it possible to correct Riemann's mistake and to issue a new critical edition of these symphonies.

avoidance of the merely conventional and in their unhindered out-pouring of a 'bold and original flow of ideas'. Such unrestrained subjectivity places Bach firmly within the aesthetic context of the *Sturm und Drang* movement. It comes as no surprise to learn that these very 'string symphonies' were regarded by contemporaries as works of genius, and earned for their composer the title *Originalgenie*.

Discussion of Genius

The discussion of genius which took place within the *Sturm und Drang* movement had its origins in England with Edward Young's *Conjectures on Original Composition* (1759). Young took the view that everyone possessed the potential for 'originality' and the ability to work creatively without regard to rules and restrictions.[115] Such ideas met with a broad resonance in Germany among the leaders of the *Sturm und Drang* (Hamann, Herder, Goethe, and others). The innumerable debates, essays, and theories about the nature and function of the *Originalgenie*, about original creation, inwardness, and subjectivity, were outward expressions in aesthetic terms of the political and ideological trend among the rising middle classes to demand universal freedom for the individual; put another way, the concept of genius that evolved in the 1770s was a manifestation of the bourgeois struggle for emancipation. Yet in view of the prevailing state of society, these demands were simply unrealistic. Post-feudal social and economic conditions gradually gave way to a capitalist society which brought its own patterns of economic dependence, so that altogether the *Sturm und Drang* movement proved to be an unsuccessful clash between 'the desire of the human will for freedom and the inevitable progress of history'.[116]

A significant contribution to the theoretical exposition of the concept of *Originalgeist*, a term used interchangeably with *Originalgenie*, was made by Johann Georg Sulzer in his *Allgemeine Theorie der schönen Künste* (1771–4). Although not a supporter of the *Sturm und Drang* movement[117]—Goethe was to attack the rationalistic and normative features of his lexicography[118]—Sulzer exerted a lasting influence on the discussion of genius in the 1770s. Regarding the specific social

---

[115] From a statement attributed to Herder, and quoted in *Geschichte der deutschen Literatur*, vi, p. 490 [Chapter 2, n. 180].

[116] J. W. von Goethe, 'Zum Schäkespears Tag', *Jugendwerke*, iii, 'Prosaschriften 1757–1775' (Berlin, 1956), p. 78.

[117] See P. Schnaus, 'Johann Georg Sulzer', *MGG*, xii, cols. 1733ff., and Ottenberg, op. cit., pp. 64ff.

[118] See *Geschichte der deutschen Literatur*, vi, pp. 510f., 870, nn. 21–2.

function of the *Originalgenie* he stressed the point that 'the most important original minds are undoubtedly those whose ideas, rather than simply benefiting professional artists in small areas of their respective fields, actually make a new and beneficial contribution to the taste of a wider public, open up new sources of enjoyment for a whole nation, and give a new lease of life to its capacity for pleasure'.[119]

The discussion of genius directed public attention onto the creative process itself and the particular manner in which artistic individuality was manifested therein: 'The original [artist] is one who bases his work on his own impressions of the world, and develops it according to his own insights.'[120] Of crucial importance, then, to the concept of genius is the creative act of the individual, derived from his 'personal impressions of the world'. Such ideas as this necessarily led to a more precise formulation of the very doctrines concerned with the nature of individuality and originality in art. In Sulzer's *Theorie* the notions of '*Originalgeist*' and 'servile, miserable imitator'[121] stand at either end of a fixed hierarchical scale of values; those who achieve 'fortuitous originality'[122] are also included.

Reichardt took his lead from such general aesthetic considerations as this, modifying them to suit the specific case of music, and relating them to compositional practice:

Every good composer sets out to observe unity in the planning and execution of his work; and every good composer has a certain style, by which he can be recognized in all his music.

The style of each composer may be more or less original: there is only one Bach,[123] whose style is utterly original and utterly his own.[124]

The original quality of Bach's style is frequently described in similar terms by other contemporary writers. According to Reichardt 'his originality of idea frequently demands original, unusual, or intense expression'.[125] For Schubart Bach's music is 'rich in invention' and 'inexhaustible in novel modulations'.[126] Burney emphasizes particularly 'his boldest strokes, both of melody and modulation'.[127] These qualities are indications of a musical language in which the individual parameters—theme, melody, harmony, dynamics etc.—come together in significant and imaginative ways, resulting in a masterly sound-

[119] J. G. Sulzer, *Allgemeine Theorie der schönen Künste*, 2nd edn., 4 vols. (Leipzig, 1792–4), iii, p. 627.
[120] Ibid., iii, p. 486.   [121] Ibid., iii, pp. 486, 625.   [122] Ibid., iii, p. 625.
[123] Carl Philipp Emanuel and not Johann Sebastian Bach is meant here.
[124] J. F. Reichardt, *Über die Deutsche comische Oper* (Hamburg, 1774), p. 15 (R/Munich, 1974).
[125] Ibid., p. 19.
[126] Schubart, op. cit., p. 178 [Introduction, n. 4].   [127] Burney, *Musical Tours*, ii, p. 218.

structure. Abrupt reversal of mood is just as likely to occur as fluid transition; no wonder that Bach was not spared the charges of 'capricious taste' and *Bizarrerie*.[128]

Bach certainly made many concessions to public taste, but as a result of his efforts to impress his personal style on even the simplest pieces, the widespread interest in his music gradually declined. It is true that individual works such as *C. P. E. Bach's keyboard sonatas with an accompaniment for violin and violoncello* and the collections 'für Kenner und Liebhaber'—the latter with significantly declining numbers of subscribers—enjoyed considerable success, yet none the less the advertisements in musical journals conveyed a different message as the years progressed. In his *Magazin der Musik* (1783–6), Cramer, whose goodwill towards Bach is beyond question, discusses countless minor composers side by side with such great masters as Gluck, Pergolesi, C. P. E. Bach, Haydn, even Mozart;[129] the columns of this journal are filled with names like Hüllmandel, Löhlein, Cambini, Vanhal, Schwanenberg, and Pleyel. A new generation was asserting itself, and new musical ideals were becoming established.

We have been looking ahead. Yet the seeds of future alienation can be seen even in the 1770s, for example in the following remarks by Burney. 'Complaints have been made against his pieces for being *long, difficult, fantastic*, and *far-fetched*.'[130] In this connection mention might also be made of the rather curious essay entitled: 'How do the two great keyboard players Carl Philipp Emanuel Bach and Alberti from Rome compare with one another?' (1780).[131] The author is in all probability Georg Joseph Vogler, composer, theorist, and founder of the Mannheim *Tonschule*. He begins, without mentioning any names, by extolling the 'merits of a worthy gentleman grown old in the outmoded system',[132] and there is no doubt that it is Bach who is meant. Normally far from restrained in his attacks (thoroughly abusive in fact in his treatment of Kirnberger[133] who replied in similar vein[134]), Vogler tempers his criticisms of Bach's music by presenting

---

[128] See n. 4 above.

[129] Incidentally the first volume of the *Magazin der Musik* contains the information that a highly promising musical career may be expected for the young Beethoven. See *Magazin der Musik*, i.1, pp. 394f. [n. 45 above].

[130] Burney, *Musical Tours*, ii, p. 218.

[131] G. J. Vogler, *Betrachtungen der Mannheimer Tonschule*, 3 vols. (Mannheim, 1778–81, R/Hildesheim etc., 1974), iii, pp. 151ff.

[132] Ibid., iii, p. 152.

[133] See Vogler's review of Kirnberger's *Kunst des reinen Satzes*, ibid., iii, pp. 258ff.

[134] Kirnberger wrote acidly to Forkel, 'I have had a letter from someone in Mannheim who tells me that Vogler is as little regarded there as anywhere else. It serves that windbag right.' Quoted in Bitter, op. cit., ii, p. 323.

them in the form of an imaginary observation from an anonymous young composer: 'Maestro, your taste is incorrect: you prefer artifice, you wish to be learned, and forget to be simple; conspicuous in all your music is the anxious quest for uniqueness, for novelty, the desire to say something never said before; in this way you pay too little attention to the formal concept . . .'[135] And to reinforce these criticisms, Vogler quotes a piece of Bach's music:

Here, for example, you have written a piece in A minor, which, instead of establishing the main key of the work at the outset, starts with four beats in A minor followed by four beats in G minor. What a way to begin, what a curious kind of music![136]

The question posed in the title still remains unanswered. In Vogler's words,

Does Bach rank beside him? [Alberti]—no, he is the greater of the two. His performance, his execution is unexceptionable. Yet well might we wish that the great man would introduce into his style more sentiment, more daintiness, more simplicity, and less artificiality (which, it must be said in his defence, the somewhat dry Northern taste still demands). By simplicity we mean not only that the notes should be straightforward, but also the key-scheme: there should be a balanced arrangement of all foreign keys around the principal key, variety within tonal unity etc.[137]

The allegations that Bach was no longer composing in a contemporary idiom and that his style conflicted with prevailing taste are serious. What not even Vogler can withhold from Bach, however, is the aura of the *Originalgenie*. 'Artifice' and failure to attend to 'the formal concept' mean in Bach's case the free unfolding of an artistic personality that delights in the unconventional and in spirited play with musical ideas, a personality which thoroughly explores both the humorous and the serious dimensions of music. Bach is 'saturated with the notion of free artistic subjectivity, which best manifests itself in the "free" style and in the "free fantasia"'.[138] In this he proves himself to be both a typical and an influential representative of the *Sturm und Drang* movement.

Bach's Family and Circle of Friends in Hamburg

On their arrival in Hamburg, Bach and his family lived at first in a flat on the Böhmerstrasse,[139] from which they soon moved into a more

---

[135] Vogler, op. cit., iii, p. 153.

[136] Ibid., p. 154. It is not clear which work is meant.

[137] Ibid., pp. 159f.

[138] J. Mainka, Introduction to C. F. D. Schubart, *Ideen zu einer Ästhetik der Tonkunst* (Leipzig, 1977), p. 20.

[139] According to *HUC*, 1768, no. 155. See Miesner, *Bach in Hamburg*, p. 32n.

spacious house in the Neueste Fuhlentwiete.[140] After visiting Bach, Voss wrote to Miller on 4 April 1774 as follows: 'Bach has a talkative wife, a rather unattractive but well-mannered daughter (Cramer described her as not particularly sensitive), a son who is a lawyer, good wine, and good beer.'[141] Johanna Maria Bach had a large household to manage, particularly since the children, with the exception of the youngest son, were living with their parents. She assisted her husband in the task of looking after his extensive music library. Bach's daughter Anna Carolina Philippina also assisted him in business matters. She was extremely well informed about the Bach family accounts, income and so on.[142]

Johann August Bach studied Law at the University of Rinteln in Schaumburg, and acquired a doctorate in June 1769. After returning to Hamburg he practised there as a lawyer.

Johann Sebastian Bach the younger received his earliest instruction in painting from Andreas Ludwig Krüger in Berlin. From 1770 onwards he studied in Leipzig with Adam Friedrich Oeser, who was also Goethe's drawing master, director of the art school in Leipzig, and a friend of Winckelmann. Oeser considered the young artist to be extraordinarily talented, and gave him as much encouragement as he could. Johann Sebastian Bach the younger submitted several works to the annual art exhibitions in Dresden. Evidence that Lessing was genuinely enthusiastic about the work of Carl Philipp Emanuel Bach's younger son is contained in a letter from the poet to the Dresden court librarian Karl Wilhelm Dassdorf:

Dearest friend, please be so good as to hand on the enclosed letter bound for Rome to Herr Bach, who is on his way there and who should be passing through Dresden very soon now. His most eager ambition is to win a position at the Dresden *Akademie* one day. I need hardly tell you how abundantly he deserves such an honour already. Yet his zeal would most certainly be doubled if it were possible at this stage to hold out to him some hope of achieving his ambition in the future, given that he believes you to be in a position perhaps to wield considerable influence in such matters. If indeed you are, then I know that you will, in order to secure for Saxony a man who promises to be no less great and original as a painter than were his forebears as musicians.[143]

In 1776 the young artist set out for Rome in order to study. His

---

[140] Ibid., p. 32.

[141] Quoted in Busch, op. cit., p. 123.

[142] For example Anna Carolina Philippina Bach was able to give detailed information about her father's finances in response to an enquiry from the authorities after Bach's death. See Miesner, *Bach in Hamburg*, pp. 14ff.

[143] G. E. Lessing, letter of 26 Sept. 1776 to K. W. Dassdorf, *Lessings Briefe in einem Band* (Berlin and Weimar, 1967), pp. 372f.

prospects looked highly promising, but Johann Sebastian became seriously ill at the beginning of 1777, and had to undergo expensive operations. The great anxiety felt by the Bach family during this period is recorded in a number of letters. On 20 June 1777 Carl Philipp Emanuel Bach wrote to Forkel as follows:

My poor son in Rome has been laid low for five months with an extremely painful illness, and is not yet out of danger. Dear Lord, how my heart suffers! Three months ago I sent him fifty ducats, and in a fortnight I must spend another 200 Reichsthalers on doctors and surgeons. I can no longer put pen to paper except to ask for support and sympathy.[144]

Before reaching the age of thirty, this talented son died in Rome on 11 September 1778.

The work of J. S. Bach the younger, Classicist and occasionally even Romantic in orientation, was well received by his contemporaries. Bach was fascinated by landscapes, mythological subjects, natural scenes with ancient temples and ruins, the world of nymphs, fauns, and shepherds, and all the time there hovered over these paintings, with all their delicate precision and detail, a visionary, idyllic mood—a fine counterpart to musical *Empfindsamkeit* [Plate 8].[145]

Carl Philipp Emanuel Bach's links with his brothers, with the exception of J. C. F. Bach, the Bückeburg Bach, were not especially close. W. F. Bach he appears not to have seen again after the move to Hamburg, although he gave him financial support from time to time;[146] and while Johann Christian Bach, who was based in London, did in fact cross the Channel on a number of occasions, nothing is known of any visit to Hamburg. Widely different in their personalities and their artistic aims, each of J. S. Bach's sons pursued his own goals independently of the others.

From 1750 onwards J. C. F. Bach was employed as *Cammer-Musicus* (from 1759 as Konzertmeister) at the Court of Count Wilhelm of Schaumburg-Lippe in Bückeburg, a position which he may well have owed to the influence of his distinguished brother, eighteen years his senior.[147] During the 1770s, the period of the Bückeburg composer's

---

[144] Quoted in Bitter, op. cit., ii, p. 113.

[145] For a discussion of his significance in the history of art, see W. Stechow, 'Johann Sebastian Bach the Younger', *De Artibus Opuscula XL, Essays in Honor of Erwin Panofsky*, ed. M. Meiss, 2 vols. (New York, 1961), i, pp. 427ff.

[146] Kirnberger wrote to Forkel, '. . . nor does his brother in Hamburg wish to have any more to do with him [W. F. Bach], for he simply squanders all his money, however much Emanuel might wish to send from Hamburg, as he has frequently done in the past.' Quoted in Bitter, op. cit., ii, p. 323.

[147] Count Wilhelm spent some time at the Court in Potsdam before employing J. C. F. Bach, and it is fairly certain that he met C. P. E. Bach there. The latter dedicated the two trio sonatas, Wq. 161, to the Count. In the princely Hausarchiv in Bückeburg, incidentally, was listed an act

fruitful collaboration with Herder, the two brothers grew closer to one another. Meetings may have taken place, particularly as Hamburg was just a day and a half's journey from the small Court in the Hanover district; and Bach's son Johann August, as mentioned earlier, attended *Collegia* in Law at Rinteln, not far from Bückeburg. The two composers helped to disseminate one another's works.[148] From J. C. F. Bach's correspondence with Gerstenberg, moreover, which touches on questions of musical aesthetics, it may be concluded that he too was in close contact with the circle of North German poets.

Owing to his social standing and his numerous connections with friends, acquaintances, and business partners, Bach moved in a wide variety of middle-class circles in Hamburg, just as he had done in Berlin. He probably travelled outside Hamburg only on rare occasions, and he appears not to have undertaken any further concert tours. Bach frequently received visitors, including not only friends but also many who were attracted by his reputation as an *Originalgenie*. These contacts were extremely important to him, as he stated in his autobiography.[149] They broadened his horizons, provided him with all sorts of stimuli for composition, and helped to refine his musical outlook. Such visits were usually celebrated in style. The poet Voss reports an outing with Bach 'to "The Raven", an inn just outside Hamburg, where we drank coffee and played ninepins. Bach told many stories about Berlin and about his father Sebastian.'[150] Bach's guests were unanimous in their praise of his hospitality.

Charles Burney's principal reason for including Hamburg in his travels through central Europe was his desire to meet Bach.[151] His description of their meeting, which occurred in October 1772, is one of the most graphic and lively accounts that we possess of Bach's life-style, his improvisation, his domestic environment, and more besides:

When I went to his house, I found him with three or four rational, and well-bred persons, his friends, besides his own family consisting of Mrs. Bach, his eldest son, who practises the law, and his daughter. He has two sons, the

're Bach, Royal Prussian court musician in Berlin'. See H. Wohlfarth, *Johann Christoph Friedrich Bach. Ein Komponist im Vorfeld der Klassik* (Berne and Munich, 1971), p. 59.

[148] See Hortschansky, op. cit., p. 201 [n. 28 above] and also advertisements in the *HUC*. Subscriptions are invited for works by the Bückeburg Bach in the issue for 26 July 1768, for example.

[149] C. P. E. Bach, 'Autobiography', p. 202. Newman, loc. cit., p. 367.

[150] J. H. Voss, letter of 2 and 3 Apr. 1774 to E. T. J. Brückner, quoted in Busch, op. cit., p. 122.

[151] Burney writes as follows: 'Hamburg is not at present, possessed of any musical professor of great eminence, except M. Carl Philip Emanuel Bach; but he is a legion! I had long contemplated, with the highest delight, his elegant and original compositions; and they had created in me so strong a desire to see, and to hear him, that I wanted no other musical temptation to visit this city.' Burney, *Musical Tours*, ii, p. 211.

youngest of whom studies painting, at the academies of Leipsic and Dresden. The instant I entered, he conducted me up stairs, into a large and elegant music room, furnished with pictures, drawings, and prints of more than a hundred and fifty eminent musicians: among whom, there are many Englishmen, and original portraits, in oil, of his father and grandfather. After I had looked at these, M. Bach was so obliging as to sit down to his *Silbermann clavichord*, and favourite instrument, upon which he played three or four of his choicest and most difficult compositions, with the delicacy, precision, and spirit, for which he is so justly celebrated among his countrymen . . .

After dinner, which was elegantly served, and chearfully eaten, I prevailed upon him to sit down again to a clavichord, and he played, with little intermission, till near eleven o'clock at night . . .[152] He is now fifty-nine, rather short in stature, with black hair and eyes, and brown complexion, has a very animated countenance, and is of a chearful and lively disposition . . .

M. Bach shewed me two manuscript books of his father's composition, written on purpose for him when he was a boy, containing pieces with a fugue, in all the twenty-four keys, extremely difficult, and generally in five parts, at which he laboured for the first years of his life, without remission.[153] He presented me with several of his own pieces, and three or four curious ancient books and treatises on music, out of his father's collection; promising, at any distant time, to furnish me with others, if I would only acquaint him by letter, with my wants.[154]

In later years this contact between Burney and Bach was maintained. Burney subscribed to some of Bach's compositions,[155] apparently in order to have at his disposal additional material for his *magnum opus*, *A General History of Music*. The fourth and final volume of this work, which appeared a year after Bach's death, contains a detailed appraisal of the composer's position in musical history.

The portrait collection mentioned by Burney,[156] which sheds light on another of Bach's interests, contained approximately 400 copper engravings, pastel drawings, oil-paintings, and silhouettes of musicians, poets, and philosophers: Johann Ambrosius Bach, J. S. Bach and his sons, Gluck, the Graun brothers, Handel, Hasse, Hiller, Haydn, Jommelli, Leopold Mozart, Neefe, Palestrina, Rameau, Schubart, Telemann; Gellert, Brockes, Gerstenberg, Klopstock, Lessing, Ramler; Rousseau, Leibniz, Luther, and many others. Bach's activity as a

---

[152] There follows the description of Bach's clavichord playing quoted on p. 169 below.

[153] Burney is referring to the two volumes of the *Well-tempered Clavier*. The German translation of this passage by Ebeling and Bode [iii, p. 215, see Chapter 1, n. 8] corrects Burney's description as follows: '. . . in all [the twenty-four] keys, a few of which were in five parts and extremely difficult. He presented me . . .'

[154] Burney, *Musical Tours*, ii, pp. 219f.

[155] These included *C. P. E. Bach's keyboard sonatas with an accompaniment for violin and violoncello* and some of the collections 'für Kenner und Liebhaber'.

[156] A survey of Bach's collection of portraits is included in the *Nachlassverzeichnis*, pp. 92–126. (See Bibliography.)

collector shows that he was well read, intellectually receptive, and motivated by a desire for a wide-ranging education. Without this breadth of outlook, in matters great and small, Bach could hardly have maintained his position as one of the most advanced German composers for so many years.

Denis Diderot, arriving in Hamburg from St Petersburg in March 1774, immediately sought Bach's acquaintance, as we know from his correspondence.[157] The proud Frenchman made his request directly, dispensing with conventional modesty:

Hamburg, 30 March 1774

Monsieur,

I am a Frenchman. My name is Diderot. I enjoy some recognition in my own country as a writer. I am the author of several plays, of which the *Père de famille* may perhaps not be unknown to you.[158] I am also the editor of the *Encyclopédie*. I am an admirer of Johann (Christian) Bach, and for a long time now my daughter, who plays your music, has taught me to admire you. She is my only child. She is a good keyboard player and knows the rules of harmony much more thoroughly than is generally the case among non-professional musicians. When Johann (Christian) Bach sent her a fortepiano from London, he included with it a sonata of his own composition.

I have just returned on the *Extrapost* from St Petersburg, with no other clothing than the house-coat which I am wearing under my fur mantle, otherwise I should not have missed the opportunity of calling on so famous a man as Emanuel. If this same Emanuel is himself a father, and if he knows how much pleasure it gives a father to be able to offer a treat to his child, he will understand the request that I make to him herewith: that he might send me some keyboard sonatas as yet unpublished, if he has any spare manuscript copies, and that he should be good enough to name his fee, which I shall pay to the messenger who delivers the sonatas to me. The only comment I shall permit myself to make is that my reputation is greater than my fortune, a predicament which I share with most men of genius, without being one of their number.

I am etc.

Diderot.[159]

---

[157] Two letters from Diderot to C. P. E. Bach were published during the composer's lifetime: in *HUC*, no. 57, 1774, and in the *Neuer gelehrter Mercur* (Altona, 1774), ii, 14. Stück. See Schmid, *Kammermusik*, pp. 45f. A few years later J. C. von Zabuesnig translated them both into German—the autograph of neither has survived. See J. C. von Zabuesnig, *Historische und kritische Nachrichten von dem Leben und den Schriften des Herrn von Voltaire und anderer Neuphilosophen unserer Zeiten* (1777). The new French complete edition of Diderot's letters, 16 vols. (1955–70) contains retranslations of both into French. See D. Diderot, *Correspondance*, ed. G. Roth and J. Varloot, xvi (Paris, 1970), pp. 49f., 51. For an English translation, see below, and p. 223. See also M. Wachs, 'Diderot's Letters to C. P. E. Bach', *Romanische Forschung*, lxxvii (1965), pp. 359ff.

[158] The *Père de famille* was performed in Hamburg in 1768. Lessing reviewed this work in the 84th article of his *Hamburgische Dramaturgie*.

[159] D. Diderot, letter of 30 Mar. 1774 to C. P. E. Bach, *Correspondance*, xvi, pp. 49f. See Appendix II for three further letters written by Diderot.

Diderot had been familiar with Bach's music for some time. More than twenty years earlier he had praised 'la force et la légèreté des tons de Bach';[160] it must have been at her father's instigation that the daughter of the French philosopher studied Bach's keyboard works. In Diderot's politically explosive book *Le Neveu de Rameau*, which had to wait until 1805 before it was translated into German (by Goethe), he expresses many ideas which, although in this case related to opera, seem equally applicable to Bach's musical language:

The passions must be strong; the musician and the lyrical poet must be full of tenderness [Goethe's translation: *Empfindsamkeit*] . . . we must have exclamation, interjection, suspension, interruption, affirmation, negation; we call, we invoke, we cry, we groan, we weep, we laugh aloud.[161]

What Diderot is saying here is not far removed from Bach's 'rhetorical principle'. According to Zoltai an important theme in Diderot's musical philosophy is the 'natural, therefore sincere and fearless expression of human nature, of intimate human feelings'.[162]

Bach conducted an extensive correspondence with acquaintances and business colleagues in other parts of Germany. He had already built up a good working relationship with the publishers Schwickert and Breitkopf in Leipzig and with Winter in Berlin. Through the mediation of Baron van Swieten, links with the Viennese firm Artaria were also established.[163]

With Ramler, whose *Auferstehung und Himmelfahrt Jesu* he set to music in 1777–8, Bach remained in correspondence until 1785.[164] The writer Anna Luise Karsch (also known as Karschin), who came from a peasant background and was deemed by Herder and Goethe to possess 'natural poetic talent', had composed a farewell ode on Bach's departure for Hamburg,[165] and she also wrote the libretto for his Passion Cantata of 1770. Might Daniel Chodowiecki have sought Bach's acquaintance in Hamburg? On 22 September 1781 the famous painter wrote as follows to Graff: 'In eight or ten days' time I am thinking of riding to Hamburg, in order to visit Meyer, Klopstock, Asmus, and Bach.'[166] Direct or indirect contact was still maintained

---

[160] D. Diderot, *Lettre sur les Aveugles* (1749). See Schmid, *Kammermusik*, p. 45.

[161] D. Diderot, *Rameau's Nephew and Other Works*, trans. Mrs. W. Jackson (London, 1926), pp. 90f. See also *Rameau's Nephew and d'Alembert's Dream*, trans. L. W. Tancock (Harmondsworth etc., 1966), p. 105.

[162] Zoltai, op. cit., p. 165 [Chapter 2, n. 76].

[163] See Hase, op. cit.; further letters to the publishers Artaria and Schwickert are contained in Nohl, op. cit. [n. 25 above], pp. 61ff.

[164] See Busch, op. cit., p. 86.

[165] The poem is printed in Bitter, op. cit., i, pp. 183f.

[166] Quoted in Miesner, 'Porträts', p. 108.

1. Carl Philipp Emanuel Bach. Engraving by J. H. Lips.

2. Carl Philipp Emanuel Bach, aged forty.
Pastel drawing attributed to A. F. Oeser, but probably by J. F. Reifenstein.

3. Frederick II playing a flute concerto in Sanssouci.
Painting by A. Menzel, 1852.

4. Royal Opera, Berlin. Contemporary engraving.

5. Music room with Silbermann harpsichord in Sanssouci.

6. (*top*) Title-page of the first edition of the
Württemberg Sonatas, Wq. 49 (Nuremberg, 1744);
(*bottom*) Sonata in A minor, Wq. 49 no. 1, from the
first edition.

7. Carl Heinrich Graun
with his wife. Oil-painting
by A. Pesne.

8. Landscape with castle by moonlight. Watercolour by J. S. Bach the
younger.

9. (*left to right*) The artist Andreas Stöttrup, Carl Philipp
Emanuel Bach, and Pastor Sturm. Pen and ink drawing by
A. Stöttrup, 1784.

10. Carl Philipp Emanuel Bach's handwriting at different stages in his life.
(*top*) Leipzig period: March in D, BWV Anh. 122; (*bottom*) Berlin period:
Alto aria 'Quia respexit' from the Magnificat, Wq. 215, 1749.

with Kirnberger, Krause, Marpurg, Agricola, and Nichelmann. Kirnberger, for example, assisted Bach in the publication of a further volume of his father's chorales.[167]

Foremost among the musicians who campaigned for a revival of interest in J. S. Bach's music in the second half of the eighteenth century was Johann Nikolaus Forkel. He frequently asked for works by the Leipzig Cantor to be sent to him from Hamburg, in order to make use of them in his Bach-biography. Many of his judgements about J. S. Bach were based on statements made by Carl Philipp Emanuel, such as the following:

The account of my late father's life given in Mizler's journal is, thanks to my participation, the most complete. The list of his keyboard compositions given there omits the following: fifteen two-part Inventions and fifteen three-part Sinfonias, as well as six short preludes. Regarding the sacred music of the deceased, it may be said that he worked on it in all humility according to the sense of the text, neither comically distorting the words, nor highlighting individual words at the expense of the overall meaning, a common fault, often suggesting laughable ideas which may elicit admiration both from the ignorant and from those who wish to appear knowledgeable. There has never been anyone who could inspect organs so acutely and yet with such honesty. His knowledge of organ-building was encyclopaedic . . . When trying out an organ, the first thing he did was to remark jovially, 'Before I do anything else, I need to know whether the organ has got good lungs', and in order to find this out, he would pull out all the stops and play in as many parts as possible. At this point the organ-builders would often turn quite pale with fright. Thanks to his great skill in harmony, he was able, on more than one occasion when accompanying a trio and feeling in good humour, to improvise a fourth part over the sparsely figured bass part in front of him, as long as he knew that the composer of the trios would not take it amiss . . .[168]

While preferring the music of J. S. Bach, Forkel did not neglect to praise the works of Carl Philipp Emanuel in numerous reviews and reports. The latter knew how to repay the compliment. Although not frequently given to making public statements on the subject of music theory, Bach published an extended discussion of the first volume of Forkel's *General History of Music* in the pages of the *Hamburgischer unpartheyischer Correspondent* in 1788.[169]

There was one composer whose music Carl Philipp Emanuel Bach liked especially, namely Georg Anton Benda.[170] The two had spent

---

[167] See Smend, op. cit., pp. 5ff. [Chapter 2, n. 198].

[168] C. P. E. Bach, letter (presumably written in the latter half of December 1774) to J. N. Forkel; quoted in *Bach Reader*, pp. 275ff.

[169] Quoted in Bitter, op. cit., ii, pp. 109ff.

[170] The *Nachlassverzeichnis* names eleven items by this composer. See *Nachlassverzeichnis*, pp. 85–9.

some years together in Frederick II's court orchestra. Bach had visited his friend in Gotha in 1754, and had given two concerts there. In 1778 Benda was engaged as Kapellmeister at the Theater am Gänsemarkt in Hamburg. There is evidence of mutual influence. The Czech scholar Zdeňka Pilková has noted numerous common stylistic features: 'the dramatic animation of the melodic line, large leaps, unexpected rests, changes in musical structure and accompaniment and so on in the space of a few bars, sudden changes of tempo'.[171] It is also conceivable that through Benda Bach was brought into closer contact with theatrical life in Hamburg. Although Lessing's attempt to set up a German national theatre there had collapsed in 1767, there were none the less some fine productions by Konrad Ernst Ackermann and Friedrich Ludwig Schröder in subsequent years.[172] Might Bach have seen Lessing's *Minna van Barnhelm*, *Emilia Galotti*, Shakespeare's *Hamlet*, *Macbeth*, *Henry IV*, or Goethe's *Clavigo* and *Götz von Berlichingen*? Did he attend the Hamburg première of Mozart's *Die Entführung aus dem Serail* in 1787?—we do not know. Further work in both Bach and Benda scholarship might possibly yield more detailed information about this in the future.

Whether Bach and Carl Stamitz were personally acquainted is another unanswerable question. The Mannheim composer, conductor, and violinist gave several concerts in Hamburg in 1785.[173] Even if a meeting between the two did occur, however, it is unlikely that it would have made an impact on the style of the seventy-one-year-old Bach at this stage.

Another of Bach's friends in Hamburg was Johann Friedrich Reichardt. In the latter's autobiography, reference is made to the time he spent in Hamburg when he had just turned twenty years of age: 'Whenever Reichardt was able to get away from the Büsch household,[174] where he spent every day, he would go to see Bach, who greatly enjoyed discussing music with him, although they were seldom able to agree.'[175] In many of his writings he paid great tribute to Bach; furthermore, the young Reichardt, still at the very beginning of his career as Kapellmeister and composer, deliberately

---

[171] Z. Pilková, 'Die Familien Bach und Benda', *Bericht über die Wissenschaftliche Konferenz zum III. Internationalen Bach-Fest der DDR 1975* (Leipzig, 1977), p. 218.

[172] For information on theatrical performances in Hamburg, see J. F. Schütze, *Hamburgische Theatergeschichte* (Hamburg, 1794, R/Leipzig, 1975); R. Schlösser, *Vom Hamburger Nationaltheater zur Gothaer Hofbühne 1767–1769* (Hamburg and Leipzig, 1895); *Geschichte der deutschen Literatur*, vi, pp. 467ff.

[173] See Eugene K. and Jean K. Wolf, 'Stamitz, (2) Carl', *New Grove*, xviii, p. 64.

[174] Reichardt lived for a short time in the home of Johann Georg Büsch.

[175] Reichardt, 'Autobiography', *AMZ*, xvi, col. 30 [n. 77 above].

modelled his style on Bach's.[176] As he wrote in 1776 to Carl Gottlieb Bock:

You know very well, my dearest friend, for how many years already, and how earnestly I have desired, how I have been burning with curiosity to come to know the great Bach really well. Now I have had this great good fortune, and I hasten to tell you as much about it as the frailty of my pen will allow. But do not expect this letter to be orderly, instead take delight in the outpourings of my most wonderfully joyful heart.

Herr Kapellmeister Bach honours me with the warmest hospitality; tirelessly and with constant good humour he plays to me all sorts of pieces, composed at various stages during his life, every time I visit him—and you can imagine how often that is, given my well-known importunity where great men are concerned—thereby giving me a most excellent opportunity to study him closely; but that is not all.

Besides this great kindness, which far exceeds all I could ask or desire from him, he helps to make my stay here as enjoyable as possible by offering me excellent hospitality in his house, and by taking me on delightful walks through the loveliest parts of Hamburg. (The areas surrounding this great trading city are exceptionally beautiful and varied. The Elbe and the Alster, of which Hagedorn has sung such warm praises . . . with their broad streams and many sailing boats and their most attractive embankments, present a truly magnificent picture. One of the great beauties of the Alster . . . is that it opens into a kind of reservoir in the city itself which is lined on either side with avenues, where one can go for quite delightful walks . . .)

Whenever I visit Herr Bach, he performs for me three, four, or even more of his sonatas . . . In each one his personal stamp can easily be recognized—the chief indication that his originality is no mere affectation—but at the same time his great variety and inexhaustible richness are evident. Every sonata has some special quality which distinguishes it clearly from any other. It would no more be possible for me to say, 'these two sonatas belong together, they constitute a pair' than to say that one was better than the other; my pride would colour my judgement, for Herr Bach's exclusive gift to me of an autograph keyboard sonata has flattered and thrilled me more than any other gifts from great men or any stroke of great good fortune could possibly do.

This is truly one of the most utterly original works that I have ever heard, and everyone, everyone to whom I play it, exclaims as if on cue, 'Never have I heard the like of this before.'

And yet, my dearest friend, I do not wish to make you too strongly desirous of hearing the work, for I can as little send it to you as I could play it to you now. Never shall the sonata leave my hands, unless I were to lose my briefcase, which I guard much more jealously than ever before, now that it contains this treasured sonata.[177]

---

[176] The deterioration of relations between the two was caused primarily by personal differences. See Miesner, *Bach in Hamburg*, pp. 26ff.

[177] Reichardt, *Briefe*, ii, pp. 7ff. [n. 68 above].

This letter conveys something of the rich emotional world and the impressionability of the *Sturm und Drang* generation. The tone is quite different from that of earlier letters, treatises, and monographs with their more sober, rationalistic style. Both in musical criticism and in music itself a new element of inner personal expression is beginning to assert itself. Emphasis is now placed on personal, subjective experience and passionate conviction. The unbounded individuality of the creative artist is all-important. In his *Schreiben über die Berlinische Musik* (1775), Reichardt has this to say:

Had you but heard how Bach brings his clavichord to life—an instrument which many people, perhaps with some justification, have long held to be dead and inexpressive, and how he manages to convey every nuance of emotion and passion—in a word, how he puts his entire soul into the music![178]

Reichardt was one of the most outspoken advocates of the ideas of the *Sturm und Drang* movement in music, according to which the expression of powerful emotions was considered the main priority. After listening to one of Bach's works, Reichardt commented:

I cannot possibly describe to you in words the way in which the whole work is aflame with intense fire; I was excited at times into a rage; the expression of pain and lamentation was no less forceful.[179]

There is no trace here of the playful pastoral scenes of Anacreontic literature.

Also new is the terminology with which Reichardt articulates his musical ideas. The term *Affekt* has been replaced in his aesthetic vocabulary by such phrases as 'expression of feelings' with overtones of *Empfindsamkeit*. What Reichardt believed to be the true nature of music he found embodied in the work of Carl Philipp Emanuel Bach. Even when in later years his attention was held by other composers, especially Gluck and Haydn, he still spoke favourably of Bach's work, as, for example, in the autobiography written in 1814, the year of his death.

Bach felt attracted by the friendly atmosphere and liberal exchange of ideas which took place at the home of the mathematician Johann Georg Büsch, director of the *Handelsakademie* founded in 1768. According to Reichardt:

... all that Hamburg had to offer by way of fine, educated young people, together with men and women of taste and sensitivity, used to gather in this

---

[178] Reichardt, *Schreiben über die Berlinische Musik*, p. 8. See also Introduction, n. 5 above.
[179] Reichardt, *Briefe*, i, p. 124 [n. 68 above]. A thorough survey of Reichardt's musical thinking is contained in G. Hartung, *Johann Friedrich Reichardt (1752–1814) als Schriftsteller und Publizist*, Diss., Halle, 1964.

noble and happy circle ... all travellers of any importance and education visited the Büsch household ... but not everyone was admitted to the inner circle which would not infrequently assemble for a pleasant evening's entertainment apart from the wider academic community.[180]

Bach was one of Büsch's closer acquaintances. It is likely that their conversations often touched upon matters connected with the 'promotion of manufacturing businesses, skills, and profitable trades'.[181] But music-making was not neglected. Reichardt directed the first performances of Bach's 'string symphonies' at Büsch's home.[182]

Among Büsch's other guests were Christoph Daniel Ebeling and Johann Joachim Christoph Bode, the former a historian and a teacher at the Hamburg Gymnasium, the latter a bookseller and publisher.[183] Both were keen music-lovers and close friends of Bach. Some of Ebeling's texts were set to music by Bach.[184] Bode took part in performances of Bach's works as a cellist in an amateur orchestra.

Bach was also on friendly terms with the doctor Johann Albert Heinrich Reimarus and his family, at whose home he used to meet a number of other poets. Gotthold Ephraim Lessing had published Hermann Samuel Reimarus's *Analogie oder Schutzschrift für die vernünftigen Verehrer Gottes* [Analogy or defence for the intelligent worshipper] in instalments and in a somewhat revised form in the *Wolfenbüttler Beiträge* between 1774 and 1777. The outspoken rejection of an orthodox exegesis of the Gospels and the criticisms of the Christian idea of Revelation, as put forward in this anonymous 'Enlightened' treatise, provoked a reaction from Hamburg's chief pastor, Johann Melchior Goeze, who was incidentally one of Bach's employers. Lessing responded acerbically and authoritatively in his well-known *Anti-Goeze* (1778). Lessing stayed in Hamburg for only three years, but during this short time (April 1767 to April 1770) and in later years he must have met Bach quite frequently.[185] The poet may have been attracted by Bach's uninhibited, humorous manner: Bach's wit he branded as 'Nuremberg-ish'.[186]

[180] Reichardt, 'Autobiography', *AMZ*, xvi, cols. 24ff. [n. 77 above].

[181] These were the aims of the 'Patriotic Society' founded in 1765, to which not only merchants and councillors, but also scholars, artists (possibly including Bach), and craftsmen belonged. See *Heimatchronik*, p. 164 [n. 31 above].

[182] See Reichardt, 'Autobiography', *AMZ*, xvi, col. 29 [n. 77 above].

[183] The two men had also translated and published Burney's travel diaries in Hamburg.

[184] Ebeling is known to have participated in the writing of the Passion Cantata, Wq. 233, 1770. He also wrote the poem 'Auf den Geburtstag eines Freundes' which was set by Bach and published in *Neue Lieder-Melodien*, 1789.

[185] Lessing visited the city many times in subsequent years.

[186] This information is supplied by Reichardt in his 'Autobiography', *AMZ*, xvi, col. 29 [n. 77 above].

In musical matters Lessing also took his lead from statements by Bach. In the *Kollektaneen* he wrote:

Bach laments the present decline of music. He ascribes this to the vogue for comic music, and informs me that Galuppi himself, one of the leading composers of musical comedy . . . has confirmed that in Italy the vogue for comic music has even driven good older music out of the churches . . . One essential feature of comic music is that it consists of practically nothing but Allegros, while Adagios are entirely neglected.[187]

Lessing showed an interest in the performance of vocal works as well: 'This winter Bach is to arrange a performance of Metastasio's Passion aria, which begins "dove son, dove corri [sic]", in the setting by Jommelli, Kapellmeister in Stuttgart.'[188] The progressive quality of Bach's style in composition remained unintelligible to Lessing, whose ideas about music hardly moved beyond the realm of early Enlightenment theory, and were largely derived from Scheibe's *Critischer Musicus*.[189]

Bach was also interested in other writers, of whom there were a great number in Hamburg and the surrounding area. Among his closer acquaintances were not only Lessing but also Klopstock, Claudius, Gerstenberg, and the poets of the 'Göttinger Grove': Voss, Hölty, Overbeck, Miller, and the von Stolberg brothers. The fact that different generations were represented here, and hence differences in literary style and attitudes, did not in the least trouble Bach, the oldest member of this circle.

Klopstock had played some part in encouraging Bach to write *Die Israeliten in der Wüste*[190] and he had helped to disseminate this work.[191] Bach set some of his poems to music, including the 'Vaterlandslied' (1773) and 'Lyda' (1774). In 1783 he wrote the cantata *Klopstocks Morgengesang am Schöpfungsfeste* (printed in 1784).

Yet one comes across the names of the writers from the 'Göttingen Grove' more frequently than Lessing or Klopstock in Bach's settings of poetry.[192] Evidently Bach was able in some sense to identify personally with their poetry. He preferred those texts with an impassioned and strongly expressive manner—in the spirit of the *Sturm und Drang*—

---

[187] G. E. Lessing, *Lessings Werke*, ed. J. Petersen and W. von Olshausen, xix: 'Kollektaneen', pp. 213f.

[188] Ibid., p. 215. [The piece in question is a recitative and aria for St Peter from Jommelli's *La Passione di Nostro Signore Gesù Cristo* (1749). The correct form of the title is 'dove son, dove corro'.]

[189] Lessing quotes extensively in the 26th section of his *Hamburgische Dramaturgie* from J. A. Scheibe's *Critischer Musicus*; see *Gesammelte Werke*, ed. P. Rilla, vi, pp. 135ff.

[190] See Bitter, op. cit., i, p. 339.

[191] See p. 122f. above, and also Miesner, *Bach in Hamburg*, p. 36.

[192] Bach is known to have set six poems by Voss, three by Miller, two by Hölty, and one each by Overbeck, L. von Stolberg, and C. F. Cramer.

because they matched his musical aims particularly well. Many of his letters offer evidence of creative collaboration with the poets. Technical matters were sometimes raised, concerning for example problems of text treatment, strophic design, or musical expression. Voss reports at the beginning of April 1774 in a letter to Brückner: Bach would 'like to adopt me as a musical poet; some of the ideas which I mentioned to him about the customary forms of lyric poetry seem to have pleased him'.[193] In another letter Voss says, 'We spoke at length about musical poetry, and he has some very sensible ideas on the subject.'[194]

Song Composition

Bach's collaboration with the poets bore rich fruit. With the anthology *Psalms translated by Dr. Cramer with melodies to sing at the keyboard* (1774) and the two collections of *Herr Christoph Christian Sturm's sacred songs* (1780 and 1781) Bach made an impression on his contemporaries comparable with that of his Gellert settings many years earlier.[195]

Of the great multitude of sacred and secular odes and songs by Bach, the song 'Lyda' is one of the loveliest. It was written at a time when *empfindsam* settings featured prominently in Bach's work, and this made him popular among contemporary readers of almanacs and lovers of literary song. Johann Heinrich Voss, who issued several such almanacs, felt confident that he knew how this song would be received:

I now have two settings of 'Lyda', both of which I must print. Reichardt's setting is attractive, and it would be an insult to him to leave it out. But Bach's setting is incomparable, so profoundly felt, so moving.[196]

Bach had set this Klopstock poem together with one by Voss, 'Die Schlummernde' ('Eingewiegt in Nachtigalltönen'), for the Göttingen *Musenalmanach*[197] of 1775. In one of the composer's letters he suggests a correction to Voss: 'If there is still time, my dear Herr Voss, would you be so good as to alter the following passage in my song "Lyda" from:

---

[193] Quoted in Busch, op. cit., p. 122.

[194] J. H. Voss, letter of 4 Apr. 1774 to J. M. Miller; quoted in Busch, op. cit., p. 123.

[195] Original titles: *Herrn Doctor Cramers übersetzte Psalmen mit Melodien zum Singen bey dem Claviere* and *Herrn Christoph Christian Sturms . . . Geistliche Gesänge mit Melodien zum Singen bey dem Claviere*. Extracts from the numerous reviews by Claudius, Schubart, and others are given in Busch, op. cit., pp. 111n. ff., 143n. ff.

[196] J. H. Voss, letter of 14 Aug. 1774 to E. Boie; quoted in Busch, op. cit., p. 125.

[197] For a discussion of the nature and origins of the *Musenalmanache*, see Ewan West, 'The Musenalmanach and Viennese Song 1770–1830', *Music and Letters*, lxvii (1986), pp. 37ff.

Ex. 63

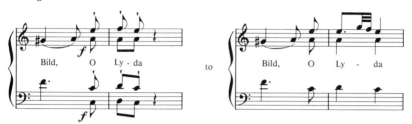

The *f* and the wedges must be omitted. The expressive phrase "O
Lyda" is more effective if it is softer.'[198] What Bach is attempting here,
then, is to bring the declamation and the meaning of the words into
conformity with the musical expression of the entire stanza. What had
seemed acceptable in the original version, and in the first moment of
artistic inspiration—a somewhat emphatic exclamation—turned out
to be inappropriate given the predominantly lyrical mood of the rest of
the song.

The same attention to detail manifested here is evident throughout
the song. Register, rhythmic motion, melodic shape, and harmonic
resources are skilfully deployed and give rise to a wide range of
expressive nuances. One moment there is a mood of lamentation—
achieved by the customary suspensions—and the next moment one of
rapture, now vehemence, now tenderness. Not only such abrupt
changes of mood, but also more fluid transitions between *Affekte* are
found here, as in the larger form of the symphony. Moreover this song
contains a few harmonic refinements and surprising turns of phrase.

Ex. 64

---

[198] C. P. E. Bach, letter of 9 Sept. 1774 to J. H. Voss, quoted in Busch, op. cit., p. 126.

One has only to think of the sudden *f* in the keyboard part, disturbing the even flow of the melody in Ex. 64.

Expressive contrasts within a small space, as in Ex. 65, constitute another personal trait in Bach's musical language.

Ex. 65

Within this simple strophic song Bach has achieved all that is necessary for the musical representation of constantly changing human feelings. It is at this point, too, that he arrives at the through-composed song.[199] He was not entirely happy with song-forms derived from the cantata, in which 'the *Affekte* do not merge into one another sufficiently'.[200] Bach, then, applied a technique of word-setting that was thoroughly suited to the style and content of contemporary lyric poetry, or at least to that of the 1770s.

Among the younger generation of poets eager to make Bach's acquaintance was Heinrich Wilhelm von Gerstenberg, who had lived in Copenhagen since 1765. It was he who made the unusual attempt to supply texts to Bach's C minor Fantasia. As Gerstenberg wrote to Nicolai on 5 December 1767:

Firstly I assume that music without words can convey only general ideas, which, however, through the addition of words become fully articulated; secondly this attempt will work only with those instrumental solos in which the expression is very clear and speech-like. With these principles in mind I have supplied a kind of text to some of Bach's keyboard works, that is to say works which were never intended to be sung, and Klopstock and everyone tell me that this is the most expressive vocal music that could ever be heard. Taking for example the fantasia in the sixth sonata written to accompany the *Versuch*, I add the text of Hamlet's soliloquy on life and death, all in short

[199] According to Gudrun Busch, Bach's first through-composed song was 'Selma' written in 1775. Ibid., p. 362.   [200] Letter from Voss to Brückner, 2 and 3 Apr., 1774, quoted ibid., p. 123.

phrases with the exception of the Largo, which represents a kind of middle state of Hamlet's shattered soul.[201]

The two artists probably met for the first time in 1777, when Gerstenberg witnessed a performance in St Catherine's Church in Hamburg of works by the composer he admired so much.

Through Gerstenberg Bach gained an entrée into artistic circles in Copenhagen. He had already been in correspondence for some years with the author of the *Critischer Musicus*, Johann Adolph Scheibe, who some forty years earlier had launched his well-known attack on J. S. Bach. But he also had links with Johann Andreas Cramer and Matthias Claudius, who lived in the Danish capital for a time. Niels Schiørring took lessons with Bach and in 1775 he became a member of the royal court orchestra in Copenhagen, where Bach's works were quite often performed. According to one of Gerstenberg's letters, the Passion Cantata had 'moved the people of Copenhagen greatly' and 'their enthusiasm had grown stronger and stronger during the seven repeat performances'.[202] Bach also supplied one or two items for inclusion in the Copenhagen publication *Kirke-Melodierne til den 1778 udgangne Psalmebog* [Church Melodies for the 1778 Psalter].[203]

Johann Heinrich Voss visited Bach in Hamburg many times. According to his description, Bach was 'a short, stout man with lively, fiery eyes, and was excellent company'.[204] Bach contributed several settings, as mentioned earlier, to the very popular Göttingen *Musen-almanache*, later published under Voss's name.

Matthias Claudius was another frequent visitor to Bach's home. The two never became close friends, however, probably on account of their very different personalities.[205] Bach set not a single poem by the editor of the *Wandsbecker Bote*, although Claudius quite often reviewed works by Bach. Some interesting accounts of what passed between them on these occasions have been preserved, such as the following conversation, recorded in one of Claudius's letters to Gerstenberg:

This morning (Tuesday) I went into the house where he goes on Sundays and found him in his night-dress; he spoke with me but I did not hear him play.

BACH: Excuse my night clothing.
CLAUDIUS: Virtuosos are often to be found thus attired.
BACH: Heavens no, they are not virtuosos, but rakes.

---

[201] Quoted in Schmid, *Kammermusik*, p. 52.
[202] Ibid., p. 53.
[203] See Busch, op. cit., pp. 154ff.
[204] Quoted in W. Herbst, *J. H. Voss*, 2 vols. (Leipzig, 1872–6), i, p. 290. See also ibid., pp. 116, 164, and Miesner, *Bach in Hamburg*, p. 41n.
[205] See Busch, op. cit., p. 96.

CLAUDIUS: I have just come from Copenhagen and bring greetings to you from Herr Pastor Resewitz, if you still remember him.

BACH: Yes, certainly; how is the musical world in Copenhagen?

CLAUDIUS: Fairly mediocre, Schobert and your brother [J. C. Bach] are the most popular composers, your music is not particularly well received.

BACH: That I must learn to live with. Schobert is also known here, he is a man of good sense, but the music that he and my brother are now producing is quite empty.

CLAUDIUS: It is easy on the ear.

BACH: It is easy enough to listen to and satisfies the ear but it leaves the heart untouched, that is my judgement of modern music, which, so Galuppi tells me, is also fashionable in Italy, with the result that one never hears an Adagio these days, only noisy Allegros, or at the most the occasional Andantino. The King of Prussia utterly detests such music, otherwise it meets with almost universal approval, and I have even made slight concessions to public taste in my sonatinas.

CLAUDIUS: It stands in relation to real music, perhaps, as humour to pathos.

BACH: The analogy is not a bad one. Music has higher aspirations, not simply to satisfy the ear, but to set the heart in motion.

(Here I looked him straight in the eye.)

CLAUDIUS: You have written some pieces in the form of musical portraits. Have you not continued this work?

BACH: No, I wrote them for particular occasions and have since forgotten them.

CLAUDIUS: They are still a new departure.

BACH: But only a small one, and the presence of words makes the task easier.[206]

Great though the initial enthusiasm of the younger generation of poets for Bach's music was, it declined noticeably from the 1780s onwards. Even Voss, who had hitherto been his most devoted follower, and had supplied the greatest number of song texts, began to look around for another composer. He alighted on Johann Abraham Peter Schulz, who, while he greatly admired Bach,[207] nevertheless represented a new outlook in his own songs, and aimed at a style of musical setting 'which would never assert itself over and above the words, nor disappear beneath them, but would match the declamation and metre of the text like a well-fitting gar-

---

[206] From a letter written by M. Claudius in 1768 to H. W. von Gerstenberg; see Busch, op. cit., pp. 93f.

[207] Schulz had originally intended to take lessons from Bach in 1764. Bach, however, sent him to Kirnberger. Schulz referred to Bach in a letter to Voss dated 23 July 1780 as the 'Non plus ultra in music'. See O. Riess, 'Johann Abraham Peter Schulz' Leben', *SIMG*, xv (1913–14), p. 182.

ment'.[208] Folk-style lyric poetry began to establish itself, thanks largely to the labours of Herder and Reichardt. The new 'folk idiom' was nourished from another source: the folk-song. Bach played no further part in this development.

The Collections 'für Kenner und Liebhaber' [for connoisseurs and amateurs]

Between 1779 and 1787 C. P. E. Bach published an ambitious series of keyboard works: *Six keyboard sonatas 'für Kenner und Liebhaber'* (1779), *Keyboard sonatas and rondos for the Fortepiano 'für Kenner und Liebhaber'* second and third sets (1780 and 1781), and *Keyboard sonatas and free fantasias, together with some rondos for the Fortepiano 'für Kenner and Liebhaber'* fourth, fifth, and sixth sets (1783, 1785, and 1787). A survey of the thirty-seven sonatas, fantasias, and rondos contained in these collections reveals an extraordinary wealth of formal devices and musical expressivity. Given the primacy of expressive language in Bach's music, he was opposed from the outset to 'tendencies towards Classical stylization and towards any kind of stereotyped form'.[209] In these sonatas he experiments with many different dimensions and methods of construction. Many are compressed into a two-movement or even a one-movement form. While the fantasias are predominantly in free metre in this collection, there are nevertheless some examples which observe strict time. The technical difficulty of some of the rondos borders on that of the fantasias, and perhaps places them beyond the reach of the amateur performer. The compositional techniques appear refined and in many respects quite novel—witness the interest shown in carefully differentiated sonorities. In these works Bach achieves a modern keyboard style with finely controlled textures. Sequences and empty repetitions are reduced to a minimum.

'Bach's imagination lives and moves so much within the particular sound of the keyboard, that this very sound draws to itself and renders fully everything that the composer wishes to express in music.'[210] Idea and expression are cast in the language of the mature artist. Seriousness and gaiety alternate. Humour is combined with irony. Passion is intensified to ecstasy, then subsides to soothing, introspective declamation. Many movements have a character entirely their own.

Compared with the other fantasias, the layout of the one in C major from the sixth set appears conventional. The barring is consistently

---

[208] Quoted from J. Mainka, *J. A. P. Schulz und die musikalische Entwicklung im Zeitalter von 'Sturm und Drang'*, Habilitationsschrift (Berlin 1970), p. 36.

[209] R. Wyler, *Form- und Stiluntersuchungen zum ersten Satz der Klaviersonaten Carl Philipp Emanuel Bachs* (Biel, 1960), p. 150.

[210] W. Georgii, *Klaviermusik*, 3rd edn. (Zurich and Freiburg im Breisgau, 1950), p. 168.

maintained, and the piece is divided into clearly separated yet inter-related sections: Presto di molto, Andante, Presto di molto, Larghetto sostenuto, Presto di molto. Bach avoids such typical fantasia-like gestures as rushing arpeggios and extended passage-work. First impressions might suggest an early work, yet they are misleading: it is in fact a typical late work, masterly in its technique, profound in its musical content. This fantasia contains expressive contrasts as powerful as any that could be imagined in Bach's music. Reichardt's description of Bach as a 'serious humorist'[211] accurately conveys the spirit of this fantasia.

The main theme is ideally suited to an exploration of different forms of humour in music (Ex. 66).

Ex. 66. Fantasia, Wq. 61 no. 6

In all three Presto sections this is the principal theme, connecting one idea with another. In the introductory first section, a quasi-exposition, the humour is still held in check. Several times the main theme makes as if to set some kind of development in motion, but sooner or later breaks off and is left 'hanging in the air'. At one such point (Ex. 67),

Ex. 67

[211] Reichardt, 'Autobiography', *AMZ*, xv (1813), col. 673.

the interval between the highest and lowest notes heard is five octaves, the entire range of the keyboard at the time.

The end of this first Presto is as humorous as anything heard so far: forcefully, and with increasing vigour, the opening motive provides an energetic conclusion. Yet this ending also possesses a momentum of its own, for its harmonic function is clearly that of a dominant to the following section. The intervening silence, such a frequent and original trait in Bach's music, signifies both separation and transition, and what is more, it heightens the listener's expectancy. The abrupt change to a totally different mood is so grating, that one wonders whether Bach has completely ignored the psychological implications of hearing music in time. How can one confront the listener with an expression of lamentation so soon after placing him in a humorous frame of mind? The answers are to be sought in Bach's spiritual and aesthetic credo. It is this same idiosyncrasy which led to Reichardt's use of the label 'serious humorist'. Accurately understood, this feature illustrates an aspect of Bach's improvisatory skills: the composer who follows the mood of the moment operates within a constant field of tension between vehement, passionate expression and introspection.

The Andante with its 'clavichord-like lyricism'[212] can only be understood in terms of Bach's concept of the 'vocally inspired' composer (Ex. 68). Nägeli speaks astutely of 'the finely chiselled, beautifully shaped ... lineaments of an expressive physiognomy with constantly changing features ...'[213]

Ex. 68

---

[212] Beurmann, op. cit., p. 81.
[213] H. G. Nägeli, *Vorlesungen über Musik* (Stuttgart and Tübingen, 1826), p. 141.

The wide-ranging tonal scheme leads from E flat major to E major, and the expression changes once again. The opening motive ushers in the second Presto section with some high-spirited pranks and finally gives way to a complete statement of the main theme, which is then heard in many different keys and registers. Frolicsome, pert playfulness is followed once again by deeply felt emotion in the almost Beethovenian Larghetto sostenuto (Ex. 69).[214]

Ex. 69

The sonorities which Bach achieves in this section easily bear comparison with the keyboard music of Haydn and Beethoven. Beginning in the bass register, he works his way up the keyboard to the highest register, with fine expressive shading throughout. The chordal writing, not unlike the Andante in tone, exudes calm, and remains untouched by the restlessness of the main theme. This Larghetto sostenuto has been variously interpreted in critical literature: Heinrich Jalowetz points out the principle, further explored by Beethoven, of 'variation by means of continuous alteration of the harmony underneath an unchanging upper part' and sees in the passage a new type of variation movement.[215] Gudrun Busch points out the lyrical character of the theme itself. For her it is 'almost an anticipation of Schubert'.[216]

Bach soon moves beyond the stable confines of G major, and works towards more distant keys. Diminished chords accumulate, and note-repetitions give the section a sense of urgency. The concluding bars break into rising arpeggios outlining diminished seventh harmonies and ending on a fermata. What will happen next? The Presto theme reappears, immediately gaining the upper hand. Without further ado a return to C major is effected, and the true reprise begins. Here too Bach's humour makes itself felt. The conclusion is constantly post-

[214] Jalowetz also points out this link with Beethoven. See H. Jalowetz, 'Beethoven's Jugendwerke in ihren melodischen Beziehungen zu Mozart, Haydn und Ph. E. Bach', *SIMG*, xii (1910–11), p. 469.

[215] Ibid.

[216] Busch, op. cit., p. 392.

poned by unexpected chromatic notes and interrupted cadences, such as the accented F in bar 188 (Ex. 70),

Ex. 70

or the A minor harmony in bar 211 (Ex. 71).

Ex. 71

Bach's intention, stated on the title-pages of the six collections, to address both the connoisseur and the amateur in his sonatas, rondos, and fantasias was a skilful act of salesmanship; that is to say Bach aimed at boosting sales by appealing to as wide an audience as possible. Naturally he was aware that in coupling the 'connoisseur' with the 'amateur' he was dealing with a wide and heterogeneous public with differing requirements and expectations, and as a composer he had to take this into account. After the lead already given by French aesthetic writers in the theory of the 'connoisseur' and the 'amateur' (Crousaz 1715, Dubos 1719), the German equivalent, 'Kenner und Liebhaber', was established in writings on music around the middle of the eighteenth century; by it was meant on the one hand an educated, rational listener, and on the other an uneducated emotional listener.[217] Listeners in each of the two categories made different demands on music:

If the qualities in a musical work which appeal to the connoisseur are those concerned with elaboration and complexity (Quantz), art, invention, and

---

[217] See E. Reimer, section 'Kenner—Liebhaber—Dilettant', *Handwörterbuch der musikalischen Terminologie*, ed. H. H. Eggebrecht (Wiesbaden, 1972ff.), p. 5.

thoroughness (Hiller), as well as order, balance, and coherence (Forkel), and summarized under the general heading of intellectual beauty . . . so in the same way the preference of the amateur, who, according to Forkel (*Theorie der Musik*, Göttingen, 1777, p. 33), 'finds pure melody adequate for the expression of every conceivable emotion and impulse of the heart', is for music which in its aesthetic effect may be categorized as 'attractive, accessible, brilliant, pleasant, and joyful'.[218]

This comparison is not in any way intended to be dismissive of the amateur. Christian Gottfried Krause, for instance, raises the latter to a status above that of the connoisseur as a judge of art, since while he may have perfectly good taste, the amateur is 'neither familiar with the rules of harmony, nor subject to other prejudices'.[219]

The success of these publications was at first quite phenomenal. Bach had launched a broadly-based advertising campaign.[220] Influential newspapers and journals such as the *Hamburgischer unpartheyischer Correspondent*, Reichardt's *Musikalisches Kunstmagazin*, Cramer's *Magazin der Musik*, and various almanacs devoted lengthy passages to exceptionally favourable accounts of this music. Reichardt believed the F minor Sonata from the third set to be unsurpassed:

I am still convinced that it is the greatest sonata that even Bach has produced; it speaks, it sings, it transports the listener through every facet of genius and art more than any other that I could imagine.[221]

The *Magazin der Musik* (1786) announced the appearance of the fifth set in the following terms:

The musical genius of the great Bach seems in fact to be inexhaustible. However often one studies his sonatas, rondos, or fantasias, of which he constantly issues new examples, and however often one compares them with one another, or with the works of other masters, one always finds that each piece is entirely new and original in its invention, while the spirit of Bach is unmistakably present in them all; this composer is literally incomparable.[222]

Bach was able to attract 519 subscribers for his first set; between them they bought almost 600 copies.[223]

[218] Ibid., p. 6.

[219] Krause, *Poesie*, p. 31 [Chapter 2, n. 74].

[220] From the list of subscribers published with the first set it is apparent that interest in these keyboard works was widespread. Subscribers from the following places are mentioned: Berlin, Brunswick, Copenhagen, Courland, Danzig, Dresden, Göttingen, Gotha, Hamburg, Hanover, Holstein, Leipzig, London, Ludwigslust, Nyburg, St Petersburg, Prague, Reval, Riga, Silesia, Stettin, Uckermark, Ulm, Hungary, Warsaw, Vienna. See also Hase, op. cit., pp. 96f.

[221] Reichardt, *Kunstmagazin*, i, p. 87 [n. 19 above].

[222] *Magazin der Musik*, ii.2, pp. 869f. [n. 45 above].

[223] See Bitter, i, p. 212. In reality the sales figures may have been much higher, for the copies remaining after the subscription period had lapsed were put on general sale. Besides, the lists of subscribers include only those who gave their names.

In spite of this promising start, interest soon declined. The sixth set, with only 288 copies sold by subscription, achieved the lowest sales figures. And Bach had not omitted to provide 'sugar' for the public here:[224] he had included rondos.[225] The reviewer in the *Magazin der Musik*, Carl Friedrich Cramer, expressed his disapproval of this: Bach, he said, had 'lowered himself to write in that genre' which was now 'so popular, infuriating, yet everywhere to be found in keyboard music, namely the rondo'.[226] Yet if Cramer assumed a corresponding decline in the quality of Bach's music, he was mistaken. Most of the rondos, especially the one in A minor from the second set and the one in E flat major from the sixth set, are among the most original of all Bach's keyboard works. Bitter quotes a lengthy extract from the A minor Rondo (Ex. 72) in order to illustrate its bold modulations.

Ex. 72. Rondo, Wq. 56 no. 5

This is by no means simply trivial, fashionable music—sufficient reason in itself for many subscribers to decide against putting their names down for subsequent sets. The familiar charge of *Bizarrerie* was renewed. Was Bach once again aiming primarily at the 'connoisseurs' when he decided to include fantasias in the fourth and subsequent collections? In 1775 he had described the composition of fantasias as not particularly lucrative:

People now ask me for six or seven more fantasias like the final piece in C minor from the *Probestücke*; I do not deny that I should very much like to write something of this kind, and perhaps I am not altogether unqualified to

---

[224] See p. 108 above.
[225] See Sonneck, op. cit., pp. 113f.
[226] *Magazin der Musik*, i.2, p. 1241 [n. 45 above].

do so; besides I have a great many sketches, which, if I had time to sort them all out, and to add to them, especially in connection with the use of all three genera,[227] would serve as good illustrations to the chapter on the free fantasia in the second part of my *Versuch*; the only difficulty is that one wonders how many people there are who like such music, understand it, and can perform it properly.[228]

It appears that Bach was unwilling to omit from these great collections a genre so characteristic and so important within his *œuvre*. The 'connoisseurs' were in any case gratified. Burney ordered extra copies, as did Dušek in Prague. Baron van Swieten bought twelve copies of each set, and Artaria bought almost as many.[229] These last two purchasers are of particular significance, since through them the Viennese Classical composers may have come into contact with Bach's late collections of keyboard music. Haydn is known to have requested Artaria in a letter of 16 February 1788 to send 'the two most recent keyboard works by C. P. Emanuel Bach'[230] and he evidently meant by this the fifth and sixth sets 'für Kenner und Liebhaber'. Did Neefe also possess copies of this music, which he might then have used in giving instruction to the young Beethoven?[231] There was a great deal to be learnt from these works, above all a musical language both 'captivating in its refinement and transparency' and 'simplified, while retaining its original emotional power'.[232]

Master of Improvisation

Bach's liking for 'bold shifts from one *Affekt* to another' in his fantasias and rondos[233] also finds expression in another area of his creative activity, namely his improvisation. The following passage is quoted from the second part of the second volume of the *Magazin der Musik* (1786):

Anyone who has heard the Herr Kapellmeister improvising on the fortepiano, if he is a connoisseur of such matters, will gladly admit that greater perfection in this art could scarcely be imagined. The greatest virtuosos who have lived here in Hamburg, and have witnessed his improvisations when he was in just

[227] i.e. *stilus gravis*, *stilus mediocris*, and *stilus humilis*, meaning the styles appropriate to church, theatre, and chamber respectively.

[228] C. P. E. Bach, letter written on 10 Feb. 1775 to J. N. Forkel. See Bitter, op. cit., i, p. 341.

[229] See the lists of subscribers published with the first editions of the collections 'für Kenner und Liebhaber'.

[230] Quoted in Schleuning, op. cit., pp. 251f. [Chapter 2, n. 144].

[231] For information concerning Bach's relationship with Neefe see Schmid, *Kammermusik*, pp. 62ff.

[232] Wyler, op. cit., p. 146 [n. 209 above].

[233] Bach, *Versuch*, i, Ch. III, par. 15.

the right frame of mind for them, have been astounded at his bold ideas and transitions, his daring, unprecedented, and yet technically correct modulations, in a word at the great wealth and rich variety of harmony with which Bach presented them, much of which was previously unknown to them; they have mopped their brows and expressed regret that they did not also possess such knowledge themselves.[234]

Bach owned some good instruments. In the *Nachlassverzeichnis* two clavichords are mentioned, one made by Christian Ernst Friederici and the other by Heinrich Wilhelm Jungcurth, an instrument-maker from Hamburg. In 1781 Bach sold a clavichord, presumably one produced at the workshop of Gottfried Silbermann, to Baron Dietrich Ewald von Grotthuss, evidently with some reluctance, for this event prompted the composition of the thoroughly melancholy rondo *Abschied von meinem Silbermannischen Claviere* [Farewell to my Silbermann clavichord].[235] Bach also possessed 'a five-octave walnut harpsichord, beautiful and strong in tone' and 'a fortepiano or Clavecin Roial made by old Friederici, in oak with an attractive sound'.[236] The following extract from a letter to Forkel written on 10 November 1773 makes clear that Bach was also well informed with regard to the construction of individual instruments:

The Friederici clavichords I greatly prefer to those of Fritz and Hass because of their good construction and the absence of octave strings in the bass, a thing I cannot bear.[237]

Although the piano was already at an advanced stage of construction by the 1770s and was gradually assuming the leading role among keyboard instruments, Bach still preferred the clavichord even in his later Hamburg years both for composition and for improvisation. The astonishing effects he was able to achieve in his performance on this instrument are recorded in numerous eye-witness accounts. Both the broad outlines and the tiny details were permeated by an expressive style of performance, precise articulation, and finely graded dynamics. In Burney's words:

In the pathetic and slow movements, whenever he had a long note to express, he absolutely contrived to produce, from his instrument, a cry of sorrow and complaint, such as can only be effected upon the clavichord, and perhaps by himself.[238]

---

[234] *Magazin der Musik*, ii.2 (1786), p. 871 [n. 45 above].

[235] With this work Bach evidently wished to demonstrate 'that it is also possible to write sad rondos'. See Georgii, op. cit., p. 167 [n. 210 above].

[236] See *Nachlassverzeichnis*, p. 92.

[237] See Bitter, op. cit., i, p. 336.

[238] Burney, *Musical Tours*, ii, p. 219.

Reichardt makes similar observations:

H[err] B[ach] can not only play you a really slow, lyrical Adagio with the most heart-rending expression, to the shame of many performers whose instruments might with much less effort be used to emulate the human voice; but he can also sustain a dotted minim at this slow tempo with all conceivable gradations of strength and weakness, both in the bass and in the treble.

Yet this is probably only possible on his very fine Silbermann instrument, for which he has written some sonatas specially, and it is only in these that such long sustained notes are to be found.

It is the same with regard to the quite extraordinary power which Herr Bach sometimes achieves in a full *fortissimo*, which would be enough to make another instrument fall to pieces; similarly with the most delicate *pianissimo*, which on another instrument would fail to speak at all.[239]

If this style of keyboard performance could so astonish contemporary audiences, how much greater must their enthusiasm have been for Bach's improvisations, which surpassed many a composition in sheer expressive originality. It was his improvisations most of all which attracted so many visitors to his house, including Burney and Reichardt. During his performance, according to Burney,

he grew so animated and *possessed*, that he not only played, but looked like one inspired. His eyes were fixed, his under lip fell, and drops of effervescence distilled from his countenance. He said, if he were to be set to work frequently, in this manner, he should grow young again.[240]

Let us draw on Reichardt's comments for comparison:

I have not yet mentioned to you the outstanding improvisations of this great man. He puts his entire soul into them, as is abundantly clear from the utter repose, one might almost say lifelessness of his body. For he retains, without moving, the posture and manner which he assumes at the outset throughout improvisations lasting for hours.

Herein he clearly demonstrates his great knowledge of harmony, and that immeasurable wealth of rare and unusual ideas, thanks to which he emerges as the greatest *Originalgenie*.[241]

Regarding the spiritual disposition of the improviser, Reichardt and Burney concur in their characterization of Bach as a performer totally absorbed by the music, one who while transported into a trance-like state (Burney: 'he looked like one inspired') adopts an impassioned tone which he then maintains for hours. The idea of 'genius' is present once again. Such improvisation enables the composer's individuality to

---

[239] Reichardt, *Briefe*, ii, pp. 16f. [n. 68 above].
[240] Burney, *Musical Tours*, ii, p. 219.
[241] Reichardt, *Briefe*, ii, p. 15 [n. 68 above].

manifest itself. It gives free rein to the play of passions. It does not place technical or formal restrictions on the composer of the kind that Bach had to observe when writing for amateur performers. And it allows the interpreter to draw on all conceivable aspects of keyboard virtuosity; scales, arpeggios, strings of chords, embellishments, rhythmic-melodic niceties, and much more besides, all combine to produce a colourful musical panorama.

While an improvisation has to forfeit such advantages as result from the rational organization of material, careful planning, shaping of detail, and attention to the architecture of a work, it is able by way of compensation to achieve greater immediacy of expression and greater freedom of musical thought. In particular Bach's harmonic language, his bold combinations of chords, his chains of modulations and resolutions, seemed quite miraculous. Yet in spite of all their extravagant ideas, his improvisations were never incoherent, as the statement by Cramer, quoted above, confirms (p. 167f.). While strict adherence to rules was set aside, at least so far as to permit 'complete unrestraint in the succession of ideas',[242] nevertheless a sense of general musical logic was retained. Bach declared more than once that for any form of improvisation, accurate knowledge both of harmonic functions and of various performance problems was essential.[243]

Bach's art of improvisation was felt to be prophetic. The most advanced musical aesthetics of the time were able to draw inspiration from it. The old doctrine of the affections with its thesis of a prevailing principal *Affekt* showed itself to be untenable in the face of such a high degree of dynamically unfolding expression. Cramer articulates newer ideas; while the remarks quoted below refer specifically to the two fantasias in the fourth set of the 'Kenner und Liebhaber' pieces, they are equally applicable to Bach's actual improvisations:

Anyone who, unlike Rousseau, does not see the essence and the entire power of music exclusively in the imitation of nature and passion, who is not altogether insensitive to instrumental music of the non-descriptive variety,

---

[242] Schleuning, op. cit., p. 165 [Chapter 2, n. 144].

[243] See for example the following extracts from the *Versuch*: 'Even though fantasias are unbarred, none the less the ear . . . demands certain proportions in the durations and the changes of harmony, and the eye demands certain proportions in the value of the notes, in order that ideas may be written down.' Bach, *Versuch*, ii, p. 326 (Mitchell, p. 430). 'A fantasia is said to be free when it is unbarred and moves through more keys than is customary in other pieces which are composed or improvised in metre. These latter require a comprehensive knowledge of composition, whereas the former require only a thorough understanding of harmony and acquaintance with a few rules of construction. Both call for natural talent, especially when actual improvisation is involved. It is quite possible for a person to have studied composition with some success and to have turned his pen to fine ends without having any gift for improvisation. But, on the other hand, a good future in composition can be assuredly predicted for anyone who can improvise, provided that he writes a great deal and does not start too late.' Ibid., pp. 325f. (Mitchell, p. 430).

and who can ascribe merit on other grounds to successions of sounds which do not correspond to specific feelings or ideas, and which sometimes hold no conspicuous attraction for the ear, will surely find such an assortment of abrupt ideas, thoughts, capriccios, in other words such free outbursts of poetico-musical inspiration . . . most fascinating listening, and all the more so the greater his familiarity with the secret rules of art and the deeper his penetration into its inner sanctum. For at every step the most diverse vistas are opened up for the intelligent music-lover. The novelty of so many frequently quite heterogeneous and yet always correctly and artistically interconnected ideas, their unexpectedness and constant surprises, given the absence of any clear theme which might register with the listener and generate expectations, the boldness of the modulations, the harmonic digressions and returns, the inexhaustible fecundity of ideas and turns of phrase, the multiplicity of the individual figures which combine to make up the whole, and the brilliant fingerwork which affords even the most inexperienced listener at least the pleasure of astonishment at hearing technical difficulties overcome: all these things suggest major and significant angles from which to view such works of art, such studies in expression as are appreciated by only a few and intelligible to only a few, and on which a man such as Bach bases no small part of his fame.[244]

While it is true that these thoughts in some ways anticipate the irrationality of early Romantic musical attitudes, such as were to be articulated some fifteen years later in Wackenroder's *Herzensergiessungen eines kunstliebenden Klosterbruders* [Confessions of an art-loving monk] (1797), this approach is in fact much better suited in general terms to the character and the resources of instrumental music and improvisation than the older doctrine of the affections had been. It follows that Bach's improvisations must themselves have had something of a Romantic flavour. The often extremely rapid alternation of radically opposed moods, and the lack of any balanced formal structure or clear architectural division, in any case point towards the idiom of later character pieces and sectional rhapsodic genres.

The Four 'Orchestral symphonies with twelve obbligato parts'

The Hamburg period also saw the composition of a second set of symphonies. Bach wrote to his Leipzig publisher Breitkopf on 30 November 1778 as follows:

Last year I wrote four grand [*gross*] orchestral symphonies with twelve obbligato parts. They are the most substantial [*grösste*] works of the kind that I have written. Modesty forbids me to say more.[245]

---

[244] *Magazin der Musik*, i.2, pp. 1250ff. [n. 45 above].
[245] Quoted in Suchalla, op. cit., p. 264.

The scoring is as follows: two horns, two flutes, two oboes, bassoon, first and second violins, violas, cellos, double-bass, and cembalo.

Apart from the E minor Symphony (1755), these were the only symphonies by Bach of which the parts were printed during his lifetime, and they are comparable in character to the six 'string symphonies': wild in their musical language, full of symphonic vigour, restless, and constantly springing surprise effects and other 'deceptions' upon the unwary listener. Once again the expressive world of *Sturm und Drang* is approached. In the process of enlarging the orchestra by adding extra 'obbligato instruments'—one performance of the symphonies in Hamburg in August 1776 involved forty players[246]—a number of important technical innovations were made.[247] The wind instruments no longer fulfil a merely supporting role, as had been the case in the Berlin works, but they are treated with much greater individuality. In particular the flutes now almost match the strings in melodic independence. Unusual combinations of instruments and contrasts of timbre are the order of the day. In bars 61–5 of the first movement of the E flat major Symphony, Wq. 183 no. 2, for example (Ex. 73), there occurs a fine though unexpected contrapuntal passage for flute, oboe, and bassoon/cello.

Ex. 73

[246] Letter from Klopstock to Schönborn dated 17 August 1776: 'How often we wish you were among us, my dear Schönborn. Yesterday, for example, when we heard four new symphonies by Bach performed by forty instrumentalists.' Quoted in Miesner, *Bach in Hamburg*, p. 36.
[247] See Suchalla, op. cit., pp. 37ff., 59f., 104.

Yet traces of concerto grosso technique are still occasionally to be found. In the opening movement of the first symphony, Wq. 183 no. 1, concertino episodes are inserted, while the slow movement of the same work contains a trio for two oboes and a bassoon. Even the bass progressions call to mind the earlier concerto style. Reminiscences of this kind are found alongside many novel technical details and procedures.

Key contrasts and corresponding changes in expression as extreme as those characteristic of this first symphony are rare even in Bach's music. He experiments with new types of *Individualthema*. One sometimes has the impression that with every main theme Bach has set himself a specific exercise in composition—bearing in mind the need to achieve symphonic unity throughout the movement. How else is the main theme of the D major Symphony (Ex. 74) to be understood than as an experiment in rhythmical and metrical acceleration and intensification?

Ex. 74. Symphony, Wq. 183 no. 1

Yet Bach does not stop there: this theme is continued over two different harmonies—B minor and G major—while the dynamic rises to *fortissimo*, only in order to fall back immediately afterwards, as so often in Bach's music, to a *piano*. In the slow movements, some of them very brief, *empfindsam* expression is allowed to prevail. The last movements of the first and fourth symphonies call to mind many a rollicking finale from the Classical symphonic repertoire with their jovial, carefree manner, as may be illustrated by Ex. 75, quoted from Wq. 183 no. 4.

If the four 'Orchestral symphonies' mark both the high point and the conclusion of Carl Philipp Emanuel Bach's personal development as a symphonist, for the present-day listener, on the other hand, they are to be

Ex. 75

regarded more as signs of a new beginning, of the genesis of a new musical language, as pointers towards the Classical symphony. We find here sounds, expressive and formal techniques which belong to a new era, but at the same time we also detect the threads which bind these works to the style of the past.[248]

Final years and late works

Bach's last years, then, were marked by intensive compositional activity and frequent improvisation at the clavichord. His other creative activities were either wholly abandoned, or else greatly curtailed. In one of the 1784 issues of *Magazin der Musik* reference is made to the fact that Bach had long since given up organizing and directing his own concerts.[249]

This is significant inasmuch as it sheds light both on Bach's position in the musical life of Hamburg in the 1780s and also on more general trends. The 'virtuoso concert' with greater emphasis on Italian, South German, and Austrian composers, was establishing itself in the North as well. Keeping up to date with repertoire, attention to all the details of concert management, from obtaining official permission and collaboration with the press to the building-up of a circle of subscribers etc.—all this would have proved too much for Bach in the end: it required professional administration. Such a thing existed in Hamburg in the hands of Johann Christoph Westphal, who was in charge of one of the largest musical establishments in Germany. According to a report in the *Hamburgischer unpartheyischer Correspondent* in 1782, Westphal used to receive 'the latest works from almost every European country at first hand, and he was in a position to report all the most

---

[248] K. Heller, Sleeve-notes to the Eterna recording of C. P. E. Bach's four 'Orchestral symphonies', No. 825923 Et.
[249] See *Magazin der Musik*, ii.1, p. 3 [n. 45 above].

interesting musical news and novelties before anyone else, through his contacts in Italy, France, England, Holland, Denmark, Sweden, and Russia'.[250] During the 1770s Bach's music was still frequently performed in Westphal's concerts alongside works by Homilius, the Benda brothers, Handel, Telemann, and Haydn.[251] Soon, however, these composers were replaced by names such as Paul and Anton Wranitzky, Mozart, Righini, Hoffmeister, Türk, Pleyel, and others.[252] In such surroundings Bach's music could no longer hold its ground.

A further factor was that even in such a large city as Hamburg it evidently did not pay to run several concert series at certain times. The general public seemed to prefer various light entertainments to serious concerts. In the *Magazin der Musik* it is reported that

during the summer all the 'beau monde' spend their time in the pleasure gardens, while in winter the clubs, assemblies, gambling-houses, picnics, balls, and banquets are so numerous and well-established, that it is only with untold difficulty that a few free hours can be found in which to squeeze a concert. On Sundays concerts are not allowed; that would offend against orthodoxy. Three or four days are post days, on which no businessman, salesman, or commercial employee ever has time to think about concerts. The remaining days are for the theatre; so only Saturday evening is left, and then everyone is recovering from the great round of feasting, gambling losses, and business, and preparing to start all over again.[253]

Bach continued to perform his church duties. As before, he borrowed portions of works by Telemann and J. S. Bach for use in his own passions, festal cantatas, Sunday cantatas, and occasional cantatas, in accordance with the practice of the period. From his father's St Matthew Passion, for example, he used, in addition to one or two choruses, the chorales 'Was mein Gott will', 'Wer hat dich so geschlagen', and 'O Haupt voll Blut und Wunden'.[254] In each of the twenty-one Passions that Bach is known to have written in Hamburg, similar borrowings from other works were made. Much the same picture emerges from a consideration of other types of church music. Two cantatas written in 1778 and 1786 begin with the opening chorus, 'Jauchzet, frohlocket' from J. S. Bach's Christmas Oratorio. The original music composed by Carl Philipp Emanuel Bach for such occasions does not stand up to comparison with his keyboard, chamber, or orchestral music. As Heinrich Miesner has pointed out, Bach transplanted Italian operatic lyricism into the Church.[255]

---

[250] *HUC*, no. 170, 1782; quoted in Sittard [n. 36 above] p. 113.
[251] See Sittard [n. 36 above] p. 114.   [252] Ibid., pp. 115ff.
[253] *Magazin der Musik*, ii.1, pp. 3f. [n. 45 above].
[254] See Miesner, *Bach in Hamburg*, p. 63.   [255] Ibid., p. 76.

With such pastiche and stylistic eclecticism, mainly born of haste, Bach was ultimately unable to satisfy the church authorities. Immediately after Bach's death a commission was set up to investigate the state of church music, with a view to carrying out extensive reforms. For reasons of respect and in view of the great esteem in which Bach had been held, the commission emphasized that there was no intention to say anything 'dishonourable' concerning the great man, but they did not neglect to point out numerous deficiencies. Yet Bach can hardly be held responsible for these: 'Given the excessive quantity of music that was required, how could it be otherwise than that many old works were reused, together with old and frequently unedifying libretti?'[256] On the other hand it must be said that Bach was not a man of the Church, and displayed little interest in bringing about significant changes in this area.

While Bach's extraordinarily prolific output declined somewhat in the 1780s owing to his advancing age, the quality of the music was nevertheless maintained in his last works. They are marked by a distinctive late style.

Besides the sonatas, rondos, and fantasias from the 'Kenner und Liebhaber' collections, which Bach continued to issue until 1787, the year before his death, the most personal instrumental works are the *Clavier-Fantasia*, Wq. 67, bearing the telling inscription 'C. P. E. Bachs Empfindungen' (1787), the three 'Quartets for Keyboard, Flute, Viola, and Bass' (1788), and the 'Concerto doppio' for harpsichord, fortepiano, and orchestra (1788).

The double concerto, with its unconventional key sequence E flat—C—E flat, is cast in Bach's humorous vein. One is struck by the way in which the two instruments engage in robust competition. Jacobi even suggests in his analysis that Bach is in some sense depicting musically the emancipation of the fortepiano here.[257] Be that as it may, Bach was in a position to observe the progress of the fortepiano towards pre-eminence, and he even played a part in the process himself.[258]

In the field of vocal music, *Die Israeliten in der Wüste* and the Passion Cantata were followed by the oratorio *Auferstehung und Himmelfahrt Jesu* (1777–8, published in 1787) on a text by Karl Wilhelm Ramler, the *Heilig* (1776, published in 1779) for double choir, and *Klopstocks Morgengesang am Schöpfungsfeste* (published in 1784). In Bach's final

---

[256] Quoted in Sittard [n. 36 above] pp. 47f.

[257] E. R. Jacobi, Preface to C. P. E. Bach, *Doppelkonzert in Es-Dur*, Wq. 47, Bärenreiter-Ausgabe 2043 (Kassel etc., 1958), pp. IVf.

[258] Van der Meer argues convincingly that the sonatas, rondos, and fantasias from the second to the sixth sets 'für Kenner und Liebhaber' were written for the piano. See Van der Meer, op. cit., pp. 35ff. [Chapter 2, n. 137].

years his output of vocal music was to decline noticeably. The *Heilig* was later arranged by Zelter, and probably formed part of the repertoire of the Berlin *Singakademie* for some years.[259] Bach thought very highly of this work.

On this piece I have worked especially hard and have been particularly daring in trying out an exceptional approach. This *Heilig* is an attempt to arouse a far greater degree of attention and emotion by means of entirely natural progressions than can be achieved by any amount of tortuous chromaticism. It is to be my swan-song in this genre, and may serve to ensure that I am not too quickly forgotten after my death.[260]

All the works mentioned here indicate how Bach continued to refine and to concentrate his style right up until his death.

Bach also took a keen interest in the printing and dissemination of his music, and he took pains to establish new contacts that would help to increase sales, for he knew well how to promote his interests. During the 1780s he became acquainted with Johann Jakob Heinrich West-phal, the Schwerin court organist, who had built up a collection of numerous manuscript copies and prints, and probably one or two autographs of Bach's music as well.[261] From one of his letters to Westphal it appears that spurious works sometimes appeared bearing Bach's name. Apparently many insignificant composers took advantage of his fame:

I thank you respectfully, most worthy Sir, for kindly sending twenty Marks, and I enclose herewith the five collections you requested, written in the violin clef. As for the manuscripts, I am sorry that you have been put to so much expense. I am sure that, apart from the copies which are faulty and of poor quality, you have encountered the same problem as many others; that is to say, you have bought a great deal of music sold in my name, which is not by me at all. I should rather like to see the incipits.[262]

On 1 January 1782, Johann Christian Bach died in London. Carl Philipp Emanuel Bach's relationship with his youngest brother had for some years been rather strained. When Matthias Claudius mentioned during an earlier conversation (quoted above on p. 159) that J. C. Bach's music together with that of Schobert enjoyed great popularity in Copenhagen, Carl Philipp Emanuel retorted somewhat

[259] See G. Schünemann, *Die Singakademie zu Berlin. 1791–1941* (Regensburg, 1941), p. 45, and Miesner, *Bach in Hamburg*, pp. 95ff.

[260] Quoted in Hase, op. cit., p. 95.

[261] Westphal's collection was later acquired by the Conservatoire Royal de Musique in Brussels. See Chapter 4, pp. 212f.

[262] C. P. E. Bach, letter of 9 Jan. 1787 to J. J. H. Westphal, quoted in Bitter, op. cit., ii, p. 305. See also M. Terry, 'C. P. E. Bach and J. J. H. Westphal. A Clarification', *JAMS*, xxii (1969), p. 108.

indignantly: 'Schobert is also known here, he is a man of good sense, but the music that he and my brother are now producing is quite empty.'[263] J. C. Bach was an artist who had achieved brilliant successes in Italy and England, had then experienced one failure after another, and yet lived in some luxury, supported by the English royal family (he was music teacher to the Queen); he had visited many central European countries, he died heavily in debt, and was quickly forgotten by London audiences. How different the artistic profiles of these two musicians were! Those intellectual, rational elements, the meditative aspects and *Bizarrerien* in Carl Philipp Emanuel Bach's music were quite foreign to that of his younger brother, who was a melodist *par excellence*, as Leopold Mozart's shrewd assessment indicates:

What is slight can still be great, if it is written in a natural, flowing, and easy style—and at the same time bears the marks of sound composition. Such works are more difficult to compose than all those harmonic progressions, *which the majority of people cannot fathom*, or pieces which have pleasing melodies, but which are *difficult to perform*. Did Bach lower himself by such work? Not at all. Good composition, sound construction, *il filo*—these distinguish the master from the bungler—even in trifles.[264]

   J. C. Bach's singing style developed during many years of contact with Neapolitan opera, and in the course of work with singers on many different European stages. Melodies such as Ex. 76

Ex. 76

Non   so __ d'on-de   vie-ne   quel   te - ne - ro af - fet - to,   quel mo - to che i - gno-to

were an inspiration to the young Mozart:

For practice I have also set to music the aria 'Non so d'onde viene', etc. which has been so beautifully composed by Bach. Just because I know Bach's setting so well and like it so much, and because it is always ringing in my ears, I wished to try and see whether in spite of all this I could not write an aria totally unlike his.[265]

The influence of J. C. Bach's music on the Salzburg composer was indeed profound, and much greater than that of the Hamburg Bach.

   [263] Quoted in Busch, op. cit., p. 93. For a discussion of Schobert's historical significance, see Georgii, op. cit., pp. 172f. [n. 210 above].
   [264] From a letter written by Leopold Mozart to his son on 13 Aug. 1778, quoted from *The Letters of Mozart and his Family*, p. 599 [n. 99 above].
   [265] From a letter by W. A. Mozart to his father written on 28 Feb. 1778, quoted ibid., p. 497.

Composing came remarkably easily to this talented musician, with the result that he wrote prolifically in many genres. J. C. Bach composed brilliant keyboard concertos (after 1768 exclusively for the piano), finely wrought chamber music, symphonies exploiting the 'singing allegro' and the thematic contrasts of the Mannheim composers, all in all a pleasant, deeply felt, and spirited kind of music. Its dissemination during the composer's lifetime could hardly be said to have been limited to particular regions; it was enthusiastically received in Italy,[266] Austria, Germany, Scandinavia, France, England, and the Low Countries.

Carl Philipp Emanuel Bach did not, as far as we know, ever revise his opinion of his brother's music. In his extensive music library, J. C. Bach was very sparsely represented with just a piano concerto, a symphony, an overture, and a 'group of compositions written in Berlin, before the author went to Italy, consisting of five keyboard concertos, one cello concerto, two trios, and three arias'.[267]

In 1784 Bach was obliged to defend a point of honour. The English journal *The European Magazine* published an anonymous article during that year in which he was accused of having criticized works by Haydn for lack of substance and craftsmanship.[268] In response, Haydn had allegedly parodied Bach's style in some sonatas, particularly in the middle movement of the E major Sonata (1773), Hob. XVI/22, imitating his 'capricious manner, odd breaks, whimsical modulations, and very often childish manner, mixed with an affectation of profound science'.[269] This report may be classed as a curiosity of musical journalism. At any rate Bach felt obliged to publish a disclaimer:

My code of conduct has never allowed me to write against anyone: thus I am particularly astonished by a passage recently printed in England in *The European Magazine*, in which I am falsely, crudely, and shamefully accused of having criticized the good Herr Haydn. To judge from the news reaching me from Vienna, and even from members of the Esterházy musical establishment, who have recently visited me, I have reason to believe that this worthy gentleman, whose work still gives me a great deal of pleasure, is as much my friend as I am his. According to my principles every master has his own particular merit, and praise or criticism do not alter this. It is the music alone which offers the best praise or criticism, and therefore I refrain from judging anybody.[270]

---

[266] 'I find all over Italy that Giardini's solos, and Bach's and Abel's overtures, are in great repute.' Burney, *Musical Tours*, i, p. 280.

[267] Bach, *Nachlassverzeichnis*, pp. 82f.

[268] 'An Account of Joseph Haydn, a Celebrated Composer of Music', *European Magazine and London Review* (Oct. 1784), reproduced in facsimile in H. C. Robbins Landon, *Haydn, Chronicle and Works*, ii, 'Haydn at Esterháza: 1766–1790' (London, 1978), pp. 496f. A German translation with a commentary by C. F. Cramer appeared in *Magazin der Musik*, ii.1, pp. 585ff. [n. 45 above].

[269] See Landon, loc. cit., p. 496.

[270] *HUC*, no. 150, 1785. Quoted in Bitter, op. cit., ii, p. 107. See also Landon, loc. cit., p. 498.

We must accept this as an indication of Bach's true feelings.

Much more important is the fact that both artists learned a great deal from one another. Bach's familiarity with Haydn's quartets, for example, may be considered proven in view of stylistic resemblances, particularly since by 1788 more than half of these works had been published and were thus accessible to him. Moreover Haydn's works were frequently performed in Hamburg,[271] the so-called 'Russian Quartets' of 1781 (op. 33) receiving a performance on 1 March 1783, for example. According to a reviewer in the *Magazin der Musik*,

These works are to be praised, and cannot be praised sufficiently, in view of their most original inspiration and the most lively and attractive wit which pervades them. I know that Bach in Hamburg . . . has expressed the utmost admiration for these works by Haydn, particularly as they were performed in so excellent a manner by Schick and Tricklir.[272]

Perhaps the clearest illustration of the interconnections that exist between the music of these two masters is to be found in Bach's three 'Quartets for Keyboard, Flute, Viola, and Bass', Wq. 93–5. Viewed technically they constitute, in Ernst Fritz Schmid's words, 'a complete breakthrough to the Viennese Classical style'.[273] All four instruments play a part in animating the texture, and are placed on an equal footing with regard to melodic importance and individuality. In places the texture of the keyboard part is fuller than almost anything found in Bach's earlier music. Even the viola, reduced in earlier concertante works to the role of a harmonic filler, is entrusted with solos. Everything in this music is extraordinarily imaginative. At times the

Ex. 77. Quartet, Wq. 94

[271] See E. F. Schmid, 'Joseph Haydn und Carl Philipp Emanuel Bach', *Zeitschrift für Musikwissenschaft*, xiv (1931–2), pp. 307f.

[272] *Magazin der Musik*, i.1, pp. 259f. [n. 45 above].

[273] E. F. Schmid, Preface to modern edition of C. P. E. Bach's three keyboard quartets, Wq. 93–5 (Kassel, 1952–71).

keyboard and the two melody instruments weave a melody between them in such a way that it is already possible, in examples such as Ex. 77 from the slow movement of the D major Quartet, to speak of a principle of motivic development.

In the Andantino of the A minor Quartet (Ex. 78) Bach achieves a rich texture through characteristic treatment of each individual instrument.

Ex. 78. Quartet, Wq. 93

Also noteworthy is the fact that Bach has entirely abandoned the continuo. All these features are undoubtedly related to techniques which Haydn had developed in his string quartets.

Yet there is another respect in which the quartets are important: they bear the imprint of an incipient Romantic idiom. The colouristic effects achieved in the slow movement of Wq. 95 by means of rippling runs in the keyboard part, constantly revealed in new lights through changing harmonic configurations, and the sometimes passionate and elegiac mood together anticipate the expression and colour of later lyrical character pieces. In this way Bach brought his art right up to the threshold of a new musical style.

In 1788 Bach published two interesting essays. One was a favourable review of the first volume of Forkel's *General History of Music* in the *Hamburgischer unpartheyischer Correspondent*. Even more significant, though, was the *Comparison between Handel and Bach* which appeared anonymously in the eighty-first volume of the *Allgemeine deutsche Bibliothek*;[274] Dragan Plamenac has established by means of elaborate detective work using textual comparisons that C. P. E. Bach was the author of this essay.[275] Bach did not wish to let Burney's remark that Handel was a better composer of organ fugues than J. S. Bach[276] pass unchallenged. In this field, he declared, his father's superiority was beyond question:

Where harmonic skill is concerned, and the genius whereby a composer invents many sections of a large work, elaborates them fully, and forms them into a single, beautiful unity, well-integrated, combining diversity with simple grandeur, in such a way as to delight even an amateur with limited understanding of the language of fugue (and others are unable to judge fugues at all): in these respects I doubt very much whether Handel's fugues could ever bear comparison with Bach's.[277]

The stand adopted here by Carl Philipp Emanuel Bach should be seen as a good example of his readiness to defend the quality and durability of his father's music.

Death and Posthumous Reputation

In a letter of 2 November 1788 Bach wrote to Westphal: 'Since 18 September I have been very ill with gout and other ailments. Now

---

[274] *Allgemeine deutsche Bibliothek*, ed. F. Nicolai, lxxxi.1 (Berlin and Stettin, 1788), pp. 295ff. The text is also found in *Bach Reader*, pp. 281ff. and *Bach-Dokumente*, iii, pp. 437ff.

[275] D. Plamenac, 'New Light on the last years of Carl Philipp Emanuel Bach', *MQ*, xxxv (1949), pp. 565ff.

[276] Bach had read this remark in the German translation of C. Burney, *An Account of the Musical Performances in Westminster Abbey* (London, 1785). It appears on p. 39 in the first part of the original in the following form: 'And, while *fugue*, *contrivance*, and a *full score*, were more generally reverenced than at present, he remained wholly unrivalled.' The German translation of this work is as follows: *Dr. Karl Burneys Nachricht von Georg Friedrich Händels Lebensumständen ...*, trans. J. J. Eschenburg (Berlin and Stettin, 1785).

[277] See *Bach Reader*, p. 283, *Bach-Dokumente*, iii, p. 439.

my health is beginning to improve.'[278] Yet this improvement turned out to be short-lived. Just six weeks later on 14 December Bach died at the age of seventy-four. Numerous obituaries appeared paying tribute to the man and his work.

Yesterday our city lost a very remarkable and famous man. At ten o'clock in the evening Herr Carl Philipp Emanuel Bach, Kapellmeister and since 3 November 1767 Director of Music in this city, passed away . . . He was one of the greatest theoretical and practical musicians, the author of the *Versuch über die wahre Art das Clavier zu spielen*, a most discerning expert in the rules of harmony and of strict musical composition, a most accurate observer of the same, and a keyboard player who in his kind has probably never been equalled. His compositions are masterpieces and will remain outstanding long after all the modern rubbish has been forgotten. In him the art of music has lost one of its greatest adornments and the name of Carl Philipp Emanuel will always be venerated. In company he was lively and vivacious, full of wit and spirit, cheerful and happy among his friends, whose deep sense of loss at his death is shared by the present writer, who had the great good fortune to be honoured with the intimate friendship of the deceased.[279]

Klopstock sketched inscriptions for two monuments which were to have been set up for Bach in Weimar and in Hamburg.[280] To this day they remain unbuilt. At this point begins the history of the reception of Bach's music, which had been foreshadowed even during his lifetime in its two most extreme forms—unlimited acclaim and total neglect.

---

[278] Quoted in Bitter, op. cit., ii, p. 307.

[279] *HUC*, no. 201, 16 Dec. 1788, probably by C. F. Cramer; quoted in Bitter, op. cit., ii, p. 123. Obituaries were also written by Reichardt, Gleim, and Klopstock. See Bitter, op. cit., ii, pp. 124f.

[280] See Bitter, op. cit., ii, pp. 124ff.

4

Carl Philipp Emanuel Bach—Aspects of Reception

'... I have only one or two of Emanuel Bach's keyboard compositions, and yet there are some which every true artist should know, not only for the great enjoyment to be derived from them, but also for the purpose of study.' (Ludwig van Beethoven writing to Breitkopf & Härtel, 26 July 1809)[1]

'I am in the process of editing some of Carl Philipp Emanuel Bach's keyboard sonatas. The work is very dry and it puts me in a bad mood.' (Hans von Bülow writing to Felix Draeseke, 16 October 1860)[2]

These two comments stand half a century apart. On the one hand there is Beethoven's admiration for the music of Carl Philipp Emanuel Bach; while recognizing a certain historical separation, he does not deny that he and Bach belong to a common tradition, and thus he draws attention to a relation between Bach's creative processes and his own. Whereas for Bülow, an admirer of Richard Wagner's work, the subtle craftsmanship and poetry of Bach's keyboard music remain a closed book. His inaccurate performing edition of the keyboard sonatas, in which the original text is sometimes altered beyond recognition, seems no more than a natural consequence of the point of view expressed here.[3]

C. P. E. Bach and the Viennese Classical composers

C. P. E. Bach may be said in the broadest sense to have formed a school of composition. From his Berlin days onwards he attracted generations of keyboard pupils, who made good use of the performing techniques, and—if they were so inclined—the compositional techniques which they learned from him. Much greater still is the number

---

[1] Beethoven, *Briefe*, i, p. 284; *Letters*, i, p. 235. [See Introduction, n. 8, where an identical reference occurs.]

[2] H. von Bülow, *Briefe und Schriften*, iv (Leipzig, 1898), p. 344.

[3] What cannot possibly be justified is Bülow's attempt to 'translate the keyboard writing of the eighteenth century into that of the nineteenth century'. See Preface to *Sechs Sonaten für Klavier allein*, ed. H. von Bülow, Edition Peters (Berlin, 1862), p. 3. This method of arrangement led to far-reaching alterations in Bach's modulation schemes, for example in bar 58 in the first movement of the F minor Sonata, Wq. 57 no. 6, the addition of inner parts, numerous expression marks, etc.

of those who learned from him indirectly through detailed study of his works, then in wide circulation, including above all the *Versuch über die wahre Art das Clavier zu spielen*. Much of Bach's music appeared in print during his lifetime; in the field of keyboard music alone there were eighteen collections, some of them issued simultaneously by several publishers,[4] to say nothing of the many individual items included in contemporary anthologies.

Reasonably precise information is available concerning the geographical dissemination of Bach's music. The extent of his influence in North Germany was discussed in some detail in the previous chapter. Yet he does not appear to have had a decisive influence on musical life in Mannheim or Vienna, to name but two centres in the South. His music did not find its way into concert programmes,[5] unlike that of his brother Johann Christian, nor did music publishers, with one or two exceptions, show much interest in it.[6] The following remarks made by Friedrich Nicolai in Vienna in 1781 are revealing:

One of the most knowledgeable of musical amateurs is Herr Reichshofrath von Braun. He admires the music of the great Philipp Emanuel Bach especially. Needless to say he has the greater part of the Viennese public against him in this matter. I myself have heard many otherwise eager and skilful music-lovers in Vienna speak of Bach not only with indifference, but with outright hostility. Kozeluch and Steffan are their idols among keyboard composers.[7]

This was because the local tradition here and throughout Southern Germany, as exemplified in the music of Johann Wenzel Anton Stamitz, Christian Cannabich, Carlo Giuseppe Toeschi, Georg Chris-

---

[4] The eighteen collections are as follows: Wq. 48–59; 61; 63, 1–6; 63, 7–12; 112–14. The sets Wq. 48–51, 54, 63, 113, and 114 were issued twice or more during the composer's lifetime. See E. F. Schmid, 'Carl Philipp Emanuel Bach', *MGG*, i, cols. 924ff. work-list, the details given in RISM, *Einzeldrucke vor 1800*, i (Kassel etc., 1971), 'C. P. E. Bach', pp. 161ff., and E. E. Helm, *Thematic Catalogue of the Works of Carl Philipp Emanuel Bach* (forthcoming).

[5] In local histories of the music of Mannheim and Vienna, there are no indications that Bach's works were frequently performed in concerts, except in isolated instances, such as those held at the home of Baron van Swieten.

[6] See W. Matthäus, *Johann André Musikverlag zu Offenbach am Main. Verlagsgeschichte und Bibliografie 1772–1800* (Tutzing, 1973). None of Carl Philipp Emanuel Bach's works is listed here. See also A. Weinmann, *Vollständiges Verlagsverzeichnis Artaria & Comp.* (Vienna, 1952, 2nd edn., 1978). In the long list of publications given here only a single item by Bach is included—announced in 1785 as '6 Sonate, Cembalo Solo'. In H. Rheinfurth, *Der Musikverlag Lotter in Augsburg (ca. 1719–1845)* (Tutzing, 1977) mention is made of nine songs by Bach in an anthology which also includes songs by Rheineck, Hiller, and Rolle. A somewhat different picture is presented by the figures for sales of sheet music. According to H. Gericke, *Der Wiener Musikalienhandel von 1700 bis 1778* (Graz and Cologne, 1960) the Viennese booksellers and music-sellers P. C. Monath, J. P. Krauss, G. Bauer, and J. T. Edler von Trattner among others, all offered works by C. P. E. Bach for sale, some of them offering a wide selection.

[7] F. Nicolai, *Beschreibung einer Reise durch Deutschland und die Schweiz im Jahre 1781*, 8 vols. (Berlin and Stettin, 1783–7), iv, p. 556.

toph Wagenseil, Matthias Georg Monn, and Joseph Anton Steffan, was so well established. It possessed not only an entirely different musical ethos, permeated with the spirit of the suite and the divertimento, but it also differed essentially from Bach's music in style.[8] All too often musical development and *Fortspinnung*—as in Steffan's work—degenerated into thematically undistinguished triadic figures, gratuitous decorations of simple melodic outlines, runs, and utterly conventional harmonic progressions.[9]

This is not to deny, however, that there were some composers in Southern Germany and Austria who drew repeatedly upon Bach's stylistic resources.[10] The three great Viennese Classical composers in particular testified more than once to the stimulating effect his work had had on them. Needless to say such influences should not be overestimated. The music of Haydn, Mozart, and Beethoven was nourished from so many sources that Bach's role in the formation of their Classical style should be seen rather as that of a stimulus, albeit a most important one.

Haydn's relationship with Carl Philipp Emanuel Bach[11] was discussed by his very first biographers, Griesinger and Dies. Griesinger gives this account:

Around this time [November 1749] Haydn discovered the first six sonatas of

[8] See the following studies: E. Bücken, *Die Musik des Rokokos und der Klassik* (Potsdam, 1927); W. Fischer, 'Zur Entwicklungsgeschichte des Wiener klassischen Stils', *Studien zur Musikwissenschaft*, iii (1915), pp. 24ff; W. S. Newman, *The Sonata in the Classic Era*, 3rd edn. (New York and London, 1983); W. S. Newman, 'Sonate', *MGG*, xii, cols. 868ff. and 'Sonata', III, 'Classical', *New Grove*, xvii, pp. 485ff. While there did exist in the eighteenth century numerous local, more or less distinctive styles of music, so-called 'schools of composition', this was none the less a time of universal communications, the musical sphere being no exception (via periodicals, concert tours, circulation of music etc.), and consequently there arose a complex network of cross-influences which has yet to be fully explored.

[9] See B. Wackernagel, *Joseph Haydns frühe Klaviersonaten. Ihre Beziehungen zur Klaviermusik um die Mitte des. 18. Jahrhunderts* (Tutzing, 1975), pp. 21ff., 44ff.

[10] See G. Hausswald, 'Der Divertimento-Begriff bei Georg Christoph Wagenseil', *Archiv für Musikwissenschaft*, ix (1952), pp. 45ff. Still to be investigated is the degree to which Wagenseil became acquainted with the prevailing styles and compositional techniques in Berlin—especially the problem of sonata form—during his travels there in 1756, and to what extent he incorporated them into his own music. W. Fischer mentions in connection with a secondary theme from a D major Symphony by Monn 'the family resemblance to numerous other "lyrical themes" by Monn himself, and to others by Gluck, Carl Philipp Emanuel Bach, etc.' W. Fischer, *Denkmäler der Tonkunst in Österreich*, xix, Part 2, vol. xxxix (Vienna, 1912, R/Graz, 1959), Introduction, p. xvii.

[11] A summary of this relationship is provided in Wackernagel, op. cit., pp. 7ff. Going further than C. H. Bitter, H. Kretzschmar, H. Jalowetz, R. Steglich, and E. Bücken, who all more or less took for granted the influence of Bach's keyboard sonatas on Haydn, H. Abert [n. 19 below] succeeded in 'establishing more convincingly the close links almost universally assumed to have existed between the two composers'. Wackernagel, op. cit., p. 8. For more recent discussions of this question, Wackernagel refers to the writings of C. Landon, G. Feder, J. P. Larsen, and K. Geiringer.

Emanuel Bach. 'I did not come away from my instrument until I had played through them all, and anyone who knows me well must realize that I owe a great deal to Emanuel Bach, that I have understood him and studied him diligently. Emanuel Bach once paid me a compliment on this score himself.'[12]

Dies's version is as follows:

Haydn ventured into a bookshop and asked for a good textbook on theory. The bookseller named the writings of Carl Philipp Emanuel Bach as the best and most recent. Haydn wanted to look and see for himself. He began to read, he understood, found what he was looking for, paid for the book, and took it away thoroughly pleased.

That Haydn sought to make Bach's principles his own, that he studied them untiringly, is apparent even in his youthful works from that period. In his nineteenth year Haydn wrote quartets which gave him a reputation among lovers of music as a profound genius, so quickly had he learnt. As time went on, he acquired Bach's later writings. In his opinion Bach's writings form the best, most thorough and most useful textbook ever published.

As soon as Haydn's musical output became available in print, Bach noted with pleasure that he could count Haydn among his pupils. He later paid Haydn a flattering compliment: that Haydn alone had understood [Bach's] writings completely and had known how to make use of them.[13]

These remarks leave no room for doubt concerning the enormous impact that Bach made on the composer eighteen years his junior.[14] This has been demonstrated with regard to Haydn's keyboard music, especially the sonatas written in the later 1760s; it applies equally, however, to the string quartets, the symphonies, and other genres, although detailed studies have yet to be carried out.[15] The two men never met in person; when Haydn passed through Hamburg on his return from London to Vienna in 1795, he met only Bach's daughter.

To a young composer the music of C. P. E. Bach offered first and foremost what might be described as a richly varied reservoir of styles. Moreover Bach and Haydn both possessed a similar artistic disposi-

[12] See *Haydn, Two Contemporary Portraits*, trans. and ed. V. Gotwals (Madison etc., 1968), p. 12. For original text, see G. A. Griesinger, *Biographische Notizen über Joseph Haydn* (Leipzig, 1810, R/1979), p. 13.

[13] Ibid., pp. 95f. For original text, see A. C. Dies, *Biographische Nachrichten von Joseph Haydn* (Vienna, 1810, R/Berlin, 2nd edn., 1962), pp. 40f.

[14] That Haydn's music also exercised an influence on Bach is suggested in Chapter 3 above. Here too further research is needed.

[15] See the texts referred to in n. 11 above. Geiringer sees in the F minor Adagio of the early string quartet, op. 2 no. 4, 'the passionate ardour ... of the North German art of Philipp Emanuel Bach', K. and I. Geiringer, *Haydn. A Creative Life in Music* (3rd edn., Sydney, 1982), p. 213. L. Somfai speaks of '[Haydn's] encounters with the music of Carl Philipp Emanuel Bach' in his book *Joseph Haydn. His Life in Contemporary Pictures* (London, 1969), p. xix. Bach's influence on Haydn quartets is also discussed by Charles Rosen in *The Classical Style*, rev. edn. (London, 1976), pp. 114f.

tion. The impassioned *Empfindsamkeit* characteristic of both composers, and the search for unusual compositional solutions should be seen as manifestations of *Sturm und Drang*.[16] Conspicuous in Haydn's music is a striving for thematic unity on the basis of a highly refined technique of motivic development. Here the influence of Bach can be seen with particular clarity, the more so since the problem of thematic treatment was by no means so acute for the pre-Classical composers of Vienna and South Germany as it was for Bach. In Monn's sonatas passage-work and scales often predominate, thus running counter to any desire for thematic unification.

Not so with Haydn: motives and themes from the opening of the movement constantly reappear in extended and intensified forms as a result of an extraordinarily rich art of melodic unfolding.[17] The imaginative transformations which Haydn is able to make of his themes may be illustrated by the extracts shown in Ex. 79, taken from the first movement of the E minor Sonata (before 1766), which is the earlier and probably original version of the Sonata Hoboken XVI/47.

Ex. 79

(Only the principal thematic configurations are shown here, not the innumerable motivic variants and individual figures.) Even Bettina

---

[16] Reichardt points out the essential affinity between Bach and Haydn. See Reichardt, *Kunstmagazin*, i, p. 25 [Chapter 3, n. 19]. In more recent C. P. E. Bach literature, as well as in Haydn literature, mention is made of the *Sturm und Drang* phase in the creative development of both men. See J. P. Larsen and H. C. Robbins Landon, 'Haydn', *MGG*, v, cols. 1857ff.; Geiringer, op. cit., pp. 252ff.; Bücken, *Rokoko*, p. 164 [n. 8 above].

[17] See Wackernagel, op. cit., p. 173 [n. 9 above].

Wackernagel, who is inclined to minimize the influence of C. P. E. Bach on Haydn in her monograph *Joseph Haydns frühe Klaviersonaten* (see n. 9), observes in connection with this striving for unity: 'No other composer who may have influenced Haydn uses a technique for achieving "thematic unity" so similar to Haydn's own in its implications for the melodic cohesion of the movement as does Bach.'[18]

And in some slow movements further affinities with Bach's musical language may be observed. Hermann Abert draws attention to Bachian stylistic features in the Largo from Haydn's Sonata in B flat major, Hob. XVI/2 (Ex. 80), citing 'the affective cantilena of the main theme with its heavy suspensions, the long-breathed melody broken up by syncopations, the varied rhythms of the consequent phrase, the rests on strong beats interrupting the melody, the figuration permeated with chromaticisms . . .'[19]

Ex. 80

'Yet the route which links Haydn with Carl Philipp Emanuel Bach is also', according to Abert, 'the route by which the master discovered himself.'[20] It is also, one might add, the route which led to Haydn's

---

[18] Ibid., p. 83.

[19] H. Abert, 'Joseph Haydns Klavierwerke', *Zeitschrift für Musikwissenschaft*, ii (1919–20), pp. 569f. [A continuation of this article is found ibid., iii (1920–1), pp. 535ff.]

[20] Quoted from K. and I. Geiringer, *Joseph Haydn. Der schöpferische Werdegang eines Meisters der Klassik* (Mainz, 1959), p. 180. [The passage quoted does not appear in the English version of this work, see n. 15 above. Geiringer does not give a source reference for the statement which he attributes here to Abert, but it appears to be a paraphrase of a point of view expressed in a number of places in Abert's article 'Joseph Haydns Klavierwerke', see n. 19 above, e.g. Part I, pp. 557, 569.]

Classical symphonies and string quartets, to the oratorios *The Creation* and *The Seasons*. In these works Haydn achieved genuine individuality, mastered new techniques, and formulated Classical ideals and humanistic utterances in an altogether new way.

Much more elusive and difficult to pin-point are the connections between the work of Carl Philipp Emanuel Bach and that of Wolfgang Amadeus Mozart. At first glance it might appear that the North German composer with his leaning towards great intensity and unbridled passions had nothing in common with the spontaneous richness of Mozart's art, its profound good humour and playful elegance, its quiet sensitivity, dramatic power, compelling tragedy, and utterly inexhaustible flow of melodic invention. And in fact Mozart stood much closer to the extrovert Italianate cantabile style of J. C. Bach.

None the less there were also links with C. P. E. Bach, and the following [apocryphal?] statement by Rochlitz is not the only evidence for this.

When Mozart visited Leipzig a few years before his death, he had passed through Hamburg shortly before, and there he had taken pains to visit Bach, by then already advanced in years; he heard Bach improvise a few times on his Silbermann instrument. During a musical soirée at the home of Doles Mozart was asked by his host for his opinion of Bach's playing, as the conversation was entirely concerned with such matters. The great man replied with his characteristically Viennese candour and directness: He is the father, we are the children. Those of us who know anything at all learned it from him; anyone who does not admit this is a . . . (this last word seemed to be connected in some way that I did not understand). What he did, Mozart continued, would be considered old-fashioned now; but the way he did it was unsurpassable. He preferred to hear me play on the organ, although I have long since been out of practice. He didn't mind that; and so he embraced me over and over again, until I almost cried out.[21]

Even if there is no proof that Mozart ever visited Hamburg, none the less his high regard for Carl Philipp Emanuel Bach is well attested in this report.

In his early years, Mozart's preoccupation with Bach's music was somewhat sporadic, his chief models being such composers as Schobert, Eckard, Abel, and J. C. Bach; after he met Baron van Swieten, that is from about 1782 onwards, it took on a new aspect. In particular Mozart made a careful study of Bach's keyboard music. Hermann Abert in his biography of Mozart describes the features which influenced the fantasias K. 394, 397, and 475: 'the strongly subjective

[21] Rochlitz, op. cit., iv, pp. 308f. n.

element, the concerto-like character, revelling in sweeping runs and arpeggios, the recitative-like features and harmonic daring'.[22] Similar influences of Bach on the development of Mozart's keyboard concertos remain to be investigated. There is an early Concerto in D major, K. 40, which contains orchestral versions of a number of solo keyboard movements by Honauer, Eckard, and C. P. E. Bach.[23]

Mozart occasionally performed Bach's works; chamber music was the most popular form of entertainment in Baron Gottfried van Swieten's Sunday concerts. Forkel's *Musikalischer Almanach für Deutschland auf das Jahr 1789* contains a report of a large-scale concert enterprise:

Vienna, 26 February 1788. On this date and on 4 March Ramler's cantata *Die Auferstehung und Himmelfahrt Christi* in the excellent setting by the incomparable Hamburg Bach was performed at the home of Count Johann Esterházy by an orchestra of eighty-six members in the presence and under the direction of that great connoisseur of music, Baron van Swieten, to universal applause from all the distinguished persons present. The Imperial Kapellmeister Herr Mozart was beating time from the score, and the Imperial Kapellmeister Herr Umlauff was at the keyboard. The performance was all the more excellent on account of the two dress rehearsals that were held. During the performance on 4 March His Lordship passed round a copper engraving of Herr Kapellmeister Bach. The princesses and countesses among the audience and all the glittering nobility admired the great composer, and there followed a great cheer and three loud bursts of applause.[24]

Beethoven's estate included a manuscript copy of *Klopstocks Morgengesang am Schöpfungsfeste* to which he had added the remark 'written by my dear father'.[25] Beethoven would have come across this work while still in Bonn. At that stage he was already a pupil of Christian Gottlob Neefe, who not only gave him a thorough grounding in the piano and the organ, in figured bass and in composition, but also aroused his literary and philosophical interests. Neefe, a highly stimulating companion and an admirer of Gellert and Klopstock, had begun his musical training under the guidance of the Leipzig Cantor Johann Adam Hiller, and by the beginning of the 1770s he had found a powerful model in Carl Philipp Emanuel Bach.[26] It need come as no surprise, therefore, that during his studies with Neefe Beethoven came

[22] Abert, *Mozart*, ii, p. 125 [Chapter 2, n. 29].

[23] The Bach piece in question was a musical portrait from *Musikalisches Mancherley*: 'La Boehmer', Wq. 117, no. 26.

[24] J. N. Forkel, *Musikalischer Almanach für Deutschland auf das Jahr 1789* (Leipzig, 1788, R/Hildesheim, 1974), p. 121.

[25] See Bitter, op. cit., ii, p. 89.

[26] Neefe's *Zwölf Klavier-Sonaten* (Leipzig, 1773, R/Düsseldorf, 1961–4, ed. W. Thoene) were dedicated to Carl Philipp Emanuel Bach. In the dedication Neefe writes: 'Since the time when you, dearest Herr Kapellmeister, presented to the public your masterly and truly tasteful

into especially close contact with J. S. and C. P. E. Bach. Thus the young composer had to grapple with a great variety of styles, ranging from the high art of 'learned' polyphonic music, as found in the *Well-tempered Clavier*, to the loosely-constructed, often almost improvisatory keyboard works of C. P. E. Bach. Yet it would be mistaken to suppose that the subtleties and the great potential inherent in the techniques of motivic development used in the collections 'für Kenner und Liebhaber' could have been fully perceived by the twelve-year-old Beethoven.

The three *Kurfürstensonaten*, WoO 47, show differing degrees of Bachian influence: the melodic invention in the E flat major Sonata is concentrated in the right hand with regular phrasing and utterly straightforward articulation, to an accompaniment of repeated-note figures and Alberti basses. Stylistically such writing has nothing in common with the much more varied textures of Bach's late keyboard music; but what may well be derived from him is this: in the same sonata the young Beethoven uses a technique of melodic development that is astonishingly advanced for one so young, and this helps to achieve thematic unity within the movement. Even the second subject turns out to be a variant of the main theme.

Concerning the Larghetto introduction to the F minor Sonata (Ex. 81) and the beginning of the Scherzando from the D major Sonata, Ludwig Schiedermair declared: 'In such agitated passages, rearing up and then storming away again, and in those violent accents and interruptions, there lives something of the revolutionary, daemonic spirit of Carl Philipp Emanuel Bach.'[27]

It might be objected that Haydn, perhaps, exerted a stronger influence on the young Beethoven. Yet there can be no doubt that Neefe, who, as mentioned earlier, grew up in the musical tradition of North Germany, would have been at pains to make his pupil familiar with Bach's sonatas. The place occupied by Haydn's work in Beethoven's education at that time cannot be assessed here. Perhaps as early as the beginning of the

keyboard sonatas, hardly any characteristic music for this instrument has been written. The majority of composers have hitherto occupied themselves with symphonies, trios, quartets, etc. And even if now and again somebody does write for the keyboard, the music is usually supplied with a violin accompaniment that may be quite arbitrary, and it might in any case be performed just as easily on many other instruments as at a keyboard. All the same it is lovers of the clavichord who constitute the greater part of the market, and for their personal enjoyment they can have little interest in anything more than a solo. It is for such people, then, that I have occupied my leisure hours by writing the present sonatas. And in dedicating them to you I hope to persuade you publicly on account of the gratitude that I owe you on account of the instruction and the pleasure which I have gained from your theoretical and practical works. If these works possess any merit at all, the principal share is unquestionably your own.'

[27] L. Schiedermair, *Der junge Beethoven*, 2nd edn. (Bonn, 1939), p. 203. [In the revised edition prepared by Ludwig-Ferdinand Schiedermair (Wilhelmshaven, 1970), the passage quoted occurs on p. 70 in a version which is not quite identical to the original.]

Ex. 81

1780s, and certainly later on in Vienna, during his brief period of
instruction from Haydn, Beethoven learned to make use in his own work
of the techniques of thematic treatment that Haydn had meanwhile
developed in the so-called 'Tost Quartets' and in the London Symphonies. We must at least regard Carl Philipp Emanuel Bach as one of the
compositional models from which Beethoven's early style was derived.
How else is Beethoven's remark of 1809 to be understood, to the effect that
Bach's keyboard works should serve every artist 'also for the purpose of
study',[28] than as an indication that Beethoven, in the course of his artistic
development, had himself drawn upon specific examples of certain
compositional approaches used by C. P. E. Bach, even if he then explored
them so much further that the original models can no longer be
recognized in the highly individual end-products?

This contention may be supported by some analytical comparisons be
tween Beethoven's F minor Sonata, op. 2 no. 1, and Bach's sonata in the
same key, Wq. 57 no. 6, from the third collection 'für Kenner und
Liebhaber'.

In the very opening bars resemblances as well as contrasts between these
two works can be observed. The main theme from op. 2 no. 1 (Ex. 82)

Ex. 82

---

[28] See the quotation with which this chapter began.

appears at first sight to be borrowed from Bach's opening thematic idea (Ex. 83).

Ex. 83

In the energetic impetus of these openings, laden with tension (though much more so in the Beethoven example than in the Bach), but above all in the omnipresence of the main theme, there are indeed resemblances between these two works. Such a comparison is questionable, however, in so far as it indirectly assumes similar intentions on the part of both composers. Even the reference to related melodic outlines and harmonic progressions is scarcely sufficient to indicate any fundamental similarity between the two works.[29] Beethoven's aims in this sonata are totally different from Bach's: he achieves a powerful drama of developmental technique which never slackens for a moment. The thematic substance is presented to the listener in an uncommonly concise and concentrated form; in the course of the first eight bars it is subjected to a gradual acceleration of harmonic rhythm, intensified by a crescendo up to *fortissimo* followed by a sudden return to *piano* to prepare for the second phrase, all this on a scale which Bach never achieved, but neither did he ever attempt it. It remains true, however, that Beethoven's 'technique of developing an entire movement from a tiny thematic cell'[30] was based on a thorough study of Bach's music.

---

[29] Attempts to suggest relationships of this kind have been made both by Jalowetz, op. cit., and by R. Oppel. The latter maintains, quite inadequately, that it is 'the overall melodic contours [which] are decisive in establishing a relationship between different pieces'. See R. Oppel, 'Über Beziehungen Beethovens zu Mozart und zu Ph. Em. Bach', *Zeitschrift für Musikwissenschaft*, v (1922–3), p. 34.

[30] J. Schmidt-Görg, 'Ludwig van Beethoven', *MGG*, i, col. 1537.

The two composers have other things in common: their zest for the unconventional, for idiosyncratic compositional procedures. When a reviewer writing for the *Allgemeine musikalische Zeitung* in 1798–9 criticized Beethoven's sonatas for piano and violin, op. 12, for their 'bizarre, laborious progression', and their 'search for unusual modulations',[31] he was almost echoing the criticisms made of Bach many years earlier.

Attention has been drawn to the 'speaking' [*redend*] quality of Bach's themes in connection with the question of a stylistic influence on Beethoven's music.[32] In fact a decisive role is played by the 'principle of rhetorical progression'[33] and other forms of instrumental declamation in Beethoven's music.[34] Let us consider first of all a work by Bach in which the principle of dialogue is clearly manifested: the harpsichord Concerto in C minor, Wq. 31 (1753). The opening tutti of the Adagio (Ex. 84) consists of a cantabile passage, laden with suspensions and finely graded dynamics, a beautiful example of introspective, *empfindsam* expressivity.

Ex. 84

The soloist answers with an instrumental recitative (Ex. 85).

Ex. 85

[31] *AMZ*, i (1798–9), col. 571.

[32] See Schering, 'Carl Philipp Emanuel Bach', especially pp. 19f., 29.

[33] H. Goldschmidt, *Die Erscheinung Beethoven* (Leipzig, 1974), p. 40. Original: 'Prinzip der gebundenen Rede'.

[34] See H. Goldschmidt, 'Vers und Strophe in Beethovens Instrumentalmusik', ibid., pp. 25ff., and, by the same author, 'Über die Einheit der vokalen und instrumentalen Sphäre in der klassischen Musik', *Deutsches Jahrbuch der Musikwissenschaft für 1966*, xi (1967), pp. 35ff.

The ensuing dialogue illustrates a feature also found in many of the fantasias: in the course of his improvisation, the 'speaking' soloist moves further and further away from the initial tonality of E flat major, and even reaches the remote key of E major via enharmonic and mediant progressions. As a result the ripieno is also drawn into these new tonal regions, and thus necessarily changes its mode of expression. So the recitative, with its harmonic mobility and rhetorical function, ensures that the *Affekt* is presented in a constantly new light.

A similar dialogue between declamatory, prose-like passages in the tutti, shown in Ex. 86,

Ex. 86

and the lyrical poetry of the solo instrument (Ex. 87)

Ex. 87

also pervades the slow movement of Beethoven's G major Piano Concerto. But here a dualistic principle is at work which raises both elements to the level of pure Classicism: 'the lament over the loss of happiness'[35] leads inevitably to a demand for the restoration of personal and communal well-being. This joyful, 'Elysian' mood[36] Beethoven then discovers in the Finale.

Meanings of this kind are not to be found in Bach's music. Yet in order to achieve such musical persuasiveness and ingenuity, Beethoven was obliged to familiarize himself with the achievements of Carl

[35] H. Goldschmidt, *Beethoven. Werkeinführungen* (Leipzig, 1975), p. 93.   [36] Ibid.

Philipp Emanuel Bach. And at least as far as the keyboard music is concerned, Beethoven passed on what he had learnt. When Carl Czerny wished to become his pupil, Beethoven said to the boy's father: 'Your son has talent; I shall instruct him myself, send him to me twice a week. Buy him at once a copy of Philipp Emanuel Bach's treatise on the true art of playing keyboard instruments, and let him bring it with him.'[37]

Viewed in the larger context of musical history, Carl Philipp Emanuel Bach can be seen to have achieved much that was new, and to have provided a base on which others could build, without being able himself to pursue his ideas to the heights of Classicism. What he began was completed by Haydn, Mozart, and Beethoven.

A Forgotten Musical Œuvre

When the publishing firm Breitkopf & Härtel failed to respond to Beethoven's request of July 1809 that they should send him music by C. P. E. Bach together with scores by Haydn, Mozart, and J. S. Bach,[38] Beethoven repeated his request on 15 October 1810.[39] When he received no reply this time either, he wrote to the Leipzig publishers a third time in a letter dated 28 January 1812: '. . . you might as well make me a present of those C. P. E. Bach scores some time', and as if to emphasize that this was not an unreasonable request, he added, 'they must be rotting with you.'[40] This remark indicates the situation regarding the cultivation and dissemination of Carl Philipp Emanuel's music in the first half of the nineteenth century. Interest in his works had declined noticeably. Breitkopf & Härtel, formerly an important business partner of Bach's,[41] did not issue a single previously unpublished work by him between 1799 and 1850.[42] Even for musical periodicals such as *Cäcilia*, *Iris im Gebiete der Tonkunst*, or the *Neue Zeitschrift für Musik*, which reported from time to time on concert performances and new appearances on the musical market, and included many reviews, Bach's name no longer carried much weight. If one is to believe a report in *Iris*, not a single symphony or oratorio by Bach was performed at Berlin concerts between 1830 and 1838. Even in the more historically conscious *Allgemeine musikalische Zeitung*, which

---

[37] Quoted in T. Frimmel, *Beethoven-Handbuch*, i (Leipzig, 1926, R/Hildesheim, 1968), p. 102.

[38] See Beethoven, *Briefe*, i, p. 284, *Letters*, i, p. 235. [See Introduction, n. 8, and n. 1 above.]

[39] Beethoven, *Briefe*, i, p. 338, *Letters*, i, p. 298. [See Introduction, n. 8.]

[40] Beethoven, *Briefe*, ii, p. 56, *Letters*, i, p. 355. [See Introduction, n. 8.]

[41] For information concerning Bach's business relations with Breitkopf & Härtel, see Hase, op. cit.

[42] See *Verzeichnis des Musikalienverlages von Breitkopf & Härtel in Leipzig* (Leipzig, 1903) for a complete survey of all the music published there until the end of 1902.

as late as 1799 described his works as 'models and exercises in the expression of deep emotions',[43] Bach's name was mentioned less and less as time went on. In short, C. P. E. Bach's music gradually passed into oblivion; the 'true art' of performing—and of hearing—his music was also lost, because its once familiar mode of communication was no longer understood.

Among the champions of the Romantic musical aesthetic—Tieck, Wackenroder, E. T. A. Hoffmann—Bach, very much a musician of the Enlightenment, had no advocate. This is surprising inasmuch as it has been possible here to detect features in his artistic profile which might be described as pre-Romantic: an improvisatory style of thought which ignored the demands of contemporary conventions and served to express a heightened subjectivity, a conception of music as a mirror of the individual's interior life, and finally the many 'Romanticisms' of his musical language itself, such as the sweeping, harmonically unstable passage-work of some of the fantasias.[44]

To E. T. A. Hoffmann, for example, Bach's music represented a stage in musical history that was already some years old, and which, measured against the achievements of the intervening generation, had since been superseded, with at the most a claim to a greater or lesser degree of historical interest.[45] But it was not simply a matter of a rejection based on aesthetic criteria or on a critical appraisal of stylistic or technical deficiencies in Bach's music; among the targets of the Romantic critics was the 'present-moment optimism' [*Gegenwartsoptimismus*] so characteristic of the Enlightenment.[46] From his vantage point, Carl Philipp Emanuel Bach had aimed to write music which would be generally accessible to a wide circle of 'Kenner und Liebhaber'. This position had been abandoned by many artists in post-Revolutionary society, and Wackenroder's theme of *Weltflucht*, for example, was scarcely compatible with C. P. E. Bach's musical philosophy. In the following brief discussion, one or two of the different aesthetic judgements passed on C. P. E. Bach's music in nineteenth-century writings will be considered.

Johann Karl Friedrich Triest in his 'Bemerkungen über die Ausbil-

---

[43] E. L. Gerber, 'Etwas über den sogenannten musikalischen Styl', *AMZ*, i (1798–9), col. 305.

[44] It is interesting that in recent discussions of Romanticism in literature similar questions have been asked about the interconnections and relationships between Romanticism and the *empfindsam*-sentimental trends of the Enlightenment and the *Sturm und Drang*. See H.-D. Dahnke, 'Zur Stellung und Leistung der deutschen romantischen Literatur', *Weimarer Beiträge*, xxiv.4 (1978), pp. 5ff.

[45] See also below.

[46] 'Aufklärerische Gegenwartsoptimismus'. A concept discussed by W. Kahl in 'Musik als Erbe. Von der Aufklärung zur Romantik', *Musikerkenntnis und Musikerziehung. Festschrift für H. Mersmann* (Kassel and Basel, 1957), p. 64.

dung der Tonkunst in Deutschland im achtzehnten Jahrhundert'[47] interpreted the history of instrumental music 'as a dialectical process in which "absolute music" rose from the "rhetorical" to the "poetic", becoming alienated from itself in the process'.[48] The works of J. S. Bach—an expression of the first stage in the process—were in essence 'only rhetorical, not poetic'.[49] In deliberate contrast to J. S. Bach, the composers of the *'galant* style' had simultaneously enriched and impoverished music; they had enriched it, in that they had imitated instrumentally 'the cantabile melody of "applied music" [*angewandte Tonkunst*] as expounded by Kant in the concepts of "attraction and emotion" [*Reiz und Rührung*]'[50] and had sought thereby to rescue music from its 'rhetorical' limitations, taking this to mean simply 'dazzling virtuosity of figural manipulation without adequate substance or truth';[51] and they had impoverished it through over-simplification of the musical language:

During the transition of absolute music from harmonic artificiality to sheer melodic vacuity, more would have been lost than gained, since the change occurred through an ill-conceived attempt to imitate theatrical style and not through a gradual inner evolution, were it not for the sudden, fortuitous emergence of a man in Germany who seized the reins of the declining art of music, who combined originality with profound learning, and opened up a path for absolute music which might otherwise never have been dreamt of.[52]

This man, 'a musical Klopstock',[53] was Carl Philipp Emanuel Bach.

The 'wealth of ideas' found in his sonatas and fantasias would 'frighten away rather than attract most musical amateurs. Yet this is not to deny its great merit; rather it enhances it, for thus did Bach show that absolute music is no mere cover for 'applied' music, nor in some way derived from it, but can achieve great things in its own right. Absolute music has no need to pose as mere prosaic or at best rhetorical play with meanings or concepts, for it is capable of reaching the heights of poetry, and poetry is all the more pure the less it is dragged down into the realm of common meaning by words (which always introduce secondary ideas)'.[54]

Thus in Carl Philipp Emanuel Bach's work, according to Triest, instrumental music of the eighteenth century reached its first peak.

However accurate Triest's evaluation may appear at first sight, it

---

[47] J. K. F. Triest, 'Bemerkungen über die Ausbildung der Tonkunst in Deutschland im achtzehnten Jahrhundert', *AMZ*, iii (1800–1), cols. 225ff. (Published in instalments—it comes to an end in col. 445.)

[48] C. Dahlhaus, 'Zur Entstehung der romantischen Bach-Deutung', *B-Jb*, lxiv (1978), p. 207. This article was to prove a powerful stimulus to the discussion of these issues.

[49] Triest, op. cit., col. 297.   [50] Dahlhaus, op. cit., p. 207.   [51] Ibid.

[52] Triest, op. cit., col. 299.   [53] Ibid., cols. 300f.   [54] Ibid., col. 301.

has its tendentious side: trapped within this narrow outlook, he is less favourably disposed towards the great musical achievements of the intervening decades. In Haydn's *Creation*, 'the supreme skill of this composer is squandered on an unworthy text, to the detriment of art'.[55] Mozart's instrumental music, it is alleged, suffers from 'overloaded accompaniments'.[56] '. . . thus one is led to the conclusion that in the field of pure music Mozart was great, very great indeed, but not unsurpassable.'[57] Notwithstanding his high regard for the other areas of Haydn's and Mozart's output, his openly-declared favourite remained Carl Philipp Emanuel Bach. Triest was especially committed to the musical culture of the Enlightenment.[58]

Triest was writing before the enormous wave of enthusiasm for the music of J. S. Bach, an enthusiasm he did not share (it would in any case have been incompatible with his philosophy); it was Felix Mendelssohn Bartholdy and Robert Schumann who later ushered it in. He was also largely unimpressed by the music of the young Beethoven, although he believed him to possess the potential to become a great artist, provided that 'the wild raving' in his music were to abate;[59] on the other hand, the Beethoven experience burst upon E. T. A. Hoffmann with sheer elemental power.

The positive evaluation that Bach's keyboard music received in Triest's essay was soon to be replaced by the complete opposite: C. P. E. Bach's music was dismissed by some writers as meaningless. The performance of Bach's keyboard works aroused E. T. A. Hoffmann's displeasure: 'Just how laughable and empty these concertos were in many places I realized only later. My teacher would usually play two harpsichord concertos by Wolf or Emanuel Bach.'[60] Simply an aversion to the music of an earlier generation?[61] A more important factor lay in the re-evaluation of the processes of eighteenth-century musical history in the light of the Romantic aesthetic. Triest's concept of 'pure poetic music' was significantly modified by E. T. A. Hoff-

[55] Ibid., col. 409.
[56] Ibid., col. 393.
[57] Ibid.
[58] This is also revealed in Triest's tribute to the Berlin music theorists Kirnberger and Marpurg, whose writings 'even today (as proof of their excellence) enjoy canonical status'. Ibid., col. 304.
[59] Ibid., col. 408.
[60] Quoted in E. T. A. Hoffmann, *Schriften zur Musik. Nachlese* (Munich, 1963), p. 467.
[61] The following is an extract from Hoffmann's *Musikfeind*: 'When a long piece of this kind was eventually over, then everyone would cry out loud and shout, 'Bravo, Bravo! what marvellous music! how expertly, how roundly played!' and would pronounce with great respect the name Emanuel Bach! The father, though, always hammered and pounded away so much, that it always seemed to me that this could scarcely be termed music.' Quoted in Hoffmann, *Schriften zur Musik*, p. 467.

mann, who adapted ideas from Wackenroder and Tieck: 'Music opens up for man an unknown world which has nothing in common with the external world surrounding him, and in which he leaves behind all particular sensations in order to abandon himself completely to inexpressible longing.'[62] Here the breakaway from the conceptual world of the Enlightenment is completed once and for all. Flight into the realm of art meant flight away from social reality. The ideals and perspectives of Enlightenment thinkers proved illusory in the light of post-Revolutionary developments.

Music, according to E. T. A. Hoffmann, was able to communicate the supernatural, the transcendental. The very quality in J. S. Bach's music which Triest still regarded as a deficiency, that is its 'rhetorical' character, was seen by Hoffmann as a manifestation of this same transcendental quality:

There are moments, usually when I have been reading widely in the music of the great Sebastian Bach, when the mathematical proportions of music, and the mystical rules of counterpoint arouse in me an inner awe. O Music!—with secret fear, yes, with trepidation do I pronounce your name!—O Sanskrit of nature expressed in sound![63]

In spite of its metaphysical overtones this evaluation of J. S. Bach by E. T. A. Hoffmann reveals the beginnings of genuinely historical thinking. J. S. Bach's counterpoint, which belongs to a different tradition from the music of Carl Philipp Emanuel, constitutes not only an unsurpassed historical achievement, but also an inexhaustible corpus of music able both to fire the creative imagination of Mendelssohn and Schumann and to be ranked on its own merit as a high point of 'absolute' music by the author of *Lebensansichten des Kater Murr*.

Certainly the proximity of Triest to Carl Philipp Emanuel Bach's music coloured his assessment of this composer.[64] E. T. A. Hoffmann, viewing Bach from a somewhat greater historical perspective, which allowed him to survey the development of musical history as far as late Beethoven, came to an altogether different assessment. For him, although he never said so explicitly, Carl Philipp Emanuel Bach's music marked the beginning of a process which culminated in the

[62] E. T. A. Hoffmann, *Musikalische Schriften*, ed. E. Istel (Stuttgart, n.d.), p. 86.

[63] Ibid., p. 96.

[64] The following statement by Triest also betrays his preference for the musical world of the Enlightenment: 'Which lover of music is there who does not name with gratitude Graun, Hasse, C. P. E. Bach etc., even if he has little or no further contact with their music?—Who will not allow that it was they who transformed the fertile seed into lovely blossoms, and who conjured up the joyful springtide which spread so lovingly over German music, hitherto almost purely mechanical, but now able at last to lay claim to the name of great art?' Triest [n. 47 above] col. 264.

works of Mozart and Beethoven.[65] In any event the idea of a large-scale historical continuity is indicated here. Schumann was to express this idea more overtly: 'As a keyboard composer he [C. P. E. Bach] was a pioneer, for his works, with their free improvisatory dynamism, while lacking the greatness of his father's music, are to be regarded as the first in this style that are connected with the period of Haydn and Mozart.'[66]

Schumann also perceived correctly the progressive features in the music of J. S. Bach's second son: 'He filed, he refined, he caused a beautiful cantilena to flow through the then predominating harmony and *Figuren*, and yet', continued the composer of the *Davidsbündlertänze*, 'as a creative musician he remained very far behind his father. As Mendelssohn once said, "it was as if a dwarf had appeared among the giants."'[67] It need come as no surprise that Schumann rated Carl Philipp Emanuel Bach's music relatively low in view of his remark about Haydn: '. . . [he] has ceased to arouse any particular interest.'[68]

In view of the kind of music being composed at the time when they were writing, Schumann and E. T. A. Hoffmann could hardly have done other than arrive at these mistaken judgements. Composers had long since adopted an altogether different style of melody, their harmonic vocabulary had been greatly enlarged, and so had the possibilities for using tone colour. Considerable technical innovations had been made in the construction of pianos. After 1821 Sébastien Erard's double escapement action, which greatly improved repetition, began to establish itself. Bach's *Versuch über die wahre Art das Clavier zu spielen* was followed by the treatises of Clementi, Cramer, Czerny, Hummel, Kalkbrenner, Moscheles, and others. The public acquired new favourites: Mozart, Weber, Spontini, and Rossini for opera, Hummel, Moscheles, and Mendelssohn for keyboard music.

In such an environment the music of C. P. E. Bach was bound to appear antiquated. The kind of reception given to the music of Bach's contemporaries may be gauged from the following review of a Passion cantata by Carl Heinrich Graun, contained in the sixth issue of *Iris im Gebiete der Tonkunst* (1835).

This work undoubtedly possesses historical interest . . . it illustrates well a gentle approach to melody and a concern for gracefulness even in the strict style . . . One also notices the emphasis on arias, and this very quality rather

---

[65] 'Haydn, Mozart, Beethoven developed a new art, the first seeds of which probably went back no further than the middle of the eighteenth century.' Hoffmann, *Musikalische Schriften*, p. 247.

[66] R. Schumann, *Gesammelte Schriften*, ii, p. 201 [Introduction, n. 11].

[67] Ibid., i, p. 11, and *On Music and Musicians*, p. 67 [Introduction, n. 11].

[68] R. Schumann, *Gesammelte Schriften*, ii, p. 54, and *On Music and Musicians*, p. 94.

spoils the work, for it gives rise to monotony and a lack of interest which in time becomes a great deficiency . . . Incidentally in our view it would be better to perform good modern music rather than old-fashioned works by composers long since dead. For the present also has its rights.[69]

It required a new historical awareness with all the consequences for music-making that that entailed to bring the 'stile antico' of J. S. Bach back to life in the context of the nineteenth century. Even Zelter expressed doubts as to whether the St Matthew Passion would succeed with the public. When Felix Mendelssohn Bartholdy performed this work with the Berlin *Singakademie* on 11 March 1829 after it had remained in obscurity for 100 years, the applause of the public was overwhelming. Thus was the Bach revival launched, the ground having been prepared for it by the Romantic musical aesthetic. The music of C. P. E. Bach, however, was denied a wider acceptance.

Yet he was not entirely forgotten, even in the nineteenth century. A small circle of music historians took an interest in Bach's music.[70] Composers discovered many original features in his work. Johannes Brahms's lively interest in the music of the past is well known. Scores, many of them in his own hand, of works by Palestrina, Schütz, J. S. Bach, Handel, Gluck, Mozart, and Beethoven formed a part of his library, and served him as an indispensable aid for his work and as a source of creative inspiration.[71] He also possessed music by C. P. E. Bach.[72] Brahms edited two of Bach's sonatas which were published by J. Rieter-Biedermann (Leipzig and Winterthur, 1864). The choice—the Sonatas in B minor, Wq. 76, and in C minor, Wq. 78, both for violin and keyboard—was his own, and he prepared the edition with characteristic scholarly precision and a profound knowledge of Bach's style. Brahms openly expressed his keen admiration for this music.[73]

Certain details in Bach's keyboard music also had an impact on the 'speaking and singing *espressivo*' in Carl Maria von Weber's sonatas.[74] Heinrich Schenker proposes, albeit very cautiously, a continuous tradition in the history of keyboard music from Bach through to

[69] *Iris im Gebiete der Tonkunst*, vi (1835), p. 72.

[70] See pp. 207f. below for further details.

[71] See F. Grasberger, *Johannes Brahms* (Vienna, 1952), pp. 124ff.

[72] See M. Kalbeck, *Johannes Brahms*, 4 vols. (Vienna and Leipzig, 1904–14), i, p. 269; F. Grasberger, *Johannes Brahms* (Vienna, 1952), pp. 124ff.

[73] The C minor Sonata, Wq. 78, for example, was performed at the end of 1863 at a concert in Vienna. See Kalbeck, op. cit., ii, p. 105. Brahms wrote in a letter that should he discover any more sonatas of such beauty, he would send them to a publisher. See Kalbeck, op. cit., ii, p. 108.

[74] E. Bücken, *Die Musik des 19. Jahrhunderts bis zur Moderne* (Wildpark-Potsdam, 1929–31), p. 64.

Chopin.[75] Certainly in artistic outlook and compositional practice these two masters stand worlds apart, and yet they nevertheless have some features in common. When Georgii, describing the most conspicuous qualities of Bach's late fantasias, refers to 'the Romantic jaggedness of form and the subjective, improvisatory expression',[76] he puts his finger on these common features. It will be the task of future Bach scholarship to treat all his music, especially the late works, to a complex comparative stylistic analysis, in order the better to elucidate such wide-ranging interconnections.

Notes on the history of Carl Philipp Emanuel Bach Scholarship I. Beginnings and first results

Scholarly consideration of Bach's music began strictly speaking while the composer was still alive. As creations of an *Originalgenie* his works attracted the attention of contemporary musical criticism and theory. Many musical journals in the eighteenth century featured detailed reviews of Bach's works, information about performances and forthcoming publications, or biographical references. Attempts were already being made, for example by Forkel, Reichardt, and Schubart, to assess more precisely Bach's artistic personality, the character and achievement of his output, and his position in musical history.

In the nineteenth century, with the onset of a musical historiography orientated towards the phenomenon of the great composer, C. P. E. Bach was either completely ignored, or else dismissed as a mere 'precursor'. The importance of his work was assessed by the extent to which it had contributed to the development of the 'golden age'[77] of Haydn and Mozart. Neither the intrinsic merit of Bach's music nor its historical setting could possibly be understood given such an approach. Writers attempted to compensate for gaps in their knowledge of the man and his music by introducing anecdotal material. Consequently there were some glaring errors.

A serious instance of this is found in an article in the *Allgemeine musikalische Zeitung* (1799–1800), which, on account of its tendency to

---

[75] 'In fact it is precisely on account of his imaginative ornamentation and passage-work that Bach can be hailed as the most truly poetic keyboard composer. I would personally go so far as to rate him higher as a composer specifically for the keyboard than even a Haydn or a Mozart, for whom orchestral and symphonic thinking had begun to undermine their idiomatic keyboard style; I would almost align him with Schumann and Chopin.' Schenker, op. cit., p. 26 [Chapter 2, n. 128].

[76] Georgii, op. cit., p. 199 [Chapter 3, n. 210].

[77] This formulation is found in W. C. Müller, *Aesthetisch-historische Einleitungen in die Wissenschaft der Tonkunst* (Leipzig, 1830), ii, p. 4, in the list of contents under the heading 'Neunter Zeitraum, von 1775 bis 1800'.

generalize, favoured the growth of legends; among other things, it
delayed for a long time an accurate assessment of the personality of
W. F. Bach.[78]

Some joker or other has characterized the three Bach brothers as artists in a
most telling manner: Friedemann (the Hallè Bach) is a master in light and
shade, Emanuel (the Hamburg Bach) in dark colours, and Christian (the
London Bach) in colourful floral designs derived from nature. Perhaps one
might distinguish them not only as artists but also, to some extent, as men (for
the two are surely inseparable) as follows: Friedemann wished in his work to
please only himself, Emanuel was more concerned to please connoisseurs *and*
amateurs, and Christian was more concerned to please amateurs and
virtuosos. Friedemann therefore repelled, Emanuel interested, Christian was
loved. Friedemann remained coarse, Emanuel cultivated, Christian polished.
Friedemann suffered want, Emanuel had enough, Christian earned enough to
live extravagantly. Friedemann moved around, Emanuel settled in Hamburg,
Christian in London. Friedemann made mostly enemies, Emanuel many
friends, Christian even more companions. Friedemann thought moderately
well of the middle brother, despised the youngest; Emanuel esteemed the
eldest highly, the youngest moderately; Christian laughed at them both.
Friedemann drank and then could not write; Emanuel did not drink but did
write; Christian drank and then wrote.[79]

This characterization is probably by Friedrich Rochlitz. Rochlitz
declared himself passionately in favour of the rediscovery of forgotten
composers,[80] although his efforts on behalf of C. P. E. Bach had no
significant practical consequences. Bach's works continued to be
performed only rarely. None the less there were some music historians—besides Rochlitz these included Nägeli, Kiesewetter, and Schilling[81]—who made efforts to secure appropriate recognition for this
composer.

---

[78] The account 'Sebastian Bach und seine Söhne' by J. P. Burmeister-Lyser printed in *Neue
Zeitschrift für Musik*, iv (Leipzig, 1836, R/Scarsdale, 1963), pp. 87ff. (published in instalments:
ends on p. 216) presents a picture of W. F. Bach just as misleading as that given some twenty
years later in Brachvogel's Friedemann Bach novel. Biographical circumstances and personal
characteristics are invented and adapted with no little sentimentality to suit the stereotype of the
'artist', amid frequent appeals to 'fate' in order to solve problems of biographical detail. Little
though W. F. Bach may have been able to assume control of his life, it would scarcely have been
possible for him—passionately committed to music as he was—to find a niche for himself in
society at the time. His biography confirms that 'the ideal of the free artist, ever-present before
him, and in search of which he discarded his ties to an official post, could not yet be realized.'
F. Blume, 'Bach, Wilhelm Friedemann', *MGG*, i, col. 1054.

[79] *AMZ*, ii (1799–1800), cols. 829f. n.

[80] Rochlitz wrote accounts of Hiller, Rolle, Reichardt, and Danzi.

[81] See the following studies: H. G. Nägeli, op. cit. [Chapter 3, n. 213]; R. G. Kiesewetter,
Geschichte der europäisch-abendländischen oder unsrer heutigen Musik, 2nd edn. (Leipzig, 1846);
G. Schilling, (ed.) 'Bach, Carl Philipp Emanuel', *Encyclopädie der gesammten musikalischen Wissen-
schaften oder Universal-Lexicon der Tonkunst*, i (Stuttgart, 1835, R/Hildesheim, 1974), pp. 38off.

Rochlitz's widely-circulated collection of essays *Für Freunde der Tonkunst* (1824–32) contains a fine article on C. P. E. Bach. The author gives numerous biographical details and offers a brief characterization of individual groups of works, with many penetrating observations on the originality of Bach's instrumental music.[82] Another text which deserves attention is *Vorlesungen über Musik* (1826) by the Swiss music theorist Hans Georg Nägeli, in which he discusses the physiognomy of Bach's music. He praises Bach's 'skill in variation both on a large and on a small scale', the 'superiority ... of his rhythms', his 'variety and perfection of construction', and 'aesthetic tenderness'.[83]

During the 1850s and 60s, musical scholarship underwent an enormous upsurge. Sources were thoroughly investigated according to more sophisticated philological methods. The first complete editions, thematic catalogues, and monographs were produced, remarkable achievements which are still today regarded as standard works. Friedrich Chrysander began to publish his pioneering work on Handel in 1858, while in 1866 there appeared Alexander Wheelock Thayer's several-volume Beethoven biography. Philipp Spitta assembled the material for his work on J. S. Bach. A thematic catalogue of the works of Gluck was produced by Aloys Fuchs in 1851, and the first edition of Ludwig Alois Friedrich von Köchel's catalogue of the works of Mozart followed in 1862.

All these activities were to benefit C. P. E. Bach research, the true beginning of which may be placed in 1868, the year in which Carl Hermann Bitter's book *Carl Philipp Emanuel Bach und Wilhelm Friedemann Bach und deren Brüder* appeared. This, the first large-scale monograph on

---

[82] Rochlitz writes as follows: 'So Emanuel Bach's keyboard pieces, especially those for solo keyboard, contain not only many virtues taught by the old school—in so far as these are compatible with the newer style—but also, quite artlessly and unaffectedly, the unique spirit, the personal emotional stamp of the composer; they exhibit plainly the unmistakable traits of that light, teasing, excitable, volatile, and whimsical personality. The more he learned to project himself as he grew older, the more he projected these very qualities; and since it was they first and foremost which led the experts (especially in Germany and England) to recognize and admire his originality, he cultivated them all the more, enlarged his range of expression, and applied them all the more rigorously; all this with such ease, variety, and skill as never to suggest that it was deliberate, but rather, however miraculously the music seemed to issue forth, always convincing the listener that it could not possibly be expressed in any other way. And this is doubtless what Papa Haydn meant when he declared Bach to have been in some sense his teacher; it was, in a word, not merely the release of the creative spirit from all that had been simply conventional in earlier music, but also the fluency or rather the complete mastery behind the individual fingerprints and changing moods of this great composer, if not in all areas of his output, then certainly in instrumental performance and composition.' Rochlitz, op. cit., iv, pp. 299f.

[83] Nägeli, op. cit., pp. 137, 140. [Chapter 3, n. 213. The original phrases are as follows: 'Kunst, im Grossen und Feinen zu variiren', 'Überlegenheit ... in seiner Rhythmik', 'Mannigfaltigkeit und Idealität der Construction', and 'ästhetisches Zartgefühl'.]

the life and work of the master, contains much documentary material
which goes back to Westphal, together with a survey of the music, but
it gives a one-sided picture of Bach, devoid of any socio-historical
context, a picture of an artist working almost entirely in a vacuum. A
fresh impulse came from a scholar who strangely had little time for
C. P. E. Bach's music: in 1897 Hugo Riemann published an essay on
the sons of the Leipzig Cantor.[84] He prefaced his ideas, however, with
the caveat that he was not in a position to reach any definitive
conclusions concerning their role in the emergence of the Classical
style, for this would require many years of detailed study. Riemann in
any event viewed the revolution that occurred in eighteenth-century
music primarily under the heading of a 'Mannheim stylistic reform'.[85]
He devoted lengthy sections of his *Handbuch der Musikgeschichte* to the
Mannheim composers and published his valuable editions of
Mannheim symphonies and chamber works in the *Denkmäler Deutscher
Tonkunst*. Attention was thus directed towards a period hitherto
neglected in musical historiography, and it was to be only a short time
before further studies of C. P. E. Bach appeared, a development which
was to continue unabated, and in which an important landmark was
reached in 1905: in that year the Belgian musicologist and archivist
Alfred Wotquenne[86] produced a work which is still indispensable for
both scholar and performer, even if open to criticism in some of its
methodology, namely his *Thematisches Verzeichnis der Werke von Carl
Philipp Emanuel Bach*.[87]

The Fate of the Bach Manuscripts

At the time when Wotquenne was working on his catalogue, the
majority of extant autographs, manuscript copies, and first editions of
Bach's music were already concentrated in two libraries, the Royal

[84] Riemann, op. cit. [Chapter 2, n. 125].

[85] See the section 'Die Mannheimer Stilreform' in H. Riemann, *Handbuch der Musikgeschichte*, ii,
Part 3 (Leipzig, 1913), pp. 127ff.

[86] Among Wotquenne's innumerable other bibliographical works may be mentioned his
Catalogue thématique des œuvres de Chr. W. Gluck (Leipzig, 1904), and a study of the works of
B. Galuppi (1902).

[87] Since Wotquenne divides Bach's works into those surviving in printed sources and those
surviving only in manuscript sources, a chronological ordering is possible only to a limited extent.
The classification adopted is also unconvincing in other respects; for example, solo keyboard
music is subdivided into sonatas and other works, with chamber music and other genres listed in
between. Since Wotquenne's day further works by Bach have been discovered, details of some of
which may be found in Schmid, 'C. P. E. Bach', Beurmann, op. cit., Busch, op. cit., Suchalla, op.
cit., P. Kast, *Die Bach-Handschriften der Berliner Staatsbibliothek* (Trossingen, 1958). For full details
see E. E. Helm, *Thematic Catalogue*, in which Bach's works are listed chronologically within each
medium.

Library in Berlin (now the Deutsche Staatsbibliothek in East Berlin) and the library of the Conservatoire Royal de Musique in Brussels. The holdings of these two libraries today constitute the core of extant Bach source material. In addition there are further sources scattered throughout the world, in private possession or else catalogued in libraries, conservatoires, concert societies, ecclesiastical establishments and so on. Nevertheless a great many printed and manuscript copies of numerous works that were in use during Bach's lifetime are now lost or unlocated. The autograph scores of *Die Israeliten in der Wüste* and *Klopstocks Morgengesang am Schöpfungsfeste* have vanished without trace. According to Ernst Suchalla only 50 out of 131 known orchestral works have survived in autograph.[88] According to RISM the first edition of the song collection *Psalms translated by Dr. Cramer with melodies to sing at the keyboard*, of which 1,050 copies were issued, is at present available in only thirty-seven libraries throughout the world.[89] Only twenty-three copies of the original edition of the Prussian Sonatas[90] are listed, while just a single set of printed parts of the E minor Symphony, Wq. 177, has been located, namely the source owned by the Library of Harvard University.[91]

It is not possible to reconstruct even approximately the route taken by the manuscripts of C. P. E. Bach's music individually. After Bach's death his widow offered his estate on sale to the public. In the *Verzeichnis des musikalischen Nachlasses des verstorbenen Capellmeisters Carl Philipp Emanuel Bach*, printed in 1790, one reads: 'Music-lovers who wish to purchase any of this estate may apply to Herr Kapellmeister Bach's widow in Hamburg.'[92] The estate consisted of:

1. Instrumental compositions.
2. Vocal compositions.
3. Mixed pieces.
4. Works by J. S. Bach, W. F. Bach, J. C. F. Bach, J. C. Bach (the London Bach), J. Bernhard Bach.
5. The Bach family archives.
6. Music by various composers.
7. Instruments.
8. A collection of portraits of famous musicians.
9. A collection of silhouettes of famous musicians, together with an appended list of various extant drawings by J. S. Bach the

---

[88] See Suchalla, op. cit., p. 141.
[89] RISM, *Einzeldrucke vor 1800*, i, p. 167 [n. 4 above].
[90] Ibid., p. 163.
[91] Ibid., p. 162.
[92] See R. W. Wade, *The Catalog of Carl Philipp Emanuel Bach's Estate*, facsimile of title-page.

younger, who died in August [*sic*, actually September] 1778 in Rome, and by some others.[93]

Thanks to good fortune and the collector's instincts of music-lovers this estate has been largely preserved, together with major works by J. S. Bach such as the St John Passion, the St Matthew Passion, the B minor Mass and the 'Art of Fugue'. That a great deal has nevertheless been lost—plenty of music was actually discarded by the composer himself—shows that Bach's heirs were hardly aware of the great value of the music in their custody:

... its value was assessed in terms of its practical usefulness without reference to the ideal status of an original manuscript according to our understanding. This can be seen particularly clearly from the auction catalogue of the estate of Anna Carolina Bach, Philipp Emanuel's daughter, a few years later in 1805, when Bach's works were no longer offered singly, but were grouped together in lots ... 'One large lot with Passion settings, dramas, cantatas, etc.' (No. 128) we read therein, and no distinction is made between autographs and copies.[94]

By far the greater part of this estate was acquired by the private scholar Georg Poelchau.[95] He had lived for some years in Hamburg and he moved to Berlin in 1813, where he worked as singer and archivist for the *Singakademie*. His extensive collection of books and music—besides the Bachiana this included autographs of works by Haydn, Mozart, and Beethoven, valuable editions of theoretical treatises from the sixteenth and seventeenth centuries, parts of the former Hamburg Opera Library, including among other things scores of Keiser's operas, plus the Schwenke estate acquired in 1824—all this he eventually offered for sale to the Royal Library in Berlin. It was only in 1841, however, five years after his death, that the sale for 6,000 Thalers was finally concluded.

Sara Levy, née Itzig, had asked Bach's widow for an accurate inventory of the music in her husband's estate within months of his death. This Johanna Maria Bach duly sent to her in a letter dated 5 September 1789,[96] and no doubt she purchased one or two items from it. Her previously-acquired collection of music probably passed to Carl Friedrich Zelter, who performed a great deal of instrumental

[93] Ibid.

[94] W. Schmieder, 'Die Handschriften Johann Sebastian Bachs', *Bach-Gedenkschrift* (Zurich, 1950), pp. 190f.

[95] G. Poelchau collected Bach manuscripts systematically. 'Thus for instance in 1814, while looking through some "papers in the estate of the pianist Palschau from St Petersburg that were being sent to the dairy", he discovered an autograph of three violin sonatas by J. S. Bach.' See Schmieder, op. cit., p. 195n.

[96] The letter is quoted in full in Bitter, op. cit., ii, pp. 307ff.

music in addition to one or two of C. P. E. Bach's larger vocal works.[97]

Zelter had in any event assembled a substantial library of music and theoretical writings in his capacity as director of the *Singakademie*, and it must be said that he did not always distinguish clearly between his own property and that of the *Singakademie*. Consequently there was a dispute after his death in 1833, which was resolved by the payment of compensation to his heirs.[98] Zelter's estate was thus acquired by the *Singakademie*. (Another part of this choral society's library of Bachiana can probably be traced back to Babette Itzig, Sara Levy's sister, and like her a passionate admirer of C. P. E. Bach's music. Babette Itzig may have left the Bach material to her grandson, Felix Mendelssohn Bartholdy, who could then have handed it on to his teacher Zelter, as Suchalla suggests.[99]) Finding itself in financial difficulties, the *Singakademie* then sold its library for 1,400 Thalers to the Royal Library in 1854.

Through gifts and purchases, the Bach collection in the Royal Library continued to grow; among other collections, the estate of the folk-song researcher Ludwig Christian Erk, that of Joseph Fischhof, a piano teacher at the Konservatorium of the Gesellschaft der Musikfreunde in Vienna, that of the Greifswald lawyer Johann Heinrich Grave, and that of the Count of Voss-Buch were acquired.

A further collection of music found its way into this library in 1914: the *Amalienbibliothek*, which has a history of its own. Anna Amalia was, as mentioned earlier, a keen collector of music by the Bachs, both father and son. She admired particularly the great vocal compositions of C. P. E. Bach, and possessed scores of the Passion Cantata, Wq. 233, the Magnificat, Wq. 215, *Die Israeliten in der Wüste*, Wq. 238, and the *Heilig*, Wq. 217.[100] Her library was bequeathed in 1787 to the Joachimsthal Gymnasium and was later dispersed still further in the estates of Schaffrath and Kirnberger, both of whom had received numerous copies of chamber works and concertos by C. P. E. Bach. This suggests that Bach's works were frequently performed during the lifetime of the Princess and of her circle of musicians, to which both Kirnberger and Schaffrath belonged. (By contrast the music collection in the King's own library contained only three items by C. P. E. Bach, compared with almost a thousand by Johann Joachim Quantz, a further indication that Frederick the Great had no particular admiration

---

[97] See Schünemann, op. cit., pp. 28, 44, 49, 83 [Chapter 3, n. 259].
[98] See Suchalla, op. cit., p. 144.   [99] Ibid.
[100] See nos. 85, 87, 88, and 170 in the *Amalienbibliothek* as listed in Blechschmidt, op. cit. [Chapter 2, n. 55].

for the music of his court harpsichordist.[101]) When the Joachimsthal Gymnasium was being moved to Templin, the Prussian authorities decided that the performing material should be transferred to the Royal Library and housed there in a separate collection as the former *Amalienbibliothek*. During the Second World War the Bach manuscripts and early editions were moved out temporarily from the Prussian State Library (as the Royal Library became known in 1918) to a variety of storage depots. Some works are since assumed to have been lost. The present Deutsche Staatsbibliothek contains the following works in Bach's autograph: keyboard sonatas and other pieces (from Wq. 49–53, 62, 65, 112, 116–18), chamber music (Wq. 75–8, 80, 84, 88–91, 143, 145–9, 151, 155, 157, 163), a sonatina with orchestra (Wq. 96), concertos (Wq. 2, 3, 7–9, 11, 12, 15, 17–20, 23, 25, 27, 30–38, 41, 44–6, 164, 165, 169, 170), symphonies (Wq. 174, 181, 183), songs (from Wq. 194, 196, 198–200, 202), 'Two Litanies' (Wq. 204), the Magnificat (Wq. 215), choruses (Wq. 218, 224, 226, 228), the Passion Cantata (Wq. 233), Passion settings (Wq. 234, 235), 'Selma' (Wq. 236), *Carl Wilhelm Rammlers Auferstehung und Himmelfahrt Jesu* (Wq. 240), Easter cantatas (Wq. 243, 244), Michaelmas cantatas (Wq. 247, 248), congratulatory cantatas (Wq. 250, 252), and other works not mentioned by Wotquenne.[102]

Another channel through which manuscript material has come down to us has its origins not in Bach's estate, but in the collection built up by Johann Jakob Heinrich Westphal, organist at the Schwerin Court. As we know, the latter corresponded with C. P. E. Bach, and acquired numerous manuscript copies, first editions, and probably even autographs of Bach's works during the composer's lifetime.[103] Moreover Westphal prepared an important thematic catalogue of Bach's works, which served Wotquenne as the basis of his own catalogue, and an equally important manuscript entitled 'Collected reports of the life and works of Herr Carl Philipp Emanuel Bach, Kapellmeister in Hamburg, together with assorted reviews and critical accounts of his published works'. After Westphal's death in 1825 his heirs tried in vain 'to deliver the collection into good hands. Proposals to offer or sell it to the Prussian or the Austrian State, the city of Hamburg, the Grand Duke of Mecklenburg, the King of Saxony,

---

[101] See G. Thouret, *Katalog der Musiksammlung auf der Königlichen Hausbibliothek im Schlosse zu Berlin* (Leipzig, 1895).

[102] See Kast, op. cit [n. 87 above].

[103] See C. P. E. Bach's letter of 9 Jan. 1787 to J. J. H. Westphal: 'In case you should want something of mine I wish you would come to me direct. I would be very glad to accommodate you without asking any real profit for myself—only enough for the copyists.' Quoted from M. Terry, 'C. P. E. Bach and J. J. H. Westphal. A Clarification', *JAMS*, xxii (1969), p. 108.

Prince Oscar of Sweden, were either abandoned or else the offers were refused.'[104] Between 1835 and 1840, François-Joseph Fétis, who had been the Director of the Brussels Conservatoire since 1833, acquired this collection, which eventually found its way into the library of that institution in 1840.[105] During the nineteenth century the Conservatoire also purchased the estate of the Marburg physician, Professor Richard Wagener, with the result that the Brussels library today owns the second largest collection of C. P. E. Bach source material after the Deutsche Staatsbibliothek, including the autographs of some solo sonatas (Wq. 123–31) and those of four of the six 'string symphonies' (Wq. 182 nos. 2–5).

Closely linked to bibliographical and scholarly investigation of these sources is the study of Bach's handwriting. In this matter important work has been done, particularly in connection with the critical reports prepared for the *Neue Bach Ausgabe* and in the *Tübinger Bach-Studien*. Detailed information has been assembled concerning Bach's style of writing at many different stages in his life [Plate 10], his copyists, types of paper, pagination, and so forth.

Georg von Dadelsen describes the characteristic features of Bach's musical script as follows:

The most conspicuous elements in general are the small and slightly tremulous note-shapes. Undoubtedly the gout which afflicted Philipp Emanuel from his thirtieth year onwards left its mark on his writing.[106]

For the young Bach, 'extraordinarily sweeping, large spacious writing' is characteristic.[107]

In spite of many changes a few elements remain unaltered from his earliest years right up to old age. In the first place mention should be made of the shape of his stave brackets and the extra thickness of lower slurs. This stands out clearly in the thickening of the lower half of void note-heads, and may be seen especially in the lengthening of letters and symbols written in a horizontal left-to-right direction, usually emphasized with strong pressure on the quill: bass-clefs, C-clefs, crotchet rests. The prominent thickening of some quaver beams is again common in later sources.[108]

For completeness mention may also be made of Bach's use of wedges to indicate staccato, while dots indicate *Bebung* and portato.[109]

---

[104] See Suchalla, op. cit., p. 146. Original source: Clemens Meyer, 'Geschichtliche Darstellung der Mecklenburg-Schweriner Hofkapelle', *Geschichtliche Darstellung der Mecklenburg-Schweriner Hofkapelle von Anfang des 16. Jahrhunderts bis zur Gegenwart* (Schwerin i. M., 1913), p. 250.

[105] Suchalla, op. cit., pp. 147f.

[106] Dadelsen, op. cit., p. 37 [Chapter 1, n. 36].

[107] Ibid.   [108] Ibid., p. 38.

[109] See Chapter 2, n. 117.

Notes on the history of Carl Philipp Emanuel Bach Scholarship II.
Continuation, Trends, and Prospects

For several decades music publishers virtually ignored C. P. E. Bach's music. The first to show an interest in it in the later nineteenth century was the French publisher Aristide Farrenc who issued a large selection of sonatas, rondos etc. in his twenty-volume collection *Le trésor des pianistes* (Paris, 1861–72). A further important publication was the Krebs Urtext edition of *Six collections of sonatas, fantasias, and rondos 'für Kenner und Liebhaber'* (Leipzig, 1895), which was subsequently reissued several times. Arnold Schering published the D minor Harpsichord Concerto, Wq. 23, in the series *Denkmäler Deutscher Tonkunst*, complete with a detailed commentary and critical report. Since then many individual works have appeared in print, admittedly with no guarantee of complete textual authenticity.

These editions were to benefit not only music-making, but also scholarship. On them Rudolf Steglich was able to base the penetrating analyses contained in his article 'Karl Philipp Emanuel Bach und der Dresdner Kreuzkantor Gottfried August Homilius im Musikleben ihrer Zeit' (1915). Steglich declared Bach's central compositional principle to be the 'thematic manipulation of pliable [*wandlungsfähig*] motives'.[110] Arnold Schering has drawn attention to another essential element of Bach's musical language: in keeping with the requirement of eighteenth-century musical aesthetics that music should 'speak', the 'rhetorical principle' is of particular significance for Bach's compositional thought.[111] Another important contribution by Schering was the attempt 'to place Bach in the paradox-ridden artistic climate of his generation, and to understand his music in terms of the general, that is to say, not specifically musical, artistic principles of that generation'.[112] And with reference to future research, he declared: 'Except for biographical studies, Philipp Emanuel Bach scholarship is still in its infancy. In future it will have to broaden its scope, and to examine critically the musical philosophy of the entire century in the process.'[113]

This challenge has since been taken up by several scholars.[114] Among the significant contributions made to Bach literature in intervening years are the writings of Miesner, Schmid, Plamenac, Beurmann, Haag, Jurisch, Busch, Müller, Randebrock, Wyler, Jacobs, Barford, Brewer, Helm, Wade, and Suchalla.[115] Monographs, analyses, and larger studies have been made of most areas of Bach's

---

[110] Steglich, op. cit., p. 112.   [111] Schering, 'C. P. E. Bach', pp. 13ff.   [112] Ibid., p. 14.
[113] Ibid., p. 29.   [114] See Bibliography.   [115] For full references see Bibliography.

output—keyboard sonatas, keyboard fantasias, keyboard concertos, chamber music, symphonies, songs, oratorios.[116] E. H. Meyer has frequently underlined the key position held by C. P. E. Bach in the development of music in the eighteenth century: 'I find it necessary to stress the continuity which links the key stages in musical Classicism: J. S. Bach–Handel, C. P. E. Bach–Gluck, and Haydn–Mozart–Beethoven.'[117] In the work of C. P. E. Bach Hanns Eisler sees an illustration of the idea of progress in music. Here it is, according to Eisler, that 'a new expressivity, a new emotional style of music, and also, from a technical point of view, music with contrasts'[118] is realized.

Since 1975 major research projects in C. P. E. Bach scholarship have been in progress at the Konzerthalle in Frankfurt an der Oder, which bears the name of the composer. In addition to the collection and cataloguing of source material, work on modern editions, and specific studies, the years ahead will see a number of scholarly publications. Recent contributions to Bach scholarship include Ernst Suchalla's critical edition of more than two hundred letters from C. P. E. Bach to J. N. Forkel and J. G. I. Breitkopf; and Eugene Helm's *Thematic Catalogue of the Works of Carl Philipp Emanuel Bach*, which will include many more works than the older Wotquenne catalogue and will arrange them chronologically within each genre, is due to appear shortly.

However plentiful the achievements of scholarship may be, Schering's demand[119] has still not been satisfied. No comprehensive study of C. P. E. Bach has yet been written. Much remains for record companies at home and abroad to discover. Good, new performing editions are needed. True, Bach's principal keyboard and chamber works— even if mostly in old editions—are now generally accessible, yet there are still numerous lacunae among works of other types. At the University of Maryland, however, work is in progress on a complete edition of Bach's works (Co-ordinating Editor: E. Eugene Helm; General Editor: Rachel W. Wade).

Composers in the German Democratic Republic have repeatedly sought inspiration from C. P. E. Bach's work.[120] Their creative energies have been channelled towards rendering this important musical

[116] Ibid.

[117] E. H. Meyer, 'Zu einigen Fragen der Periodisierung der Musik des 17. und 18. Jahrhunderts', *Musik der Renaissance—Aufklärung—Klassik* (Leipzig, 1973), p. 30. See also pp. 199, 202, 218, 227f.

[118] H. Eisler, 'Inhalt und Form', *Materialien zu einer Dialektik der Musik* (Leipzig, 1973), p. 310.

[119] See p. 214 above.

[120] Works by Bach have even been used as direct models by Lothar Voigtländer in his *Variationen über ein Thema von Carl Philipp Emanuel Bach* (1972), and by Willy Focke in his *Epitaph für Carl Philipp Emanuel Bach* (1975).

heritage of direct use for modern composition. In such a work as Paul
Dessau's *Bach Variationen für grosses Orchester* (1963) this objective is
realized.[121]

What of performances of C. P. E. Bach's music in the concert-hall?
They are seldom heard, although the keyboard and chamber works are
more frequently performed than the songs, oratorios, and symphonies.
Yet, to consider the case of the German Democratic Republic alone, it
must be said that there are certain music festivals and concert series,
such as the annual Bach festivals or the *Stunde der Musik* in which works
by this master have long since been included. Signs of new activity can
be detected: a 'Carl Philipp Emanuel Bach Archive' has been established in conjunction with the Hamburg *Bach-Gesellschaft*, founded in
1985, which includes among its members such distinguished performers and scholars as Gustav Leonhardt, Rudolf Serkin, and Karl

[121] Dessau borrowed Bach's theme 'Bauerntanz' from Part III of the second volume of
J. P. Kirnberger's *Die Kunst des reinen Satzes in der Musik* (Berlin and Königsberg, 1779), p. 53, in
which commentaries by Kirnberger and C. P. E. Bach are also supplied. Dessau himself has has this
to say about his treatment of Bach's theme: 'For many years I hesitated to use the "Bauerntanz"
by Carl Philipp Emanuel Bach as a theme for variations. There was a particular reason for this,
namely that even without variation this piece already possesses an extremely complex structure,
which seemed to me to act as an obstacle to the kind of arrangement that is involved in variation
form. While the theme itself moves in crotchets and quavers, it is accompanied by the same theme
in minims and crotchets (i.e. in augmentation).

Ex. 88. Theme from Paul Dessau, *Bach Variationen für grosses Orchester*

In the fifth bar a third voice enters with the main theme in inversion (i.e. ascending lines are
replaced by descending lines and vice versa). In the second eight-bar section of the "Bauerntanz",
Philipp Emanuel begins with the latter half of the first section, but with the parts exchanged (i.e.
the upper voice now appears underneath), and he concludes the second section with the first four
bars of the first section. The third section of the dance is a repetition of the first. Thus we are faced
with a highly complex ternary form (ABA), which, as mentioned earlier, is not ideally suited to
variation treatment using those learned devices which Carl Philipp Emanuel Bach has
anticipated.' P. Dessau, *Notizen zu Noten* (Leipzig, 1974), p. 93.

Geiringer; in Potsdam and Berlin the Friends of the Cultural Union of the German Democratic Republic take pains to ensure that Bach's music receives attention. The *Singakademie* in Frankfurt an der Oder plans to add to its repertoire before 1988, the bicentenary of Bach's death, three of his major vocal works, *Die Israeliten in der Wüste, Carl Wilhelm Rammlers Auferstehung und Himmelfahrt Jesu,* and the Magnificat. With the formation of the 'Carl Philipp Emanuel Bach Chamber Orchestra' at the *Staatsoper Berlin* under the direction of Hartmut Haenchen, an excellent ensemble has appeared which specializes in the authentic performance of Bach's music. All too often, however, one meets a certain resistance to this music. Concert programmes of many soloists and orchestras continue to centre around the 'classics'. The fact that a good interpretation of, for example, Bach's sonatas 'für Kenner und Liebhaber' demands extensive knowledge of the art of ornamentation in the eighteenth century, or that the performance on a modern concert grand of works conceived for the gentle tone of the clavichord presents problems, ought to act as a challenge rather than a disincentive. At this point some responsibility must be laid at the doors of music schools and conservatoires, which ought not only to educate students in the knowledge of the conventions and peculiarities of performing practice in the music of that period, and develop proficiency in such matters, but also to encourage greater openness towards this hitherto largely neglected heritage. Let there be no misunderstanding: this is not a matter of banal antiquarianism, whereby anything and everything is judged worthy of preservation. Not even an appeal to the fame and acclaim which the composer enjoyed during his lifetime would be sufficient justification for a Bach revival. It is the intrinsic quality of C. P. E. Bach's music which gives rise to the hope that it will be more widely cultivated in future.

APPENDIX I

Chronological Table

1714   Carl Philipp Emanuel Bach, second son of Johann Sebastian Bach, is born on 8 March in Weimar. (Wilhelm Friedemann had been born on 22 November 1710.)

1717   The family moves to Cöthen, where Johann Sebastian Bach becomes Court Kapellmeister to Prince Leopold of Anhalt-Cöthen. Philipp Emanuel attends the Latin School.

1720   Bach's mother, Maria Barbara, dies in July.

1721   Johann Sebastian Bach marries Anna Magdalena Wilcke on 3 December.

1723   Johann Sebastian Bach takes up office as Music Director and Cantor at the Thomaskirche in Leipzig. Carl Philipp Emanuel is entered as a pupil at the Thomasschule. His father is in charge of his musical education.

1731   Carl Philipp Emanuel matriculates as a student of Law at Leipzig University on 1 October. He writes one of his first compositions, a 'Menuet pour le clavessin', Wq. 111.

1732   Bach's brother Johann Christoph Friedrich, later to become Kapellmeister in Bückeburg, is born on 21 June.

1733   In August Bach applies unsuccessfully for the post of organist at the church of St Wenceslaus in Naumburg.

1734   Bach continues his studies at the University of Frankfurt an der Oder, where he also gives keyboard lessons and directs 'a musical *Akademie*' as well as 'all the public concerts on ceremonial occasions'.

1735   Bach's brother Johann Christian, later to be known as the 'Milan Bach', or the 'London Bach' is born on 5 September.

1738   Bach enters the service of the Crown Prince of Prussia (later King Frederick the Great) as Court Harpsichordist. Based initially in Ruppin and Rheinsberg, the Court moves to Berlin in 1740.

1741   A year after Frederick's accession to the throne Bach is confirmed in his appointment as Court Harpsichordist with a starting salary of 300 Thalers a year. He takes over responsibility for accompanying the evening concerts in the royal palaces in Berlin and Potsdam. In musical circles he mixes with Quantz, the Benda brothers, the Graun brothers, Agricola, Nichelmann, Krause, and Marpurg, while in the literary sphere his companions in Berlin are Lessing, Ramler, Gleim, and Sulzer. In August Johann Sebastian Bach travels to Berlin.

1742   The six so-called 'Prussian' keyboard sonatas, Wq. 48, are published in Nuremberg.

1743   For health reasons, on account of his gout, Bach travels to Bad Teplitz in Bohemia.

1744   At the beginning of the year Carl Philipp Emanuel marries Johanna Maria Dannemann (born on 10 December 1724), the daughter of a

Berlin wine merchant. The six so-called 'Württemberg' keyboard sonatas, Wq. 49, are published in Nuremberg.

1745   Bach's son Johann August, later to pursue a legal career, is baptized on 10 December.

1747   Johann Sebastian Bach visits the Court of Frederick the Great in Potsdam on 7 and 8 May. On 4 September Carl Philipp Emanuel's daughter Anna Carolina Philippina is born.

1748   Bach's son Johann Sebastian, later to become a painter and to die in Rome at the age of thirty, is baptized on 26 September.

1750   Bach's father dies on 28 July. Carl Philipp Emanuel inherits large portions of his father's estate. He applies unsuccessfully for his father's job in Leipzig. Johann Christian lives with his elder brother until 1754, and receives musical instruction from him.

1751   In January Bach travels to Halberstadt, where he stays with the poet Gleim, and to Brunswick.

1753   The first volume of the important didactic work *Versuch über die wahre Art das Clavier zu spielen* is published. (The second volume was to follow in 1762.) In the same year Bach's application for the post of Cantor at the church of St John in Zittau is turned down.

1756   Beginning of the Seven Years War.

1758   *Herr Professor Gellert's sacred odes and songs with melodies* are published in Berlin. This popular song collection was to be issued five times during Bach's lifetime. On account of the dangerous proximity of the Russian army, Bach sets off in August with his wife and children to spend a few months in Zerbst with the family of his friend Johann Friedrich Fasch.

1760   The 'Six keyboard sonatas with varied repeats', Wq. 50, appear in print.

1767   Princess Anna Amalia of Prussia appoints Bach her personal Kapellmeister.

1768   In March Bach takes up the post of City Director of Music at the five principal churches in Hamburg. As in Berlin his home becomes a popular meeting place for many artists (Lessing, Klopstock, Gerstenberg, Voss, Forkel, Reichardt). Bach appears in public as a conductor (his first concert takes place on 28 April 1768) and frequently performs on the harpsichord and clavichord.

1772   In September the English music historian Charles Burney visits Bach in Hamburg. A description of their meeting is given in Burney's *The Present State of Music in Germany, the Netherlands, and United Provinces* (London, 1773). The German translation of this book by C. D. Ebeling and J. J. C. Bode, which was published in Hamburg in 1773 as *Tagebuch einer musikalischen Reise*, ii–iii, contains Bach's autobiographical sketch.

1773   In response to a commission from the Austrian imperial family's ambassador to Berlin, Baron Gottfried van Swieten, Bach composes his six 'string symphonies', Wq. 182.

1775   The first edition of the oratorio *Die Israeliten in der Wüste* is published. In the same year Bach conducts Handel's *Messiah* in Hamburg. (The first German performance had taken place in 1772 under Michael Arne, also in Hamburg.)

1779 The first of the six collections of sonatas, free fantasias, and rondos 'für Kenner und Liebhaber' appears in print. (The others were to follow in 1780, 1781, 1783, 1785, and 1787.)

1780 The Leipzig publisher Schwickert issues the four 'Orchestral symphonies with twelve obbligato parts', Wq. 183.

1786 Bach performs the Credo from his father's B minor Mass, BWV 232, at a concert in Hamburg 'for this city's medical Institute for the Poor'.

1788 Carl Philipp Emanuel Bach dies on 14 December. Klopstock and Gleim write obituaries in verse. The greater part of his musical estate is acquired by the collector Georg Poelchau.

APPENDIX II

Three Letters from Denis Diderot

To C. P. E. Bach   Hamburg, 31 (?) March 1774

Monsieur,

I did not dare to expect such an obliging reply from you. Since I do not have the honour of being known to you, I was obliged perhaps to speak a little less modestly of myself than I should. I had to recommend myself to you. My name is certainly not unknown, though I may not be so famous as you are. I shall act on your suggestion. Engage a copyist, or two if necessary. I shall gladly meet all the costs, and if, as I hope, you will accept a fee yourself, monsieur, then a local businessman will perform the transaction on my behalf. You may send the music which you promise me to my friend His Excellency Prince Galitzin, Ambassador to the Empress of Russia in the Hague, with whom I shall spend at least two or three months. Monsieur Emanuel, I count on you to keep your promise. It is not enough to be a genius, one must also keep one's word faithfully.

I am, etc.

Diderot.[1]

To F. M. Grimm   2 November 1769

My daughter has devoured the music you brought for her. I thank you for it, in the expectation that she will thank you herself when she returns from the country again. This Müller, this Emanuel (Bach), this Müthel, have a unique power which I rather admire. Moreover, since their music is difficult, you can imagine how much it has increased my daughter's skill in reading and in dexterous fingering—a good deal of technical proficiency is needed to play these composers in any event; there is plenty to occupy both hands and more besides. It would be a source of great pleasure to her if you were to hear her perform some of these pieces, and especially if you would give her some lessons in accompaniment. If you would like to consult Naigeon for further news, he will oblige you. I believe that she will be a good player, but I am practically certain that she will be a musician, and that she will learn the theory of this art well, unless some future husband should ruin everything, spoil her figure, and take away her appetite for study.[2]

To F. M. Grimm   28 June 1770

Do not forget that you were going to write to Eckard to ask for a volume of sonatas in unusual keys by Emanuel Bach. If he possesses the volume, he must send it to you. If someone else possesses it, he must acquire it for you. Have the title-page copied and then send the volume back immediately . . .[3]

---

[1] *Correspondance*, xvi, p. 51 [Chapter 3, n. 158]. Also quoted in Schmid, *Kammermusik*, p. 46.
[2] *Correspondance*, ix, pp. 189f. The passage quoted is only an extract from the letter.
[3] *Correspondance*, x, pp. 78f. The passage quoted is only an extract from the letter.

APPENDIX III
Work-List

Among the numerous lists and catalogues, old and new, of Bach's works, the following deserve particular attention:

1. The list of works included in Bach's 'Autobiography', first published in *Carl Burney's der Musik Doctors Tagebuch seiner musikalischen Reisen*, iii (Hamburg, 1773), pp. 199ff. (See Bibliography.)
2. *Silhouetten jetztlebender Gelehrten en Bou-Magie. Erstes Heft. Nebst einem von ihnen selber durchgesehenen Verzeichnis ihrer Schriften* (Hamburg, 1778).
3. *Verzeichnis des musikalischen Nachlasses des verstorbenen Capellmeisters Carl Philipp Emanuel Bach* (Hamburg, 1790); reprinted in instalments in *B-Jb*, xxxv-xxxvii (1938, 1939, 1940–8). A facsimile edition of the *Nachlassverzeichnis* with detailed commentary by R. W. Wade has been published as *The Catalog of Carl Philipp Emanuel Bach's Estate. A Facsimile of the Edition by Schniebes, Hamburg, 1790* (New York and London, 1981).
4. J. J. H. Westphal, *Thematisches Verzeichnis der Werke C. Ph. E. Bachs*, manuscript, Bibliothèque Royale, Brussels, Fonds Fétis 5218 (a second copy is located in the Deutsche Staatsbibliothek, East Berlin).
5. J. J. H. Westphal, *Gesammelte Nachrichten von dem Leben und den Werken des Herrn Carl Philipp Emanuel Bach Kapellmeister in Hamburg nebst einer Sammlung verschiedener Recensionen und Beurtheilungen seiner herausgegebenen Werke*, manuscript, Bibliothèque Royale, Brussels, Fonds Fétis 4779.
6. Wotquenne, A., *Thematisches Verzeichnis der Werke von Carl Philipp Emanuel Bach (1714–1788)* (Leipzig, 1905; R/Wiesbaden, 1964).
7. List of works by E. E. Helm in 'Carl Philipp Emanuel Bach', *The New Grove Dictionary of Music and Musicians*, ed. S. Sadie, i (London etc., 1980), pp. 855ff. Reprinted with minor revisions in *The New Grove Bach Family* (London, 1983), pp. 288ff. An abbreviated version containing further minor revisions is supplied below.
8. E. E. Helm, *Thematic Catalogue of the Works of Carl Philipp Emanuel Bach* (forthcoming).

Useful catalogues of works in particular genres are contained in:

D. M. Berg, *The Keyboard Sonatas of C. P. E. Bach. An Expression of the Mannerist Principle*, Diss., State University of New York at Buffalo, 1975.

E. Beurmann, *Die Klaviersonaten Carl Philipp Emanuel Bachs*, Diss., Göttingen, 1953.

G. Busch, *C. Ph. E. Bach und seine Lieder* (Regensburg, 1957).

R. M. Jacobs, *The Chamber Ensembles of C. P. E. Bach Using Two or More Wind Instruments*, Diss., State University of Iowa, 1963.

E. Suchalla, *Die Orchestersinfonien Carl Philipp Emanuel Bachs nebst einem thematischen Verzeichnis seiner Orchesterwerke* (Augsburg, 1968).

R. W. Wade, *The Keyboard Concertos of Carl Philipp Emanuel Bach. Sources and Style* (Ann Arbor, 1981).

The following work-list is an abbreviated and updated version of that supplied by Eugene Helm for *New Grove*. Works in the 'possibly authentic', 'doubtful', and 'spurious' categories have been omitted, as have references to manuscript sources and to printed editions made after Bach's death. For fuller details concerning these and other matters, see E. E. Helm, *Thematic Catalogue* (no. 8 above).

Both the Helm numbering and the Wotquenne numbering (if any) are given for each work listed below. A table of concordances between the Wotquenne numbering used throughout the text of this book and the Helm numbering is supplied on pp. 245ff.

SOLO KEYBOARD

Editions

There follows a list of published collections of keyboard music by Bach which appeared during his lifetime, together with the catalogue numbers of the works which they contain.

Sei sonate . . . che all'augusta maesta di Federico II ré di Prussia (Nuremberg, 1742 or 1743): H. 24–9; Wq. 48 [1742].

Sei sonate . . . dedicate all'altezza serenissima di Carlo Eugenio duca di Wirtemberg (Nuremberg, 1744): H. 30–1, 33, 32, 34, 36; Wq. 49 [1744].

Sechs Sonaten . . . mit veränderten Reprisen (Berlin, 1760), ded. to Princess Amalia of Prussia: H. 136–9, 126, 140; Wq. 50 [1760].

Fortsetzung von Sechs Sonaten (Berlin, 1761): H. 150–1, 127–8, 141, 62; Wq. 51 [1761¹].

Musikalisches Allerley (Berlin, 1761): H. 2, 40, 63, 66, 69, 109–13, 123, 155, 773–4 [1761²].

Musikalisches Mancherley (Berlin, 1762–3): H. 59, 77, 81, 92–5, 118–20, 171–2, 562, 584, 590, 601 [1763¹].

Zweyte Fortsetzung von sechs Sonaten (Berlin, 1763): H. 50, 142, 158, 37, 161, 129; Wq. 52 [1763²].

Clavierstücke verschiedener Art (Berlin, 1765): H. 190, 144, 165, 145, 166, 693, 179, 146, 167, 147, 168, 694, 191, 695, 148, 169–70, 149, 101.5; Wq. 112 [1765].

Kurze und leichte Clavierstücke mit veränderten Reprisen und beygefügter Fingersetzung für Anfänger (Berlin, 1766): H. 193–203; Wq. 113 [1766¹].

Sechs leichte Clavier-Sonaten (Leipzig, 1766): H. 162, 180–2, 163, 183; Wq. 53 [1766²].

Six sonates, op. 1 (Paris, before 1768): H. 55, 19, 56, 67, 18, 48, 54 [54 not indicated in the title] [1768¹].

Kurze und leichte Clavier-Stücke mit veränderten Reprisen und beygefügter Fingersetzung, ii (Berlin, 1768): H. 228–38; Wq. 114 [1768²].

Six sonates . . . à l'usage des dames (Amsterdam, 1770): H. 204–5, 184, 206, 185, 207; Wq. 54 [1770¹].

Musikalisches Vielerley, ed. C. P. E. Bach (Hamburg, 1770): H. 69, 155, 210, 214–25, 227, 240–1, 598, 698 [1770²].

Sechs Clavier-Sonaten für Kenner und Liebhaber, i (Leipzig, 1779): H. 244, 130, 245, 186, 243, 187; Wq. 55 [1779].

Clavier-Sonaten nebst einigen Rondos... für Kenner und Liebhaber, ii
  (Leipzig, 1780): H. 260, 246, 261, 269, 262, 270; Wq. 56 [1780].
Clavier-Sonaten nebst einigen Rondos... für Kenner und Liebhaber, iii
  (Leipzig, 1781): H. 265, 247, 271, 208, 266, 173; Wq. 57 [1781].
Clavier-Sonaten und freye Fantasien nebst einigen Rondos... für Kenner
  und Liebhaber, iv (Leipzig, 1783): H. 276, 273–4, 188, 267, 277–8; Wq. 58
  [1783].
Clavier-Sonaten und freye Fantasien nebst einigen Rondos... für Kenner
  und Liebhaber, v (Leipzig, 1785): H. 281, 268, 282–3, 279, 284; Wq. 59
  [1785].
Clavier-Sonaten und freye Fantasien nebst einigen rondos... für Kenner und
  Liebhaber, vi (Leipzig, 1787): H. 288, 286, 289–90, 287, 291; Wq. 61
  [1787].

The dates given in square brackets at the end of each of the above entries serve
to identify the publications concerned in the following list of solo keyboard
works by C. P. E. Bach; the appearance of one of these dates in round brackets
without a corresponding place-name against an entry in this section of the
work-list indicates the inclusion of the work in question in the corresponding
publication.

Helm	*Wotquenne*	
1	[BWV Anh. 122–5]	March, D; Polonoise, g; March, G; Polonoise, g: 1730–1 [nos. 16–19 in *Clavierbüchlein für Anna Magdalena Bach*]
1.5	111	Menuet, C, 1731 (Leipzig, 1731)
2	62/1	Sonata, B flat, 1731, rev. 1744 (1761[2])
3–6	65/1–4	4 sonatas, F, a, d, e, 1731–3, rev. 1744
7–12	64/1–6	6 sonatinas, F, G, a, e, D, E flat, 1734, rev. 1744
13	65/5	Sonata, e, 1735, rev. 1743
14	118/7 [269]	Minuet (by Locatelli) with variations, G, 1735
15–19	65/6–10	5 sonatas, G, E flat, C, B flat, A, 1736–8, rev. 1743–4 [1st movt. of 16 = BWV Anh. 129, no. 27 in *Clavierbüchlein für Anna Magdalena Bach*], 18–19 (1768[1])
20	62/2	Sonata, G, 1739, in *Nebenstunden der berlinischen Musen*, i (Berlin, 1762)
21	65/11 [266]	Sonata, g, 1739
22	62/3	Sonata, D, 1740, in F. W. Marpurg: *Clavierstücke mit einem practischen Unterricht* (Berlin, 1762–3)
23	65/12	Sonata, G, 1740
24–9	48	6 sonatas, F, B flat, E, c, C, A, 1740–2 (1742)
30–34	49/1–2,4,3,5	5 sonatas, a, A flat, B flat, e, E flat, 1742–3 (1744)
32.5	65/13	Sonata, b, 1743
36	49/6	Sonata, b, 1744 (1744)
37	52/4	Sonata, f sharp, 1744 (1763[2])
38–41	62/4–7	4 sonatas, d, E, f, C, 1744, 38–9 in *Oeuvres mêlées*

Helm	Wotquenne	
		(Nuremberg, 1755–65), 40 (1761²), 41 in *Collection récréative* (Nuremberg, 1760–1)
42	65/14	Sonata, D, 1744
43	65/15	Sonata, G, 1745
44	118/3	Minuetto con V variationi, C, 1745
45	122/1	Sinfonia, G, 1745
46–9	65/16–19	4 sonatas, C, g, F, F, 1746, 48 (1768¹)
50	52/1	Sonata, E flat, 1747 (1763²)
51–2	65/20 [266, 268]; 65/21	2 sonatas, B flat, F, 1747
53	69	Sonata 'a due tastature', d, 1747
54	118/4	Arioso con VII variazioni, F, 1747 (1768¹)
55–7	62/8; 65/22–3	3 sonatas, F, G, d, 1748, 55 (1768¹) and in *Tonstücke . . . vom Herrn C. P. E. Bach und andern classischen Musikern* (Berlin, 1762, 2/1774 as *C. P. E. Bachs, Nichelmanns und Handels Sonaten und Fugen*), 56 (1768¹)
58–61	62/9–10; 65/24–5	4 sonatas, F, C, d, C, 1749, 58 in *Oeuvres mêlées* (Nuremberg, 1755–65), 59 (1763¹)
62	51/6	Sonata, G, 1750 (1761¹)
63	62/11	Sonata, G, 1750 (1761²)
64	65/26	Sonata, G, 1750
65	118/5	Allegretto con VI variazioni, C, 1750
66	62/12	Sonata, e, 1751 (1761²)
67–8	62/13; 65/27	2 sonatas, D, g, 1752, 67 in *Raccolta delle più nuove composizioni* (Leipzig, 1756) and (1768¹)
69	118/1	24 Veränderungen über das Lied: Ich schlief, da träumte mir, F, 1752, variations 1–17 (1761²), variations 18–24 (1770²)
70–5	63/1–6; 202/M without text	18 Probestücke in 6 Sonaten, C, d, A, b, E flat, f, 1753; bound with exx. for *Versuch*, i [see 868]
75·5	119/7	Fantasia e fuga a 4, c.1755
76	119/1	Duo in contrap. ad 8, 11 & 12 mit Anmerkungen, a, by 1754, in F. W. Marpurg: *Abhandlung von der Fuge* (Berlin, 1754), 'Anmerkungen' [?by Marpurg]
77–8	62/14; 65/28	2 sonatas, G, E flat, 1754, 77 (1763¹)
79	117/17	La Borchward, polonoise, G, 1754
80	117/18	La Pott, minuet, C, 1754, in *Raccolta delle più nuove composizioni* (Leipzig, 1756)
81	117/26	La Boehmer, D, 1754; (1763¹)
82	117/37	La Gause, F
83	65/29	Sonata, E, 1755
84–7	70/3–6 [265]	4 organ sonatas, F, a, D, g, 1755
89–90	117/19–20	La Gleim, rondeau, a; La Bergius, B flat: 1755,

Helm	Wotquenne	
		in *Raccolta delle più nuove composizioni* (Leipzig, 1756)
91	117/21	La Prinzette, F, 1755, in *Raccolta delle più nuove composizioni* (Leipzig, 1757)
92–5	117/23–5, 27	L'Herrmann, g; La Buchholz, d; La Stahl, d; L'Aly Rupalich, C: 1755; (1763¹)
96–8	117/34–5, 39	La Philippine, A; La Gabriel, C; La Caroline, a: 1755
99	119/2	Fuga a 2, d, 1755, in F. W. Marpurg: *Fugen-Sammlung*, i (Berlin, 1758)
100	119/3	Fuga a 3, F, 1755 in *Tonstücke . . . vom Herrn C. P. E. Bach und andern classischen Musikern* (Berlin, 1762, 2/1774 as *C. P. E. Bachs, Nichelmanns und Handels Sonaten und Fugen*)
101.5	112/19 [119/5]	Fuga a 3, g, 1755 (1765)
101–2	119/4,6	Fuga a 3 mit Anmerkungen, A: Fuga a 4, org. mit Anmerkungen, E flat: 1755, 101 in *Raccolta delle più nuove composizioni* (Leipzig, 1757), both in F. W. Marpurg: *Clavierstücke mit einem practischen Unterricht* (Berlin, 1762–3)
104	122/2	Sinfonia, F, ?1755 or later, in F. W. Marpurg: *Raccolta delle megliore sinfonie* (Leipzig, 1761–2)
105–6	62/15; 65/30	2 sonatas, d, e, 1756, 105 in *Raccolta delle più nuove composizioni* (Leipzig, 1757)
107	70/7 [265]	Preludio, org, D, 1756
108	116/18	Andantino, F, 1756, in F. W. Marpurg: *Kritische Briefe über die Tonkunst* (Berlin, 1760)
109	117/28	La complaisante, B flat, 1756 (1761²)
110–13	117/30–33	Les langueurs tendres, c; L'irrésoluë, G; La journalière, c; La capricieuse, e: 1756 (1761²); 110 also as La memoire raisonée
114	117/36	La Louise, D, 1756
115	122/3	Sinfonia, e, ?1756 or later, lost
116–20	62/16–20	5 sonatas, B flat, E, g, G, C, 1757, 116–17 in *Oeuvres mêlées* (Nuremberg, 1755–65), 118–20 (1763¹)
121	65/31 [266]	Sonata, c, 1757
122	117/22	L'Auguste, polonoise, F, 1757, in *Raccolta delle più nuove composizioni* (Leipzig, 1757)
123	117/29	La Xénophon-La Sybille, C sharp, 1757 (1761²)
124–5	117/38, 40	L'Ernestine, D; La Sophie, aria B flat: 1757
126	50/5	Sonata, B flat, 1758 (1760)
127–9	51/3–4; 52/6	3 sonatas, c, d, e, 1758, 127–8 (1761¹), 129 (1763²)
130	55/2	Sonata, F, 1758 (1779)
131–2	62/21–2	2 sonatas, a, b, 1758, 131 in *Oeuvres mêlées*

Helm   *Wotquenne*

		(Nuremberg, 1755–65), 132 in *Collection récréative* (Nuremberg, 1760–1)
133–4	70/1; 70/2 [265]	2 sonatas, A, B flat, org, 1758, 134 in *III sonates . . . par Mrs. C. P. E. Bach, C. S. Binder e C. Fasch* (Nuremberg, n.d.); cf 135
135	65/32	Sonata, A, 1758 or later; [rev. of 133]
136–40	50/1–4, 6	5 sonatas, F, G, a, d, c, 1759 (1760); 138 cf 334
141–2	51/5; 52/2	2 sonatas, F, d, 1759, 141 (1761¹), 142 (1763²)
143	65/33	Sonata, a, 1759
144–9	112/2,4,8,10,15,18 [117/8,5,9,6,10,7]	Fantasia, D; Solfeggio, G; Fantasia, B flat; Solfeggio, C; Fantasia, F; Solfeggio, G: 1759 (1765)
150–2	51/1–2; 65/34	3 sonatas, C, B flat, B flat, 1760, 150–1 (1761¹) [cf 156–7]
153	116/21	Allegro, C, 1760
154	116/22	Polonoise, g, 1760
155	118/2	Clavierstück mit [22] Veränderungen, A, 1760; theme and variations 1–17 (1761²), theme and variations 18–22 (1770²)
156–7	65/35–6	2 sonatas, C, 1760 or later; revs. of 150
158	52/3	Sonata, g, 1761 (1763²)
159	116/15	Minuet, C, by ?1762
160	117/14	Fantasia, D, by 1762, pubd in *Versuch*, ii [cf 870]
161	52/5	Sonata, E, 1762 (1763²)
162	53/1	Sonata, C, 1762 (1766²)
163	53/5	Sonata, C, 1762 (1766²)
164	68	Veränderungen und Auszierungen über einige meiner Sonaten, completed 1762 or later
165	112/3 [116/9]	Minuet, D, 1762–5 (1765)
166	112/5 [116/10]	Alla polacca, a, 1762–5 (1765)
167–72	112/9,11,16–17 [116/11–14]; 116/1,2	Minuet, D; Alla polacca, g; Minuet, A; Alla polacca, D: 1762–5 (1765) Minuet, Polonoise, E flat, by 1763 (1763¹)
173	57/6	Sonata, f, 1763 (1781)
174–8	65/37–41	5 sonatas, A, B flat, e, D, C, 1763
179	112/7	Sonata, d, 1763 (1765)
180–3	53/2–4,6	4 sonatas, B flat, a, b, F, 1764 (1766²)
184–5	54/3,5	2 sonatas, d, D, 1765 (1770¹)
186–7	55/4,6	2 sonatas, A, G, 1765 (1779)
188–9	58/4; 65/42	2 sonatas, e, E flat, 1765, 188 (1783)
190	112/1	Concerto, hpd solo, C, 1765 (1765)
191	112/13 [122/4]	Sinfonia, hpd solo, G, 1765 (1765)
192	65/43	Sonata, A, 1765–6
193– 203	113/1–11 [113/3 = 117/15]	Allegro, G; Arioso, a; Fantasia, d; Minuet, F; Alla polacca, C; Allegretto, d; Alla polacca, D; Allegretto, A; Andante e sostenuto, g; Presto, B flat; Allegro, d: 1765–6 (1766¹)

Helm	Wotquenne	
204–7	54/1,2,4,6	4 sonatas, F, C, B flat, A, 1766 (1770[1])
208	57/4	Sonata, d, 1766 (1781)
209	60	Sonata, c, 1766 (Leipzig, 1785)
210–13	62/23; 65/44–6	4 sonatas, g, g, B flat, E, 1766, 210 (1770[2])
214–19	116/3–8	Minuet, D; Alla polacca, C; Minuet, C; Alla polacca, D; Minuet, F; Alla polacca, G: 1766 (1770[2])
220–22	117/2 [271]; 117/3–4	3 solfeggios, c, E flat, A, 1766 (1770[2])
223–5	117/11–13	3 fantasias, G, d, g, 1766 (1770[2])
226	118/6	Romance, avec XII variations, G, 1766
227	122/5	Sinfonia, hpd solo, F, 1766 (1770[2])
228–38	114/1–11 [114/7=117/16]	Allegro di molto, d; Andantino e grazioso, B flat; Presto, c; Minuet, G; Alla polacca, D; Alla polacca, E flat; Fantasia, d; Allegro, E; Allegretto, A; Andante, C; Poco allegro, e: 1767 (1768[2])
240	62/24	Clavier-Sonate mit veränderten Reprisen, F, 1769 (1770[2])
241	117/1	Clavierstück für die rechte oder linke Hand allein, A, by 1770 (1770[2])
242		Concerto, hpd solo, 1770
243–7	55/5,1,3; 56/2; 57/2	5 sonatas, F, C, b, G, a, 1772–4, 243–5 (1779); 246 (1780), 247 (1781)
248	65/47	Sonata, C, 1775
249–54	116/23–8	Sechs leichte Clavier-Stückgen, C, F, D, G, B flat, D, 1775; intended as a set; cf 259
255–8		Allegro, D; Allegro, F; Allegretto, D; Minuet, F: ?1775
259	118/10	Variationes mit veränderten Reprisen, C, 1777 or later; on theme of 534, which is a set of variations on 249
260–2	56/1,3,5	3 rondos, C, D, a, 1778 (1780)
263	118/9 [270]	12 Variationes über die Folie d'Espagne, d, 1778
264	120	[75] Cadenzen, 1778 or later, written for his own concs. and sonatas
265–8	57/1,5; 58/5; 59/2	4 rondos, E, F, B flat, G, 1779, 265–6 (1781), 267 (1783), 268 (1785)
269–71	56/4,6; 57/3	2 sonatas, F, A; Rondo, G: 1780, 269–70 (1780), 271 (1781)
272	66	Abschied von meinem Silbermannischen Claviere, in einem Rondo, e, 1781
273–4	58/2,3	Sonata, G; Rondo, E: 1781 (1783)
275	118/8	Canzonetta der Herzogin von Gotha, mit 6 Veränderungen, F, 1781, pubd as Canzonette fürs Clavier von einer Liebhaberin der Musik

Helm   *Wotquenne*

		(Gotha, 1781), incl. variations by G. Benda, C. F. Cramer, Golde, Scheidler, Scherlitz, A. Schweitzer
276–9	58/1,6,7; 59/5	Rondo, A; 3 fantasias, E flat, A, F: 1782, 276–8 (1783), 279 (1785)
280	65/48	Sonata fürs Bogen-Clavier, G, 1783
281–4	59/1,3,4,6	2 sonatas, e, B flat; Rondo, c; Fantasia, C: 1784 (1785)
285		Fughetta on the name 'C. Filippo E. Bach' [C-F-E-B-A-C-H], F, 1784; cf 867
286–91	61/2,5,1,3,4,6	2 sonatas, D, G; Rondo, E flat; Fantasia, B flat; Rondo, d; Fantasia, C: 1785–6 (1787)
292–7	63/7–12	VI sonatine nuove, G, E, D, B flat, F, d, 1786, pubd in 868 (2/1787) also pubd as 2 sonatas of 3 movts (Leipzig, 1786)
298–9	65/49,50	2 sonatas, E flat, G, 1786
300	67	Freie Fantasie fürs Clavier, f sharp, 1787
301–9	116/19,20,29–35	Allegretto, F; Allegro, D; Minuet, G; Minuet, G; Minuet G; Minuet F; Minuet D; Polonoise, A; Minuet, D
310–14	116/36–40	Allegro di molto, A; Allegro E; Allegro, B flat; Presto, a; Minuet, D
315–18	116/41–4	4 polonoises, F, A, B flat, E flat
319–22	116/45–8	2 marches, F, D; 2 minuets, C, G
323–31	116/49–57	Polonoise, D; Langsam und traurig, a; Allegro, C; Allegro ma non troppo, E flat; Allegro C; Allegro, G; Allegro, E flat; Allegro, D; Allegretto grazioso, C
333		La Juliane, F
334		Variations, C, late variant of 3rd movt of H. 138
336		5 Choräle mit ausgesetzten Mittelstimmen, kbd, no text: O Gott du frommer Gott, Ich bin ja Herr in deiner Macht, Jesus meine Zuversicht, Wer nur den Lieben Gott, Komm heiliger Geist
337		Chorale: Wo Gott zum Haus nicht gibt, a 4, bc

CONCERTOS AND SONATINAS WITH ORCHESTRA

Editions

Concertos, hpd/org, vns, insts (London, *c.*1753): H. 414, 417, 429; Wq. 11, 14, 25 [1753].

A Second Sett of Three Concertos, org/hpd, insts (London, *c.*1760): H. 421, 428, 444; Wq. 18, 24, 34 [1760].

Helm	Wotquenne	
403	1	Conc., a, hpd, str, 1733, lost, rev. 1744
404	2	Conc., E flat, hpd, str, 1734, lost, rev. 1743 as op. 2 (Paris, n.d.)
405	3	Conc., G, hpd, str, 1737, lost, rev. 1745
406	4	Conc., G, hpd, str, 1738
407	5	Conc., c, hpd, str, 1739, lost, rev. 1762
408	46	Conc. doppio, F, 2 hpd, 2 hn, str, 1740
409–10	6–7	2 concs., g, A, hpd, str, 1740
411–13	8–10	3 concs., A, G, B flat, hpd, str, 1741–2
414	11	Conc., D, hpd, str, 1743 (Nuremberg, 1745), and (1753)
415–17	12–14	3 concs., F, D, E, hpd, str, 1744, 417 (1753) and (Berlin, 1760)
418–21	15–18	4 concs., e, G, d, D, hpd, str, 1745, 421 (1760)
422–5	19–22	4 concs., A, C, a, d, hpd, str. 1746–7, 425, rev. 1775
427	23	Conc., d, hpd, str, 1748
428	24	Conc., e, hpd, str, 1748 (1760)
429	25	Conc., B flat, hpd, str, 1749 (Nuremberg, 1752) and (1753)
430–32	26; 166; 170	Conc., a, hpd, str, 1750; versions for fl, str, ?1750 and for vc, str, ?1750
433	27	Conc., D, hpd, str, with 2 ob, 2 tpt/hn, 2 fl ad lib, timp ad lib, 1750; 2nd version for str, 2 hn
434–6	28; 167; 171	Conc., B flat, hpd, str, 1751; versions for fl, str, 1751 and for vc, str, ?1751
437–9	29; 168; 172	Conc., A, hpd, str, 1753; versions for fl, str, ?1753, and for vc, str, ?1753
440–43	30–33	4 concs., b, c, g, F, hpd, 2 vn, b, 1753–5
444–5	34; 169	Conc., G, org/hpd, str, 1755 (1760); version for fl, str, ?1755 or later
446	35	Conc., E flat, org/hpd, 2 hn, str, 1759
447–8	36–7	Conc., B flat, hpd, str, 1762; conc., c, hpd, 2 hn, str, 1762
449–52	96–9	4 sonatinas, D, G, G, F, hpd, 2 fl, 2 hn, str, 1762
453	109	Sonatina . . . con 18 stromenti, D, 2 hpd, 2 fl, 2 ob, bn, 2 hn, 3 tpt, timp, 2 vn, va, vc, vle, 1762
454	38	Conc., F, hpd, str, 2 fl ad lib, 1763
455–7	100; 102–3	3 sonatinas, E, D, C, hpd, 2 fl, 2 hn, str, 1763
458	106	Sonatina I, C, hpd, 2 fl, str, 1763 (Berlin, 1764); cf 460
459	110	Sonatina, B flat, 2 hpd, 2 fl, 2 hn, str, 1763
460	101	Sonatina, C, hpd, 2 fl, 2 hn, str, 1763 or later; rev. of 458
461–4	107–8; 104–5	Sonatinas, II, III, F, E flat; 2 sonatinas, F,

Helm	Wotquenne	
		E flat; hpd, 2 fl, str, 1764–5, 463–4 [revs. of 461–2] also 2 hn, 461 (Berlin, 1764), 462 (Berlin, 1766)
465–8	39; 164; 40; 165	Conc., B flat, hpd, str, 1765, version for ob, str, ?1765; Conc., E flat, hpd, str, 1765, version for ob, str. ?1765
469	41	Conc., E flat, hpd, 2 fl, 2 hn, str, 1769
470	42	Conc., F, hpd, 2 hn, str, 1770
471–6	43/1–6	Sei concerti, F, D, E flat, c, G, C, hpd, str, with 2 hn, 2 fl ad lib, 1771 (Hamburg, 1772)
477–8	44–5	2 concs., G, D, hpd, 2 hn, vn, va, b, 1778
479	47	Conc. doppio, E flat, hpd, pf, 2 fl, 2 hn, str, 1788

CHAMBER MUSIC WITH OBBLIGATO KEYBOARD

502	71	Sonata, D, hpd, vn, 1731, rev. 1746
503	72	Sonata, d, hpd, vn, 1731, rev. 1747
504	73	Sonata, C, hpd, vn, 1745
505	83	Sonata, D, hpd, fl, ?1747 or later
506	84	Trio, E, hpd, fl, ?1749 or later
507	74	Sonata o vero sinfonia, D, hpd, vn, 1754
508–9	85–6	2 sonatas, G, hpd, fl, 1754–5
510	88	Sonata, g, hpd, va da gamba, 1759
511–14	75–8	4 sonatas, F, b, B flat, c, hpd, vn, 1763
515	87	Sonata, C, hpd, fl, 1766
516–21	92	Sei Sonate, E flat, E flat, E flat, B flat, E flat, B flat, hpd, cl, bn, after 1767
522–4	90	[3] Claviersonaten, i, a, G, C, hpd, vn, vc, 1775 (Leipzig, 1776)
525–30	89	Six Sonatas, B flat, C, A, E flat, e, D, hpd/pf, vn, vc, 1775–6 (London, 1776)
531–4	91	[4] Claviersonaten, ii, e, D, F, C, hpd, vn, vc, 1777 (Leipzig, 1777); 534 variations on 249 [cf 259]
535	79	Arioso con variazioni, A, hpd, vn, 1781
536	80	Clavier-Fantasie mit Begleitung (C. P. E. Bachs Empfindungen), f sharp, hpd, vn, 1787
537–9	93–5	3 quartets, a, D, G, hpd, fl, va, [vc], 1788
540		[Sonata], e, kbd, melody inst., frag.
541		[Sonata], G, kbd, va

SOLO SONATAS FOR WIND AND STRINGS

548	134	Sonata, G, fl, bc, by ?1735
549	135	Solo, g, ob, bc, by ?1735
550–6	123–9	7 sonatas, G, e, B flat, D, G, a, D, fl, bc, 1735–40

Helm	Wotquenne	
557	138	Solo, g, vc, bc, 1740, rev. 1769, lost
558–9	136–7	2 solos, C, D, va da gamba, bc, 1745–6
560–1	130–1	2 sonatas, B flat, D, fl, bc, 1746–7
562	132	Sonata, a, fl, 1747 (Berlin, 1763) and in *Musikalisches Mancherley* (Berlin, 1762–3)
563	139	Solo, G, harp, 1762
564	133	Sonata, G, fl, bc, 1786

TRIO SONATAS

566		Trio . . . mit Johann Sebastian Bach gemeinschaftlich verfertigt, vn, va, bc, by ?1731, lost
567–71	143–7	5 sonatas, b, e, d, A, C, fl, vn, bc, 1731, rev. 1747; ?569 composed jointly by J. S. and C. P. E. Bach [cf BWV 1036]
572–5	148–51	4 sonatas, a, C, G, D, fl, vn, bc, 572 1735, rev. 1747, 573 1745, 574 1747, 575 1747
576–7	154–5	2 sonatas, F, e, 2 vn, bc, 1747; 576 cf BWV Anh. 186
578–9	161/2,1	Sonata, B flat, fl, vn, bc, 1748; Sonata, c, 2 vn, bc, 1749: pubd as *Zwey Trio* (Nuremberg, 1751)
580–1	162, 152	Trio, E, 2 fl, bc, 1749; trio G, fl, vn, bc, 1754
582	156	Sinfonia, a, 2 vn, bc, 1754
583–4	157–8	2 sonatas, G, B flat, 2 vn, bc, 1754, 584 (Berlin, 1763) and *Musikalisches Mancherley* (Berlin, 1762–3)
585		Sinfonia a tre voce, D, 2 vn, bc. ?1754
586	153	Sonata, G, fl, vn, bc, 1755
587–9	159, 163	Sonata, B flat, 2 vn, hpd, 1755; versions as trio, F, va, b rec, hpd, 1755, and trio, bn, b rec, hpd, ?1755
590	160	Sonata, d, 2 vn, bc, 1756, variant in *Musikalisches Mancherley* (Berlin, 1762–3)

OTHER CHAMBER

598	140	Duett, e, fl, vn, 1748, in *Musikalisches Vielerley* (Hamburg, 1770)
599	141	Duetto, d, 2 vn, 1752, lost
600	81	Zwölf kleine Stücke mit 2 und 3 Stimmen, 2 fl/2 vn, hpd, 1758 (Berlin, 1758)
601	192	Zwey Menuetten, C, 2 fl, 2 bn, 3 tpt, timp, 2 vn, bc, by 1762, in *Musikalisches Mancherley* (Berlin, 1762–3)
602–3	189/1–2	2 minuets, D, 2 fl, 2 cl, 2 vn, bc, ?*c*.1765

Helm	*Wotquenne*	
604–5	190/1,3	Polonoise, D, 2 cl, 2 vn, bc; Polonoise, a, 2 vn, bc: *c.*1765
606–9	189/8, 190/2,4,5	Minuet, D, 2 fl, 2 cl, 2 hn, 2 vn, bc: Polonoise, G, 2 vn, bc; Polonoise, D, 2 cl, 2 hn, 2 vn, bc; Polonoise, C, 2 vn, b: ?*c.*1766
610–13	115/1–4	4 kleine Duetten, B flat, F, a, E flat, 2 hpd, ?after 1767
614–19	185/1–6	VI Märsche, D, C, F, G, E flat, D, 2 ob, 2 cl, bn, 2 hn, after 1767
620	186	2 kleine Stücke, C, F, 2 cl, bn, 2 hn, after 1767, lost
621	188	Marcia . . . für die Arche, C, 3 tpt, timp, after 1767
622	189/3	Minuet, G, 2 fl, bn, 2 hn, 2 vn, bc, ?before 1768
623–6	189/4–7	4 minuets, G, G, F, D, 2 fl, 2 hn, 2 vn, bc, ?before 1768
627	190/6	Polonoise, A, 2 vn, bc, ?before 1768
628	82	Zwölf 2- und 3-stimmige kleine Stücke, 2 fl/2 vn, hpd, 1769 (Hamburg, 1770)
629–34	184/1–6	VI sonate, D, F, G, E flat, A, C, 2 fl, 2 cl, bn, 2 hn, 1775
635	193	[30] Stücke für Spieluhren, auch Dreh-Orgeln, no. 2, 1775 or later
636	142	Duett, C, 2 cl
637	187	2 Märsche, F, D, 2 ob, bn, 2 hn
638	191	Zwo abwechselnde Menuetten, D, 2 fl, 2 ob, 2 hn, 3 tpt, timp, str, bc

SYMPHONIES

648	173	Sinfonia, G, str, 1741
649	174	Sinfonia, C, 2 fl, 2 hn, str, 1755, also without hns/fls
650	175	Sinfonia, F, 2 fl, 2 bn, 2 hn, str, 1755; wind pts. opt.
651	176	Sinfonia, D, 2 fl, 2 ob, 2 hn, 3 tpt, timp, str, 1755; wind and timp pts. opt.
652	177	Sinfonia, e, str, 1756 (Nuremberg, 1759)
653	178	Sinfonia, e, 2 fl, 2 ob, 2 hn, str, ?1756
654–6	179–81	3 sinfonias, E flat, G, F, 2 ob, 2 hn, str, 1757–62; wind pts. opt.
657–62	182	Sei sinfonie, G, B flat, C, A, b, E, str, 1773; for G. van Swieten
663–6	183	[4] Orchester-Sinfonien mit 12 obligaten Stimmen, D, E flat, F, G, 2 fl, 2 ob, bn, 2 hn, 2 vn, va, vc, cb, 1775–6 (Leipzig, 1780)

WORKS FOR SOLO VOICE

Editions

Oden mit Melodien (Berlin, 1762): H. 677, 670, 679, 673–4, 680, 678, 683, 681, 671, 675, 672, 682, 676, 684, 689–92, 687; Wq. 199 [1762].

Helm	*Wotquenne*	
669	211	3 arias: Edle Freiheit, Götterglück; Himmels Tochter, Ruh der Seelen; Reiche bis zum Wolkensitze: T, str, bc, ?by 1738
670–2	199/2,10,12	3 songs: Schäferlied (M. von Ziegler), 1741; Der Zufrieden (Stahl), 1743; Die verliebte Verzweifelung (Steinhauer), 1743: (1762) and in *Sammlung verschiedener und auserlesener Oden* (Halle, 1737–43)
673–5	199/4,5,11	3 songs: Die Küsse (N. D. Giseke); Trinklied (J. W. L. Gleim); Amint (E. von Kleist): 1750–3 (1762) and in *Oden mit Melodien*, i (Berlin, 1753), 673–5 in *Lieder der Deutschen mit Melodien* (Berlin, 1767–8)
676	199/14	Die märkische Helene (G. E. Lessing), 1754 (1762) and in F. W. Marpurg: *Historisch-kritische Beyträge*, i.1 (1754)
677–8	199/1,7	2 songs: Die sächsische Helene (Gleim); Dorinde (Gleim): 1754 or 1755 (1762) and in *Oden mit Melodien*, ii (Berlin, 1755) and *Lieder der Deutschen mit Melodien* (Berlin, 1767–8)
679–80	199/3,6	2 songs: Lied eines jungen Mägdchens (Fräulein von H [?Lessing]); Der Morgen (F. von Hagedorn): 1756 (1762), 679 in *Berlinische Oden und Lieder* (Leipzig, 1756), 680 in F. W. Marpurg: *Neue Lieder zum singen beym Claviere* (1756)
681–4	199/9,13,8,15	4 songs: Die Biene (Lessing); Die Küsse (Lessing); Der Stoiker; Serin: 1756–7 (1762) and in *Berlinische Oden und Lieder* (Leipzig, 1756)
685		La Sophie, aria, 1757
686	194	[55] Geistliche Oden und Lieder mit Melodien (C. F. Gellert), 1757 (Berlin, 1758); 5 nos. in *Lieder und Arien aus Sophiens Reise* (Leipzig, 1779), 9 nos. in *Fünfzig und sechs neue Melodien* (Memmingen, 1780), no. 1 in *Musikalische Blumenlese* (Zurich, 1786)
687	199/20	Herausforderungslied vor der Schlacht bey Rossbach (Gleim), 1758 (1762)
688	202/A	Freude, du Lust der Götter und Menschen (C. M. Wieland), 1760, in *Drey verschiedene*

Helm	Wotquenne	
		Versuche eines einfachen Gesanges für den Hexameter (Berlin, 1760)
689–92	199/16–19	4 songs: Auf den Namenstag der Mademoiselle S.; Der Traum; Die Tugend (A. von Haller); Doris (von Haller): 1761–2 (1762)
693–5	202/B/1–3, [112/6,12,14]	3 songs: Das Privilegium (N. D. Giseke); Die Landschaft; Belinde (K. W. Müller): 1762–5 in *Clavierstücke verschiedener Art*, i (Berlin, 1765)
696	195	Zwölf geistliche Oden und Lieder als ein Anhang zu Gellerts geistliche Oden und Liedern mit Melodien (no. 4: L. F. F. Lehr, nos. 8, 10, 11: A. L. Karsch), 1764 (Berlin, 1764)
697	232	Phillis und Thirsis, cantata, 2 S, 2 fl, bc, 1765 (Berlin, 1766)
698	202/D	Bachus und Venus (H. W. von Gerstenberg), 1766, in *Musikalisches Vielerley* (Hamburg, 1770)
699	201 [264]	Der Wirth und die Gäste (Gleim), 4 solo vv, kbd, 1766 (Berlin, 1766, rev. 2/1790) and in *Notenbuch zu des akademischen Liederbuches erstem Bändchen* (Dessau and Leipzig, 1783)
700–1	200/10,20	Belise und Thyrsis; An eine kleine Schöne (Lessing): before 1767; 700 also as Allgütiger! gewohnt Gebet zu hören
702–8	200/6,8,11,12, 15,17,19	7 songs (J. H. Röding, J. H. Lüttkens, C. D. Ebeling, J. C. Unzer), after 1767
709–11	202/C/1–3	3 songs: Der Unbeständige ('W.'); Phillis (von Kleist); An die Liebe (von Hagedorn): c.1768, in *Unterhaltungen* (Hamburg, 1768–70)
712–17	202/C/4–9	6 songs (some by D. Schiebeler), 1769, in *Unterhaltungen* (Hamburg, 1768–70)
718–21	202/C/10–13	4 songs (Schiebeler, Karsch, von Gerstenberg, D. P. Scriba), 1770, in *Unterhaltungen* (Hamburg, 1768–70)
723	237	Der Frühling, cantata (Wieland), T, str, bc, 1770–2
724–9	202/E/1–6	6 songs (D. B. Münter), 1772–3, in *D. B. Münters erste Sammlung geistlicher Lieder mit Melodien* (Leipzig, 1773)
730–2	202/O/2; 202/F/1,2	3 songs: Klagelied eines Baueren (Miller); Vaterlandslied (F. G. Klopstock); Der Bauer (Miller): c.1773, 731–2 in *Göttinger Musenalmanach . . . 1774* (Göttingen, 1774)
733	196	[42] Übersetzte Psalmen mit Melodien (J. A. Cramer), 1773–4 (Leipzig, 1774)

Helm	Wotquenne	
734-5	200/9,22	Der Frühling (Miller), ?1773-82; Die Grazien, cantata (von Gerstenberg), 1774
736-7	202/G/1,2	Die Schlummernde (Voss); Lyda (Klopstock): 1774, in *Göttinger Musenalmanach . . . 1775* (Göttingen and Gotha, 1775) [cf 732]
738	202/I/1	Trinklied für Freye (Voss), 1775, in *Musenalmanach*, ed. J. H. Voss (Hamburg, 1776); cf 732
739	236	Selma (Voss), cantata, S, 2 fl, 2 vn, va, bc, ?1775
739.5	202/I/2	Alternative version of 739, 1775, in *Musenalmanach*, ed. J. H. Voss (Hamburg, 1776); cf 732
740-3	200/13,21; 202/O/1,4	4 songs: Trinklied (L. C. H. Hölty), 1775-82; An Doris (von Haller), 1775-6; Auf den Flügeln des Morgenroths (C. F. Cramer), ?1775-6; Da schlägt des Abschieds Stunde (Metastasio, trans. J. J. Eschenburg), ?1775-6
744-5	202/H; 200/1	An den Schlaf, 1776; Todtengräberlied (Hölty), 1776-82: 744 in *Die Muse*, i (Leipzig, 1776)
746	202/J	Selma (Voss), 1777, in *Musenalmanach*, ed. J. H. Voss (Hamburg, 1778) [not same as 739 or 739.5]
747-8	200/14,5	Aus einer Ode zum neuen Jahr; An die Grazien und Musen (Gleim): ?1777-82
749	197	[30] Geistliche Gesänge (C. C. Sturm) (Hamburg, 1780)
750-1	202/K/1,2	Fischerlied (C. A. Overbeck); Tischlied (Voss): 1780, in *Musenalmanach*, ed. J. H. Voss (Hamburg, 1781)
752	198	[30] Geistliche Gesänge, ii (Sturm) (Hamburg, 1781)
753-4	202/L/1,2	Lied (F. L. von Stolberg); Das Milchmädchen (Voss): 1781, in *Musenalmanach*, ed. J. H. Voss (Hamburg, 1782)
755-60	200/2-4,7,16,18	6 songs: Lied der Schnitterinnen (Gleim); Nonnelied; Das mitleidige Mädchen (Miller); Bevelise und Lysidor (J. A. Schlegel); Mittel, freundlich zu werden (Gleim); Ich hoff auch Gott mit festem Muth (E. von der Recke): 755-9 by ?1782, 760 1785
761-2	214; 231	Fürsten sind am Lebensziele, aria, S, str, bc, lost; Freudenlied (auf die Wiederkunft des Herrn Dr. C. aus dem Bade), 2 S, bc, 1785
763		[Die Alster] (von Hagedorn), and Harvestehude (von Hagedorn), ?c.1788

Helm	*Wotquenne*	
764	202/N/1–12	12 Masonic songs, 1788, in *Freymaurer-Lieder mit ganz neuen Melodien von den Herren Capellmeister Bach, Naumann und Schulz* (Copenhagen and Leipzig, 1788), also in *Allgemeines Liederbuch für Freymaurer*, iii (Copenhagen, 1788)
765–6	202/O/3,5	Kommt, lass uns seine Huld besingen (J. A. Cramer); Die schönste soll bey Sonnenschein
767	213	D'amor per te languisco, arietta, S, 2 fl, bc

CHORAL

774–826 are for solo vv, chorus, orch, 827–40 are mostly for chorus, orch; the
Passions include much material by J. S. Bach and Telemann.

772	215	Magnificat, S, A, T, B, SATB, 2 fl, 2 ob, 2 hn, 3 tpt, timp, str, bc, 1749
773–4	205–6	Der Zweyte Psalm, SATB; Der Vierte Psalm, S, A, bc: by 1761, in *Musikalisches Allerley* (Berlin, 1761)
775	238	Die Israeliten in der Wüste (D. Schiebeler), oratorio, solo vv, SATB, 2 fl, 2 ob, bn, 2 hn, 3 tpt, timp, str, bc, 1769 (Hamburg, 1775)
776	233	Passions-Cantate (L. Karsch), solo vv, SATB, 2 fl, 2 ob, 2 bn, 3 hn, timp, str, bc, 1770
777	240	Auferstehung und Himmelfahrt Jesu (C. W. Ramler), oratorio, S, T, B, SATB, 2 fl, 2 ob, bn, 2 hn, 3 tpt, timp, str, bc, 1777–80 (Leipzig, 1787)
778	217	Heilig, SATB, SATB, 2 ob, bn, 3 tpt, timp, str, bc, 1778 (Hamburg, 1779); used in 2 cantatas from 823 and 824
779	239	Morgengesang am Schöpfungsfeste (Klopstock), ode, solo vv, SSTB, 2 fl, 2 vn, 2 va, vc, bc, 1783 (Leipzig, 1784)
780	204	Zwey Litaneyen aus dem Schleswig-Holsteinischen Gesangbuche, SATB, SATB, bc, 1786 (Copenhagen, 1786) [cf 871]
781	203	[14] Neue Melodien zu einigen Liedern des neuen Hamburgischen Gesangbuchs, 1v, bc, 1787 (Hamburg, 1787)
782		St Matthew Passion, by 1768–9, lost
783–5		3 Passions: St Mark, by 1769–70; St Luke, by 1770–71; St John, by 1771–2, lost
786		St Matthew Passion, by 1772–3, lost

Helm	Wotquenne	
787–9		3 Passions: St Mark, by 1773–4; St Luke, by ?1774–5; St John, by 1775–6, lost
790		St Matthew Passion, by 1776–7, lost
791–3		3 Passions: St Mark, by 1777–8; St Luke, by 1778–9; St John, by 1779–80, lost
794		St Matthew Passion, by 1780–1, sketches
795		St Mark Passion, by 1781–2, lost
796		St Luke Passion, by 1782–3, incl. recit. and aria
797		St John Passion, by 1783–4, incl. 2 arias, recit.
798		St Matthew Passion, by 1784–5, lost
799		St Mark Passion, by 1785–6, lost
800	234	St Luke Passion, by 1786–7
801		St John Passion, by 1787–8, lost
802	235	St Matthew Passion, by 1788, ?composer's last work
803	244	Oster-Musik (Cochius), cantata, 1756
804–5	242, 241	Oster-Musik, cantata, by 1778, Oster-Musik, cantata, 1778 or later; 804 partly borrowed from J. S. Bach; 805 incl. 778
807	243	Oster-Musik, cantata, by 1784; pt. ii lost
808		MSS of Oster-Musik for 1768–9, 1771, 1775, 1781–2, 1787, lost, mostly borrowed from other works
809–11	248, 245	3 Michaelis-Musik, cantatas, c.1769–c.1772; 809 sources inc.; 811 lost
812	247, 212	Michaelis-Musik, cantata, c.1775, incl. Wq. 212, aria
814	246	Michaelis-Musik, cantata, by 1785 [incl. 778]
815	249	Weihnachts-Musik, cantata, 1775
816		At least 4 lost MSS of Weihnachts-Musik
817		Herr, lehr' uns thun, cantata, 1769, collab. G. A. Homilius, lost
818		Der Gerechte, ob er gleich, cantata, 1774, after Johann Christoph Bach
819		Meine Seele erhebt den Herrn, cantata, collab. 'Hoffmann', lost
820		At least 4 lost MSS of Sonntagsmusik
821–4	250–3	c.30 congratulatory cantatas, variously entitled Einführungsmusik, Jubelmusik, Serenata, Oratorio, Musik am Dankfest, Trauungs-Cantate, Dank-Hymne, Geburtstags-Cantate, 1768–87, occasional works for Hamburg, often incl. borrowed material
825	207	Veni, Sancte Spiritus, after 1767
826	208	4 Motetten, nos. 1–3 after 1767, no. 4 c.1781
827–8	218–19	Einchöriges Heilig; Sanctus: after 1767

Helm	Wotquenne	
829	216	Spiega, Ammonia fortunata, occasional work, 1770
830	221	Mein Heiland, meine Zuversicht, ?Sonntagsmusik, 1771
831	222	Wer ist so würdig als du, 1774
832	223	Zeige du mir deine Wege, 1777; ?part of Sonntagsmusik, 1777
833	225	Gott, dem ich lebe, 1780
834–5	226–7	Amen, Amen, Lob und Preis; Leite mich nach deinen Willen: 1783; ?part of Sonntagsmusik 1783
836–7	228–9	Meine Lebenszeit verstreicht, 1783; Meinen Leib wird man begraben, ?1788; funeral music
838		Merkt und seht; ?from Passion
839–40	209–10	Antiphonia, 4 vv; Amen, 4 vv: lost
841		Wirf dein Anliegen auf, arr. of anon. motet, lost
842	(Wotquenne, p.96n.)	10 Choräle (Graf von Wernigerode), 4 vv, by 1767
843		Naglet til et Kors paa Jorden, chorale, by 1781, in Kirke-Melodierne til den 1778 udgangne Psalmebog (Copenhagen, 1778)
844		3 chorales, by 1785, in Vollständige Sammlung der Melodien . . . des neuen allgemeinen Schleswig-Holsteinischen Gesangbuchs (Leipzig, 1785)
845		Chorale, by 1786, in Vierstimmige alte und neue Choralgesänge (Berlin, 1786)
847		Tpt and timp parts added to C. H. Graun: Te Deum, after 1756, lost
848		Inst introduction to Credo of J. S. Bach: B minor Mass, 1768, or later
854		Various acc. recits added to works by other composers, lost
859		Sey mir gesegnet, aria from choral work

THEORETICAL WORKS

867	121	Miscellanea musica, technical exercises collected by Westphal, incl. 285 and various sketches, some for 536
868	254	Versuch über die wahre Art das Clavier zu spielen, mit Exempeln und achtzehn Probe-Stücken in sechs Sonaten erläutert, i (Berlin, 1753, reissues 1759, 1780, rev. 2/1787) [for Probe-Stücke, see 70–75, 2nd edn., incl. 292–7]
869	257	'Einfall einen doppelten Contrapunct in der Octave von 6 Tacten zu machen, ohne die

Helm	Wotquenne	
		Regeln davon zu wissen', *c.*1757, in F. W. Marpurg: *Historisch-kritische Beyträge zur Aufnahme der Musik*, iii (Berlin, 1757) [a permutational scheme of composition]
870	255	*Versuch über die wahre Art das Clavier zu spielen . . . in welchen die Lehre von dem Accompagnement und der freyen Fantasie abgehandelt wird*, ii (Berlin, 1762, reissues, 1780, 1787, rev. 2/1797)
871	204	Zwey Litaneyen aus dem Schleswig-Holstein-ischen Gesangbuche, SATB, SATB, bc, 1786 (Copenhagen, 1786) [contains nearly 100 different harmonizations of 1 motif, cf 780]

APPENDIX IV

Concordances of Wotquenne numbers (Wq.) with Helm numbers (H.)

Wq.	H.	Wq.	H.	Wq.	H.	Wq.	H.
1	403	43/2	472	53/5	163	61/4	290
2	404	43/3	473	53/6	183	61/5	287
3	405	43/4	474	54/1	204	61/6	291
4	406	43/5	475	54/2	205	62/1	2
5	407	43/6	476	54/3	184	62/2	20
6	409	44	477	54/4	206	62/3	22
7	410	45	478	54/5	185	62/4	38
8	411	46	408	54/6	207	62/5	39
9	412	47	479	55/1	244	62/6	40
10	413	48/1	24	55/2	130	62/7	41
11	414	48/2	25	55/3	245	62/8	55
12	415	48/3	26	55/4	186	62/9	58
13	416	48/4	27	55/5	243	62/10	59
14	417	48/5	28	55/6	187	62/11	63
15	418	48/6	29	56/1	260	62/12	66
16	419	49/1	30	56/2	246	62/13	67
17	420	49/2	31	56/3	261	62/14	77
18	421	49/3	33	56/4	269	62/15	105
19	422	49/4	32	56/5	262	62/16	116
20	423	49/5	34	56/6	270	62/17	117
21	424	49/6	36	57/1	265	62/18	118
22	425	50/1	136	57/2	247	62/19	119
23	427	50/2	137	57/3	271	62/20	120
24	428	50/3	138	57/4	208	62/21	131
25	429	50/4	139	57/5	266	62/22	132
26	430	50/5	126	57/6	173	62/23	210
27	433	50/6	140	58/1	276	62/24	240
28	434	51/1	150	58/2	273	63/1	70
29	437	51/2	151	58/3	274	63/2	71
30	440	51/3	127	58/4	188	63/3	72
31	441	51/4	128	58/5	267	63/4	73
32	442	51/5	141	58/6	277	63/5	74
33	443	51/6	62	58/7	278	63/6	75
34	444	52/1	50	59/1	281	63/7	292
35	446	52/2	142	59/2	268	63/8	293
36	447	52/3	158	59/3	282	63/9	294
37	448	52/4	37	59/4	283	63/10	295
38	454	52/5	161	59/5	279	63/11	296
39	465	52/6	129	59/6	284	63/12	297
40	467	53/1	162	60	209	64/1	7
41	469	53/2	180	61/1	288	64/2	8
42	470	53/3	181	61/2	286	64/3	9
43/1	471	53/4	182	61/3	289	64/4	10

Wq.	H.	Wq.	H.	Wq.	H.	Wq.	H.
64/5	11	65/50	299	95	539	114/5	232
64/6	12	66	272	96	449	114/6	233
65/1	3	67	300	97	450	114/7	234
65/2	4	68	164	98	451	114/8	235
65/3	5	69	53	99	452	114/9	236
65/4	6	70/1	133	100	455	114/10	237
65/5	13	70/2	134	101	460	114/11	238
65/6	15	70/3	84	102	456	115/1	610
65/7	16	70/4	85	103	457	115/2	611
65/8	17	70/5	86	104	463	115/3	612
65/9	18	70/6	87	105	464	115/4	613
65/10	19	70/7	107	106	458	116/1	171
65/11	21	71	502	107	461	116/2	172
65/12	23	72	503	108	462	116/3	214
65/13	32.5	73	504	109	453	116/4	215
65/14	42	74	507	110	459	116/5	216
65/15	43	75	511	111	1.5	116/6	217
65/16	46	76	512	112/1	190	116/7	218
65/17	47	77	513	112/2	144	116/8	219
65/18	48	78	514	112/3	165	116/9	165
65/19	49	79	535	112/4	145	116/10	166
65/20	51	80	536	112/5	166	116/11	167
65/21	52	81	600	112/6	693	116/12	168
65/22	56	82	628	112/7	179	116/13	169
65/23	57	83	505	112/8	146	116/14	170
65/24	60	84	506	112/9	167	116/15	159
65/25	61	85	508	112/10	147	116/16	338
65/26	64	86	509	112/11	168	116/17	338
65/27	68	87	515	112/12	694	116/18	108
65/28	78	88	510	112/13	91	116/19	301
65/29	83	89/1	525	112/14	695	116/20	302
65/30	106	89/2	526	112/15	148	116/21	153
65/31	121	89/3	527	112/16	169	116/22	154
65/32	135	89/4	528	112/17	170	116/23	249
65/33	143	89/5	529	112/18	149	116/24	250
65/34	152	89/6	530	112/19	101.5	116/25	251
65/35	156	90/1	522	113/1	193	116/26	252
65/36	157	90/2	523	113/2	194	116/27	253
65/37	174	90/3	524	113/3	195	116/28	254
65/38	175	91/1	531	113/4	196	116/29	303
65/39	176	91/2	532	113/5	197	116/30	304
65/40	177	91/3	533	113/6	198	116/31	305
65/41	178	91/4	534	113/7	199	116/32	306
65/42	189	92/1	516	113/8	200	116/33	307
65/43	192	92/2	517	113/9	201	116/34	308
65/44	211	92/3	518	113/10	202	116/35	309
65/45	212	92/4	519	113/11	203	116/36	310
65/46	213	92/5	520	114/1	228	116/37	311
65/47	248	92/6	521	114/2	229	116/38	312
65/48	280	93	537	114/3	230	116/39	313
65/49	298	94	538	114/4	231	116/40	314

Wq.	H.	Wq.	H.	Wq.	H.	Wq.	H.
116/41	315	117/35	97	144	568	184/4	632
116/42	316	117/36	114	145	569	184/5	633
116/43	317	117/37	82	146	570	184/6	634
116/44	318	117/38	124	147	571	185/1	614
116/45	319	117/39	98	148	572	185/2	615
116/46	320	117/40	125	149	573	185/3	616
116/47	321	118/1	69	150	574	185/4	617
116/48	322	118/2	155	151	575	185/5	618
116/49	323	118/3	44	152	581	185/6	619
116/50	324	118/4	54	153	586	186	620
116/51	325	118/5	65	154	576	187	637
116/52	326	118/6	226	155	577	188	621
116/53	327	118/7	14	156	582	189/1	602
116/54	328	118/8	275	157	583	189/2	603
116/55	329	118/9	263	158	584	189/3	622
116/56	330	118/10	259	159	587	189/4	623
116/57	331	119/1	76	160	590	189/5	624
117/1	241	119/2	99	161	578-9	189/6	625
117/2	220	119/3	100	162	580	189/7	626
117/3	221	119/4	101	163	588	189/8	606
117/4	222	119/5	101.5	164	466	190/1	604
117/5	145	119/6	102	165	468	190/2	607
117/6	147	119/7	75.5	166	431	190/3	605
117/7	149	120	264	167	435	190/4	608
117/8	144	121	867	168	438	190/5	609
117/9	146	122/1	45	169	445	190/6	627
117/10	148	122/2	104	170	432	191	638
117/11	223	122/3	115	171	436	192	601
117/12	224	122/4	191	172	439	193	635
117/13	225	122/5	227	173	648	194	686
117/14	160	123	550	174	649	195	696
117/15	195	124	551	175	650	196	733
117/16	234	125	552	176	651	197	749
117/17	79	126	553	177	652	198	752
117/18	80	127	554	178	653	199/1	677
117/19	89	128	555	179	654	199/2	670
117/20	90	129	556	180	655	199/3	679
117/21	91	130	560	181	656	199/4	673
117/22	122	131	561	182/1	657	199/5	674
117/23	92	132	562	182/2	658	199/6	680
117/24	93	133	564	182/3	659	199/7	678
117/25	94	134	548	182/4	660	199/8	683
117/26	81	135	549	182/5	661	199/9	681
117/27	95	136	558	182/6	662	199/10	671
117/28	109	137	559	183/1	663	199/11	675
117/29	123	138	557	183/2	664	199/12	672
117/30	110	139	563	183/3	665	199/13	682
117/31	111	140	598	183/4	666	199/14	676
117/32	112	141	599	184/1	629	199/15	684
117/33	113	142	636	184/2	630	199/16	689
117/34	96	143	567	184/3	631	199/17	690

Wq.	*H.*	*Wq.*	*H.*	*Wq.*	*H.*
199/18	691	202/E/4	727	228	836
199/19	692	202/E/5	728	229	837
199/20	687	202/E/6	729	230	795
200/1	745	202/F/1	731	231	762
200/2	755	202/F/2	732	232	697
200/3	756	202/G/1	736	233	776
200/4	757	202/G/2	737	234	800
200/5	748	202/H	744	235	802
200/6	702	202/I/1	738	236	739
200/7	758	202/I/2	739.5	237	723
200/8	703	202/J	746	238	775
200/9	734	202/K/1	750	239	779
200/10	700	202/K/2	751	240	777
200/11	704	202/L/1	753	241	805
200/12	705	202/L/2	754	242	804
200/13	740	202/M	See H.7	243	807
200/14	747	202/N	764	244	803
200/15	706	202/O/1	742	245	810
200/16	759	202/O/2	730	246	814
200/17	707	202/O/3	765	247	812
200/18	760	202/O/4	743	248	809
200/19	708	202/O/5	766	249	815
200/20	701	203	781	250	821 l
200/21	741	204	780,871	251	821 g
200/22	735	205	773	252	821 f
201	699	206	774	253	821 m
202/A	688	207	825	254	868
202/B/1	693	208	826	255	870
202/B/2	694	209	839	256	868 (and 873, a
202/B/3	695	210	840		spurious addition)
202/C/1	709	211	669	257	869
202/C/2	710	212	812	258	874 (spurious)
202/C/3	11	213	767	259	See Wq. 113
202/C/4	12	214	761	260	See Wq. 113
202/C/5	713	215	772	261	See Wq. 113
202/C/6	714	216	829	262	See Wq. 113
202/C/7	715	217	778	263	776
202/C/8	716	218	827	264	699
202/C/9	717	219	828	265	See Wq. 70
202/C/10	718	220	855	266	21, 51, 121
202/C/11	719	221	830	267	See Wq. 113.
202/C/12	720	222	831	268	51
202/C/13	721	223	832	269	14
202/D	698	224	798	270	263
202/E/1	724	225	833	271	220
202/E/2	725	226	834	272	386 (spurious)
202/E/3	726	227	835		

Wq. 273–8 lists portraits of the composer, not dealt with in H.
Wq. 279 is the *Nachlassverzeichnis*.

SELECT BIBLIOGRAPHY

Useful bibliographies are found in the *Bach-Jahrbücher*, and in the sections 'Family History' and 'Johann Sebastian Bach' (by C. Wolff) and 'Carl Philipp Emanuel Bach' (by E. E. Helm) in 'Bach Family', *The New Grove Dictionary of Music and Musicians*, ed. Stanley Sadie, i (London etc., 1980), pp. 782, 836ff., 862f. (For slightly updated versions see *The New Grove Bach Family*, London, 1983, pp. 27ff., 215ff., 305f.) A comprehensive bibliography will be included in *C. P. E. Bach Studies*, ed. S. L. Clark (forthcoming, Oxford, 1988).

BACH, C. P. E., *Versuch über die wahre Art das Clavier zu spielen*, 2 vols. (Berlin 1753–62; R (facs.)/Leipzig and Wiesbaden, 1957). Trans. and ed. W. J. Mitchell as *Essay on the True Art of Playing Keyboard Instruments* (New York and London, 1949).

BACH, C. P. E., 'Autobiography', contained in C. Burney, *Tagebuch einer musikalischen Reise*, iii, trans. C. D. Ebeling and J. J. C. Bode (Hamburg, 1773; R/Kassel etc., 1959), pp. 199ff. For a translation into English, see under W. S. Newman below.

BACH, C. P. E., Letters. These are contained in: *Letters of Distinguished Musicians*, collected L. Nohl, trans. Lady Wallace (London, 1867); La Mara, *Musikerbriefe aus fünf Jahrhunderten*, i (Leipzig, 1886); E. Bücken, *Musikerbriefe* (Leipzig, 1940); E. Suchalla, *Briefe von Carl Philipp Emanuel Bach an Johann Gottlob Immanuel Breitkopf und Johann Nikolaus Forkel* (1985). Letters are also quoted in the texts by C. H. Bitter (1868), F. Chrysander (1869), S. L. Clark (1984), H. von Hase (1911), E. R. Jacobi (1970 and 1974), H. Miesner (1929 and 1932), C. Petzsch (1965), E. F. Schmid (1931), O. G. Sonneck (1906–7), and M. Terry (1969) which are listed below.

BACH, C. P. E., and AGRICOLA, J. F., *Obituary of J. S. Bach*, quoted in *Bach Reader*, pp. 215ff. Originally published in L. Mizler, *Musikalische Bibliothek*, iv (Leipzig, 1754; R/Hilversum, 1966), pp. 166ff.

Verzeichnis des musikalischen Nachlasses des Verstorbenen Capellmeisters Carl Philipp Emanuel Bach, (Hamburg, 1790); reprinted with notes by H. Miesner as 'Philipp Emanuel Bachs musikalischer Nachlass', *B-Jb*, xxxv (1938), pp. 103ff., xxxvi (1939), pp. 81ff., xxxvii (1940–8), pp. 161ff. See also R. W. Wade below.

Bach-Dokumente, 3 vols. (Kassel etc., 1963–72). i: Schriftstücke von der Hand Johann Sebastian Bachs. ii: Fremdschriftliche und gedruckte Dokumente zur Lebensgeschichte Johann Sebastian Bachs 1685–1750. iii: Dokumente zum Nachwirken Johann Sebastian Bachs 1750–1800.

The Bach Reader. A Life of Johann Sebastian Bach in Letters and Documents, ed. H. T. David and A. Mendel (New York, 1945, rev. 2nd edn., 1966).

BARFORD, P., *The Keyboard Music of C. P. E. Bach* (London, 1965).

BARFORD, P., 'Some Afterthoughts by C. P. E. Bach', *Monthly Musical Record*, xc (1960), pp. 94ff.

BAUMGART, E. F., 'Ueber harmonische Ausfüllung älterer Claviermusik, hauptsächlich bei Ph. Em. Bach', *[Leipziger] Allgemeine musikalische Zeitung*, v (1870), pp. 185ff., 193ff., 210f., 209f.

BERG, D. M., *The Keyboard Sonatas of C. P. E. Bach. An Expression of the Mannerist Principle*, Diss., State University of New York at Buffalo, 1975.

BERG, D. M., 'Towards a Catalogue of the Keyboard Sonatas of C. P. E. Bach', *JAMS*, xxxii (1979), pp. 276ff.

BERG, D. M., 'C. P. E. Bach's "Variations" and "Embellishments" for his Keyboard Sonatas', *The Journal of Musicology*, ii (1983), pp. 151ff.

BESSELER, H., 'Bach als Wegbereiter', *Archiv für Musikwissenschaft*, xii (1955), pp. 1ff.

BEURMANN, E., *Die Klaviersonaten Carl Philipp Emanuel Bachs*, Diss., Göttingen, 1953.

BEURMANN, E., 'Die Reprisensonaten Carl Philipp Emanuel Bachs', *Archiv für Musikwissenschaft*, xiii (1956), pp. 168ff.

BITTER, C. H., *Carl Philipp Emanuel und Wilhelm Friedemann Bach und deren Brüder*, 2 vols. (Berlin, 1868; R/Leipzig, 1973).

BITTER, C. H., *Die Söhne Sebastian Bach's* (Leipzig, 1883).

BODKY, E., 'C. P. E. Bach's Influence on the Viennese Masters', *Bulletin of the American Musicological Society*, xi (1948), p. 38.

BRAUSS, M., 'Manierismus. Ästhetische und didaktische Aspekte einer Kompositionstechnik am Beispiel des Instrumentalen Rezitativs bei C. Ph. E. Bach', *Musik und Bildung*, xvii (1985), pp. 416ff.

BREWER, R. H., *The Two Oratorios of C. P. E. Bach in Relation to Performance*, Diss., University of Southern California, 1965.

BROWN, A. P., 'Joseph Haydn and C. P. E. Bach: The Question of Influence', *Haydn Studies: Washington 1975*, pp. 158ff.

BURNEY, C., *The Present State of Music in Germany, the Netherlands, and United Provinces* (London, 1773), ed. P. Scholes as *Dr. Burney's Musical Tours*, ii (London, 1959).

BUSCH, G., *C. Ph. E. Bach und seine Lieder* (Regensburg, 1957).

BYRT, J. C., *Form and Style in the Works of J. S. and C. P. E. Bach*, Diss., Oxford University, 1970.

CANAVE, P. C. G., *A Revaluation of the Role Played by Carl Philipp Emanuel Bach in the Development of the Clavier Sonata* (Washington D.C., 1956).

Carl-Philipp-Emanuel-Bach-Konzepte, ed. H.-G. Ottenberg, i (Frankfurt an der Oder, 1983).

C. P. E. Bach Studies, ed. S. L. Clark (forthcoming, Oxford, 1988).

CHAMBLEE, J. M., *The Cantatas and Oratorios of Carl Philipp Emanuel Bach*, Diss., University of North Carolina, 1973.

CHERBULIEZ, A. E., *Carl Philipp Emanuel Bach. 1714–1788* (Zurich and Leipzig, 1940).

CHRYSANDER, F., 'Eine Klavier-Phantasie von Karl Philipp Emanuel Bach mit nachträglich von Gerstenberg eingefügten Gesangsmelodien zu zwei verschiedenen Texten', *Vierteljahrsschrift für Musikwissenschaft*, vii (1891), pp. 1ff.

CHRYSANDER, F., (ed.), 'Briefe von Karl Philipp Emanuel Bach an G. M. Telemann', *[Leipziger] Allgemeine musikalische Zeitung*, iv (1869), pp. 177ff., 185ff.

CLARK, S. L., 'The Letters from Carl Philipp Emanuel Bach to Georg Michael Telemann', *The Journal of Musicology*, iii (1984), pp. 177ff.

CLARK, S. L., *The Occasional Choral Works of C. P. E. Bach*, Diss., Princeton University, 1984.

COHEN, P., 'Theorie und Praxis der Clavierästhetik Carl Philipp Emanuel Bachs', *Musikforschung*, xxxi.2 (1978), pp. 221ff.

CRAMER, H., 'Die Violoncell-Kompositionen Philipp Emanuel Bachs', *Allgemeine Musikzeitung*, lvii (1930), pp. 316ff.

CRAMER, H., 'Einiges zu Ph. E. Bachs Kammermusik', *Allgemeine Musikzeitung*, lvii (1930), pp. 519f.

CRICKMORE, L., 'C. P. E. Bach's Harpsichord Concertos', *Music and Letters*, xxxix (1958), pp. 227ff.

DAHLHAUS, C., 'Si vis me flere . . .', *Musikforschung*, xxv (1972), pp. 51f.

DAYMOND, E. R., 'Carl Philipp Emanuel Bach', *Proceedings of the Musical Association*, xxxiii (London, 1907), pp. 45ff.

DERR, E. S., 'Beethoven's Long-Term memory of C. P. E. Bach's Rondo in E flat, Wq. 61 no. 1 (1787) manifest in the Variations in E flat for piano, op. 35 (1802)', *MQ*, lxx (1984), pp. 45ff.

DIETRICH, F., 'Matthias Claudius und C. Ph. E. Bach', *Zeitschrift für Hausmusik*, ix (1940), pp. 73ff.

DRUMMOND, P., *The German Concerto. Five Eighteenth-Century Studies* (Oxford, 1980).

FISCHER, K. VON, 'C. Ph. E. Bachs Variationenwerke', *Revue Belge de Musicologie*, vi (1952), pp. 190ff.

FISCHER, K. VON, 'Arietta Variata', *Studies in Eighteenth-Century Music. A Tribute to Karl Geiringer on his Seventieth Birthday*, ed. H. C. Robbins Landon (London, 1970), pp. 224ff.

FISCHMAN, N., 'Estetika F. E. Bacha', *Sowjetskaja musyka*, xxviii (1964), book viii, pp. 59ff.

FLUELER, M., *Die Norddeutsche Sinfonie zur Zeit Friedrichs d. Gr. und besonders die Werke Ph. Em. Bachs*, Diss., Berlin, 1908.

FOX, P. R., *Melodic Nonconstancy in the Keyboard Sonatas of C. P. E. Bach*, Diss., Cincinnati, 1983.

FRIEDLAENDER, M., 'Ein ungedrucktes Lied Philipp Emanuel Bachs', *Jahrbuch der Musikbibliothek Peters für 1899*, vi (1900), pp. 65ff.

GEIRINGER, K., 'Artistic Interrelations of the Bachs', *MQ*, xxxvi (1950), pp. 363ff.

GEIRINGER, K. AND I., *The Bach Family. Seven Generations of Creative Genius* (London, 1954; R/1980).

GEIRINGER, K., *The Music of the Bach Family: An Anthology* (Cambridge, Mass., 1955; R/New York, 1980).

GODT, I., 'C. P. E. Bach his Mark', *College Music Symposium (USA)*, xix.2 (fall 1979), pp. 154ff.

HAACKE, W., *Die Söhne Bachs* (Königstein im Taunus, n.d.).

HAAG, C. R., *The Keyboard Concertos of Karl Philipp Emanuel Bach*, Diss., University of California at Los Angeles, 1956.

HAGER, N. B., *Rhythm and voice-leading as a facet of style: keyboard works of Johann*

Sebastian Bach, Carl Philipp Emanuel Bach, and Mozart, Diss., City University of New York, 1978.

HASE, H. VON, 'Carl Philipp Emanuel Bach und Joh. Gottl. Im. Breitkopf', *B-Jb*, viii (1911), pp. 86ff.

HELM, E. E., *Thematic Catalogue of the Works of Carl Philipp Emanuel Bach* (forthcoming).

HELM, E. E., 'The "Hamlet" Fantasy and the Literary Element in C. P. E. Bach's Music', *MQ*, lviii (1972), pp. 277ff.

HELM, E. E., *Music at the Court of Frederick the Great* (Norman, Okla., 1960).

HELM, E. E., 'Carl Philipp Emanuel Bach', *The New Grove Dictionary of Music and Musicians*, ed. Stanley Sadie, i (London etc., 1980), pp. 844ff. Reprinted with minor revisions in *The New Grove Bach Family* (London, 1983), pp. 251ff.

HELM, E. E., 'An Honorable Shortcut to the Works of C. P. E. Bach', *Music in the Classic Period. Essays in Honor of Barry S. Brook* (New York, 1985), pp. 85ff.

HELM, E. E., 'To Haydn from C. P. E. Bach: Non-tunes', *Haydn Studies: Washington 1975*, pp. 382ff.

HELM, E. E., 'Six Random Measures of C. P. E. Bach', *Journal of Music Theory*, (1966), pp. 19ff.

HOFFMANN-ERBRECHT, L., 'Klavierkonzert und Affektgestaltung. Bemerkungen zu einigen d-Moll Klavierkonzerten des 18. Jahrhunderts', *Deutsches Jahrbuch der Musikwissenschaft*, xvi (1971), pp. 86ff.

HOFFMANN-ERBRECHT, L., 'Johann Sebastian und Carl Philipp Emanuel Bachs Nürnberger Verleger', *Die Nürnberger Musikverleger und die Familie Bach, Materialien zu einer Ausstellung des 48. Bach-Festes der Neuen Bach-Gesellschaft* (Nuremberg, 1973), pp. 5ff.

HOLSCHNEIDER, A., 'C. Ph. E. Bachs Kantate "Auferstehung und Himmelfahrt Jesu" und Mozarts Aufführung des Jahres 1788', *Mozart-Jahrbuch* (1968–70), pp. 264ff.

JACOBI, E. R., 'Das Autograph von C. Ph. E. Bachs Doppelkonzert in Es-dur für Cembalo, Fortepiano und Orchester (Wq. 47, Hamburg, 1788)', *Musikforschung*, xii (1959), pp. 488ff.

JACOBI, E. R., 'Five hitherto unknown letters from C. P. E. Bach to J. J. H. Westphal', *JAMS*, xxiii (1970), pp. 119ff.

JACOBI, E. R., 'Three Additional Letters from C. P. E. Bach to J. J. H. Westphal', *JAMS*, xxvii (1974), pp. 119ff.

JACOBS, R. M., *The Chamber Ensembles of C. P. E. Bach Using Two or More Wind Instruments*, Diss., State University of Iowa, 1963.

JALOWETZ, H., 'Beethoven's Jugendwerke in ihren melodischen Beziehungen zu Mozart, Haydn und Ph. E. Bach', *SIMG*, xii (1910–11), pp. 417ff.

JURISCH, H., *Prinzipien der Dynamik im Klavierwerk Philipp Emanuel Bachs*, Diss., Tübingen, 1959.

JURISCH, H., 'Zur Dynamik im Klavierwerk Ph. E. Bachs', *Bericht über den Internationalen Musikwissenschaftlichen Kongress Kassel 1962* (Kassel etc., 1963), pp. 178ff.

KAHL, W., 'Geschichte, Kritik und Aufgaben der K. Ph. E. Bach-Forschung', *Beethoven-Zentenarfeier, Internationaler Musikhistorischer Kongress* (Vienna, 1927), pp. 211ff.

KELLAR, A., *The Hamburg Bach: Carl Philipp Emanuel Bach as Choral Composer*, Diss., State University of Iowa, 1970.

KIRKPATRICK, R., 'C. P. E. Bach's "Versuch" Reconsidered', *Early Music*, iv. 4 (October 1976), pp. 384ff.

KRICKEBERG, D., 'Ein Hammerflügel von Johann Heinrich Silbermann (1776) im Musikinstrumenten-Museum des Staatl. Instituts für Musikforschung in Berlin', *Bachwoche Ansbach 1979*, pp. 47ff.

LISCO, J. D., *C. P. E. Bach and the fantasia*, M.A. Diss., University of Kentucky, 1978.

LORINCE, F. E., *A Study of Musical Texture in Relation to Sonata-Form As Evidenced in Selected Keyboard Sonatas from C. P. E. Bach through Beethoven*, Diss., University of Rochester, 1966.

MARKS, P. F., *Sturm und Drang in the Instrumental Music of C. P. E. Bach, Haydn, and Mozart*, Diss., University of Washington (in preparation).

MEER, J. H. VAN DER, *Die klangfarbliche Identität der Klavierwerke Carl Philipp Emanuel Bachs* (Amsterdam, 1978).

MERSMANN, H., 'Ein Programmtrio Karl Philipp Emanuel Bachs', *B-Jb*, xiv (1917), pp. 137ff.

MIESNER, H., *Philipp Emanuel Bach in Hamburg* (Leipzig, 1929; R/Wiesbaden, 1969).

MIESNER, H., 'Ungedruckte Briefe von Philipp Emanuel Bach', *Zeitschrift für Musikwissenschaft*, xiv (1931–2), pp. 224ff.

MIESNER, H., 'Die Grabstätte Emanuel Bachs', *B-Jb*, xxxi (1934), pp. 164f.

MIESNER, H., 'Urkundliche Nachrichten über die Familie Bach in Berlin', *B-Jb*, xxix (1932), pp. 157ff.

MIESNER, H., 'Beziehungen zwischen den Familien Stahl und Bach', *B-Jb*, xxx (1933), pp. 71ff.

MIESNER, H., 'Graf von Keyserlingk und Minister von Happe, zwei Gönner der Familie Bach', *B-Jb*, xxxi (1934), pp. 101ff.

MIESNER, H., 'Aus der Umwelt Philipp Emanuel Bachs', *B-Jb*, xxxiv (1937), pp. 132ff.

MIESNER, H., 'Porträts aus dem Kreise Philipp Emanuel und Wilhelm Friedemann Bachs', *Musik und Bild. Festschrift Max Seiffert* (Kassel, 1938), pp. 101ff.

MITCHELL, W. J., 'C. P. E. Bach's Essay. An Introduction', *MQ*, xxxiii (1947), pp. 460ff. The same article is also printed as the introduction to Mitchell's translation of the *Essay* (See under Bach, *Versuch*).

MITCHELL, W. J., 'Modulation in C. P. E. Bach's "Versuch"', *Studies in Eighteenth-Century Music. A Tribute to Karl Geiringer on his Seventieth Birthday*, ed. H. C. Robbins Landon (London, 1970), pp. 333ff.

MÜLLER, J.-P., 'La Technique de l'accompagnement dans la musique du xviii-ème siècle tirée du traité de C. P. E. Bach, *Versuch über die wahre Art das Clavier zu spielen*', *Revue Belge de Musicologie*, xxiii (1969), pp. 3ff.

MÜLLER, W., *Das Ausdrucksproblem in der Klaviermusik C. Ph. E. Bachs*, Diss., Saarbrücken, 1959.

MÜLLER, W., 'Die Artikulation im Klavierwerk C. Ph. E. Bachs', *Annales Universitatis Saraviensis*, ix, F. 1, pp. 51ff.

NEWLIN, D., 'C. P. E. Bach and Arnold Schoenberg. A Comparison', *The Commonwealth of Music. Gedenkschrift C. Sachs* (New York, 1965), pp. 300ff.

NEWMAN, W. S., 'Emanuel Bach's Autobiography', *MQ*, li (1965), pp. 363ff.

O'DOUWES, H., 'Carl Philipp Emanuel Bach als Koorcomponist', *Mens en Melodie*, xiii (1958), pp. 115ff.

OPPEL, R., 'Über Beziehungen Beethovens zu Mozart und zu Ph. E. Bach', *Zeitschrift für Musikwissenschaft*, v (1922–3), pp. 30ff.

OTTENBERG, H.-G., 'Carl Philipp Emanuel Bach. Komponist im Umfeld Lessings. Erforschung und Pflege eines wenig bekannten Erbes in der DDR', *Musik und Gesellschaft*, xxix (1979), pp. 144ff.

OTTENBERG, H.-G., 'Zur Fantasieproblematik im Schaffen Carl Philipp Emanuel Bachs', *Studien zur Aufführungspraxis und Interpretation von Instrumentalmusik des 18. Jahrhunderts*, xiii (Blankenburg, 1981), pp. 74ff.

OTTENBERG, H.-G., 'Zum Verhältnis von BWV 745 und Wq. 65 no. 10', *B-Jb*, lxxii (1986).

PETZSCH, C., 'Ein unbekannter Brief von Carl Philipp Emanuel Bach an Ch. G. von Murr in Nürnberg', *Archiv für Musikwissenschaft*, xxii (1965), pp. 208ff.

PILKOVÁ, Z., 'Die Familien Bach und Benda', *Bericht über die Wissenschaftliche Konferenz zum III. Internationalen Bach-Fest der DDR 1975* (Leipzig, 1977), pp. 215ff.

PILKOVÁ, Z., 'Die Cembalosonaten Jiří Bendas und ihre Beziehung zu den Kompositionen C. Ph. E. Bachs für Tasteninstrumente', *Studien zur Aufführungspraxis und Interpretation von Instrumentalmusik des 18. Jahrhunderts*, vi.1 (Magdeburg and Leipzig, 1978), pp. 67ff.

PLAMENAC, D., 'New Light on the last Years of Carl Philipp Emanuel Bach', *MQ*, xxxv (1949), pp. 565ff.

POOS, H., 'Harmoniestruktur und Hermeneutik in C. Ph. E. Bachs fis-moll Fantasie', *Kongress-Bericht Berlin 1974*, pp. 319ff.

RANDEBROCK, E., *Studie zur Klaviersonate Carl Philipp Emanuel Bachs*, Diss., Münster, 1953.

REESER, E., *The Sons of Bach*, trans. W. A. G. Doyle-Davidson (London, 1949).

RIEMANN, H., 'Die Söhne Bachs', *Präludien und Studien*, iii (Leipzig, 1897), pp. 173ff.

RIXMAN, E. E., *The Sacred Cantata 'God hath awakened the Lord' ('Gott hat den Herrn aufgeweckt') by Carl Philipp Emanuel Bach, in Relation to its Performance*, Diss., University of Southern California, 1969.

ROCHLITZ, F., 'Karl Philipp Emanuel Bach', *Für Freunde der Tonkunst*, iv (Leipzig, 1832), pp. 271ff.

ROSE, G., 'Father and Son: some attributions to J. S. Bach by C. P. E. Bach', *Studies in Eighteenth-Century Music. A Tribute to Karl Geiringer on his Seventieth Birthday*, ed. H. C. Robbins Landon (London, 1970), pp. 364ff.

ROSE, J. M., *The Harmonic Idiom of the Keyboard Works of C. P. E. Bach*, Diss., University of California Santa Barbara, 1970.

SALZER, F., 'Über die Bedeutung der Ornamente in Philipp Emanuel Bachs Klavierwerken', *Zeitschrift für Musikwissenschaft*, xii (1929–30), pp. 398ff.

SCHENKER, H., 'A Contribution to the Study of Ornamentation', trans. Hedi Siegel, *The Music Forum*, iv (1976), pp. 1ff.

SCHERING, A., 'Carl Philipp Emanuel Bach und das "redende Prinzip" in der Musik', *Jahrbuch der Musikbibliothek Peters für 1938*, xlv (1939), pp. 13ff.

SCHMID, E. F., *Carl Philipp Emanuel Bach und seine Kammermusik* (Kassel, 1931).

SCHMID, E. F., 'Joseph Haydn und Carl Philipp Emanuel Bach', *Zeitschrift für Musikwissenschaft*, xiv (1931–2), pp. 299ff.

SCHMID, E. F., 'Carl Philipp Emanuel Bach', *Die Musik in Geschichte und Gegenwart (MGG)*, i (Kassel and Basel, 1949–51), cols. 924ff.

SCHMIDT, C., 'Philipp Emanuel Bach und das Clavichord', *Schweizerische Musikzeitung*, xcii (1952), pp. 441ff.

SCHULENBERG, D., *The Instrumental Music of Carl Philipp Emanuel Bach* (Ann Arbor, 1984).

SHERWOOD, A. K., *Two keyboard sonatas of Johann Christian Bach and Carl Philipp Emanuel Bach: a historical perspective*. Diss. North Texas State University, 1979.

SINCERO, D., 'La Sonata di Filippo Emanuele Bach', *Rivista Musicale Italiana*, v (1898), pp. 677ff.

SONNECK, O. G., 'Zwei Briefe C. Ph. Em. Bachs an Alexander Reinagle', *SIMG*, vii (1906–7), pp. 112ff.

STEGLICH, R., 'Karl Philipp Emanuel Bach und der Dresdner Kreuzkantor Gottfried August Homilius im Musikleben ihrer Zeit', *B-Jb*, xii (1915), pp. 39ff.

STEVENS, J. R., *The Keyboard Concertos of Carl Philipp Emanuel Bach*, Diss., Yale University (Connecticut), 1965.

STOLJAR, M. M., 'First Settings of Klopstock: C. P. E. Bach and Gluck', *Poetry and Song in Late Eighteenth-Century Germany. A Study in the Musical Sturm und Drang* (London etc., 1985), pp. 59ff.

SUCHALLA, E., *Die Orchestersinfonien Carl Philipp Emanuel Bachs nebst einem thematischen Verzeichnis seiner Orchesterwerke* (Augsburg, 1968).

SUCHALLA, E., *Briefe von Carl Philipp Emanuel Bach an Johann Gottlob Immanuel Breitkopf und Johann Nikolaus Forkel* (Tutzing, 1985).

TERRY, M., 'C. P. E. Bach and J. J. H. Westphal. A Clarification', *JAMS*, xxii (1969), pp. 106ff.

TOWN, S., 'Sechs Lieder von Christian Fürchtegott Gellert (1715–1769) as set by Carl Philipp Emanuel Bach and Ludwig van Beethoven: a comparative analysis', *National Association of Teachers of Singing Bulletin, USA*, xxxvi.5 (March-June 1980), pp. 30ff.

VRIESLANDER, O., *Carl Philipp Emanuel Bach* (Munich, 1923).

VRIESLANDER, O., 'Carl Philipp Emanuel Bach als Theoretiker', *Von neuer Musik* (Cologne, 1925), pp. 222ff.

WACHS, M., 'Diderot's Letters to C. P. E. Bach', *Romanische Forschung*, lxxvii (1965), pp. 359ff.

WADE, R. W., *The Keyboard Concertos of Carl Philipp Emanuel Bach. Sources and Style* (Ann Arbor, 1981).

WADE, R. W., ed., *The Catalog of Carl Philipp Emanuel Bach's Estate. A Facsimile of the Edition by Schniebes, Hamburg, 1790* (New York and London, 1981).

WAGNER, G., 'Motivgruppierung in der Expositionsgestaltung bei C. Ph. E. Bach und Beethoven. Zur kompositionsgeschichtlichen Kontinuität im 18. Jahrhundert', *Jahrbuch des Staatlichen Instituts für Musikforschung* (1979), pp. 43ff.

WIEN-CLAUDI, H., *Zum Liedschaffen Carl Philipp Emanuel Bachs* (Reichenberg, 1928).

WOTQUENNE, A., *Thematisches Verzeichnis der Werke von Carl Philipp Emanuel Bach* (Leipzig, 1905; R/Wiesbaden, 1964).

WYLER, R., *Form- und Stiluntersuchungen zum ersten Satz der Klaviersonaten Carl Philipp Emanuel Bachs* (Biel, 1960).

YOUNG, P. M., *The Bachs. 1500–1850* (London, 1970).

ZERASCHI, H., 'C. Ph. E. Bachs Komposition "für eine Drehorgel"', *Beiträge zur Musikwissenschaft*, iii (1961), pp. 61ff.

GLOSSARY OF NAMES

ABEL, CARL FRIEDRICH (1723–87). German gamba player and composer, resident in London from 1759, joint organizer with J. C. Bach of a series of subscription concerts 1765–82.

ACKERMANN, KONRAD ERNST (1712–71). German actor and producer, built a permanent theatre in Hamburg in 1764.

AGRICOLA, JOHANN FRIEDRICH (1720–74). German composer and musical theorist, pupil of J. S. Bach, from 1751 court composer to Frederick the Great, co-author with C. P. E. Bach of the obituary of J. S. Bach published in Mizler, *Musikalische Bibliothek* (1754); author of the well-known treatise *Anleitung zur Singekunst* (1757; this work consists of Agricola's translation of P. F. Tosi, *Opinioni de' cantori antichi e moderni*, together with detailed commentary).

ALBERTI, DOMENICO (*c.*1710–*c.*1740). Italian composer, harpsichordist, and singer. Active in Venice and Rome.

D'ALEMBERT, JEAN LE ROND (1717–83). French encyclopaedist, physicist, and mathematician.

ALTNICKOL, JOHANN CHRISTOPH (1719–59). German composer, pupil and son-in-law of J. S. Bach.

ANNA AMALIA (1723–87). Princess of Prussia, sister of Frederick the Great, pupil of Kirnberger, owner of a large collection of music which was acquired by the Royal Library in Berlin (now divided between the Staatsbibliothek Preussischer Kulturbesitz and the Deutsche Staatsbibliothek) in 1914.

ARNE, MICHAEL (1741–86). English composer. Conducted the first public performance in Germany of Handel's *Messiah* in Hamburg in 1772.

ARTARIA. Viennese firm of music publishers existing from the middle of the eighteenth century. Issued works by C. P. E. Bach among others.

BACH, ANNA CAROLINA PHILIPPINA (1747–1804). Daughter of C. P. E. Bach.

BACH, ANNA MAGDALENA, née Wilcke (1701–60). Second wife of J. S. Bach, stepmother of C. P. E. Bach.

BACH, CATHARINA DOROTHEA (1708–74). Daughter of J. S. Bach by his first marriage.

BACH, JOHANN AUGUST (?ADAM) (1745–89). Elder son of C. P. E. Bach. Became a lawyer.

BACH, JOHANN AMBROSIUS (1645–95). Father of J. S. Bach, *Stadtmusikus* in Erfurt.

BACH, JOHANN BERNHARD (1676–1749). Organist in Erfurt, Magdeburg, and Eisenach.

BACH, JOHANN CHRISTIAN (the Milan or London Bach) (1735–82). Youngest son of J. S. Bach, worked as a composer in Italy and England, a strong influence on Mozart.

BACH, JOHANN CHRISTOPH FRIEDRICH (the Bückeburg Bach) (1732–95). Second youngest son of J. S. Bach, Konzertmeister and Kapellmeister at the Court of Bückeburg, and also a composer.

BACH, JOHANN ELIAS (1705–55). Private secretary to J. S. Bach and tutor of his younger children.

BACH, JOHANN GOTTFRIED BERNHARD (1715–39). Son of J. S. Bach by his first marriage, organist in Mühlhausen and Sangershausen.

BACH, JOHANN SEBASTIAN the younger (1748–78). Younger son of C. P. E. Bach, became a painter.

BACH, JOHANNA MARIA, née Dannemann (1724–95). Wife of C. P. E. Bach.

BACH, MARIA BARBARA (1684–1720). Daughter of J. M. Bach, first wife of J. S. Bach, mother of W. F. and C. P. E. Bach.

BACH, VEIT (died before 1577). An ancestor of the Bach family.

BACH, WILHELM FRIEDEMANN (1710–84). Eldest son of J. S. Bach, well-known as organist and harpsichordist in addition to being a composer.

BAUMGART, E. FRIEDRICH (1817–71). German scholar and teacher.

BAUMGARTEN, ALEXANDER GOTTLIEB (1714–62). German philosopher and aesthetician.

BENDA, FRANZ [František] (1709–86). Bohemian violinist and composer, Konzertmeister at the Court of Frederick the Great from 1771.

BENDA, JOHANN (GEORG) [Jan Jiří] (1713–52). Bohemian violinist and composer, who, like his brothers (above and below), was a member of Frederick the Great's court orchestra.

BENDA, GEORG (ANTON) [Jiří Antonín] (1722–95). Bohemian composer, Royal *Cammer-Musicus* in Berlin from 1742, Court Kapellmeister in Gotha from 1750, brother of F. Benda and of J. G. Benda, composer of keyboard music, Singspiele, and melodramas etc.

BIRNSTIEL, FRIEDRICH WILHELM. Berlin music publisher *c.*1750–82.

BOCK, CARL GOTTLIEB (1746–1829). Childhood friend of J. F. Reichardt.

BODE, JOHANN JOACHIM CHRISTOPH (1730–93). German publisher, oboist, and composer, collaborator with Ebeling in the translation into German of Burney's *Tagebuch einer musikalischen Reise*. (See Bibliography.)

BÖHMER, JOHANN SAMUEL FRIEDRICH (1704–72). German jurist, attached to the University of Frankfurt an der Oder.

BÖHMER, JUSTUS HENNIG (1674–1749). German jurist, father of the above.

BRAUN, JOHANN GOTTLIEB VON. Imperial Councillor in Vienna.

BREITKOPF, JOHANN GOTTLOB IMMANUEL (1719–94). German music publisher, pioneered a method of printing music with divisible and movable type in 1755. His extensive correspondence with C. P. E. Bach was lost during the Second World War.

BREITKOPF & HÄRTEL. German music publishing house in Leipzig, the main publisher of C. P. E. Bach's works in the eighteenth century.

BROCKES, BARTHOLD HEINRICH (1680–1747). German poet, founder of the *Deutschübende Gesellschaft* (1715), author of Passion texts set severally by R. Keiser, Handel, Telemann, etc.

BRÜCKNER, ERNST THEODOR JOHANN (1746–1805). Clergyman in Gross-Viehlen, later in Neubrandenburg, tragedian and poet.

BRÜHL, COUNT HEINRICH VON (1700–63). Prime Minister under Friedrich August II of Saxony (King August III of Poland) from 1746.

BÜLOW, HANS VON (1830–94). German pianist, conductor, and scholar.

BURNEY, CHARLES (1726–1814). English music historian, author of *The Present State of Music in France and Italy* (1771), *The Present State of Music in Germany, the Netherlands, and United Provinces* (1773), and *A General History of Music* (1782–9). In 1772 he visited C. P. E. Bach in Hamburg.

BÜSCH, JOHANN GEORG (1728–1800). German economist, and Professor of Mathematics in Hamburg.

CAMBINI, GIUSEPPE MARIA (1746–1825). Italian violinist and composer, resident in Paris from the 1770s.

CANNABICH, JOHANN CHRISTIAN (1731–98). German composer, from 1758 Konzertmeister of the Mannheim court orchestra, and from 1774 Director of instrumental music there.

CARL EUGEN (1728–93), Duke of Württemberg. Keyboard pupil of C. P. E. Bach.

CAUDELLA, PHILIPP. Austrian composer and teacher.

CHODOWIECKI, DANIEL (1726–1801). German painter, etcher, and draughtsman, resident in Berlin from 1743, provided illustrations for literary and scholarly publications including works by Lessing, Gellert, Klopstock, Goethe, and Schiller.

CLAUDIUS, MATTHIAS (1740–1815). German lyric poet and journalist. Editor of the *Wandsbecker Bote* (1770–5).

CLEMENTI, MUZIO (1752–1832). English composer, pianist, teacher, music publisher, and piano manufacturer of Italian origin.

CRAMER, CARL FRIEDRICH (1752–1807). German publisher, editor of *Magazin der Musik* (1783–7), and of the anthology *Flora* (1787) containing songs by Gluck, Kunzen, and Reichardt, as well as C. P. E. Bach's C minor Fantasia.

CRAMER, JOHANN ANDREAS (1723–88). German theologian, historian, and lyric poet, joint founder of the *Bremer Beiträge*, author of psalm translations set to music by C. P. E. Bach.

CRAMER, JOHANN BAPTIST (1771–1858). German pianist and teacher, resident in England after 1800. Like Clementi he was also a music publisher.

CROUSAZ, JEAN PIERRE DE (1663–1750). French philosopher, aesthetician, and mathematician.

CZERNY, CARL (1791–1857). Austrian composer, pianist, and teacher.

DANZI, FRANZ (1763–1826). German composer and cellist.

DASSDORF, KARL WILHELM (1750–1812). Archivist in Dresden.

DESSAU, PAUL (1894–1979). German composer, resident in East Berlin from 1948.

DIDEROT, DENIS (1713–84). French encyclopaedist and author.

DIES, ALBERT CHRISTOPH (1755–1822). German landscape painter and music historian, biographer of Haydn.

DOLES, JOHANN FRIEDRICH (1715–97). German composer, from 1755 to 1789 Cantor at the Thomaskirche in Leipzig.

DOTZAUER, JUSTUS JOHANN FRIEDRICH (1783–1860). German cellist and composer.

DRAESEKE, FELIX AUGUST BERNHARD (1835–1913). German composer and teacher.

DRESE, JOHANN SAMUEL (died 1716). Court Kapellmeister in Weimar from 1683 until his death.

DRESE, JOHANN WILHELM (1677–1745). Son of the above, Court Kapellmeister in Weimar from 1717.

DRUSINA, BENEDICTUS DE (born early sixteenth century). German lutenist.

DUBOS, ABBÉ JEAN-BAPTISTE (1670–1742). French aesthetician.

DUŠEK [Duschek], FRANTIŠEK XAVER (1731–99). Bohemian pianist, teacher, and composer.

DUSSEK [Dusík], JAN LADISLAV [Johann Ladislaus] (1760–1812). Bohemian pianist and composer. Studied with C. P. E. Bach.

EBELING, CHRISTOPH DANIEL (1741–1817). German scholar and writer on music, translator of Burney's travel diaries, and a member of C. P. E. Bach's circle of acquaintances in Hamburg.

ECKARD, JOHANN GOTTFRIED (1735–1809). German pianist and composer, resident in Paris from 1758.

EISLER, HANNS (1898–1962). German composer, resident in East Berlin from 1949.

ERARD, SÉBASTIEN (1752–1831). French piano manufacturer.

ERDMANN, GEORG (1682–1736). Russian Imperial Councillor, resident in Danzig, childhood friend of J. S. Bach.

ERK, LUDWIG CHRISTIAN (1807–83). German editor of folk-songs and teacher.

ERNESTI, JOHANN HEINRICH (1652–1729). Rector of the Thomasschule in Leipzig from 1684 to 1729.

ESTERHÁZY, COUNT JOHANN NEPOMUK (1754–1840). Member of the Hungarian aristocratic family of Esterházy.

ESTERHÁZY, PRINCE NICHOLAS JOSEPH (1714–90). Another member of the family and Haydn's patron.

EULER, LEONHARD (1707–83). Swiss mathematician, physicist, and astronomer.

FARRENC, JACQUES HIPPOLYTE ARISTIDE (1794–1865). French music publisher and scholar.

FASCH, JOHANN FRIEDRICH (1688–1758). German composer, Court Kapellmeister in Zerbst from 1722.

FASCH, KARL FRIEDRICH CHRISTIAN (1736–1800). German composer and harpsichordist, son and pupil of J. F. Fasch, Frederick the Great's second harpsichordist, and founder of the Berlin *Singakademie* in 1791.

FÉTIS, FRANÇOIS-JOSEPH (1784–1871). Belgian music historian and composer.

FISCHHOF, JOSEPH (1804–57). Austrian pianist and teacher.

FONTENELLE, BERNARD LE BOVIER DE (1657–1757). French writer and philosopher.

FORKEL, JOHANN NIKOLAUS (1749–1818). German music theorist, resident in Göttingen, author of important theoretical works, including *Musikalisch-kritische Bibliothek* (1778–9), *General History of Music* (1788–1801), as well as the first historical biography of J. S. Bach (1802).

FREDERICK THE GREAT (1712–86). King Frederick II of Prussia (1740–86), son of King Frederick William I.

FREDERICK WILLIAM I (1688–1740). King of Prussia (1713–40).

FREDERSDORFF, MICHAEL GABRIEL (1708–58). Private Chamberlain to Frederick the Great, also a flautist.

FRIEDERICI, CHRISTIAN ERNST (1709–80). German piano- and organ-builder. C. P. E. Bach possessed a clavichord made by Friederici.

FRITZ, BARTHOLD (*c.*1697–1766). German clavichord- and organ-builder.

FUCHS, ALOYS (1799–1853). Austrian official, collector of sheet music.

FUX, JOHANN JOSEPH (1660–1741). Austrian composer and music theorist, author of the treatise on counterpoint *Gradus ad Parnassum* (1725).

GALUPPI, BALDASSARE (1706–85). Venetian composer, a crucial figure in the development of *opera buffa*.

GELLERT, CHRISTIAN FÜRCHTEGOTT (1715–69). German poet; many of his *Geistliche Oden und Lieder* (1757) were set to music by C. P. E. Bach.

GERSTENBERG, HEINRICH WILHELM VON (1727–1823). German poet and critic, author of the play *Ugolino* (1768); his cantata *Die Grazien* was set to music by C. P. E. Bach and appeared in Lübeck in 1789.

GESIUS, BARTHOLOMÄUS (*c.*1560–1613). German composer and Cantor, based in Frankfurt an der Oder for much of his life.

GESNER, JOHANN MATTHIAS (1691–1761). German scholar, from 1730 to 1734 Rector of the Thomasschule in Leipzig.

GIARDINI, FELICE DE (1716–96). Italian violinist and composer, resident in London.

GLEIM, JOHANN WILHELM LUDWIG (1719–1803). German poet, principal representative of the German Anacreontic movement in poetry.

GOEZE, MELCHIOR (1717–86). German theologian, representative of Lutheran Orthodoxy.

GÖRNER, JOHANN GOTTLIEB (1697–1778). German organist and composer.

GÖSCHEN, GEORG JOACHIM (1752–1828). German bookseller and publisher.

GOTTSCHED, JOHANN CHRISTOPH (1700–66). German poet, author of important theoretical works, including *Versuch einer kritischen Dichtkunst* (1730), and *Grundlegung einer deutschen Sprachkunst* (1748).

GRÄFE, JOHANN FRIEDRICH (1711–87). German song-composer.

GRAFF, ANTON (1736–1813). Swiss painter.

GRAUN, AUGUST FRIEDRICH (1698 or 1699–1765). German composer and church musician.

GRAUN, CARL HEINRICH (1703 or 1704–1759). German composer, Kapellmeister at the Court of Frederick the Great from 1740, important as an opera composer, and widely known for the Passion Oratorio *Der Tod Jesu* (1755).

GRAUN, JOHANN GOTTLIEB (1702 or 1703–1771). German violinist and composer, in the service of the Prussian Crown Prince (later King Frederick the Great) from 1732, prolific writer of instrumental music.

GRAUPNER, JOHANN CHRISTOPH (1683–1760). German composer, active mainly in Darmstadt.

GRAVE, JOHANN HEINRICH (lived until at least 1810). Lawyer in Greifswald. Collector of C. P. E. Bachiana.

GRIBNER, MICHAEL HEINRICH (1682–1734). German jurist.

GRIESINGER, GEORG AUGUST (died 1828). German writer, biographer of Haydn.

GROTTHUSS, DIETRICH EWALD VON (1751–86). Baron in Courland.

HAFFNER, JOHANN ULRICH (1711–67). German virtuoso lutenist and music publisher.

HAGEDORN, FRIEDRICH VON (1708–54). German lyric poet and writer of fables.

HAMANN, JOHANN GEORG (1730–88). German writer on the philosophy of religion.

HAPPE, FRANZ WILHELM VON (1687–1760). Prussian minister and diplomat, whose sons Ludwig Wilhelm and Ernst Wilhelm were studying at the University of Frankfurt an der Oder in 1735.

HARRER, JOHANN GOTTLOB (1703–55). German composer, successor of J. S. Bach as Cantor at the Thomaskirche in 1750.

HASS, HIERONYMUS ALBRECHT. German instrument-maker in the eighteenth century.

HASSE, JOHANN ADOLPH (1699–1783). German composer, main representative of *opera seria* around the middle of the eighteenth century.

HEINECCIUS, JOHANN GOTTLIEB (1681–1741). German jurist.

HELLFELD, JOHANN AUGUST (1717–82). German jurist.

HERDER, JOHANN GOTTFRIED VON (1744–1803). German critic, theologian, and philosopher, the leading figure of the *Sturm und Drang* literary movement.

HERING, CARL GOTTLIEB (1766–1853). German music teacher and composer.

HERING, JOHANN FRIEDRICH (earliest documentation dated 1773). Berlin musician.

HILLER, JOHANN ADAM (1728–1804). German composer and musical theorist, the first Kapellmeister of the Gewandhaus in Leipzig, from 1789 to 1801 Cantor at the Thomaskirche, author of important theoretical works, including *Wöchentliche Nachrichten und Anmerkungen die Musik betreffend* (1766–70).

HOFFMANN, ERNST THEODOR AMADEUS (1776–1822). German poet, writer on music, and composer.

HOFFMEISTER, FRANZ ANTON (1754–1812). German composer, church organist, and music-seller.

HÖLTY, LUDWIG CHRISTOPH HEINRICH (1748–76). German poet, member of the 'Göttingen Grove', co-editor of the Göttingen *Musenalmanach*.

HOMILIUS, GOTTFRIED AUGUST (1714–85). German composer, pupil of J. S. Bach, from 1755 Cantor at the Kreuzschule and Director of Music at the three principal churches in Dresden.

HONAUER, LEONTZI (*c.*1735–after 1790). Alsatian composer, active in Paris.

HÜLLMANDEL, NICOLAS-JOSEPH (1751–1823). Alsatian pianist and composer, pupil of C. P. E. Bach.

HUMMEL, JOHANN NEPOMUK (1778–1837). Austrian composer and pianist. Pupil of Mozart.

ITZIG, ISAAK DANIEL. Jewish banker in Berlin.

ITZIG, BABETTE, married name Salomon (1749–1825). Daughter of the above, grandmother of Felix Mendelssohn Bartholdy.

JADIN, LOUIS-EMMANUEL (1768–1853). French composer and keyboard player.

JANITSCH, JOHANN GOTTLIEB (1708–*c.*1763). German jurist and composer, member of the Court orchestra of Frederick the Great, organizer of a popular series of weekly concerts.

JOMMELLI, NICOLÒ (1714–74). Italian composer, principally of opera. Active for much of his life in Stuttgart.

JUNGCURTH, HEINRICH WILHELM. German instrument-maker, became a citizen of Hamburg in 1782. C. P. E. Bach owned a clavichord made by him.

KALKBRENNER, FRIEDRICH WILHELM MICHAEL (1785–1849). German pianist and teacher.

KARSCH, ANNA LUISE, known as 'die Karschin' (1722–91). German poetess, close to the literary circle around J. W. L. Gleim and K. W. Ramler.

KEISER, REINHARD (1674–1739). German composer, principal composer of the Hamburg opera from 1696.

KEYSERLINGK, HEINRICH CHRISTIAN VON (1727–87). Son of Hermann Carl Reichsgraf von Keyserlingk (1696–1764), who was acquainted with J. S. Bach's family.

KIESEWETTER, RAPHAEL GEORG (1773–1850). Austrian music historian.

KIRNBERGER, JOHANN PHILIPP (1721–83). German music theorist and composer, pupil of J. S. Bach, became teacher of composition and Kapellmeister to Princess Anna Amalia of Prussia in 1754, author of important theoretical works including *Die Kunst des reinen Satzes* (1771–9), and *Grundsätze des General Basses als erste Linien zur Composition* (1781).

KLOPSTOCK, FRIEDRICH GOTTLIEB (1724–1803). German poet, author of many odes, and of the biblical poem *Messias* (1748–73), lived in Hamburg from 1770, where he was a friend of C. P. E. Bach.

KNOBELSDORFF, GEORG WENZESLAUS VON (1699–1753). German architect and painter.

KOZELUCH [Koželuh], LEOPOLD (Jan Antonín) (1752–1818). Bohemian composer and pianist, settled in Vienna in 1778.

KRAUSE, CHRISTIAN GOTTFRIED (1719–70). German jurist, music theorist and composer, an important representative of the first Berlin school of song composition, author of the theoretical treatise *Von der musikalischen Poesie*.

KREBS, JOHANN LUDWIG (1713–80). German organist and composer, pupil of J. S. Bach.

KRENGEL, GREGOR (*c.*1550–94 or later). German lutenist, active in the second half of the sixteenth century in Frankfurt an der Oder.

KRÜGER, ANDREAS LUDWIG (1743–1803). German painter, active in Berlin, teacher of J. S. Bach the younger.

KUHNAU, JOHANN (1660–1722). German composer, Cantor at the Thomaskirche in Leipzig from 1701.

KUSSER, JOHANN SIGISMUND (1660–1727). German composer, active at the Hamburg opera.

LAMETTRIE, JULIEN OFFRAY DE (1709–51). French physician and philosopher.

LANGE, GREGOR (*c.*1550–87). German Cantor and organist, active in Frankfurt an der Oder and Breslau.

LAUTENSACK. Prussian privy councillor and adviser to King Frederick the Great on military and financial affairs.

LAVATER, JOHANN CASPAR (1741–1801). Swiss writer, closely connected with the German *Sturm und Drang* movement (together with Herder and Goethe), author of *Physiognomische Fragmente zur Beförderung der Menschenkenntnis und Menschenliebe* (1775–8).

LEIBNIZ, GOTTFRIED WILHELM (1646–1716). German philosopher, mathematician, and political adviser.

LESSING, GOTTHOLD EPHRAIM (1729–81). Critic, aesthetician, and the first German dramatist of lasting importance.

LEVY, SARA, née Itzig (1761–1854). Daughter of the Jewish banker I. D. Itzig, great-aunt of Felix Mendelssohn Bartholdy.

LINNAEUS, CARL (1707–78). Swedish naturalist.

LIPS, JOHANN HEINRICH (1758–1817). Swiss copper engraver and painter.

LÖHLEIN, GEORG SIMON (1725–81). German pianist, violinist, and composer.

MARCHAND, LOUIS (1669–1732). French organist and composer.

MARPURG, FRIEDRICH WILHELM (1718–95). German musical theorist, author and editor of important treatises and musical periodicals, including *Der critische Musicus an der Spree* (1749–50), *Historisch-kritische Beyträge zur Aufnahme der Musik* (1754–62, 1778), *Abhandlung von der Fuge* (1753–4), and *Kritische Briefe über die Tonkunst* (1759–63).

MARTINI, PADRE GIOVANNI BATTISTA (1706–84). Italian musical theorist and composer.

MATTHESON, JOHANN (1681–1764). German musical theorist and composer, author of important treatises, including *Critica musica* (1722–5), *Der Musicalische Patriot* (1728), *Der Vollkommene Capellmeister* (1739), and *Grundlage einer Ehren-Pforte* (1740).

MAUPERTUIS, PIERRE LOUIS MOREAU DE (1698–1759). French mathematician, physicist, and geographer, became President of the Royal Academy in Berlin in 1741.

MEIER, GEORG FRIEDRICH (1718–77). German philosopher and aesthetician.

MEINECKE, CARL. American composer, pianist, and organist of German origin, active in the early nineteenth century.

MENCKE, JOHANN BURKHARD (1675–1732). German historian and writer.

MENDELSSOHN, MOSES (1729–86). German philosopher and writer, representative of the so-called 'popular philosophy of the Enlightenment', principal work *Morgenstunden* (1785), grandfather of Felix Mendelssohn Bartholdy (1809–47).

MENZEL, ADOLPH VON (1815–1905). German painter, artist, and draughtsman.

METASTASIO, PIETRO (real name Trapassi) (1698–1782). Italian poet and librettist.

MILLER, JOHANN MARTIN (1750–1814). German lyric poet, member of the 'Göttingen Grove'.

MIZLER, LORENZ CHRISTOPH (1711–78). German writer on music. Founder of the *Societät der musikalischen Wissenschaften* in Leipzig in 1738, and editor of the *Neu eröffnete Musikalische Bibliothek* (1736–54).

MONN, MATTHIAS GEORG (1717–50). Austrian composer, organist in Vienna.

MOSCHELES, IGNAZ (1794–1870). German pianist, composer, and conductor.

MOSER, JOHANN JAKOB (1701–85). German jurist and Pietist.

MÜTHEL, JOHANN GOTTFRIED (1728–88). German composer, active in Riga, and an important composer for the keyboard.

NÄGELI, HANS GEORG (1773–1836). Swiss writer and publisher.

NEEFE, CHRISTIAN GOTTLOB (1748–98). German composer, teacher of Beethoven.

NICHELMANN, CHRISTOPH (1717–62). German harpsichordist, composer, and musical theorist, principal work *Die Melodie nach ihrem Wesen sowohl, als nach ihren Eigenschaften* (1755).

NICOLAI, CHRISTOPH FRIEDRICH (1733–1811). German writer and publisher, founder of two major periodicals of the German Enlightenment: *Briefe, die neueste Literatur betreffend* (1759–65), *Allgemeine Deutsche Bibliothek* (1759–1805), the latter containing numerous reviews of compositions by C. P. E. Bach.

OESER, ADAM FRIEDRICH (1717–99). German painter, etcher, and sculptor, director of the Leipzig *Kunstakademie*, teacher of J. S. Bach the younger.

OVERBECK, CHRISTIAN ADOLF (1755–1821). German lyric poet, member of the 'Göttingen Grove'.

PISENDEL, JOHANN GEORG (1687–1755). German violinist and composer, employed in the Dresden court orchestra. Pupil of Vivaldi.

PITTANUS, FRIEDRICH (born *c.*1568). German Cantor and composer, active in Frankfurt an der Oder.

PLEYEL, IGNACE JOSEPH (1757–1831). Austrian composer, piano manufacturer, and publisher, active in France. Pupil of Haydn.

POCHHAMMER, JOHANN SEBASTIAN (1719 or 1720–80). Cantor in Berlin.

POELCHAU, GEORG (1773–1836). German musical archivist, and owner of an extensive collection of music including numerous autographs, manuscript copies, and first editions of works by Bach.

PÖLLNITZ, KARL LUDWIG, FREIHERR VON (1692–1775). Prussian officer, appointed by Frederick the Great in 1740 to the post of Principal Master of Ceremonies.

PRAETORIUS, MICHAEL (1571 or 1572–1621). German composer and musical theorist, whose principal work was the treatise *Syntagma musicum* (1615–20).

QUANTZ, JOHANN JOACHIM (1697–1773). German flautist, composer, and musical theorist, employed at the Court of Frederick the Great from 1741, composer of numerous concertos and solos for the flute, and author of the treatise *Versuch einer Anweisung die Flöte traversiere zu spielen* (1752).

RAMLER, KARL WILHELM (1725–98). German poet, a central figure in the Berlin Enlightenment, author of odes in Classical metres, and of texts set to music by C. P. E. Bach among others.

RAUPACH, HERMANN FRIEDRICH (1728–78). German composer and Kapellmeister.

REICHA, ANTOINE [Antonín] (1770–1836). French composer and musical theorist of Bohemian origin.

REICHARDT, JOHANN FRIEDRICH (1752–1814). German composer and writer on music, author of *Briefe eines aufmerksamen Reisenden die Musik betreffend*

(1774–6), *Schreiben über die Berlinische Musik* (1775), *Musikalisches Kunstmagazin* (1782–91).

REIFENSTEIN, JOHANN FRIEDRICH (1709–93). German painter, whose work includes a portrait of C. P. E. Bach.

REIMARUS, HERMANN SAMUEL (1694–1768). German philosopher, disciple of Christian Wolff.

REIMARUS, JOHANN ALBERT HEINRICH (1729–1814). German doctor and natural scientist, son of the above.

RELLSTAB, JOHANN KARL FRIEDRICH (1759–1813). German music publisher and composer.

RESEWITZ, FRIEDRICH GABRIEL (1729–1806). German theologian and journalist, continued Lessing's *Literaturbriefe* for a time.

RICHTER, FRANZ XAVER (1709–89). Bohemian composer, violinist, and singer in the court orchestra of the Elector Palatine at Mannheim.

RICHTER, JOHANN CHRISTIAN (1689–1744). Oboist in the court orchestra at Dresden.

RICHTER, JOHANN CHRISTOPH (1700–85). Court organist in Dresden.

RIGHINI, VINCENZO (1756–1812). Italian composer and conductor.

RIOTTE, PHILIPP JAKOB (1776–1856). German composer and conductor. Active in Vienna.

ROCHLITZ, JOHANN FRIEDRICH (1769–1842). German writer on music. Editor and publisher of the *Allgemeine musikalische Zeitung* (from 1798).

ROLLE, JOHANN HEINRICH (1716–85). German composer. Active mainly in Magdeburg.

ROUSSEAU, JEAN-JACQUES (1712–78). French philosopher, writer, composer, and music theorist.

RUST, FRIEDRICH WILHELM (1739–96). German violinist and composer, pupil of C. P. E. Bach, active in Dessau from 1766.

SACK, JOHANN PHILIPP (1722–63). German composer, co-founder of the *Musikübende Gesellschaft* (1749), from 1755 organist at Berlin Cathedral.

SALIERI, ANTONIO (1750–1825). Italian composer, Kapellmeister in Vienna.

SCHAFFRATH, CHRISTOPH (1709–63). German composer, member of the orchestra kept by the Crown Prince of Prussia, later King Frederick the Great.

SCHALE, CHRISTIAN FRIEDRICH (1713–1800). German composer, cellist in the court orchestra at Berlin.

SCHEIBE, JOHANN ADOLPH (1708–76). German music theorist and composer, author of *Critischer Musicus* (1745).

SCHICK, ERNST (1756–1815). German violinist of Netherlandish origin.

SCHIEBELER, DANIEL (1741–71). Canon and poet in Hamburg, author of heroic poems, epigrams, and romances, as well as the libretto of C. P. E. Bach's oratorio *Die Israeliten in der Wüste*.

SCHILLING, GUSTAV (1803–81). German writer on music and lexicographer.

SCHIØRRING, NIELS (1743–98). Danish composer and instrumentalist, pupil of C. P. E. Bach, harpsichordist at the Royal Court in Copenhagen.

SCHMID, BALTHASAR (1705–49). German music publisher in Nuremberg, who issued the fourth part of J. S. Bach's *Clavierübung*, and the *Canonic Variations*, etc., as well as works by Telemann and the Bach pupils C. P. E. Bach, J. L. Krebs, Nichelmann, and J. N. Tischer.

SCHMID, MARIA HELENA, née Volland (1710–91). Wife of Balthasar Schmid, who continued her husband's business after his death.

SCHOBERT, JOHANN [Jean] (*c.*1720–67). German composer and pianist, a pioneer of chamber music with obbligato keyboard, active in Paris.

SCHRÖDER, FRIEDRICH LUDWIG (1744–1816). German actor and producer, director of the theatre in Hamburg from 1771 to 1780, from 1786 to 1798, and from 1811 to 1812.

SCHUBART, CHRISTIAN FRIEDRICH DANIEL (1739–91). German poet, composer, and writer on music, well-known for his *Ideen zu einer Ästhetik der Tonkunst* (published by L. Schubart in 1806).

SCHULZ, JOHANN ABRAHAM PETER (1747–1800). German composer and musical theorist, the leading representative of the second Berlin school of song composition, composer of numerous songs and oratorios.

SCHWANENBERG, JOHANN GOTTFRIED (1740–1804). German composer and Kapellmeister, active in Brunswick.

SCHWENKE, CHRISTIAN FRIEDRICH GOTTLIEB (1767–1822). German composer, successor to C. P. E. Bach as Director of Music at the five principal churches in Hamburg and Cantor of the Johanneum.

SCHWICKERT, ENGELBERT BENJAMIN. Leipzig publisher who issued among other things a revised edition of C. P. E. Bach's *Versuch über die wahre Art das Clavier zu spielen.*

SILBERMANN, GOTTFRIED (1683–1753). German organ-builder and instrument-maker. C. P. E. Bach owned a clavichord made by him.

SONNENFELS, JOSEF (1733–1817). Austrian writer and journalist.

SONNENKALB, JOHANN FRIEDRICH WILHELM (1732–85). German organist and Cantor at Dahme. Alumnus of the Thomasschule in Leipzig.

SPONTINI, GASPARO LUIGI PACIFICO (1774–1851). Italian composer and conductor, active in Paris and associated principally with French serious opera.

STAHL, GEORG ERNST (1713–72). Court Councillor and physician in Berlin.

STÄHLIN, JACOB VON (1709–85). German historian, member of the Academy of Sciences at St Petersburg.

STAMITZ [Stamic], CARL (1745–1801). German composer and violinist of Bohemian origin, and son of J. W. A. Stamitz.

STAMITZ [Stamic], JOHANN WENZEL ANTON [Jan Václav Antonín] (1717–57). Bohemian composer and violinist, founder of the 'Mannheim School'.

STARKE, FRIEDRICH (1774–1835). German composer. Eventually settled in Vienna.

STEFFAN, JOSEPH ANTON (1726–97). Bohemian composer, active in Vienna.

STEIBELT, DANIEL (1765–1823). German itinerant pianist and composer.

STEIN, FRIEDRICH (1784–1809). German composer and pianist, son of the piano- and organ-builder J. A. Stein.

STEINACKER, CARL (1785–1815). German bookseller and composer.

STOLBERG, COUNT CHRISTIAN ZU (1748–1821). German lyric poet, dramatist, and translator, member of the 'Göttingen Grove', and co-editor of the *Musenalmanach.*

STOLBERG, COUNT FRIEDRICH LEOPOLD ZU (1750–1819). German lyric poet, dramatist, journalist, and translator, member of the 'Göttingen Grove'.

STÖLZEL, GOTTFRIED HEINRICH (1690–1749). German composer and Kapellmeister at Gotha.

STURM, CHRISTOPH CHRISTIAN (1740–86). German theologian, preacher at the church of St Peter in Hamburg, and one of the poets whose works were set to music by Bach.

SULZER, JOHANN GEORG (1720–79). German philosopher and aesthetician, principal theoretical work *Allgemeine Theorie der schönen Künste* (1771–4).

SWIETEN, GOTTFRIED BERNHARD BARON VAN (1733–1803). Austrian diplomat of Netherlandish origin.

TELEMANN, GEORG MICHAEL (1748–1831). German composer and musical theorist. Grandson of G. P. Telemann.

THOMASIUS, JAKOB (1622–84). Rector at the Thomasschule in Leipzig.

TIECK, JOHANN LUDWIG (1773–1853). German poet, theorist, and critic.

TOESCHI, CARLO GIUSEPPE (1722–88). Italian composer and violinist, pupil of J. W. A. Stamitz.

TOST, JOHANN. Violinist employed from 1783 to 1789 in the orchestra of the Esterházy princes.

TRICKLIR, JEAN BALTHASAR (1750–1813). French cellist and composer of German descent.

TRIER, JOHANN (1716–90). German organist and Director of Music at Zittau.

TRIEST, JOHANN KARL FRIEDRICH (1764–1810). Pastor in Stettin.

TÜRK, DANIEL GOTTLOB (1750–1813). German composer, theorist, and teacher. Cantor in Halle.

UMLAUFF, IGNAZ (1746–96). Austrian composer and conductor, active in Vienna.

VANHAL, JOHANN BAPTIST (1739–1813). Czech composer and violinist, active in Vienna.

VINCI, LEONARDO (1690–1730). Italian composer, mainly of opera.

VOGLER, GEORG JOSEPH (1749–1814). German composer, musical theorist, and organ virtuoso.

VOLTAIRE, FRANÇOIS-MARIE (1696–1778). French philosopher and writer.

VOSS, JOHANN HEINRICH (1751–1826). German poet and translator, leading figure of the 'Göttingen Grove', editor of the *Göttingen Musenalmanach*, author of texts set by C. P. E. Bach.

VOSS-BUCH, COUNT OTTO KARL FRIEDRICH VON (1755–1823). Provost of the Cathedral at Havelberg.

WACKENRODER, WILHELM HEINRICH (1773–98). German literary and art theorist, principal works *Herzensergiessungen eines kunstliebenden Klosterbruders* (1797), and *Phantasien über die Kunst für Freunde der Kunst* (1799, ed. L. Tieck).

WAGENER, ANTON. Hamburg Senator and Mayor in the eighteenth century.

WAGENER, GUIDO RICHARD (1822–96). Professor of Anatomy. Collector of C. P. E. Bachiana.

WAGENSEIL, GEORG CHRISTOPH (1715–77). Prolific Viennese composer and pianist.

WAISSEL, MATTHÄUS (*c.*1540–1602). German composer and lutenist, active for part of his life in Frankfurt an der Oder.

WESTPHAL, JOHANN CHRISTOPH the elder (1727?–1799). German music publisher.

WESTPHAL, JOHANN JAKOB HEINRICH (1756–1825). German organist and harpsichordist, collector of C. P. E. Bachiana.

WILHELM ERNST, Duke of Sachsen-Weimar (1662–1728). J. S. Bach's patron (1708–1717).

WILHELM, Count of Schaumburg-Lippe (1724–77). J. C. F. Bach's patron.

WILLICH, JODOCUS (*c.*1486–1552). German scholar, humanist, and musical theorist, Professor at the University of Frankfurt an der Oder.

WILMS, JOHANN WILHELM (1772–1847). Netherlandish composer and organist.

WINCKELMANN, JOHANN JOACHIM (1717–68). German art theorist, pioneer of Classical archaeology.

WINTER, GEORG LUDWIG (died before 1772). Berlin publisher.

WINTERFELD, CARL GEORG AUGUST VIVIGENS VON (1784–1852). German music historian.

WINTHEM, JOHANNA ELISABETH VON (1747–1821). Klopstock's second wife.

WOLF, ERNST WILHELM (1735–92). German composer and Kapellmeister, Court Kapellmeister in Weimar from 1768.

WOLFF, CHRISTIAN (1679–1754). German philosopher, rationalist representative of Enlightenment philosophy.

WÖLFL, JOSEPH (1773–1812). Austrian pianist and composer.

WOTQUENNE, ALFRED (1867–1939). Belgian music historian and archivist.

WRANITZKY, ANTON (1761–1826). Moravian composer and violinist.

WRANITZKY, PAUL (1756–1808). Moravian composer and violinist. Brother of the above.

YOUNG, EDWARD (1683–1765). English poet.

ZELENKA, JAN DISMAS (LUKÁŠ?) (1679–1745). Bohemian composer, employed from 1710 to 1745 as a bass-player in the court orchestra at Dresden, where he also directed and composed church music.

ZELTER, CARL FRIEDRICH (1758–1832). German composer and musical theorist, director of the Berlin *Singakademie* from 1800, friend of Goethe, teacher of Felix Mendelssohn Bartholdy.

ZIEGLER, CHRISTIANE MARIANE VON (1695–1760). German poetess, author of cantata librettos.

ZOPPIS, FRANCESCO (1715–81). Venetian opera composer, employed for a time at Bonn and later at St Petersburg.

INDEX OF WORKS

BY C. P. E. BACH

GENERAL INDEX